# *ON YOUR*

CW00868702

# ON YOUR OWN

A practical guide to independent living

## JEAN SHAPIRO

PANDORA PRESS

LONDON, BOSTON AND HENLEY

First published in 1985
by Pandora Press
(Routledge & Kegan Paul plc)
14 Leicester Square, London WC2H 7PH,
England

9 Park Street, Boston, Mass. 02108, USA and

Broadway House, Newtown Road,
Henley on Thames, Oxon RG9 1EN, England

Set in 10/11pt Palatino
by Input Typesetting Ltd, London
and printed in Great Britain
by The Thetford Press Ltd,
Thetford, Norfolk

Library of Congress Cataloging in Publication
Data
Shapiro, Jean, 1916–
  On your own.

  Bibliography: p.
  Includes index.
  1. Widows—Life skills guides. 2. Divorced
women—Life skills guides. 3. Middle aged
women— Life skills guides. I. Title.
HQ1058.S53  1985    646.7    85–591

ISBN 0–86358–027–0 (C) |507
    0–86358–045–9 (P)

British Library CIP data also available

Editor: Jane Hawksley
Designer: Flo Henfield
Desk Editor: Beverley Stern
Illustrations: Janos Marfy, Howard Pemberton,
Jenny Smith

With thanks for additional assistance from:
Betty Dowden, Kate Figes, Format
Photographers and *Good Housekeeping*
magazine for permission to use photographs
for artist's reference, the Automobile
Association, Helen Mott, Hugo Rose, Michele
Swing

# CONTENTS

My thanks are due to the many women whose experiences have contributed to this book. Some have been quoted directly; but letters written to me at *Good Housekeeping* have also enabled me to appreciate and focus on the particular problems of the divorced and widowed when they are faced for the first time in their lives with being alone.

I should also like to thank Jane Hawksley, who gave me the idea; my agent, Gill Coleridge, for her unfailing interest, concern and advice; and Diana Harris, an invaluable aide at *GH* since 1979. Diana Austen and Bob Tattersall gave me useful contacts at the planning stage.

I am especially indebted to Sonya Mills, for advice on house maintenance and DIY.

My friends Rhoda Brawne, Pat Land, Helen Utidjian and Anne Woolf have helped me in more ways than they knew. I thank them, and Monte Shapiro, for his support and encouragement through the writing of this book and in all my work over the years.

# PART I
# FACING THE FUTURE

*Ahead of you is a bewildering array of unfamiliar tasks. But don't feel swamped – this book will help you, step by step, to find your way.*

# CHAPTER 1
# WHAT IT'S ALL ABOUT

You're a woman now planning for the first time to tackle life on your own – and this book is for you. You've had years – maybe almost your whole life – depending on other people to cope with some of the more difficult aspects of modern living. Money and banks; insurance; social security; rates and taxes; red tape and officialdom: household repairs; organising holidays; looking after a car: these are just some of the jobs that many women thankfully leave to the men in their lives, while *they*'re occupied with bringing up children, doing the domestic chores, and, very likely, fitting in paid work outside the home as well. That was more than enough. You may well have left everything else to your husband. And we haven't mentioned what may have been an even greater dependence – the emotional support of a sharing, caring relationship and the companionship that's now been lost, either suddenly or over a long, agonising period when everything seemed to be collapsing and your whole future was in doubt.

Perhaps you're going through a divorce, or the decree has just come through. Now you're one of the statistics that tell us that one in three existing marriages will founder. You never thought it would happen to you, but it has. Or perhaps you have recently suffered bereavement, the loss of your husband or lover, and have joined the ranks of the 3,200,000 widows now living in Britain: that is, one in six women. Perhaps you're young, with school-age children. Or you may be fifty years old and going through the menopause, just at this time of emotional upheaval. Or are you an older woman, brought up at a time when you weren't expected ever to be able to stand on your own two feet?

At first glance it may seem that these groups don't have much in common. But wait a minute. Although you may *feel* very differently about the loss you've suffered, or about your position as an older or a younger person, right now you share with the other groups something that's crucial. You're having to cope alone. Whatever the cause of your being in this situation, gradually, painfully, perhaps, you have to build a new life for yourself, and become for the first time, an independent person. No matter into which group you fall, it won't be easy, and that's why this book has been written. It's intended as a signpost on the road.

Much of the information, suggestions and advice you'll find in the following pages is based on the experiences of the many women who have contributed in some way to the making of this book. Part of my job over the last seventeen years has been to act as 'agony aunt', trying to help magazine readers in a huge variety of situations. Among the thousands of letters I've received, inevitably there have been many concerned with just the sort of problems you're facing now. Every one has received a personal reply. Through consulting files built up over the years, increased knowledge of sources of information, contact with self-help groups and specialist organisations, familiarity with the difficult decisions a lone woman has to make, and an appreciation, too, of the uniqueness of every individual, I've now felt able to produce a handbook aimed at helping *you*.

It's as comprehensive as any short handbook can be. We look together not only at the very practical matters you're having to deal with now, but at your emotional life and the obstacles that can make it even more daunting to cope with day-to-day living. Loneliness, stress, depression and health worries may seem overwhelming when you've no one to give you support. These problems are real, not to be dismissed as personal weakness, hidden from the world through shame, or tackled with no better resource than the proverbial 'stiff upper lip'. Most of the women quoted in the following pages have experienced every kind of negative feeling. Some of them still do. Others, with the passing of time, a little help from their friends, and knowledge of where to get information and advice, have emerged happier, more alive, self-sufficient people than they ever hoped to be. Whatever you're feeling now, I think you can do that, too.

Since separate books – some good, some useless, some patronising – have been written about almost every subject covered here, it must be obvious that every aspect of life can't be tackled in one book. Whenever it's appropriate, though, I've listed other publications (most available in public libraries) that provide more detail, if that's what you need. Similarly, helpful organisations are given in relevant places throughout the book; and a complete list of these, with their addresses, can be found in the 'Directory of useful organisations' at the end of the book.

You probably won't need to read this book straight through, though most chapters will be of use to you at some time. For instance, if you've recently been bereaved, you should find some help in Chapter 3. If you're divorcing, read Chapter 2 and skip Chapter 3. Whether you're widowed or divorced, most of Chapters 4, 5 and 6 will concern you. If housing is your main problem, turn to Chapter 7. When you feel that loneliness is the worst feature of your present life, read Chapters 11 and 12. If you have children, Chapter 14 could be helpful. A middle-aged woman could find some answers to her problems in Chapter 16, and an older woman could be helped by consulting Chapter 20. If you plan to take on paid work, or go back to full- or part-time education, Chapter 8 is for you. If you're a car owner who hasn't a clue about regular maintenance, look at Chapter 10. If, like so many of us, you hardly know the difference between a screwdriver and a chisel and you can't tackle simple electrical repairs, Chapter 9 will help you. And everyone, no matter what her age, wants more than ever now she has to depend on her own strength, to keep fit and healthy: there's plenty on diet, exercise and healthy living in Chapter 15. You may not now be able to afford the sort of holiday you've been used to – but you do need to take a break from time to time, and there are some holiday suggestions and planning tips in Chapter 18.

Because you, the reader, don't want an over-optimistic appraisal of what it's like to be alone, or alone with children, this is a serious book. You don't want to be told how to be Superwoman, though, or jollied along, or made to feel guilty because some of the time you feel overwhelmed and everything just seems too much to cope with. What you do want, and what this book aims to give you, is some guidance now and in the future. It aims, too, to show that there are satisfactions to be gained, rewards to be won, and perhaps a new kind of enjoyment in a life in which you take full responsibility for yourself. Of course there are challenges – they're there to be met.

It won't happen all at once, but there will come a time when you know that you've won through. You have a future. Of course it's different from the past – but maybe it's none the worse for that. You'll accept that you're on your own, and that you can achieve things of your own. You are your own woman.

*Because many of the women whose experiences are quoted in this book wish to remain anonymous, all have been given fictitious names.*

# CHAPTER 2
# DIVORCE:
# Picking up the pieces

**This chapter gives you a brief summary of the procedures in divorce and its immediate aftermath. Procedures described in the first part of the chapter apply to England and Wales. There are some differences in Scottish law, and these are summarised on pp. 28–9.**

When a marriage has reached breaking point – and since 1969 'irretrievable breakdown' (with a variety of definitions of exactly what that means) has been the sole ground for divorce – it is almost inevitable that emotions run high. Bitterness and a desire for revenge may cloud the judgment at a time when level-headedness is most needed. That is why do-it-yourself divorce, though possible, may in some cases not be desirable. Unless the divorce is undefended and likely to be very straightforward, or you are an experienced administrator, a hardened negotiator, and persistent with it, you may need help. But if you do decide on a DIY divorce, because you and your husband are in broad agreement about the details, see p. 20 for a rundown on procedure.

## A first step

You'll probably have talked your situation over with friends and relatives, and may have received conflicting advice. But once you have made up your mind at least to consider divorce, your first step is to get legal advice. This may be helpful even if you later decide to do-it-yourself. But if you already have a solicitor, s/he may not be the best person to help you at this point. You need to contact someone who is used to handling 'matrimonial' cases. You may find him or her through personal contacts. But if not, the Citizens Advice Bureau (see telephone directory or public library) or, in cities, a Law Centre, will provide a list of solicitors experienced in divorce.

Your major anxiety about getting a divorce may be the cost of a solicitor's advice and the subsequent court action.

But you can find out very early in the proceedings just how much these costs will be. In theory, at least, it is possible for anyone to get a divorce, whatever her means, provided she has grounds (see p. 15). The CAB or Law Centre can provide leaflets outlining the 'Green Form' and 'Legal Aid' schemes, including the current financial limits.

Most solicitors operate the 'Green Form' scheme. Initially, they will advise you, free, whether or not you are entitled to advice under this scheme. This is decided on the basis of a means test, so on the first interview you should provide evidence of 'disposable income' and 'disposable capital' (the value of your possessions, but not your home or furniture). Your husband's income and capital will not be taken into account, since you are in dispute with him. On the basis of this means test, the solicitor will tell you what the cost (if any) of your contribution to legal advice will be, and will probably ask for this contribution before proceeding further.

You may prefer to start with a brief session with a solicitor under the '£5 for half an hour' scheme. The Legal Aid Solicitor's list, which you can see at the CAB or Law Centre, lists around 7,000 solicitors operating Legal Aid, and those asterisked will give basic advice under the £5 scheme, whatever your means. You should make it clear that this is what you are seeking. You may actually be eligible under the 'Green Form' scheme to pay less than £5 for this advice, and the solicitor will explain this to you. It may be that on the basis of this half-hour consultation you will decide that you can cope with a do-it-yourself divorce.

| **Unreasonable behaviour** | *Jessie cited her husband's 'unreasonable behaviour' as a ground for divorce. She complained that he slept for most of the day and walked around the house at night, preventing her and their children from sleeping. She had tried to persuade him to change his habits but had not been successful. She also claimed that because he slept in the daytime he couldn't get a job.* |
| :--- | :--- |
| | *The husband maintained that his behaviour was not unreasonable, because in the recession he could not get employment, and that it suited his 'time clock' to be awake at night. He had offered Jessie and the children ear plugs to cut out the noise of his movements, but Jessie refused to use them because she was afraid of fire or burglary.* |
| | *The court held that the husband's behaviour was unreasonable since he appeared to have made no attempt to stop walking about or playing the radio, which had caused distress to Jessie and the family.* |

# Grounds for divorce

It will save time, and possibly money, if you are clear from the beginning what the grounds for divorce actually are.

## Grounds for divorce

The petitioner has to show that:
1 The marriage has lasted for one year.
2 That s/he is resident or domiciled in England or Wales.
3 That the marriage has irretrievably broken down. In practice this means that the petitioner must cite one or more of the following grounds:
   a The other spouse has committed adultery, and the petitioner finds it intolerable to live with him or her.
   b The spouse has behaved unreasonably.
   c Both partners want a divorce and have been living apart for at least two years.
   d The other spouse has been in desertion for at least two years.
   e Wife and husband have been living apart for at least five years. In this case it is normally possible to get a divorce even if the other partner doesn't want it.

Of these grounds, 3b is the one most likely to cause uncertainty, but in fact the courts interpret 'unreasonable behaviour' fairly liberally, and will accept that the behaviour complained about is seen as intolerable by the petitioner in her particular circumstances, taking into account that the spouse has not attempted to modify it. For an example of 'unreasonable behaviour' that was disputed, see p. 14.

'Living apart' (see 3 c, d and e) involves separation for continuous periods – though short (less than six months') attempts to get together again don't count. What is meant here is living in separate households. Separate bedrooms in the same dwelling would not count as 'living apart', though occupying completely separate areas with separate cooking facilities probably would. Ask a solicitor.

---

*Lilian has been married for twenty-seven years. Her children are grown-up. She feels her marriage is 'dead'.*

*'We really have nothing in common. He watches sport on TV or goes to the pub every night and goes to football matches at weekends. He's not interested in me or my friends. Sex has just died out – the one thing we've agreed on is that it doesn't work for us any more. He's perfectly reasonable and polite, just bored and boring. I have quite a nice job, but I do think there's more to life than work, housework, cooking and sleep. He doesn't see it like that. I suppose he's quite content to have a good housekeeper and a comfortable home. Anyway, he really does nothing that the divorce court would call 'unreasonable'. I've asked a solicitor about it, and she says that while he doesn't want a divorce it's going to be difficult for me to get one. I know that if I left, after five years he could get a divorce. But I don't think he'd bother. Women like me are trapped. We can't afford to take off on our own.'*

**The man who won't give ground(s)**

## Contesting divorce after five years

After the couple have lived apart for at least five years, a divorce may be granted even if the other partner doesn't want it (see p. 15, 3d). But very exceptionally indeed, the court may refuse to grant a divorce if doing so would cause grave financial or other hardship. In practice, however, this provision has scarcely been used. Although it would seem that a woman with several young children could suffer great financial hardship if there were a divorce, it is generally accepted that a reduction of living standards of both parties is to be expected and this would not be considered 'grave financial hardship'.

One case which was initially successful involved a sixty-three-year-old woman caring for an invalid son. The court held that divorce would involve grave hardship for this woman. The husband appealed against the decision, but in the meantime the son died, and the divorce was granted. Possibly if the son had lived the original decision would have held good – but evidently the husband's solicitor must have thought he had a good case while the invalid son was alive.

In another case, following a breakdown in her marriage a Sicilian woman took her baby son back to Sicily. After five years the husband sought a divorce, but the wife objected on religious grounds and because her son would be ostracised in Sicily, since he would be the child of divorced parents. She regarded these as 'hardships' but the decree was granted despite this.

From these two cases it is clear that in the vast majority of situations it would be almost impossible to invoke this clause in the 'five year separation' rules, and that the original reasons for inserting these exceptions – that women might need protection from suffering serious deprivation as a result of a divorce they did not want – may have been just a sop to placate those who believe that the courts don't always treat women fairly. It is also evident that it is not possible to contest after five years' separation on religious grounds.

## If you go ahead

When you and the solicitor decide that there are grounds for seeking a divorce, you can still get advice under the Green Form scheme – but it's important to stress that the advice and assistance you get in an *undefended* divorce case does not include the actual court proceedings. This scheme is not 'Legal Aid' which does cover court proceedings (see below). You should be able to get funding to cover up to £75 worth of the solicitor's fees, but as we've seen (p. 14) you must undergo a means test if you have advice under this scheme. This will normally cover the drafting of the divorce petition and general advice on any problems associated with the divorce, and perhaps some correspondence. Though the solicitor can tell the client what to do, the actual filing of the petition has to be done by the petitioner. The only exceptions are when cases are complicated – or when there is a dispute between the spouses about finance or arrangements for any children. In such cases *and when the divorce is defended*, Legal Aid may be available.

Remember that in addition to any legal fees, court fees are payable if these will amount to rather less than £50. Your solicitor or the Citizens' Advice Bureau will tell you what to do if you are unable to pay the court fees.

**Legal Aid**
If you are the petitioner, you may be eligible for Legal Aid – as may your husband be as respondent. We are assuming here that you are the petitioner, but of course the same rules apply throughout if the positions are reversed. As with the Green Form scheme, you can get advice without charge to tell you whether you are eligible for Legal Aid, but the process is slower, because the solicitor has to put your case before the Legal Aid authorities. Unless you have already had a review of your means because you have applied for Family Income Supplement or Supplementary Benefit, you will have to be interviewed at the local Department of Health and Social Security office, to decide whether you are eligible. If you are, the contribution you must pay towards the costs of your legal advice will be assessed. You may be told what the maximum amount of your contribution could be, taking into account that, as a result of the divorce, you may in the future have the means to make this contribution. *This is a point that needs to be watched*: if there is a dispute about the family home, for instance, you could find yourself having to sell your share in order to pay for the legal aid you have received to enable you to get this share!

You may also be told what your actual contribution in the initial stages will be, and you may be able to arrange to pay this by instalments. Your solicitor will be notified, and at that point you can decide whether or not to take up the offer of Legal Aid.

The certificate received by the solicitor will tell her or him what work can be done for you on Legal Aid. This normally includes all the advice needed to cover the problems associated with your divorce, and also court attendance if this is necessary in a *defended divorce* case.

---

## Legal Aid

Legal Aid and advice under the Green Form scheme do not cover a solicitor's attendance in court if the divorce is undefended. If the divorce is defended (that is, contested by the respondent – your husband) your solicitor can represent you in court under the Legal Aid scheme.

---

## Free Legal Aid?

You may think you qualify for free legal aid – but watch it! Mavis had legal aid when she petitioned for divorce from Peter. She didn't have to pay for this when the proceedings were started. But at the hearing, the judge ordered Peter to pay a lump sum of £10,000 to her. Her costs came to £3,500, and Peter was ordered to pay £1,000 of these. The Law Society, which administers the legal aid scheme, had first charge on Mavis's assets (the £10,000) so she found herself liable for £2,500 (the full cost, £3,500, minus Peter's share). Thus her original lump sum shrank to £7,500.

Joyce was awarded a lump sum of £2,000. Although her legal costs came to a little more than this, she was exempted from payment because her assets were less than £2,500.

*See further examples concerning the statutory charge on money and property in the Consumers' Association Guide listed on p. 30.*

# Money before divorce

If you have been left with no means of support, and you have not yet taken action to get a divorce or are in process of doing so, you can apply to the magistrates' court for maintenance from your husband. You can do this without a solicitor. Go to the magistrates' court in the county in which you or your husband live, tell the warrant officer that you wish to apply for a maintenance order, and fill in a form. You will then be told to appear before a magistrate, who will satisfy her- or himself about your need, and then issue a summons against your husband. The court staff will see that the order is served on your husband. Again, we are assuming that it is you, the wife, who is without means. If, for example, your husband were unemployed and you were in work, and had left him with the children, the position might be reversed.

It may be a week or more before the case is heard, so if the need for money is pressing, you will have to apply to the DHSS for Supplementary Benefit (see p. 00).

Both partners must appear before the magistrate(s) who hear the application in private. If the husband fails to appear without good reason, the court can order him to do so, and failure to appear at an adjourned hearing will involve a heavy penalty.

The court must decide that the husband (or wife) has failed to provide the spouse or children with reasonable maintenance, or that he or she has behaved in such a way that it is not reasonable for the spouse to live with him or her, or that he has deserted the spouse. The amount awarded including the sum (if any) for children will depend on the individual case. It will generally approximate to the 'one-third' rule (see p. 23) but may be rather less; the magistrates will probably not order the husband to pay a sum in maintenance that would leave him on less than the Social Security 'subsistence' level. Since this would probably result in the wife not having enough for her needs, she would have to apply for Supplementary Benefit as above. This is particularly likely if the husband is unemployed.

If you find yourself without means for living expenses *after* the filing of a divorce petition, but before your case comes to court, you can apply to the divorce court – that is, the county court if the divorce is undefended, otherwise the High Court – for 'maintenance pending suit'. The amount which the court decides your husband must pay is not necessarily the amount ultimately payable when the divorce has gone through, but should be sufficient to enable you to maintain yourself and any dependent children for the time being.

---

*Mira's husband walked out on her and did not tell her where he was living. He left her with no money for the rent and living expenses – she was earning less than £20 a week in her part-time job. She decided to consider applying for a divorce, but in the meantime needed money to meet her debts. The Citizens' Advice Bureau explained to her how to apply for a maintenance order, and that before this came through she could get something from the DHSS under the Supplementary Benefit system. Finding this out took half a day, because of the queue at the CAB. She couldn't leave her children again the same day, so had to spend another morning at the DHSS local office before being seen by an official there. After some searching and embarrassing questions she was granted Supplementary Benefit to cover her rent for the week – but the fact that she'd missed half a day's work wasn't taken into account. 'If it hadn't been for my mother giving me £10 for food for the rest of the week until I had to go before the magistrate for the maintenance order we'd have just about starved. As it was I had to get another two weeks' money on Supplementary Benefit before my husband paid up.'*

**Money before divorce**

---

# Do-it-yourself divorce

If you intend to make a financial claim it is not desirable to go it alone. However, it may be useful to explain what has to be done if you decide to handle the whole matter yourself, because a rundown on the procedure to be followed will also enable you to see just what is involved if a solicitor is advising you, and to keep a check on what is happening. *Remember that this applies only to undefended divorce* (i.e. when your husband is not opposing the granting of a divorce). As we've seen, you will need legal help if he is defending, and this can be free or very cheap according to your means.

See below for a step-by-step guide.

## Do-it-yourself divorce

This is a step-by-step guide for anyone handling the divorce for herself or to enable her to check on progress if a solicitor is involved. Remember, this refers to *undefended divorce* only.

**What to do:**

1 Get a copy of the marriage certificate.

2 Go to the county (divorce) court and ask for form D8 – this is the standard divorce petition form. You will need three copies – four if you are citing adultery. If there are children in full-time education you will also need three copies of form D8A. Finally, you should ask for the notes on guidance on filling in the forms and the essential free booklet 'Undefended Divorce' which will help you with your DIY divorce.

3 Fill in all the copies of D8 and D8A (if applicable), using the guidance notes and 'Undefended Divorce'.

4 You are now ready to start divorce proceedings. Take to the court office:

    a Two (or three, see above) copies of form D8 and form D8A (if applicable).

    b The marriage certificate.

    c A fee of £35 (ask for exemption if your means are limited – take proof of this).

    *Note that if you are claiming a share in your family home you may have to register your claim and for this you really need to consult a solicitor.*

5 The court will now send the respondent (your husband) a copy of your petition (D8) and a copy of D8A, which is the Statement of Arrangements for Children (if applicable); a Notice of Proceedings form; and an Acknowledgment of Service form which he has to return to show that he has received these documents and that he does not intend to defend the petition.

6 Now the court send you, the petitioner, a copy of the Acknowledgment of Service form; a form for you to ask for Directions for Trial; and a standard form of affidavit for you to fill in. This affidavit states on what grounds you are making your petition and the evidence you have to support it.

7 Take the completed affidavit and the copy of Acknowledgment of Service to a solicitor or court official and sign them in front of her or him. The solicitor will charge a small fee. The court official does not charge. Send the documents to the court along with the form asking for Directions for Trial.

8 A registrar will consider the affidavit and evidence. If he is satisfied that the evidence is sufficient to entitle you to a divorce, he will send copies of a certificate to both spouses. At the same time, if there are children he will notify you of the date for an appointment before the judge 'the children's appointment'). On that day, in a private hearing, which should be attended by both parents, he will consider the arrangements you have proposed for the children. If the judge is not satisfied with your proposals, he will adjourn the proceedings until you come up with a more acceptable solution, and he may possibly ask for a welfare officer's report. This could involve a visit to your home by the welfare officer, whether or

not you are already involved with the social services social worker.

9 Once the 'decree nisi' has been pronounced, both spouses are sent copies, and also a copy of the judge's order about the children.

10 Ask at the court for a standard form of application to make the decree nisi 'absolute', and send it to the court at least six weeks after the decree nisi.

11 The court now makes the decree absolute, and a certificate to that effect is sent to both spouses. This means that the divorce is now completed and both of you are now free to marry again if you wish.

Depending on the length of time taken by the preliminary stages, and on the speed at which the court has been able to put your case on its list for a hearing, a straightforward, undefended divorce can be granted within a few months or up to a year of the initiation of proceedings.

*Note:* If it is your husband rather than you who initiates the divorce proceedings as petitioner, the procedures outlined above will be exactly the same, so for 'you' read 'your husband' and for 'your husband' read 'you'.

## Court attendance

If no children are involved, there is no need for either partner in an undefended divorce to attend court in person when the hearing takes place. Everything is done by post. However, you may attend the court if you wish.

## Cutting the cost

Although you may wish to 'do-it-yourself' primarily to avoid solicitors' fees, it's sensible to find out how much the divorce is likely to cost you if you do employ a solicitor. You could find that you have very little to pay, or even nothing at all, if your financial situation allows you to take full advantage of legal aid. For how to find this out, see p. 17.

# Alternatives to divorce

Before the 1970s and the simpler divorce laws, various forms of separation order were more common than they are today. However, if a couple do not want to divorce they can simply decide to separate, making an informal arrangement for maintenance of wife or husband and children, if necessary. Apart from the possibility that one or both partners will not stick to the agreement, there is also a possible difficulty over taxation, since the income tax inspectorate may not be willing to give each partner a separate tax allowance unless there is a *formal* separation agreement. It is usually much better to take legal advice and have a proper *deed of separation* drawn up.

A magistrate's *separation order* is usually applied for in circumstances where there is danger of violence to the spouse or the children. The violent spouse (usually the man, of course) can be ordered to be excluded from the marital home. A solicitor or a Women's Aid Centre can advise. A maintenance order (see p. 18) can also be applied for in the magistrates' court.

Then there is the rare 'judicial separation'. This is an alternative to divorce, but to obtain it the petitioner still has to prove that one of the five grounds cited on p. 15 applies. There is no 'one year rule', however. Following a judicial separation neither partner is free to remarry. It must be remembered, though, that after five years' separation either partner can get a divorce if s/he has grounds for doing so. Thus the religious scruples that are usually the cause for a petition for judicial separation rather than divorce can be overruled.

Finally, there is *annulment*. There are a number of possible grounds for this, chief among them being non-consummation, bigamy, irregularity in the original marriage formalities or – if proceedings are started within one year of marriage – pregnancy by another man at the time of the marriage. Marriages may be pronounced *void* or *voidable*: i.e. in the first instance according to the law no marriage took place, in the second there was a marriage but it was defective. *Annulment is unusual and complicated, and legal advice is needed.*

**Non-consummation**

*Melody was twenty-five when she married John, thirty-nine. They had not had sexual relations before marriage, because both believed that this was wrong. Melody was not too disturbed when 'nothing happened' in the first few weeks as she felt that John had been over-tired at work and by the excitement of the wedding. However, as time went on, she found her own advances to him being received first, with indifference, and then actually repulsed. Eventually he insisted on sleeping in a separate room and finally he told her that the idea of sex disgusted him and that he would never be willing to have relations with her.*

*Melody consulted her doctor and later, a solicitor. After some time – and a medical examination, which showed that she was a virgin – she was able to get an annulment of the marriage, and has since remarried. If she had not been a virgin, the case would have been more difficult to prove: she would have had to get John to testify that he had not had and would not have 'marital relations'.*

# Money after divorce

No matter which court has dealt with the divorce or separation, you can apply for maintenance for yourself and any children or adopted children of the marriage. For 'maintenance pending suit' see p. 19.

The divorce court can divide the family assets and property at the time of the divorce. Over recent years certain guidelines have evolved, and even though every set of circumstances is different, it is possible to give a rough guide about what will probably happen following your separation or divorce.

The basic rule has been that a wife (particularly if she has had children) would be allotted something like one-third of the family assets, and one-third of the couple's gross combined income. The main asset is usually the family home, but it can also be money in the bank or other valuable property. The gross income is the regular sum received by both partners – or by only one of them if both do not earn.

When you file your petition for divorce, you can include with it a request for interim maintenance for yourself and/or for your children. As soon as the proceedings have started, you should apply for maintenance in the long term, and this must be supported by an 'affidavit of means' setting out your finances and your estimate of those of your husband. Once the maintenance order has been made, you should ask for it to be registered in the magistrates' court

## Maintenance change

Under the Matrimonial and Family Proceedings Act 1984 the court must consider whether it should terminate the financial obligations of each party towards the other after the divorce, and when it would be fair and reasonable to do so. It has to consider the income of each party, their earning capacity and their property and other financial resources, taking into account:
• Financial needs, obligations and responsibilities now and in the foreseeable future
• Age of the parties
• How long the marriage has lasted
• The family's standard of living before the breakdown of the marriage

• Any physical or mental disabilities
• Any contributions made by either party to the family's welfare (in money or in kind)
• In certain circumstances, the 'conduct' of the parties (this is discussed in the Consumers' Association book listed on p. 30)
• The value of any future benefits (e.g. pension rights) either party may lose as a result of the divorce.
*At the time of going to press it is too early to assess just how this new legislation will work in practice. Many believe that it could disadvantage still further the woman left on her own after years of marriage.*

– this is to ensure that you can take action if your husband stops paying. (For further information see Chapter 6.)

Clearly it has not always been possible to apply the 'one-third' rule to property. The court, therefore, has powers to re-allocate all your property between you. In the case of a house, it can order one of you to transfer it to the other; or to share it; or to settle it on trust to one spouse; or to sell it and share the proceeds.

**Maintenance – two views**

*Alice is fifty-three. She married at nineteen and had three children, all now grown-up. She never had a 'proper job' as she stayed at home between leaving school and getting married, to help her mother with younger children, and after she had her own children she looked after them until the youngest was in her late teens. She is now divorced.*

*When her husband left her for a younger woman Alice decided to go to college as a 'mature student' and train to be a teacher. Although she had no dependent children she felt entitled to accept maintenance for herself from her ex-husband because during their partnership she had seen her job as looking after their children and this had prevented her from training or following a separate career. Even when, after four years' study, she became a qualified teacher, she regarded the maintenance that she was still receiving as some compensation for the lack of seniority in her profession that prevented her from earning as much as she would have done if she had not stayed at home with the children. 'I have no qualms about accepting the money the court ordered,' she says. Under the new legislation, her 'earning capacity' might have been taken into account, despite her age.*

*Rose is a divorced woman of fifty-seven. Her children are off her hands. With two short interruptions when her children were born she has been able to carry on with her job throughout her marriage and after it broke up. She is earning well and does not wish to be obligated towards her former husband by accepting any maintenance from him. 'I am lucky to be in this position,' she admits. 'I might feel differently if I had not been able to make such a good career for myself, despite having children. My only worry now is old age – my pension alone won't be nearly as good as the joint ones would have been, since my ex-husband is now a very high earner and will get a large pension.' But she feels that her financial independence is something that is worth more than relative affluence in the future.*

When there are young children, it is usual for the mother to have them living with her, and thus she is the one likely to be able to stay in the family home, at least until the youngest child has left full-time education; and the fact that she has a home is taken into account when the court fixed the amount of maintenance to be paid to her and the children. When the home is a rented one, there are no problems about transferring the tenancy to the wife.

Inevitably every couple's circumstances are different, but if you can bear in mind that *if you have dependent children* the probability is that the court will award you something like 25–30 per cent of joint assets and income, you will have something upon which to base future plans. Even before recent changes in the law, however, if you were childless, the marriage had been of short duration and you had a good job, the court could decide that the 'one-third rule' should not apply. You might have decided, law or no law, to adopt a 'clean break' policy and ask for nothing from your former husband. Recent legislation has confirmed this; following a great deal of pressure from a campaign representing, in the main, the interests of better-off ex-husbands, in late 1984 the law was changed, and now the court has to consider whether to terminate the financial obligations of each partner towards the other, having regard to income and potential earning capacity and financial resources. 'Conduct' of the parties is also considered. See p. 30.

Women's organisations have been very critical of the new legislation, which may be particularly hard on middle-aged women whose 'earning capacity' is somewhat notional, particularly at a time of high unemployment.

Of course there are some women who feel that even if they have children they would prefer financial independence, and will make every effort to provide for themselves and their children without taking anything from the former husband. Others, aware that women's earnings are often inadequate to keep a family, don't ask for maintenance for themselves but will try to ensure the children's wellbeing by claiming maintenance for them: and this may have tax advantages, too.

Older women, many of whom have spent years at home looking after children, feel that they have a strong case for compensation by their husbands for the loss of career prospects that the long break from employment has entailed. Two different viewpoints on this are expressed by the women quoted on p. 24.

# Custody, care and control

One of the documents that must be lodged by the petitioner is the Statement of Arrangements for Children (see form D8A, p. 20). This records the proposals for the care and custody of the children, and the judge has to approve these. Both parents have to attend the judge's chambers (see p. 20) and even in an undefended case, the court hearing. (It is only when there are no children that divorce through the post is possible.) The court is concerned only with arrangements for children under sixteen, unless they are in full-time education, when the limit is eighteen; there is no limit for handicapped children.

Parents are usually able to make a satisfactory agreement about their children. It is common for the mother to have the children living with her (called 'care and control'), but the father to have legal custody. This means that he has to take major decisions about them, while the mother is in charge of day-to-day arrangements (see p. 28 for an example). This arrangement is called a 'split order'. If you have good reason to believe that this sort of agreement is undesirable, of course you can ask the court to order a different arrangement.

When the court decides about care, control and custody, it will also want to be satisfied about the arrangements for access by the parent with whom the children are not living.

If the parents cannot agree about custody, this does not mean that the divorce comes into the category of 'defended'. But it may be wise to get a solicitor's advice.

In deciding the outcome of disputed cases, the judge will normally take a report from a welfare officer, who will visit the parents and discuss the children and their relationship with them and any new partner with whom one or other parent may now be living.

Further reports from a child's school, social worker or other concerned professionals may be asked for. And if s/he is considered old enough – around ten or more – her or his feelings will be discussed with the child and taken into account. The prime consideration is held to be the welfare of the child.

## Lesbian mothers

The best explanation of the rights of lesbian mothers, including the legal position in the event of divorce, is *Lesbian Mothers on Trial* published by the Rights of Women, 52 Featherstone Street, London EC1 price £2.00 including postage.

As we shall see from Liz's story (see below) this whole area of care and custody can be fraught with problems, and despite initial agreement about the children it is all too possible for resentment to build up on both sides. Fathers sometimes use the fact that they have only limited access to their children as an excuse to default on maintenance payments, and mothers may block access because payments are in arrears. The children in such a case can be used as pawns in a bitter war of attrition.

This kind of dispute may even lead to one parent trying to remove the child, by force or otherwise, and taking her or him out of the country. Even though this may seem unlikely in your case, it's as well to be aware of the procedure for making a child a 'ward of court'. This is done by application to the High Court (through a solicitor – Legal

---

**Access and maintenance**

*On her divorce, the court awarded Liz a sum in maintenance for herself and her two children that she felt should have been just about adequate for their needs. Her former husband was to have access to the children – he could see them on alternate weekends and have them to stay with him and his new partner overnight once a month.*

*'Things went all right for a while, but two things happened. First, he started to fall behind with the money, then he started to let the children down – promising to come and see them and not turning up. I had to handle their upsets over this and try not to let them see how rotten I thought he was to behave like that. They got really confused and difficult and I felt the whole thing was so unfair – I was short of money and I had these disturbed children to cope with. So when he did finally arrive to take them out I said he couldn't unless he paid me the money he owed.*

*'It was a horrible situation – I'd never imagined that I could behave like that, depriving the children of their father so that in a way he would have to pay to see them. I suppose I was even more bitter about it all because by this time he had landed a very good job and could easily pay me more than the court had ordered. So it was all very complicated. I've been back to the court, and the result is that for the moment, anyway, I'm getting a bit more money and he's seeing the children more regularly. But our divorce, which was going to be so "civilised" has worked out really badly. I know I'm not the only woman in this position – far too many find that they go on fighting about money and access arrangements long after everything should be settled. And it's the children who suffer most of all.'*

---

Aid is available for this) and may be accomplished very quickly. When the application is granted, the child may not be taken out of the country without the court's permission. This procedure would not apply if the child is taken abroad on a short holiday, of course, but it's as well to get the other parent's permission if at all feasible.

Another matter that can arise is the desire of one parent to change the child's surname. Normally this cannot be done without the other parent's consent, but the courts can override this, although it seldom happens.

---

**Custody, care and control**

*Brian was given custody of Jennifer, twelve, and Martin, ten. Their mother, Jane, was given care and control. Martin was a 'difficult' child and Brian felt that he needed to go to a boarding school that had a reputation for helping such children. Jane believed that she could handle Martin herself, that she would prefer to keep him at home, and that it would be better for him to go to the same comprehensive school as his sister, who was happily settled there. But the 'custody' order meant that Brian could have the last word in deciding about Martin's school.*

*Jennifer felt she was old enough to go to the local disco and stay out late. Jane made a rule that the disco was out of bounds during term-time. Jennifer appealed to Brian to overrule her mother, but he rightly said that this was a matter for Jane to decide as she had 'care and control' and this was not a question of a major decision about the child's future.*

---

## Divorce in Northern Ireland

The law and procedure for divorce in Northern Ireland are much the same as in England and Wales. The main differences are that there are no 'postal' or 'special procedure' divorces (this means that both parties must attend the court and give evidence in person); that you can choose in the case of an undefended divorce whether to go to the county court or the High Court; that legal aid is available for all divorce proceedings; and that the Matrimonial Homes Act does not operate.

## Divorce in Scotland

There are some procedural differences and in some cases different terminology is used, but, broadly, getting a divorce in Scotland follows much the same lines as in England and Wales.

Your Citizens' Advice Bureau can provide you with a useful and comprehensive booklet – 'Getting Divorced? A Guide to Divorce in Scotland' – and this sets out very clearly the procedure to be followed, whether or not you get advice from a solicitor.

You can ask for a divorce in Scotland if you or your spouse have lived in Scotland for at least a year (holidays don't count) before you apply for divorce, or if Scotland is your permanent home and you intend to remain permanently in Scotland in the foreseeable future.

The ground for divorce in Scotland, as in England, is irretrievable breakdown of the marriage (see pp. 15–21). But there is one difference:- whereas in England the marriage must have lasted one year before proceedings can be started, in Scotland there is no minimum period during which you must have been married before you can apply for divorce on grounds of unreasonable behaviour or adultery. And in the case of adultery, you can have had a trial reconciliation for up to three months (six months in England). But as in England, if you are citing two years' mutually agreed separation, you may have spent six months in a trial reconciliation (see 3c and d, p. 15).

The terms used when referring to maintenance are different:- the regular weekly or monthly payment made to the parent with custody is called 'aliment', and the regular sum paid to the spouse is called 'periodical aliment'. Scottish courts don't have the power to order the transfer of ownership of the family home from one spouse to the other, but they can order the payment of a lump sum to compensate for the loss of any contributions made to the value of the family's home. As in England, it is wise to take legal advice about this point, since once you are no longer married, your rights of occupancy of your home will cease, unless you have taken steps to secure them.

Until very recently, all divorces in Scotland were handled by the Court of Session in Edinburgh, but since last year the law has been changed and they may also be dealt with by the local Sheriff Court. The system of free or cheap legal aid is broadly similar to that in England and Wales.

One big difference is that a Scottish divorce is final once the court has granted it – there is no period of decree nisi. In Scotland a DIY divorce can be completed in about two months. DIY divorce in Scotland is not possible when one spouse intends to make a financial claim at the time of the divorce (in England and Wales it is permissible, but probably unwise – see p. 19).

# Still undecided?

The majority of women reading this book will have reached the point of no return as far as their marriage is concerned. But if you are still not quite sure whether or not your marriage could be revived, and you feel that talking things over with an experienced counsellor could help, there is a Family Conciliation Service in some towns, and if there is one near you the Citizens' Advice Bureau will tell you. Unfortunately Government cuts have meant that some of the fifteen or so Family Conciliation Service units that were operating in 1982 are no longer functioning. Marriage Guidance Counsellors tend to have a somewhat 'do-gooding' middle-class image – justified in some cases – but even though they are trained not to give actual advice, they can provide a sounding board which some of their clients find useful. You are asked to pay what you can afford.

You don't have to stick with your counsellor if you find her or him less than helpful and understanding, but it's worth trying a few interviews to see whether s/he is able to assist you to clarify your thoughts and feelings. Appointments can be made by telephone (local directory) but unless your case is desperate you may have to wait.

Although many women feel particularly friendless and isolated at this time, there are women's groups in most areas, and women's centres in many towns, and even if you have never been part of a group before, you could find support and friendship in one of these. Many older women will have been through difficult divorces themselves and so will be particularly understanding and supportive. A Woman's Place in London can give you a contact address, and read Chapter 12.

## Where to get help

Wherever you live in the United Kingdom you will probably find that the local Citizens' Advice Bureau is the best source of preliminary information and advice. The address is in the telephone directory or you can ask for it at the public library.

The CAB can supply booklets and leaflets. 'Undefended Divorce' is available free from the county court, and is essential reading.

Look in the reference section of your public library for books giving more detailed information. *Divorce: Legal Procedures and Financial Facts* edited by Edith Rudinger, published by the Consumers' Association, is fairly easy to follow. If you need your own copy, it can be ordered from a bookshop. Make sure you get the most recent edition (1984), which briefly outlines recent changes in the law. Three free leaflets on legal aid are obtainable from the Law Society. 'Guide for the Petitioner Acting without a Solicitor' is free from the Divorce Registry.

# CHAPTER 3
# BEREAVEMENT:
## Picking up the pieces

**In this chapter we look at some of the practical things that have to be done following the death of a partner. A brief rundown on immediate action is followed by an explanation of the formalities that have to be gone through in the first few weeks and months. The procedures described apply to England and Wales, but where there are differences in Scottish law these are summarised on p. 41.**

Whether the death of your partner was sudden or following prolonged illness you are in a state of shock. If you have had to do the nursing yourself or have spent long hours at a hospital bedside you feel physically and emotionally drained. Yet it is at this time, when you have just been through what may have been the most devastating experience of your life, that there are certain inescapable formalities that have to be attended to. Just because you are in shock, for the first few days you may feel numbed, and function almost automatically. It is only some days later that the full force of your new situation may hit you. Don't feel at this early stage that you 'ought' to be able to cope. Get help from friends and relatives – especially adult daughters and sons if you are close to them. The time to struggle for independence will come later.

## Immediate action

Most readers will consult this book after the funeral, when they are wondering about the next steps to take in the seemingly endless process of completing the formalities connected with death in the family. For those not yet at this stage, the following is a very brief summary of the action to be taken once death is confirmed. The undertaker (funeral director) will guide you through the process. And the books mentioned on p. 36 will help fill in the details and advise you on procedures and choices. Everything may seem daunting, but people *do* cope.

## Immediate action

**If the death was at home,** you should inform the family doctor; relatives; possibly clergy; and, if the death was accidental or as a result of violence, the police.

If the doctor was attending the patient during his or her last illness, s/he will give you: a sealed envelope containing a free certificate showing the cause of death, and addressed to the Registrar of Deaths; and a formal notice stating that s/he has signed the medical certificate and telling you how to register the death.

If the doctor did not attend the patient during his or her last illness, or within 14 days of death; or if s/he is not certain of the cause of death; or if death was sudden or resulted from an accident, violence, or industrial disease, s/he will report the death to the coroner.

**When the death was in hospital** the ward sister will inform you or another close relative. You or the relative will have to go to the hospital to collect the possessions, and if the deceased person was not an in-patient, identify the body.

As with a death at home, the hospital doctor will give you a certificate of death. You may be asked for permission to perform a *post mortem*. If the death was sudden, the hospital doctor will carry out the procedure of reporting to the coroner, as outlined above.

**If the coroner is notified** he may decide to hold an inquest. He will usually hold a preliminary hearing within a few days of the death; this is for identification only. After this the coroner will normally release the body for burial or cremation, and if the post mortem showed that the death was from natural causes, a notification to the Registrar. When the coroner has not been able to find the cause of death, some weeks later an inquest to determine this will be held, possibly with a jury. Once this is completed, the coroner will send a cause of death certificate to the Registrar.

### Registering the death

The local Registrar of Births, Marriages and Deaths is listed in the telephone directory. You cannot register a death reported to the coroner until he has issued the required certificate (see above). But if the death was not reported to the coroner, you or a close relative or someone present at the death must register it within five days (see p. 33)

# The funeral

### Arranging the funeral

Although in theory it would be possible to make all the arrangements for a funeral yourself, in practice this is something for which you do have to engage an undertaker or funeral director. Someone who is a member of the National Association of Funeral Directors has to abide by a Code of Practice agreed with the Office of Fair Trading, and must give you an estimate of costs for a 'basic funeral'. He should also be able to give you information about the costs for anything you require over and above this basic price.

## Registering the death

You must take with you:
- the medical certificate;
- the deceased person's National Health card if you have it;
- any war pension order book if you have it;

The Registrar will want to know;
- date and place of death;
- the deceased person's usual address;
- full names and surnames of the deceased person (and maiden name for a woman);
- his or her occupation (and her husband's if she was a married woman);
- his or her date of birth and the town, county and country of birth;
- your date of birth, if you were married to the deceased person, or her husband's date of birth if she was a married woman;
- whether the deceased person was receiving any state benefits.

The Registrar will register the death and give you:
- a certificate of disposal (unless the coroner has already issued this). You will need to give this to the undertaker (funeral director) before burial or cremation can take place; and
- a certificate of registration of death. You need this for the DHSS office so that you can claim a death grant and, if applicable, widow's benefit (see p. 43.)

You will need extra copies, for which you will have to pay, to claim on insurance policies and for other purposes. It is advisable to get at least three of these, but you can get extra copies later if necessary;
- booklets on welfare benefits to which you might be entitled;
- form PR48 which explains how to get a Grant of Probate.

---

You will find that even the simplest funeral can cost £250 or more (1984). The statutory death grant can be used towards this cost, but is likely to be only a fraction of the total. If you are on or near Supplementary Benefit levels you may get Supplementary Benefit to pay for the funeral; arrange this at the local Social Security office before arranging the funeral. It is obviously a great advantage to have had a joint bank account on which you can draw for immediate expenses. Usually, the deceased person's estate will be used to meet the funeral costs, but this may only be available after probate has been granted. Meanwhile, building societies or banks may be prepared to release up to £1,500 on production of a death certificate.

The funeral director will explain the procedure for burial, and will provide a form of application to the cemetery which you or an executor must sign before burial can take place. For a cremation there are other formalities. You will need the disposal certificate obtained from the Registrar, plus two cremation certificates signed by your family doctor and another doctor – fees are normally payable. You or the funeral director will also need a cremation certificate signed by the medical referee of the crematorium – the fee is usually included in cremation charges – and two forms signed by the executor or you as next-of-kin. One of these applies for the cremation, the other gives instructions for disposal of the ashes.

**After the funeral**
Once the immediate formalities are completed – probably after the funeral has taken place – you have other matters to attend to.

## After the funeral

You should:
- return any pension or welfare benefit book to the local office of the DHSS;
- go through the will (if there is one);
- apply for the death grants and any other welfare benefits (see p. 43);
- inform the deceased person's bank and insurance companies of the death;
- return any season tickets to the authorities involved so that refunds can be obtained;
- if you are using the deceased person's car, get a new insurance certificate;
- inform credit card companies, but don't pay outstanding accounts;
- decide who is to be the personal representative(s) – see below;
- once this is done, start to administer the estate (for checklist see p. 38).

# The will

**The personal representative**
If there is a will, it is likely that someone, or more than one person, will have been appointed as executor (executrix, if a woman). If there is no will, or no executor has been named, then you must decide who is to act in dealing with all the financial and other matters arising out of the death. In either event, this is a very time-consuming and possibly complicated job, particularly if there is a large amount of property or money involved, with a number of investments, insurance policies, bank accounts and so on to be dealt with. If the estate is a small one, with assets consisting perhaps only of money in a current bank account, a house or flat, and some savings in a building society account, and if the person who has died has left all his or her property to the partner, the job of the personal representative will be a lot easier. It is easier still all round if the bank account was a joint one and the ownership or tenancy of the house or flat was in both names.

One of the executors nominated in the will may be a solicitor, and in this case it was obviously intended that the whole process of getting a Grant of Probate and winding up the estate should not be a burden on the surviving partner or any other family member or friend. And it may well be that, even if you have been appointed executrix, faced with the possibly complicated job of dealing with your partner's affairs, you will decide that you need to hand it over to an experienced solicitor. You are within your rights to do this.

Of course getting this sort of help is not cheap. The 'estate' will eventually be charged the solicitor's fees, which means that there will be that much less left for you or another legatee. But if the provisions of the will are complicated, and the amount of assets and property involved is substantial, you may feel that this would be money well spent. Legal fees for probate work are charged on a time basis, plus about 25–30 per cent for clerical work, plus 1 per cent of the gross value of the estate. VAT is added to the bill. Thus for a fairly substantial estate you could find yourself (or the estate) with a solicitor's bill of around £2,000. If the assets are much smaller, the bill would be less. You are entitled, and advised, to ask the solicitor for a rough estimate of the costs before entrusting him with this work.

If the solicitor takes no part in administering the estate, merely taking out Grant of Probate (or, when there is no will, Letters of Administration) s/he will probably charge only 1/6 per cent of the total estate, and much less time would be spent, so that the eventual cost could probably be reckoned in hundreds rather than thousands of pounds.

When no solicitor has been nominated as executor in the will, or there is no will, and you decide to use the services of one, it's important to ask around for recommendations, if at all possible. A friend may have had good or bad experiences with one particular firm. You can get a list of solicitors from the Citizens' Advice Bureau; or your bank may be able to recommend someone – but unless you are willing for the estate to be debited with a very large sum

---

## Grant of probate

When someone has left a will appointing an executor or executrix that person is called a 'personal representative'. If there is no will, the personal representative is known as an 'administrator'. In either case, s/he has to get an official document, issued by the High Court, to show that s/he has legal authority to deal with the property.

Executors are said to 'prove the will', and the document they get from the High Court is the 'Grant of Probate'. Administrators get a Grant of Letters of Administration. The estate cannot be distributed until the Grant of Probate or Letters of Administration have been obtained. But for the winding up of a small estate, see p. 37.

of money, remember that although banks can and do take over the whole business of getting probate and administering the estate, and are usually very efficient in doing so, their charges are even higher than those of the High Street solicitors.

### When there is no will

If a person dies 'intestate', the first £40,000 (1984) of his or her estate goes to the surviving spouse (unless they were divorced) and then to children or other relatives. The rules governing intestacy are summarised on p. 37.

### Administering the estate

If you decide to administer the estate and apply for Grant of Probate on a do-it-yourself basis – and most people who undertake this do so in order the save the very substantial fees of solicitors – you must appreciate that this can be a very long and tedious business. Depending on your circumstances and personality, it could be that having to get on with all this work in the immediate aftermath of bereavement may have a good effect on you. You may feel that this is a job to do, something to occupy your mind for at least part of each day. On the other hand, if it is going to involve great effort and impose an even greater strain on you than you have already been suffering, you may feel it would be just too much to undertake at this time.

If someone else has been appointed executor, or is willing to be the personal representative, s/he too, will have to consider the pros and cons of 'doing it yourself'.

For those who do decide to administer the estate personally, the steps outlined on p. 38 are the ones that have to be taken. This can only be a brief outline: you are advised to consult a book such as the Consumers' Association's *Wills and Probate* (this should be in your public library), though the DHSS leaflet D49 *'What to Do When, After A Death'*, may prove comprehensive enough.

| | |
|---|---|
| **Unmarried and intestate** | *Joyce lived with Colin, who was married to someone else, for over 20 years. He died, leaving no will. By law all Colin's property should go to his estranged wife and children. But a 1976 Act of Parliament allowed Joyce to challenge Colin's family's right to the whole of his estate. Since the relationship had lasted so long, Joyce would be entitled to a substantial share – after a lot of legal hassle and high fees. Had Colin left a will, leaving everything to Joyce, his wife could have contested the will and might have received something.* |

**Winding up a small estate** The procedures outlined on pp. 38–9 may seem rather daunting if the amount of money and property left by the deceased person is very small. Fortunately it is normal practice, in the case of a small estate, not to need a Grant of Probate. If the amount held by a bank, building society, etc. is less than £1,500 in each case, those institutions may, at their discretion, pay out the money without seeing a Grant of Probate.

### Intestacy

When someone dies 'intestate' i.e. without making a will, there are certain rules to be followed – and they may or may not conform to what the deceased person would have wished, or in some cases, may be very unjust to those who are left. This is why every adult should make a will, especially if her or his estate is likely to amount to more than a few hundreds of pounds in total. However, if you are now in the position of a dependent whose partner did not make a will – who died 'intestate' – a brief and necessarily summarised account of the rules governing intestacy follows.

If the estate is quite a large one you should undoubtedly consult a solicitor or, at the very least, a book such as the Consumers' Association's *Wills and Probate*.

## When there is no will (intestacy)

If the person who has died has left no will, his or her estate is distributed in this order:

• If the total estate is less than £40,000 everything goes to the widow or widower.

• If the estate is larger, the widow or widower inherits the furniture, car, personal effects and the first £40,000 (which includes any house or flat). Since many relatively modest dwellings are now worth at least £40,000, a widow or widower could find that there was little or nothing beyond the house and personal effects; and s/he might even have to sell this to meet other calls on the estate (see p. 40).

• Once the widow or widower has the above share, the rest of the estate is divided into two: one half to any children equally, the other half as a life interest for the widow or widower (i.e. s/he gets the income from any property, shares, etc. until her or his death.) On the surviving spouse's death, the half-share is divided equally between the children.

• If there is no wife or husband, the estate is divided equally between the children. If there is a wife or husband, but no children, s/he gets everything up to £85,000 and half of the rest. The other half will go to other relatives.

• If an unmarried man or woman dies intestate, the property is divided between his or her parents, or, if they are dead, between his or her brothers and sisters.

• There are provisions for the distribution of the estate if none of these relatives survives.

*The amounts referred to above could change. For up-to-date figures consult DHSS leaflet D49.*

## Administering the estate

These are the steps the executor or executrix or personal representative will have to take:

• Make sure that the immediate post-funeral procedures outlined on p. 34 have been carried out.

• Look at all papers and documents and find out where all the assets and property are.

• Consult the bank about balance, interest and any bank charges in connection with the deceased person's account(s). Ask about securities held by the bank in his or her name.

• Ask a bank to open an 'executor's account'.

• Write to insurance companies notifying them of the death and sending the death certificate. Ask how much is payable on life insurance. Ask for a claim form.

• List any shares held by the deceased person. The bank manager should be able to tell you their value at the date of death.

• Notify the building society if there is a mortgage. Enclose the death certificate. Ask how much was owed at the date of death.

• Decide on the value of any property – house or flat – owned by the deceased person. You may know roughly what similar property in the locality is worth. This value has to be agreed by the District Valuer later.

• Send a copy of the death certificate to any employer or pension fund and ask for details of any sum due on death.

• Send a copy of the death certificate to the Savings Certificate Office, Durham, if the deceased person held any savings certificates, and ask when they were bought and what their value was on the date of death.

• Similarly for Premium Bonds – write to the Bond and Stock Office, Lytham St Annes, Lancs.

• Send a copy of the death certificate to any building society or other savings scheme with the deposit book and ask for it to be completed on the date of death. Ask for a withdrawal form.

• Try to estimate the value of all the personal effects of the deceased person. You may need to consult a secondhand dealer or in the case of a car, a local garage.

• Notify the relevant Inland Revenue office of the death. Ask whether a refund or tax payment are due.

• Make a list of people to whom money is due.

• Make a list of people from whom money is owed.

Now you will be able to go ahead to complete all the forms you need to apply for Probate or Letters of Administration. You need to:

• Write to the nearest Probate Registry or Probate Office (address in telephone directory) for forms 38, 44, 37B and 40. It is obligatory to complete forms 38 and 44, but forms 37B and 40 are required only when there is real property such as a house, flat or land. Form 44 is concerned with Capital Transfer Tax (see Chapter 6, p. 117), and you may find that if the estate is small and it is all to pass to the surviving spouse you will not need to fill in any CTT forms.

• Send all completed forms to the Probate Registry – whose address you will have been given – with the death certificate, the will (keep a copy), and a covering letter, stating whether you wish to attend the Probate Registry or the Probate Office, and also dates and times when you cannot attend.

You will be given an appointment for interview, where any problems will be discussed. You will have to swear a formal oath about CTT and sign a Capital Transfer Tax Warrant. A few weeks later you will receive a set of forms, which are applications for the

Grant of Probate. You must complete and return these, with a copy of the will, and a cheque for the CTT payable to Inland Revenue. The Capital Transfer Tax Account Form explains how this sum is arrived at. (You may have to borrow from the bank to meet this, but if you had a joint account you may be able to settle this without borrowing. If there is anything in National Savings it is possible to use this account to pay the tax bill – ask the tax office.) You must also pay the probate fee, which is based on the amount of net estate. Send all these with a covering letter asking for the Grant of Probate, and for two copies.

About three weeks later you will receive the Grant of Probate and the two copies.

Now you are ready to deal with the estate and to distribute any legacies. This is the procedure to follow:
• Open a bank account in the name of the estate.
• Collect any money owed to the deceased person – e.g. insurance, sums in bank accounts and building societies, unclaimed pension, etc. and pay these sums into the estate's bank account. To claim these sums you will probably need to supply a copy of the Grant of Probate to each of the persons or institutions from whom money is owed.
• Claim any tax refund from the Inland Revenue.
• Pay all debts owed by the deceased person, including funeral expenses and Capital Transfer Tax. If necessary you will have to sell the person's assets to meet these debts and these will be: firstly, anything not covered by the will; secondly, whatever sum is necessary from the 'residue' whose disposition has been mentioned in the will; if this is not enough, any property the person has earmarked for payment of debts (surprisingly, this is not the first call on the estate for settlement of debts). After that, legacies in money; and finally, property specifically bequeathed, taking a proportion of the proceeds from the sale of each of these legacies.
• Place notices in the London Gazette (this is an official publication, despite its title not confined to the London area) and if the deceased person owned any land, local papers in the area. You can get forms to do this from Oyez Publishing Limited: ask for forms Pro 36A, 36B and 36C. Wait for two months before distributing the estate, otherwise the executor is personally liable for meeting any debts.

If there is any possibility that someone – a child, lover or ex-wife, for instance – might claim something from the estate, wait six months before distributing the estate.
• Sell off anything not mentioned in the will and not wanted by any beneficiary. CTT may be payable – apply to the Inland Revenue on form D3.
• Finally, distribute the assets; costs of storage, insurance, etc. since the death, or legal fees connected with conveyancing of land are met by the beneficiary.
• All income from property, dividends, etc. since the date of the death is owed to the relevant beneficiaries.
• After one year, if any money is due to a beneficiary has not been paid, s/he is entitled to interest at 5 per cent per annum.

**Without a will**

*Jim died in an accident, aged fifty-eight. He left a wife, Betty, and daughter Maggie and son Peter, in their twenties. The house was worth £65,000 and was in Jim's name, and thus part of his estate. After deductions of the outstanding mortgage and other debts, and with additions from insurance and other assets, the whole estate came to £70,000. Because Jim had died without leaving a will, Betty inherited his personal belongings, plus £25,000. The rest of the assets – in their case £45,000 – was divided by two. One half (£22,500) was split between each child immediately; the other half would eventually go to them equally, but Betty could have the interest from it – 'life interest'.*

*But since the main asset of the estate was the £65,000 house, in law Betty would probably have to sell it in order for her children each to receive their half of the £22,500. If they were not willing to wait for their money, or if Betty failed to raise it in some way, she would find herself without her house.*

*The above is an example only. Check current figures.*

As can be seen from the summary on p. 37 it is obvious that in many cases the lover of someone who dies intestate can be in a very bad position. She may have lived with that person for many years, sharing a house, income and other assets, but on her or his death everything could go to an undivorced spouse or to other relatives. It is possible in these circumstances to make a claim on the estate, but there is no guarantee of success, and in the event of litigation, failure could be very costly.

## Procedures in Scotland

Most of the procedures described here also apply to Scotland, but some of the terminology is different and there are other small variations. For example, an executor or executrix obtains 'confirmation of the estate' rather than Grant of Probate, and s/he 'in-gathers' the estate before distributing it. You also deal with the sheriff clerk – the address can be found in the telephone book or from a Citizens' Advice Bureau – for most official purposes. On the page opposite you will find a brief summary of procedures in Scotland, and some suggestions for where to get further information.

# Wills in Scotland

If no executor is named in the deceased person's will, or if there is no will, a solicitor or the sheriff clerk will arrange for the Court to appoint an executor – normally the surviving spouse or next-of-kin.

The executor must:
• List all money, furniture, savings, house or other property – the 'estate'.
• Pay Capital Transfer Tax (see pp. 39 and 117).
• Obtain confirmation of the estate (similar to Grant of Probate). In-gather the estate. Distribute the estate.

All estates whose gross value is less than a current limit are classed as small estates. To find the current figure, ask at the local Citizens' Advice Bureau or the sheriff clerk's office. If the estate is small, you can manage to get confirmation without the help of a solicitor. You need only pay the statutory confirmation fee. Although the sheriff clerk will help with this, he cannot give you further advice once the confirmation is issued.

**If there is a will.** Go to the sheriff clerk's office with:
• The will.
• Personal details of the deceased person and his/her family.
• A full list of the person's estate and its value at the date of death.
• A death certificate.
The sheriff clerk will complete all the necessary documents, and if he does not need any further information, he will issue confirmation within a few days.

**If there is no will.** Supply the sheriff clerk with details as above. A similar procedure is followed, except that it may be necessary to obtain a 'bond of caution' (pronounced 'kayshun') – a guarantor's agreement from an individual or an insurance company that the executor will carry out his duties properly and insure against losses in handling the estate. You may need to bring two witnesses on a further visit, to establish your identity.

**After confirmation of the small estate has been obtained** you will need to proceed to in-gather and distribute the deceased person's property, producing the confirmation to obtain payments from banks, insurance companies and so on. If there are many items in an estate, situated in different places, the sheriff clerk will on request provide for any individual item a certificate of confirmation which is a substitute for the full confirmation for that item. This can speed things up, but a small fee is payable for each certificate.

There are certain rules to be followed in the case of intestacy – they are not quite identical to those in force in England and Wales but the Scottish Home and Health Department has a leaflet 'Rights of Succession' which you can get free from the Citizens' Advice Bureau or the Scottish Home and Health Department.

**General information and advice.**
The Home and Health Department publishes a basic booklet *What to Do After a Death* – obtainable as above.

The Scottish Association of CAB's with the Scottish Legal Education Trust have published *In the Event of Death* by David Nichols and this too is obtainable from your local Citizens' Advice Bureau, or the public library. This book covers all the information an executor is likely to need.

# Widows' National Insurance allowances

When a husband dies, his widow may be entitled to certain National Insurance allowances. In order to qualify, you must have been married to him on the day he died (it doesn't matter if you have been separated for years as long as you weren't divorced by decree absolute at his death). These benefits are explained in leaflets obtainable from your local Social Security office – ask for NP35 and NP36. There is also NI51, which is more detailed.

*For the first 26 weeks* after your husband's death, if you are under 60 you are probably entitled to a widow's allowance. (If you are over 60, or your husband was getting the retirement pension when he died this allowance is not payable.) To entitle you to this allowance your husband must have paid enough NI contributions; if for some reason he has not paid enough contributions, special rules may still make it possible for you to get the widow's allowance.

To get the allowance, fill in the form at the back of the special death certificate you were given when you registered the death, and take or send it to the local Social Security office – post offices will supply a special postage paid envelope for this. You will then be sent a claim form (form BW1). Complete it and return it as soon as possible, with your birth and marriage certificates – but if you haven't copies of these certificates, send the form anyway.

You will get a book of orders to cash at the post office: benefit is paid weekly in advance. You should cash each order within three months of the date printed on it.

Before the end of the 26 weeks you will be sent information about any other benefits to which you may be entitled, including possible child benefit increase. If you are sixty or over, you may be paid graduated pension and additional retirement pension, calculated on your own contribution and that of your husband. Leaflet NI 196 tells you the current rates of benefit.

---

## No widowers' allowance

It is assumed that a wife is dependent on her husband, and that she needs an immediate allowance after his death. There is no such provision for a widower, who is assumed a) to be earning or in receipt of some form of social security in his own right and b) not dependent on his wife's earnings.

---

*After the first 26 weeks* you may get basic widowed mother's allowance *or* widow's pension, *and* any additional pension your husband earned, though this may be reduced by any pension paid you by your husband's former employers. The NI widow's pension depends upon your husband's NI contributions – not yours.

*A widowed mother's allowance* is payable if you have a child under nineteen whose father was your late husband; or for whom he was entitled to child benefit at the time of his death; or for whom he would have been entitled to benefit if the child were under sixteen or not living abroad. You are also entitled to a widowed mother's allowance if you are pregnant by your late husband. You *may* be entitled to an increase for a child of a previous marriage if you would normally be entitled to child benefit for that child.

*A widow's pension* may be payable if you were forty or over when your husband died and you are not already getting the widowed mother's allowance; or if you are 40 or over when the widowed mother's allowance ends. You can find the current rates of widow's pension in leaflet NI 196.

You may also be entitled to an additional pension over and above the widowed mother's allowance or widow's pension. This is based on your husband's earnings since April 6 1978.

Details of how to claim are explained in leaflet NP35, which you should already have. Benefit is paid weekly in advance, and you must cash the orders at your chosen post office within three months of their date. If you return to work your benefit will not be reduced. Widow's benefit is taxable and must be included in your tax return.

It is important to understand that these benefits are dependent upon the NI contributions that your late husband has made – if you are in any doubt about whether or not you qualify, leaflet NP 36 sets out the conditions quite clearly, and if you are still not sure, ask to speak to someone at the local Social Security office.

## Further information

For further advice and help contact the National Association of Widows, Chell Rd, Stafford ST16 2QA.
For local support groups for widows contact CRUSE, 126 Sheen Rd, Richmond, Surrey TW9 1UR.

# Advice and further help

It's a good idea when you attend the local Social Security office to pick up any relevant leaflets, since you may find that there are other payments you are entitled to – attendance allowance, invalidity pension, invalid care allowance and so on. If you find the people in the Social Security office difficult to talk to, the staff in the Citizens' Advice Bureau are more likely to be approachable and are used to dealing with problems rather than simply giving official information. If there's a Law Centre near you, you might find help there in sorting out any legal difficulties, and the Widows' Advisory Trust, set up by the National Association of Widows has local Advisory Centres in about 20 areas. Counsellors there will help you sort out practical worries, but, even more important, will provide a 'listening ear'. As the Trust's information material says, a widow's greatest need is to talk out her worries and fears with someone who has herself been through the same kind of experience: 'We consider that this service helps to prevent the mental ill-health so prevalent among widows . . . Never should a widow feel alone and isolated.'

For a discussion of your feelings after a bereavement, see the next chapter.

# CHAPTER 4
# TAKE TIME TO THINK

**Whether you have suffered bereavement or have been through a divorce, coming to terms with what has happened and your changed circumstances can be a long process. It may not be wise to rush into quick decisions. This chapter discusses the beginnings of building your new life.**

Possibly for the first time ever, you are on your own. You have been through a sad or a bitter experience and the loss of the very person with whom you have previously shared troubles, and perhaps have leaned on, has left you feeling truly bereft. In the aftermath of that loss it's difficult to believe that you will ever be the same person again. You don't know what to do.

Perhaps the first thing to accept is that in important ways you never will be that same person again. If, like so many women, you have lived your life up till now in the shadow of other people – parents, husband, lover – it is very hard indeed to emerge from that shadow and face the cruel light of day – alone. You can no longer be the woman who deferred to others, allowed someone else to make decisions for her, lacked the confidence to assert her needs and rights. You have to take charge of yourself. But not all at once. It will be a slow process. Depending on the suddenness or otherwise of the loss and the experiences leading up to it, you may find that becoming a really independent person is something to aim for months or even years ahead. The important thing is to begin.

## After the divorce

Few couples can divorce without some bitterness. Even if you were never really happy in your marriage, there must have been some apparently good reason for marrying in the first place – unless, of course, it was really a shotgun wedding. So you have suffered either slow disillusionment or terrible shock. Perhaps you carried on with an unsatisfactory marriage for years because you had children and thought that they shouldn't be subjected to the emotional and material deprivations of a 'broken home'. Perhaps you suffered as a deserted wife or because your husband had relations with someone else, and you found this intolerable. Perhaps you were physically battered or treated with contempt. Or perhaps in all sorts of subtle ways you just didn't get on and living together gradually became impossible. Most people go into marriage expecting that the relationship will satisfy their needs for love and companionship and mutual support. They don't expect to reach a point where divorce seems the only answer: the common 'it can't happen to me' belief is strong.

If you now feel that marrying when you did or tying yourself down with the man you chose were terrible mistakes, you are probably blaming yourself for your lack of sense and judgement. Your self-respect suffers and you feel even more depressed and unsure of yourself. What you now have to come to terms with is that you probably did make a mistake. But if you look at the way you were brought up, the expectations that the books that you read, the magazines you bought and the people around you drummed into you as a young woman, can you really blame yourself for accepting what everyone else seemed to take for granted? When everyone seemed to expect you to marry and live happily ever after it would have been hard – perhaps impossible – to resist and run the 'risk' of being 'left on the shelf'. Looking back on your marriage you'll probably decide that at least part of the reason for it was all this pressure; and that sexual attraction with all the restrictions on sexual expression that were current at the time you married contributed to the pressure. The need for security and perhaps a need to get away from home could have been factors, too. You probably wanted children.

So can you really blame yourself? Only if you somehow believe that you should have been a superwoman, able to resist all pressure, firm and mature of judgement even when you lacked experience, and that somehow you failed.

Perhaps the first step in overcoming the sad and even devastating feelings that are undermining you now is to treat yourself with the same tolerance and sympathy that you would extend to someone else who had suffered as you have. The past is past. Of course there may be lessons to be learned from what has happened, and the time to begin to apply them is now. Self-blame is a negative thing and can only slow up the process.

# After bereavement

Your partner's death may have been sudden and unexpected, but even if it was not, you will certainly need a lot of time to come to terms with it. For the first days or weeks you will have felt numbed, then possibly disbelieving, as your feelings gradually return. Then, as you struggle to accept what has happened, the full force of grief and desolation hits you. You may even feel like blaming the person who has died. You may feel guilty because you didn't always behave well, or love him enough.

This is the time when you need the love and support of those around you. You need to feel free to talk about the person you have lost, to talk endlessly perhaps. And yet you feel that others can't understand you and will feel uncomfortable and embarrassed if you express your grief. People these days are becoming rather more understanding of these needs and you will probably find that at least one or two relatives or friends are willing and anxious to give you their full attention and support. Don't, with the mistaken aim of sparing them, try to bottle up your feelings. Those near you need to be needed – they will feel helpless if their desire to give you their support is frustrated. And if you don't to some extent 'give way' to your grief the emotional wound you have suffered will take longer to begin to heal.

If you are quite alone – if you are without close friends, and relatives aren't available – there are Bereavement Counselling Services in some towns. You could ask the local Social Services Department whether there's one in your area. Or you could contact the Widows' Advisory Service to ask for the nearest counsellor. Counsellors with these services are experienced people who know how to help a bereaved person through the early stages of learning to accept what has happened, working through her grief and beginning to pick up the threads of life again. They are able to give practical advice, too (see Chapter 3).

## A useful book

*All in the End is Harvest* by Agnes Whitaker is 'an anthology for all who grieve'. Published by Darton Longman and Todd in association with CRUSE (see Chapter 3, p. 43) the book aims to answer the needs of bereaved people to understand their feelings and the emotional experiences in the aftermath of their loss. The Introduction is by Dr Colin Murray Parkes, pioneer in bereavement counselling.

# Dangerous decisions

Certain decisions have to be made in the immediate period following a divorce or bereavement. They were outlined in Chapters 2 and 3. But sometimes following a painful experience there's an urge to take action in the hope that doing so will take one's mind off the loss, or because there seems to be some financial or other urgent pressure that make a big change imperative.

This can be dangerous. Elizabeth, whose husband had died in tragic circumstances, felt completely unable to return to their home after the funeral. Her daughter with whom she was staying impetuously offered her the chance to remain with her – she, too, was deeply upset at the time and felt that offering her mother a home was more than a gesture. She wanted to help.

The older woman's home was sold and most of her possessions with it. At first all went well. Elizabeth had a room of her own and appreciated the comfort of her daughter's presence when she needed it. In return she felt useful as a baby-sitter. But soon the constrictions of living on top of each other and the need for more space for a growing family made for tensions and finally serious quarrels. 'I simply had to get out,' says Elizabeth. 'But I had nowhere to go. I felt I was ruining their lives, however hard I tried to make myself scarce and not interfere with the children's upbringing. I simply longed for my old home, but we'd sold it at a low price when I was in such a state after my husband died. And who would give me a mortgage as a single person over retirement age? In the end I did move, into a poky, dark flat. I'm not happy there; if only I hadn't been so hasty I could have remained where I was – the mortgage was paid off and I had just enough pension to live on there. I'd advise anyone in the same situation to wait several months before deciding on a move that really may not be in anyone's best interests.'

Another woman, who escaped the marital home and an impossible marital situation by returning to her old home town, also bitterly regrets the move. In her fifties and with two teenage daughters she found that, contrary to expectations, she had lost touch with girlhood friends, most of whom had moved away. While a particularly messy and acrimonious divorce was going through, the family suffered additional hardship through lack of money, lack of tolerable housing and the disruption of the girls' education. 'I still think I was right to get out,' she says, 'and at the time I did feel that the farther away from my husband I was the safer we'd be. But I could have made the move much less drastic if I'd thought things out more carefully. Just at the time when I needed most support I was completely isolated, hundreds of miles from friends who could have given it.' This woman is now desperately trying to save enough money to enable her to make another move. Her adult children would like to help; but they have young families and are themselves stretched to the limit to make ends meet.

Faced with a completely new situation – and this can be frightening – like these women you may panic. How can you cope, with very little money, a house or flat that costs more than you realised to run, unfamiliar paperwork to deal with, a car you either can't drive or can't maintain? You feel desperate, trapped.

It may well be that a radical change in your life is needed. But not yet. Perhaps you should ask yourself what difference a delay of a few months will make? It's a well-known fact, backed by a lot of research findings, that 'life changes' are hazardous to mental health, and that the more changes coincide, and the more radical they are, the greater the danger of breakdown or depressive illness. Difficult as it is at this time – following one of the most traumatic of all life changes – you must try to act calmly and take time to think. This applies just as much to the way you handle your day-to-day living as to the way you handle relationships with people (see Chapters 11 and 12).

## Taking stock

While you're thinking things out you can start to prepare for the independent life that lies ahead. Already you've had a good deal of organising to do and documents to attend to. Now is the time to take a calm look at exactly what your income is going to be, how much money – if any – is in the bank or in savings. If you don't know already, try to make an exact estimate of how much money will be coming in weekly or monthly from all sources. Then, with the help of past bills, receipts or any accounts your partner or you may have kept, try to estimate the regular outgoings such as rent or mortgage repayments, rates, fuel, insurances, house and car maintenance (if applicable), and so on. Then make a realistic assessment of your living expenses – food, clothing, outgoings and entertainment, tv rental, holidays. To this total add, say, 10 per cent for unexpected expenses, and see how well the income and expenditure columns balance. Very many future decisions may depend on just this vital step on your road to independence. With this basic information appreciated and absorbed you will be in a far better position to decide how you're going to live your life from now on. And you will never again be prey to the vague panic that comes to everyone who doesn't really know how she stands, but fears the worst. More than that – you will have begun to train yourself to manage your money and manage your life – alone. We look at this in detail in Chapter 6, and there's a section on budgeting at the end of Chapter 5.

When you look at how you stand financially, you may be in for a shock. It need not be an unpleasant one. Janet, at forty-eight, found herself a widow when her husband died following an accident at work. She had brought up three children and had just been intending to try to find a part-time job when the blow fell. She had not been planning to go back to work because they were hard up, but because she had been getting bored at home and wanted to *do* something. All the same, when her husband died she had the feeling that without his income she and the family would be very short of money – only the eldest was earning. However, when she took the time to work out the position, she realised that with her state allowance added to the income from the lump sum she was eventually awarded because her husband had been the victim of an industrial accident, the life insurance he had taken out, and some savings they had made over the years, she was not in such a bad position after all. If she could manage to supplement their income with part-time work – and she was lucky enough to find a job within a few weeks of deciding to look for one – the family could cope quite well. 'I had always left the money side of things to my husband,' Janet says, 'so I really had no idea how we stood. But we never lived extravagantly and although we do have less money coming in, we really haven't had to change our lives very much. I don't worry about the next few years now; it's my old age that may not be so rosy.'

Molly, though, had a very different experience. Left with two quite young children when her husband deserted her, when the divorce went through she was awarded maintenance for herself and the children. It wasn't much, but she budgeted carefully and thought she knew exactly where she stood. After some months, though, maintenance payments became irregular and she had to go to Social Security whenever the money didn't come in. Eventually the payments ceased altogether. 'The Social Security people took over', she says, 'but by that time my ex-husband was working abroad and there was no way they could get the money off him under an "Attachment of Earnings" order. So now we're totally dependent on Social Security. The kids have free school meals, we get Housing Benefit, I buy all our clothes at jumble sales, but every now and again I have to beg Social Security for an extra payment for something we need. I can't get a job now, but I plan to study – do a TOPS course or something – so that I can go to work when the children are a bit older. If there *is* work. . . .' Sadly, no amount of planning could have improved Molly's situation; but willy-nilly she has had to develop her own resources, and her flat on a large London estate is evidence of her ability to create pleasant surroundings for the family despite the lack of money. 'At first I was helpless – hopeless,' Molly claims. 'Now I'm tough.'

Once you've taken a realistic look at the problems of daily living you may, like Molly, have to adapt to a totally new lifestyle. Now is the time to think ahead; must you move house? What would be the snags as well as the advantages of living with relatives? Should you retrain or go back to work? How can you plan for old age? These are some of the questions you have to ask yourself. Already you've come quite a long way from the despair and feelings of inadequacy that you experienced immediately after your loss. Don't underestimate what you've already been able to do. It's prepared you to make decisions, to know where you're going now. You can already glimpse a future for yourself.

# CHAPTER 5
# PRIORITIES

**After the stock-taking of the last few months it's time to begin to put your plans into action. In this chapter we look at the first steps you may need to take.**

Ingrid was devastated when she discovered that, for a number of years, her husband had been involved in a relationship with her 'best friend'. There was no way she could forgive either of them for what she saw as their treachery. Although he had been quite happy to maintain the two relationships and was very reluctant to leave the home in which he had enjoyed all the comforts provided by a nurturing wife, he agreed to a divorce – but very much on his terms. Ingrid was too numbed to fight, her solicitor was far from helpful, and the result was that she and her children were left with much too small an income to maintain anything like the rather high standard of living they'd been used to.

Perhaps it was fortunate that Ingrid was unable to follow up her immediate, panic plan to sell up everything and make a radical change as soon as the divorce was through. Like many women in her position her physical and emotional health broke down and she just wasn't fit to take any action. It was some months before she recovered sufficiently to start to take stock of the position as it really was, and to get together the strength to change her solicitor, go back to the court and get the terms of the divorce settlement changed. She was able to clear the debts she'd incurred while she was out of action; and as a result of her stock-taking was able to see that if she could return to her old job, cut down on the frills that had made life pleasant but were by no means essential, and take the children into her confidence so that they, too, made fewer extravagant demands, they could cope reasonably well.

But just as important as the relative financial security she now experienced were her feelings of achievement at coming through the whole horrible nightmare with a positive plan for the future of herself and the children. Before her children were born she had been a teacher, and since her specialist subject was one that was in demand despite teacher unemployment, she was appointed to the staff of a nearby comprehensive and for the first time for more than two years she began to enjoy life again. Her positive feelings rubbed off on to her domestic life, too. She was amazed to find that she could cope quite well with the home decorating and gardening that her husband had always paid to have done by outside labour, and that her children quickly became competent helpers, too. And she began to make new friends, and make the effort to see old ones.

Ingrid's story shows just how desirable it is to wait until you're in a better emotional state before carrying out any definite plans. Not everyone, fortunately, has to go through the experience of breakdown before coming to this point, but it is worth taking into account the strong probability that for a while you haven't been as capable as you would like to be. However, once you feel better, and you're really able to carry out any plans you've been considering, it's time to get them clear in your mind and maybe even write them down as a kind of timetable or balance sheet.

# First things first

Although by far the most important task you're going to have to carry out is personal rehabilitation, without a relatively ordered and secure background it's unlikely that you'll be able to discover who you are, what your needs are and how you're going to be able to live as a non-dependent human being.

If you've been getting a lot of help and support from relatives and friends now is the time to see how much you can manage without them. As we've seen, there's no shame in having had to rely rather heavily on moral support through the difficult months. But if, consciously or not, you've been using someone else as a buffer against the outside world and transferring to him or her the responsibility for running your life and dealing with the practicalities – the sort of relationship which perhaps you now realise made you over-dependent on your former partner – you may feel it's got to stop. This may be a hard thing to do, as much for the person you have been leaning on as for you. But without being hurtful or ungrateful you should now put it to anyone who has been helping you in this way that you feel that you must now begin to stand on your own two feet. Bear in mind that having someone in a dependent relation to him or her may have met deep needs in the person concerned, and he or she may be unwilling to give up the relationship. But perhaps the experience of your earlier partnership may have convinced you that dependence of this kind wasn't really in your own best interests and you mustn't let it happen again.

In later chapters we'll be looking at practical details in greater depth, but for a start now you'll want to make lists of the steps you need to take if your life is to be well-organised and as satisfying as possible in your new circumstances.

## Security

If you have never lived on your own before, or you have not done so for many years, you may feel nervous about being alone in the house at night. The best thing to do is to put your mind at rest as far as you can by checking on the security of your home and taking effective steps to remedy deficiencies. You can ask at your local police station for a visit by one of their crime prevention officers, whose job it is to advise you exactly how to protect your home. He or she will assess whether your home is secure and suggest possible improvements. Good locks are expensive, but it is probably worth it for your peace of mind.

**Books and Publications**
*Securing Your Home*, edited by Edith Rudinger, published by the Consumers' Association.

The Home Office has published a booklet, 'Protect Your Home', available free from police stations, Citizens' Advice Bureaux and libraries.

The British Insurance Association wil send you (free in exchange for a stamped addressed envelope) a leaflet called 'No Place Like Home – For Thieves' which gives basic precautions you should take, and includes a check list for identifying valuable objects. Write to them at Aldermary House, Queen Street, London EC4 1TU.

# Money and housing

Top of almost every woman's list must come decisions about where she, and the children if she has them, are going to live, and what they're going to live on.

In the case of divorce both these matters may have been settled by the court, particularly if there are children. However, if you believe that circumstances have changed or for some other reason it seems that you should be receiving more financial support than you are, *if you or your solicitor think that you have a good case* it is always open to you to return to the court and ask for the order to be changed, in the light of the new situation.

Of course, like Molly whose case was outlined in Chapter 4, you may be totally dependent on Social Security, either because your former husband has disappeared or because he, too, is living on Social Security. In this situation it may be unrealistic to suggest that you try to increase the regular Social Security payments, though you may be able to make special claims to enable you to meet certain non-recurring expenses.

The situation regarding your housing may be rather more complicated. If you have custody of children, you will probably have been enabled by court order to continue to live in the marital home. The problem may be, however, that because the marital home usually represents such a large part of a couple's assets, your ex-husband may have been relieved of the obligation to pay maintenance for you, and you may find it impossible to meet the expenses connected with running the home. And if you then sell with the idea of buying or renting cheaper accommodation, the court may have ordered that when the home is eventually sold, your ex-husband has a right to part of the proceeds. Thus you could be faced with trying to find a smaller, cheaper dwelling for a sum less than the asking price for *any* housing in your area – let alone an amount that would provide you with a surplus to eke out any maintenance that would then be due to you. In such circumstances you really do need to think things over very carefully, seek advice from one of the counselling organisations and possibly from your solicitor. The obvious solution – getting a job, starting some form of work at home, or letting part of your house – may not be practicable, but if such schemes are possible in your circumstances, they're discussed in some detail later in this book (see Chapters 7 and 8).

### If you're a widow

Similar problems to those of the divorced or separated woman are faced by someone who has lost her partner through death. But some of the difficulties are even harder to resolve. If you have been left with few or no financial resources, no secure housing or perhaps a house that is impossible to keep up on the income you now have, you may still be able to take the sort of action – getting a job, letting a room or taking in a lodger – that some women see as possible solutions to lack of money. But when for various reasons these options aren't open to you, Social

Security may be your only (inadequate) shield from severe want and it's then that getting in touch with the National Association of Widows and its linked Widows' Advisory Trust (see p. 44) could be invaluable. Local advisers can help you find out about re-training, prepare appeals to the relevant tribunals and even – so far as funds allow – help you to get financial help from the Advisory Trust, as well as assisting you with any day-to-day problems that crop up. Chapter 6 of this book ('Money') will give you more detailed information about the Social Security benefits for which you may be eligible.

# Financial planning

Chapter 6 will give you detailed information on possible future sources of income, but now is the time to sit down and work out exactly what your financial problems are. If you have been left relatively well off, there won't be so much urgency calculating whether or not you can make ends meet. But you may not be making the best use of your money, or you may have a 'cash flow' problem – your in-coming money may not coincide with demands for overheads. There's no point finding out, too late, that you have debts you can't pay; which could have been avoided with better planning and budgeting.

The first thing to do is to work out whether you have unpaid bills or debts – either left by your partner, or caused by the end of your relationship, or which have gradually built up since you have been on your own. If you do have any debts or unpaid bills, you need to get them sorted out as quickly as possible. If they are debts which your ex-partner has left you with, it may have come as a great shock to discover that bills haven't been paid. You need good advice to find out exactly which of these debts are your responsibility. If you are already using a solicitor to sort out a will, your divorce or maintenance, then ask the solicitor for advice. Otherwise you should go to the local Citizens' Advice Bureau or other advice centre. It is very complicated to work out whether or not you must pay certain debts and what the consequences may be. For example, if there are unpaid electricity or gas bills and the supply was in your partner's name, you shouldn't have to pay them. But you may need help to negotiate this with the fuel board. You must find out which debts are your responsibility and get advice on the best ways of dealing with them and paying them off.

## Working out your budget

If you are struggling on from week to week on Supplementary Benefit, or on a Retirement Pension, the idea of drawing up a workable budget may seem laughable. The time-honoured collection of envelopes or tins marked 'Rent', 'Gas', 'Grocer' and so on may be the nearest you get to allocating your income reasonably between all the different calls upon it. And with a very limited income it may still be the only way. But sticking even to this simple system can be very hard – if shoes unexpectedly need mending it may be impossible to avoid borrowing from 'Gas' – because you know that the gas bill isn't due for another month, and somehow you will have to pay back the money before then.

If you are forced to adopt this method it is important to try to pay yourself – or the tin – back by as large instalments as you can manage. Although the gas and electricity boards are supposed to deal sympathetically with people getting into arrears with their payments, in practice thousands are disconnected from these vital services every winter. If you have young children you should be treated more leniently, but you will have to pay eventually. If you should find yourself threatened with disconnection, seek immediate advice from the Citizens' Advice Bureau or from the Social Security office with which you normally deal. Don't wait to be cut off.

But even if your income is well above subsistence level, you'll still need to draw up a monthly or an annual budget – and, ideally, stick to it.

Once you know what your outstanding debts and over-heads are, you need to work out whether you have enough income to cover all your overheads and expenses – not just the day to day ones but the irregular and unexpected bills, too. It may be that you simply don't have enough income to cover all your outgoings; or you may not be budgeting as well as you could. One really major difficulty with budgeting is that income tends to come either weekly or monthly; whereas bills either arrive at longer intervals or come unexpectedly. Either way having the right money at the right time can be a problem. There are ways of coping with this, but first you need to work out exactly what your income will be for the next twelve months; how often and in what form it will be paid; and exactly what your expenses are going to be for the next year.

| Working out your budget | List 1: Fixed outgoings/ essential overheads | List 2: Regular daily living expenses | List 3: Irregular expenses |
|---|---|---|---|
| | Rent or mortgage repayments Rates Water rates (if applicable) Property insurances Household contents insurance Car insurance Car tax Subscriptions, union dues Personal insurance Fuel (estimated monthly) Telephone (estimated monthly) Childminding (if applicable) Nursery or school fees | Food and household supplies – remember to include supermarket, butcher, milk, bread, fruit and vegetables, health food, fish, chemist Books and newspapers Lunches out (if applicable) School dinners (if applicable) Entertaining Amusements Child's allowance or pocket money (if applicable) Drink and cigarettes (if applicable) Dry cleaning Medicines Fares Necessary work expenses TV rental or estimated annual expenditure on repairs Garden Car petrol, oil, parking fees | Clothing – assess annual expenditure, divide by 12 for monthly 'allowance' Dentist Holiday – assess annual expenditure, divide by 10 to calculate monthly savings (omitting Christmas and holiday month) Presents Household repairs and decorations Household goods and furniture purchases (if applicable) Car servicing, repairs, tyres, accessories |

**Income.** First work out your income for the next twelve months. Only list income which you are sure will be available to you – any additional money will then come as a bonus. Work out exactly when it is paid and in what form (for example, your Child Benefit may get paid *monthly directly into your bank account*, but your wages are paid *cash each week*). Working out the way your money flows will help you decide the best forms of budgeting and saving schemes.

**Expenditure.** Next, work out all your expenses and overheads for the next twelve months. You should make three separate lists: *one* for your fixed outgoings or overheads – rent, rates, mortgage, electricity, gas, telephone, etc.; *the second* for regular daily living expenses, should list weekly needs – food, soap, household utensils and items, fares, pet food, light bulbs, minor repairs, dry cleaning, etc. *The* *third* list is for irregular and unexpected expenses – clothes, shoes, holidays, large repair bills.

For an idea of the sort of fixed outgoings common to most households, whether you're a woman on your own or you have dependents, refer to the box on p. 58

Draw up your own list – some of the items in the table won't apply to you, but there may be others that are not included. The items in List 1 'Fixed outgoings', are the 'untouchables', and you should avoid borrowing from the sums allocated to them except in the direst of emergencies. To estimate amounts, look at last year's bills. Having written down your estimate of all these fixed outgoings, you are now faced with deciding how to budget for the other regular expenditures which may be more flexible. To prompt you, look at List 2 on p. 58. Your estimates will be realistic if you can look back at expenditure in the recent past. What is your average milk bill? How much did you spend at the supermarket last week and the week before? How often do you entertain friends? How often do you – or would you like to – go to the cinema? And for List 3, 'Irregular items', what did your most recent holiday cost? How much was the last bill for the car service? If these last were matters that your husband dealt with exclusively and you can't find recent bills or records, ask friends whose expenditure might be comparable.

With each list add together the total expenses for the year (work out a weekly figure for List 2 and multiply by 52). Each total should then be increased by 10 per cent to take account of inflation and allow for extra consumption. The three together represent your estimated expenditure for the year.

If your total income for the year is well above your estimated expenditure, fine. But you need to work out whether it is paid to coincide with the time when expenses actually occur. If not, you need to plan budgeting. (See below.)

If your income is approximately the same as or actually *below* your expenditure, then you are going to have to do some hard thinking:

*1 Is there any way to increase your income or capital?* Check Chapter 6 to see if there are any social security benefits you should be claiming; can you get more maintenance from your ex-partner? Would it be realistic to look for some paid work? (But check Chapter 6, pp. 86–7, to see if you would be better off working.)

Don't think about taking any sort of loan, unless you are

100 per cent sure that either you are expecting a lump sum payment in the near future (like, for example, your share of a property settlement) or your income is about to increase dramatically (for example, if you are starting a full time job in three months' time). Otherwise, don't – if your income isn't sufficient to meet your present overheads, it isn't big enough to pay off interest on a loan. If you do decide a loan would be possible – ask your bank manager. A bank manager will be able to work out what kind and size of loan you could realistically pay off and will charge a 'fair' rate of interest. Whatever you do, *never* use a commercial money lender or loan company. You will end up with debts you can never clear and your income will be wasted paying off huge sums of interest.

*2 Is there any way to reduce your estimated expenditure for the year?* Take each list in turn. Are there any items you could reasonably do without? Can you make your winter coat last another year, or manage with your raincoat and a thick lining? Then take each list and see if there are any items where you could reduce expenditure or get better value for money. Could you cut your meat bill by substituting other forms of protein? (See the section on 'Diet' in Chapter 15.) Most of the items in List 1, such as housing costs, are likely to be beyond your control, but there may be some (for example, house insurance) where if you looked around you might be able to get the same cover for less money. If you have to have repairs done, always get at least three estimates – you can save a lot of money this way.

You may have to draw on resources you never knew you had. Later in this book you will find do-it-yourself suggestions that may enable you to look after the maintenance of your house, car, bike and garden – in fact, take over the role traditionally assigned to the 'man of the house'. Many women have done it, more are learning. But there are other traditions, too, that you needn't break with. If you don't know how to do it already, you could start to make clothes for yourself and for your family. Your local library has books on knitting, sewing and dressmaking. You may be able to learn from a friend, or you may be able to get to adult education classes to develop skills to help you cut the cost of living.

*Making your income meet your overheads.* Whatever your income you will have to plan carefully if you are going to meet all your overheads as they fall due; and avoid spending money which should have been earmarked, for example, for the winter electricity bill, or on new school shoes for the children. Perhaps your partner took responsibility for paying the budgeting bills, overheads and repairs and you handled day to day expenses.

It is essential to work out ways of either avoiding large irregular bills or finding savings or budgeting schemes so you will have sufficient money when the bill has to be paid. There is nothing worse than the worry of unpaid bills which you cannot meet – and it is a worry that you can avoid. Obviously, the lower your income, the more difficulty you will have putting money aside for bills when you don't have sufficient for daily living, but it is even more essential to work out a saving plan and stick to it. You should take each list of overheads in turn:

**List 1.** *Fixed outgoings/essential overheads*: these are all essential items. Whether they have to be paid weekly, monthly or quarterly, you *must* have the money to pay them as they fall due.

*If your main income is paid monthly into a bank account*, banks have a variety of schemes to help you to budget and pay bills by instalments. The easiest method of budgeting is to try to arrange for all major overheads to be met through monthly instalments which are paid out by the bank a day or two after your income reaches the bank. Rates, electricity and gas can all be paid monthly either by bank standing order or directly by you to the authority. Bills which can only be paid quarterly or half yearly will need money putting aside each month.

*If your main income is paid weekly in cash*, it will be more difficult to budget for large quarterly or monthly bills. You will have to put money aside each week and either save it yourself in a bank, post office or building society account, or find out how many of your overheads can be paid off through weekly budget schemes. For example, gas and electricity bills can be met through budget saving stamps and other schemes. Ask at the local showroom for details. There are similar schemes for telephone and TV licences.

You must now deduct the amount of your weekly or monthly income which is needed to pay off List 1 overheads from your total weekly or monthly income.

The balance is the maximum you can spend on List 2 and 3 expenses. Depending on your circumstances, you must decide the best way to split the rest of your income between Lists 2 and 3. You may prefer to put a set amount each month or week into a savings account, which will be there to meet List 3 needs, such as shoes, clothing and repair bills. Until you become more confident at manipulating your income across the competing demands on it, this may be the safest method. It may leave you a little short on weekly cash, but you will have the security of knowing that money is there for unexpected expenses.

**List 2.** *Regular daily living expenses*: You have already calculated the amount of weekly cash you need for day-to-day expenses. Unless you have plenty of surplus money, you must be disciplined and keep to this

---

If you have income which is paid irregularly or at a different time from your main income (for example, maintenance payments, child benefit or interest from savings), you could decide to use this money to pay bills. It could be paid into a savings account and accumulate and be available either to pay List 1 overheads or List 3 expenses.

---

## What can banks offer?

Banks can provide a variety of accounts which provide safe and flexible ways of storing your money. They can also advise you on a number of financial and legal transactions; for example, making a will, investing your spare money, or buying a property.

If you do not have a bank account, or you had a joint account with your partner and he did all the financial transactions, the prospect of using a bank and writing cheques can be pretty daunting. Whether or not you are used to banks, at this point in your life you need to find out which banks can offer you the best services to meet your needs. Different banks offer a variety of services and schemes. There is no reason why you must let one bank handle all your money. You may, for example, want a current account at a bank that has low – (or no) – service charges and is near your home. But a different bank may offer a really advantageous saving scheme. Bank managers may try to persuade you that it is in your interest for them to handle all your financial affairs. It is true that if the manager knows about your financial circumstances, the bank can be more sympathetic and flexible in meeting your needs. For example, if you are likely to overdraw on your current account, you should always let the bank manager know in advance, explain what is causing the difficulty and tell them how long you think the problem will last. But this should not stop you shopping around and putting your money with lots of different banks if they offer you the services you need.

weekly limit. Whatever you do, you cannot afford to overspend on List 2. In fact, weekly housekeeping is probably where your financial skills will come to the fore. You've had plenty of experience of scrimping and saving. If you have taken care of all the overheads in List 1 and can feel secure that money is set aside to pay all of those, you can start manipulating your weekly housekeeping money, to see where you could make savings. Do it on a week-to-week basis, otherwise the savings from one week will disappear in the next week's expenses. If you do underspend one week, put the money away – for example, in a building society account.

**List 3.** *Irregular expenses*: It is almost impossible to forecast when most of these expenses will occur, so you need to be sure that there is money set aside to meet the essential ones as they arise. Any money set aside to pay for List 3 items should be kept in a savings account so that it is earning some interest.

If anything needs repairing or you have to use builders always get at least three estimates. They will vary a great deal, both about what needs to be done, and how much it will cost. Some repair jobs will be emergencies, but with other jobs you can, to some extent, control when to have them done. Try to spread them out so they don't coincide with other big bills or expenses. For example, you tend to get bigger bills in the winter, and builders often charge more then than they do in the summer. If you have a bank account, a *budget account* can help to deal with List 3 expenses.

## Budget accounts

Different banks offer very varied kinds of budget account. But the basic principle is the same. You agree to pay a certain amount each month into the account. You get a cheque book and can then use the account to pay bills as they occur. Over the year, the account should balance out – the amount you have paid in will have covered all the year's bills. But during the year there will have been times when the account was overdrawn and others when it was in credit. The service charges on budget accounts can be high, although some banks pay *you* interest when the account is in credit. But they are a good way of spreading your financial burdens. Imagine for example, that you know you have five or six big bills that all fall due in January, and nothing else until May. Your monthly income for January couldn't meet all those bills, so you use the budget account and make it up over the next few months.

Find out about all the possible budget schemes and costs before deciding which, if any, would help you.

You also need to decide whether you want to do most of your regular expenditure and budgeting using cash or through a bank account. This will depend on how you are paid, what your main expenses are and what you feel most comfortable with.

### Keeping accounts

Once you've worked out your budget, you'll have to think of an easy way of recording expenditure. Few women can keep a meticulous account of how much they spend on separate items in the weekly food bill, but it's worth taking some time working to a system that isn't irksome and fiddly, but that works for *you*.

One method that's been successful is to get a durable cash notebook and enter in it everything spent – not item by item, but under various headings – over the month. You do this using the right-hand pages, while on the left you record your income from all sources. If you don't fancy breaking your expenses down into items like 'Meat', 'Milk', 'Fruit' and so on, you can have general headings like 'Food'. On p. 65 you will see an example that will give you an idea of how this system might work for a woman with a teenage daughter.

A very important part of this method is to keep a record at the back of the cash book of all your fixed outgoings. Check with the example on p. 58. Some will be outgoings like annual subscriptions that occur only in a certain month of the year. Others will be items like rates, rent, mortgage repayments, insurance premiums and so on that may be payable monthly.

Assuming that you are keeping your accounts on a monthly basis, at the beginning of each month you enter on the left-hand page your income for that month. If you are paid monthly, you will probably have received your month's salary at the end of the previous month. If you are receiving maintenance, or are living on Social Security, these sums may come in weekly, so you would have to enter them each week.

On the right-hand page, which is kept for expenditure, before you do anything else you enter the fixed outgoings for that month, consulting your list at the back of the book. Some will be one-off payments that occur only in that month, and don't reappear until the same month the following year. Others will be the same every month, or until circumstances change.

When you've entered all these sums on both pages, if

you add up the income items and then the expenditure items so far, and then subtract expenditure from income, you will have a very good idea of how much you have to manage on for the rest of the week or the month. Then you continue to enter other items, as you spend, on the right-hand page – see example.

This may sound very tedious – it is – but a system like this, or any other that works for you, can give you peace of mind; and that may be worth the trouble. Keeping

| March | Income | | | March | Expenditure | |
|---|---|---|---|---|---|---|
| | Salary after tax & NI | £350 | | | Fixed outgoings | |
| | | | | | Rent | £80 . 50 |
| | Allowance for Melanie | 60 | | | Rates | 20 . 00 |
| | | | | | Gas | 15 . 00 |
| | Interest on savings | 8 | | | Save for insurances | 15 . 00 |
| | | | | | Union sub | 2 . 00 |
| | | | | | Telephone | 15 . 00 |
| | | £418 | | | Holiday fund | 10 . 00 |
| | Fixed outgoings | £157 . 50 | | | | £157.00 |
| | Income | 418 | | | Spent | |
| | Less fixed expenditure | 157 . 50 | | | Supermarket | £49.75 |
| | | | | | Butcher | 12 . 00 |
| | March expenses | £260.50 | | | Fish | 4 . 50 |
| | | | | | extra fruit | 2 . 80 |
| | | | | | Milk | 7 . 50 |
| | Actual expenditure | £201.75 | | | extra bread | 2 . 20 |
| | | | | | chemist | 1 . 80 |
| | | | | | cleaner | 1 . 50 |
| | | | | | Shoe repairs | 2 . 00 |
| | | | | | School blazer | 20 . 50 |
| | | | | | Tights | 1 . 20 |
| | | | | | P's present | 2 . 00 |
| | | | | | Concert | 2 . 50 |
| | | | | | Entertaining | 8 . 40 |
| | | | | | Melanie's pocket money | 15 . 00 |
| | | | | | Sweater | 8 . 90 |
| | | | | | Newspapers | 6 . 00 |
| | | | | | Elec. bill | 25 . 00 |
| | | | | | Fares | 28 . 00 |
| | | | | | | £201.55 |

records, too, can be very helpful in assessing future needs, seeing where you may have gone wrong, in fact in being realistic about your financial situation. It could be useful, too, should you need to produce some sort of evidence when you make a claim for increased maintenance, or to help you make a realistic claim for Social Security purposes.

However, there are simpler methods of keeping tabs on your income and expenses. An adaptation of the system shown on pp. 64–5 would be to enter in your cash book on the right-hand page all the sums drawn as cash, without itemising how you spend this money. For instance, if you draw £25 weekly to meet current expenditure on food, fares etc., you would simply enter 'Cash £25' four to five times for the month, and at the end of the month total up everything on this right-hand page, as in the example shown, and subtract it from the 'Income' entered on the left-hand page.

A crude method of keeping accounts for anyone with a bank account is simply to use the spaces provided in most cheque books to enter the balance in your account, and then, on the drawing up of each cheque, subtract that sum from the balance, to give you the total remaining in the account. This works best for people whose monthly outgoings can't be easily estimated – that is, there are few 'fixed outgoings' – and who pay their way by cheque rather than by banker's order.

No matter which method you use, if you have a bank account you should make sure that you see a statement at fixed intervals – usually quarterly, but you can ask the bank to provide you with this monthly – so that you can check your personal accounts against this statement. To avoid bank charges you should keep a minimum sum (fixed by the bank) in the account at all times if possible. Some banks make no charge as long as you keep in credit. It's well worth checking what the rule is for your bank, and change to another bank that doesn't charge if you think it likely that you will often need to spend more than the limit allowed by your present bank. After all, if you have that much money over and above what you spend each month, you might as well get the interest on it, rather than the bank!

**Lump sums, bequests and savings**
To many readers of this book, concern about what to do with 'capital' must seem like a bad joke. However, there are widows, divorced women and those in well-paid jobs

who may find themselves in possession of 'spare' money; and certainly those who do have a capital sum from which they may need the interest to supplement a low income, or who need to spread a lump sum over a few bad years, can be faced with making important decisions.

Most banks don't give interest on current accounts, and those that do have very low interest rates, so it's never sensible to keep more money in your current account than you need for current expenses. If you keep monthly records by one of these suggested methods you'll soon see whether your income exceeds your regular expenditure. You will then be in a position to put the excess into some form of savings.

Building societies are the most common resting-places for spare money. Since they offer so many different schemes, and these change rapidly from month to month, in line with the current economic conditions, it's impossible here to give a rundown or a 'best buy'. You will need to watch their advertisements and get their literature before you can decide which scheme suits you best. The basic decision to make is whether you are likely to need extra money to meet an unforeseen emergency, and/or whether you prefer to get a higher rate of interest by leaving your money in the building society account for a specified number of years. Remember that if you do opt for the fixed term type of investment and you have to withdraw your money earlier, you will lose some interest. This could mean that it would have been better to put the money into an 'instant withdrawal' or 'seven-day withdrawal' account in the first place. Perhaps the most sensible solution for those with a fairly large amount to invest is to place a proportion of the money in each type of account.

Remember that if you don't pay at least basic income tax it is not advantageous to use a building society account, since the society pays tax at the basic rate on your money, and you can't reclaim it from the Inland Revenue.

The government offers various ('tax paid') schemes, some 'index-linked' – again you will have to read current literature and advertisements to decide which is the best scheme for you. Most such schemes do involve tying up your money for a specified length of time, with some form of penalty for earlier withdrawal – i.e. loss of some interest.

If what to do with your money is a major concern, it's sensible to watch the 'personal finance' pages of the news-papers, for generally useful and informative articles which keep readers up-to-date. Unless you are keenly interested and willing to play the market – and few will be in a position to do this – it's probably better to play safe and go for a form of investment that can never make your fortune but won't be risky either; or to seek advice from an accountant, investment counsellor or a very knowledgeable friend. Just make sure s/he does know what's what, and isn't making assumptions about you and your financial circumstances that aren't valid. If it's vital to you not to risk your money, don't allow yourself to fall for 'dead certs' – whether they come in the form of shares in an 'up-and-coming' company or a racehorse! Beware of any scheme which seems to promise impossible gains.

**It's never easy**
All this said, however, it would be unrealistic to believe that the money problems that almost every woman left on her own has to face can be solved by turning to the state or the voluntary sector, or by finding some magical inner resource for herself. When you've really had time to take stock of what has happened and is happening to you, you may begin to look with more critical eyes than ever before at the position of women in our society – and ask questions. Why are you now in the position of having to struggle so hard just to keep your head above water? Why are you having to beg from the state or depend on charity hand-outs? Why are you constantly worried almost to the point of desperation just because, at an earlier stage in your life, you accepted the dependent role that everyone around you – including the media, the advertising industry and all the powers-that-be – assigned to you?

After all that, not surprisingly you accepted that education and training weren't really important for a girl whose main job would be to get married and have children. You accepted that once you had those children, they were primarily your responsibility and that you were just lucky if you had some 'help' from your partner. Now – and maybe you blame yourself, or another individual, or maybe it was a blow of fate – all this conventional and convenient protection has been snatched away from you. Once these questions have come into your mind you may decide that in looking for a solution to your own problems you have to join with others in fighting for a change in the position and role of all women; we'll be looking later in this book at some of the groups, organisations and forms of political action that may contribute to this vast and necessary change in the way we live.

# Relationships: you're still vulnerable

At this time of getting yourself together to face the future, it won't be easy to break the habits of a lifetime and gain instant practical and emotional independence.

'As a newly-divorced woman, still quite young, I was amazed to find that male neighbours and colleagues, and even men who had been friends when I was part of a couple, seemed to think that I'd be desperate for sex or that I was "fair game" in some way,' says Maggie. 'I must admit that I did feel very much at a loss for all sorts of practical help, and I may have given the impression when I asked someone to move a wardrobe or explain a tax problem that I needed more than just that. Or perhaps they thought I ought to pay in that way for what they'd just done for me. They acted surprised and angry when I showed them the door.'

Like very many women, Maggie is too ready to see this sort of situation as being somehow her own fault. If only she hadn't invited this man into her house while she was alone, she wouldn't have provided him with an opportunity, or excuse, to make a pass at her. If only she hadn't been so naively friendly, another wouldn't have been able to interpret her attitude as an invitation to him to leap into bed with her. Psychologists sometimes talk about 'blaming the victim'. This means that when things go wrong in personal relationships others are all too ready to say that the person who suffers the most is the one who invited trouble. A battered wife – say – has somehow brought her trouble on herself. She 'asked for it'. Maggie, too, is 'blaming the victim' – but in this case, the victim is herself. She's acting as the unconscious spokesperson for a society that's very ready to excuse male aggression on those very 'asking-for-it' grounds. Behave in a normal, friendly way, or seek ordinary human support and help, say so many lone women, and it's seen as 'your fault' if you're misinterpreted.

But many other women admit that in their depression and state of low self-respect they made bad mistakes in attempting to form new relationships too soon. It's very easy, particularly for a woman who feels she has been rejected, to rush into an ill-considered relationship in an attempt to heal her bruised feelings. If sexual needs are strong – and you are aware that this is the basis of your drive to replace a former partner – you may indeed find the relationship meets these needs. But if you are expecting much more than this, you could be leaping into something fraught with potential emotional dangers to yourself and to your new partner. If you've already been deeply hurt it can be extremely damaging to be the centre of new storms which may end, yet again, in the wreck of all your hopes.

This wariness may be difficult to maintain. 'More than anything I missed the comfort and warmth, the cuddles in bed. I found it very hard to have no one to talk to about the day's events, or to share my worries about the children. Sex wasn't nearly as important to me,' explains another woman. 'When I was in a pub with a friend I was chatted up by a lone man and somehow I found myself inviting him back to the house. Nothing happened that time, but after we met again – he seemed a pleasant enough guy – he wanted to go to bed with me and I thought 'why not?' It wasn't very satisfactory, but I felt really sorry for him, because he started to tell me all about the rotten life he'd had, the wife who'd left him, and so on. In no time at all he'd moved in with me and the children. That was the beginning of a terrible time. He started to become completely dependent on me, jealous of my friends, made impossible demands, upset the children. For several months he really ruined my life. Just when I was beginning to get over my divorce and learning to live independently, I found myself being leaned on, part of a couple again, and an unsatisfactory one at that. It took a lot to dislodge him and he made me feel cruel and guilty in the process. Never again!'

To avoid the perils of over-dependence – or, as in this woman's case, of forming a relationship with someone whose dependence on you may become very damaging – you'll need to be both self-aware and tough. If at this stage you can be realistic about assessing your needs – practical, sexual and emotional – you could become honest enough with yourself to know how to get what you need, give what you can, and remain free to act as your own person.

**The need for sex**
Any woman on her own has the option to remain celibate. Some, after a lot of trials and some errors, conclude that for them this is the only way to live. For these women, sexual tensions can be released by masturbation, and the need for loving and caring can be met by involvement in relationships with family and friends, absorption in work or commitment to some cause.

For the majority, though, sexual needs do present a problem, and, as we've seen, this is because their sexuality is so bound up with other needs and drives which it seems that only sexual relationships can meet. In assessing your own situation your future attitudes and actions will be greatly influenced by how you weigh up your own particular needs and expectations now.

To you, sex may mean a lot more than the act itself, the physical pleasure it gives you, the sense of release and relaxation. If you have never experienced those joys, on the other hand, you may be very well aware of what you have been missing and all the more conscious of a deep need. It's helpful to ask yourself what, to you, is the most important thing about sex.

For some women physical satisfaction isn't nearly as important as love – however we interpret that over-worked word. And it's only in a sexual relationship, many believe, that it's possible to express and receive love at the deep level which can satisfy this need. It's true that in the society in which we live touching, caressing, cuddling, complete physical involvement with another person are usually sanctioned only by sexual relationships – or, if not too intense, in parent–child ones. To be able to express and receive love may mean so much to you that, if you see sexual involvement as the only means of finding it, you may be willing to take on everything else that such a relationship can entail – aware that while you are still recovering from your recent experiences you *are* vulnerable, and your needs may be affecting your judgement.

To most women – especially those whose previous relationships have foundered, causing them to feel unwanted, unattractive, rejected – finding a new sexual partner can represent reassurance. Someone finds you sexy, interesting, worthwhile, and it's a great boost to your morale. But could it be that you are accepting the idea that personal worth can be measured only, or mainly, in terms of sexual attractiveness? And isn't that the kind of belief that you, now on your way towards independence, acceptance of and respect for yourself should be questioning? Telling yourself – as one 'agony aunt' has suggested – that since someone (your former partner) once found you attractive you must still be attractive and therefore you don't need to worry, can be intended to encourage self-confidence. But that self-confidence, surely, would be founded on acceptance of other people's values, set and maintained by *un*acceptable male values. If this kind of rationalisation influenced you, you would be colluding with the view of women sex objects. Is that what you want?

### Odd-woman-out?

A sexual relationship with a new partner, too, can attract you for another, social reason. As a widow or divorced woman you have almost certainly already experienced some awkwardness in relationships with other people. It's all too easy to feel odd-woman-out and unfortunately there are colleagues and acquaintances who will encourage this feeling. You believe – again because of accepted stereotypes – that as a single person you're a failure. And there are practical problems that are very real, however we may try to deny their existence.

'I'd go to a concert alone, maybe the theatre,' says Caroline, 'but when it comes to going out for a meal – no. I'd go to a small café all right, but not a proper restaurant. Even with another woman – except at lunch time when it's more acceptable – I feel embarrassed.'

And almost every woman on her own can tell of occasions when she hasn't received an expected invitation, or, even worse, has been teamed up with a single incompatible man just because they're both partnerless. No wonder, then, that this discrimination against single people forces some into relationships whose chief purpose seems to be to proclaim to the world that they're not rejected and alone. Once again, you can accept and collude with such values – or by your actions deny their validity. But it isn't easy.

### A father figure?

Another potent rationalisation which could lead you into a heterosexual relationship for which you may not be ready is the widespread belief that children need a father. It's quite true – and we'll be looking at this in some detail later – that death and divorce can seriously upset the children in the family. If you have young or teenage children you will already have experienced some of the problems. But it's by no means certain that these will be solved by the introduction of a new man into the situation, and few women have found that entering into a new relationship 'for the sake of the children' really works out. Still less is it likely to be wholly satisfactory, if at the same time, you deceive yourself into believing that this is what you are doing, when in fact it is your needs alone that are being met. Far better to face reality and accept that for once you are putting yourself first, that you are entitled to do so, and that if your new partner and the children get on well together, that's a bonus.

If to you sex is a means to an end – children – either because you've never had a child or because you want more, think carefully. At this stage in your life it's very probable that a new sexual involvement will be temporary. Some women are perfectly prepared to take on the problems inherent in bringing up a child alone. If this is a conscious decision, planned despite the understanding of what it may mean in the future, it's not an irresponsible one. Why should anyone's strong need to have a child be frustrated because she isn't willing to pay the price – the loss of personal independence that most long-term heterosexual relationships involve? But if you really don't know how difficult it may be to cope alone with a demanding, exhausting baby, or an awkward adolescent, if you can't see any likelihood of back-up from friends and relatives, and if your new relationship is deliberately, or potentially, a fairly casual one, it may be wise to decide that this particular need of yours has to be met in other ways.

Yet another need that leads people into sexual relationships is the desire for friendship, understanding and support. It's very true that a good relationship can provide just this sort of comforting background, easing, through sharing, many of the difficulties of life as well as the pleasures. You may indeed be fortunate at this stage in finding that your sexual needs are met by just such a person; but remember that once already you probably expected all this from a relationship – and that however good the sex was, if the partnership ended in separation or divorce you almost certainly didn't find it.

Most damaging to your self-respect, yet totally understandable in many situations, is another very potent reason for entering into a new relationship. Put baldly – money. As a widow or divorced woman you are more than likely to be suffering some degree of deprivation of everything that money can buy. If only you were more financially secure a far better life would be possible; you could pay for the various services you need but now have to do for yourself, or go without; your children could have more treats, better clothes. Never, never, did you think that you would be the sort of woman who would, in effect, sell herself for the sake of financial security. But think again. You and your friends may not have 'married for money' but didn't the financial standing of a possible partner have any bearing on your choice? If you were in a good job – and your boyfriend had earning potential – you may have been the major earner for a while. But in the long term you did expect his contribution to the budget to be the greater one; and the majority of women even today do enter into marriage with the idea that they will be, largely, 'kept'. Already, they, and probably you, have done something, in the form that society sees as completely acceptable, that you now may begin to see as degrading. Once more, if you go into such a relationship again, shouldn't it be with your eyes open – because you genuinely have no alternative? But better, can you use this book, and the other resources we'll be looking at, to secure for yourself some real economic, and hence, personal independence? At that point you will have given yourself a real choice: we'll be discussing this in Chapter 13.

**Your own woman**
Questioning, as we've been doing, the motives behind the drive to form a new relationship may be an uncomfortable process. It would be easier, while you are still in a somewhat raw state and trying to keep your head above water both practically and emotionally, to sweep aside these awkward questions. But putting them, and groping towards answers that will make some sense to you individually, seem to be vital processes on the way to understanding the situation in which you find yourself and the sort of society that has put you there. Nothing can place you in a better position to take charge of your own future. And that's what, from now on, you'll be aiming to do.

# PART II
# PRACTICAL MATTERS

*Now is the time to develop new skills – not just from necessity but also because to do so will build up your confidence.*

# CHAPTER 6
# MONEY

**In this section we look in detail at the sort of money problems you may be having as a woman on your own; and at the sources of income available to you, including social security benefits, pensions and maintenance. We go on to look at tax, insurance, and using your money to plan for the future.**

*This section has been prepared with the assistance of Lynda Bransbury, Information Officer of the National Association of Citizens' Advice Bureaux.*

As a woman on your own you don't need a book like this to tell you that your biggest worry is almost certainly money – where it comes from, where it goes, and how, if possible, to get more.

In addition to all the emotional upheaval, women who have lost their partners will nearly always find they are financially worse off than they were. If, after several weeks or months on your own, your income doesn't seem capable of meeting your needs, don't panic and don't blame yourself for being a bad manager. There are many reasons why life on your own is likely to be a financial struggle. Whether or not you were working, your life style must, to some extent, have depended on your partner's income and financial circumstances. Whatever financial provision your partner has made for you – for example, maintenance, life insurance or pension – it is unlikely to reflect in real terms either his financial and practical contribution to your daily lives nor your present cost of living. You are now struggling to maintain the same standard of living without his involvement – so it's not surprising that you are finding it difficult. You may also find that your overheads have dramatically increased, particularly if you have children or have had to move home as a result of your separation or bereavement.

One of the main reasons for your financial difficulties is the effect on women of the inbuilt assumptions in Britain about family life. There is still a belief that families should consist of a male breadwinner and a woman whose main role is to run the home and rear children. In reality this is no longer the typical British family: the National Council for One-Parent Families estimates that there are around one million one-parent families in the United Kingdom and that about one in seven families with children is headed by a lone parent. Even two-parent families tend to depend more and more on both partners working. But these assumptions about family life mean that now that you are on your own you will find it difficult to replace both the financial and practical support you have been used to. It is very important not to be defeated, but you are going to have to be realistic and hard-headed about the obstacles that face you. It's also important to realise that they are not your fault and not of your making. For example, whatever your age, if you have spent several years in the traditional women's role, you may find it very difficult to get a well-paid job. The hours you can work may be limited if you have young children and you may have to pay a lot of your income on child care. If you haven't worked for some years, your age, lack of skills and experience will go against you. The present high levels of unemployment will also mean lots of competition.

If you have children, you don't need to be told how much they cost. Now that you are on your own, you will also have discovered that there is very little financial help available with the costs of child-rearing. The government has always acknowledged the heavy financial burden caused by bringing up children and in recent years has made a token contribution towards it in the form of child benefit and married man's tax allowance. But again, the assumptions about family life mean that the state places financial responsibility for children firmly on the family – and, too, the assumption is that the woman stays at home while the man goes out and earns an adequate income. You will be finding that Social Security benefits neither adequately replace income from employment nor meet the real cost of living for you and your children. You will also find there is little help available if you try to juggle the conflicting tasks of finding or keeping a job, running your home and bringing up your children.

If you are a widow, your husband may have made financial provision for you during his lifetime. Aside from this, or in the event he did not do so, your sources of income are state benefits and earnings from your own employment.

If you have separated from your partner, the amount you are getting in maintenance, however generous or regularly paid – which it often isn't – probably won't be enough to live on. Your partner may have voluntarily agreed to a reasonable financial settlement, but if you had to go to court for a maintenance order, you will know that judges tend to award absurdly low amounts for wives and children to live on. There are court orders made every day which award a mother less than a third of the costs of rearing a growing child. Even with a court order, you cannot be sure that your ex-partner will pay and while the court has the powers to punish him, this is little help to you if the money still doesn't come through. Society has pushed you into a position of financial dependence, but it is also structured to prevent you benefiting financially from divorce or separation. The new law on divorce and maintenance which came into effect in October 1984 shows how anxious our institutions are to prevent women from gaining any financial independence or dignity. Under the new rules it is even more difficult for women to get adequate maintenance orders. Maintenance may be reduced or refused unless there are no prospects of employment and the wife is regarded as 'not to blame' for the breakdown of the marriage. This change in the legislation reflects the attitudes of the courts and the Law Commission on divorce. The spectre of the ex-wife living in luxury on alimony has created a concern to protect men from exorbitant maintenance payments and obscures the real hardship most women face on divorce or separation.

Another reason for financial difficulties may be the increased overheads you face living on your own. For example, paying for household repairs which your partner did himself; you may have to pay the full cost of rent or mortgage to stay in your own home, or pay someone to look after your children if you want to keep your job. Your partner may have taken responsibility for paying large bills and overheads and you may have no experience of large-scale budgeting. While you are learning to deal with all the household overheads and how to get the best deal on costs, you may find you spend more than you need. You will learn in time how to keep your overheads to a minimum, but initially your cost of living may be high at a time when you can least afford it.

You have every right to feel angry about your present financial situation. If you have adopted the traditional female role within your partnership you probably gave up your own chances of education, promotion or a career. Your effort, support, or, for example, willingness to move around the country, may have directly contributed to your partner's job prospects and increased income over the years. It may possibly have seemed like a fair division of responsibilities and work while you were living together, both of you doing the things you enjoyed and were good at. But now you are on your own, you may be finding that you're not getting a fair share or reward for all those years of work.

But even though you recognise all this, it's now up to you. You are going to *have* to overcome some of these obstacles and challenge the assumptions society has made about you; you are going to have to shed the dependent role that has been pushed upon you. You have a right to an independent income, whether from benefits or employment, and you will need to be determined and fight hard to make sure that you are getting all the income to which you are entitled and taking up every opportunity that you can. If you find it difficult, it's not because of your inadequacy, it's because things are loaded against you. It won't be easy and it may take some time. At this stage you need to plan and work out what is available both in the immediate future and in the longer term. Your first task is to work out how much income you have and whether you can make ends meet. You will then need to check whether there is anything you can do to increase your income and what the best choices are for you.

## Assessing and maximising your income

In Chapter 5 we looked at managing your money on a day-to-day basis and at planning your expenditure in relation to your income. But now that you have got through the first few weeks or months of confusion, shock or bitterness and you are beginning to take full charge of your affairs, you need to look in greater detail at the sources of income available to you.

However rich or poor you were, you may never have had to bother about money matters before. But money must now be your most important priority. It is essential if you are to develop a full and active life on your own. Money is your passport to a new and independent life, to dignity and self respect. You owe it to yourself and your family to ensure that you aren't losing out on any income that is available to you, and to plan your financial future. In order to do this you need a few basic bits of information – what money there is around that you aren't getting; how one source of income can affect another. For example, if you're not working but would like a job, you need to know how your other income would be affected by any earnings. Equally, if you are working but finding life a struggle, you need to find out if there is any way of increasing your income. You can then plan what you want to do, what is available to you and what is realistic both in the immediate future and the longer term. This section should point you in the right direction; it won't give you all the answers but may provide the right questions to ask, and tell you where to go for further information.

### Using the Social Security system

Once you have worked out which sources of income apply to you, apply for all the Social Security benefits that could help you. We are considerably luckier than our mothers and grandmothers. When they lost their husbands, most of them would have been dependent on the goodness of their families or on charity. But things have changed: you have a real chance of economic independence. People have struggled long and hard for the benefits, grants and training opportunities that do now exist. You should take full advantage of what does exist. If you are looking for further information or advice on any money matter you should contact your local Citizens' Advice Bureau, or the relevant government department. There are also lots of publications and leaflets produced by government departments and voluntary organisations to give you an idea of what money is available. Some of these leaflets use jargon which can be confusing or misleading. But it's worth studying them closely if you think they apply to you and asking for an explanation if you're not clear what they mean. We have tried to give you the correct leaflet name and number when we mention different kinds of income and benefits but there are lots more. Your local DHSS office, reference library or CAB should have most of them.

### What income can you have?

You can use the charts here which list the different kinds of income for women in different situations. Find the chart that applies to you. For example, if you are a woman aged 45 who is not working or is temporarily off work, use *Chart 1*, but if you are 53 and working part time use *Chart 3*.

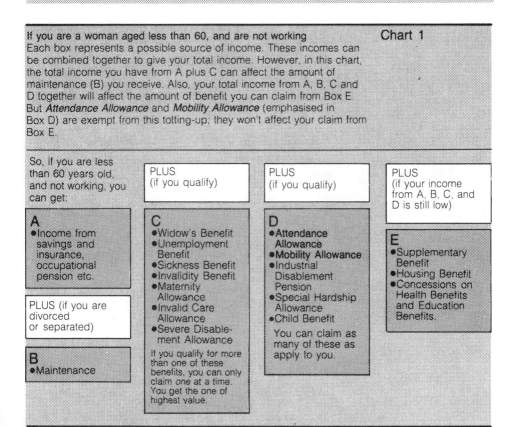

If you are a woman aged less than 60, and are not working    **Chart 1**
Each box represents a possible source of income. These incomes can
be combined together to give your total income. However, in this chart,
the total income you have from A plus C can affect the amount of
maintenance (B) you receive. Also, your total income from A, B, C and
D together will affect the amount of benefit you can claim from Box E.
But *Attendance Allowance* and *Mobility Allowance* (emphasised in
Box D) are exempt from this totting-up; they won't affect your claim from
Box E.

So, if you are less than 60 years old, and not working, you can get:

**A**
- Income from savings and insurance, occupational pension etc.

PLUS (if you are divorced or separated)

**B**
- Maintenance

PLUS (if you qualify)

**C**
- Widow's Benefit
- Unemployment Benefit
- Sickness Benefit
- Invalidity Benefit
- Maternity Allowance
- Invalid Care Allowance
- Severe Disablement Allowance

If you qualify for more than one of these benefits, you can only claim one at a time. You get the one of highest value.

PLUS (if you qualify)

**D**
- **Attendance Allowance**
- **Mobility Allowance**
- Industrial Disablement Pension
- Special Hardship Allowance
- Child Benefit

You can claim as many of these as apply to you.

PLUS (if your income from A, B, C, and D is still low)

**E**
- Supplementary Benefit
- Housing Benefit
- Concessions on Health Benefits and Education Benefits.

The boxes list the different kinds of income that it is possible to get. But the charts will not tell you if you do or do
not qualify for a particular sort of income. For example,
*Chart 1* lists both widow's benefit and maintenance, but
you could only claim the first if you were a widow and the
latter if you were separated or divorced. All the charts will
do is give you an idea of which sorts of income you can
get at the same time and when entitlement to one kind of
income affects whether you can get another.

This section is intended simply to signpost you to the
different sorts of income. If you want further information
on the benefits listed, check in the text. Some of the benefits
are not described in this chapter because only a small
number of people can claim them. The DHSS produces
leaflets on all Social Security benefits. These are available
from any local DHSS offices, Citizens' Advice Bureau, some
public libraries and larger post offices.

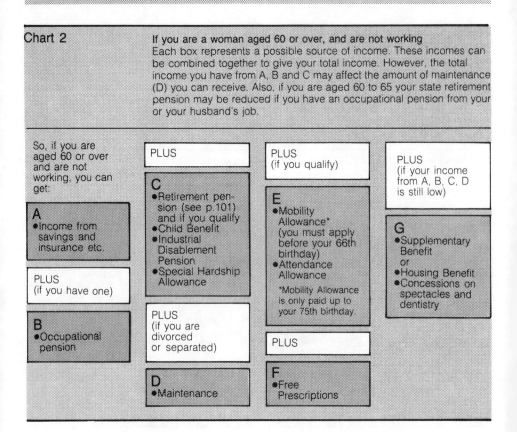

**Chart 2**

If you are a woman aged 60 or over, and are not working
Each box represents a possible source of income. These incomes can be combined together to give your total income. However, the total income you have from A, B and C may affect the amount of maintenance (D) you can receive. Also, if you are aged 60 to 65 your state retirement pension may be reduced if you have an occupational pension from your or your husband's job.

So, if you are aged 60 or over and are not working, you can get:

**A**
• Income from savings and insurance etc.

PLUS
(if you have one)

**B**
• Occupational pension

PLUS

**C**
• Retirement pension (see p.101) and if you qualify
• Child Benefit
• Industrial Disablement Pension
• Special Hardship Allowance

PLUS
(if you are divorced or separated)

**D**
• Maintenance

PLUS
(if you qualify)

**E**
• Mobility Allowance* (you must apply before your 66th birthday)
• Attendance Allowance

*Mobility Allowance is only paid up to your 75th birthday.

PLUS

**F**
• Free Prescriptions

PLUS
(if your income from A, B, C, D is still low)

**G**
• Supplementary Benefit
or
• Housing Benefit
• Concessions on spectacles and dentistry

**How will your working affect your other income?**
**If you are already working,** then you need to know what benefits you might be able to get *on top* of your earnings. Use *Chart 3* and *Chart 4* to do this. If you are a lone parent you may also have the choice between claiming Family Income Supplement (FIS) and Supplementary Benefit.

Making the Choice:
**Family Income Supplement** is paid to people with children who are in low-paid work. As a lone parent you must be working *at least* 24 hours per week (couples can only claim if one of them is working at least 30 hours).

**Supplementary Benefit** is paid to people who are not in full time work and whose income is below supplementary benefit level. So part-time workers can qualify, but you can only claim supplementary benefit if you are working *less* than 30 hours per week.

**If you are a woman aged under 65 and working**    **Chart 3**

Each box represents a possible source of income. These incomes can be combined together to give your total income. However, your income from Box A will affect the amount of maintenance you can get. Also, your total income from A, B and C together will affect the amount of benefits you can claim from D, E or F. But Attendance Allowance and Mobility Allowance (emphasised in Box C) are exempt from this totting-up; they won't affect your claim from Boxes D, E or F.

So, follow the version which applies to you.

---

**If you are aged under 65 and are working 30 hours or more per week**

**A**
- Earnings
- Income from savings, insurance

PLUS
(if you are separated or divorced)

**B**
- Maintenance

PLUS
(if you qualify)

**C**
- Social Security
- Widow's Benefit
- Child Benefit and One Parent Benefit
- **Attendance Allowance**
- **Mobility Allowance**
- Special Hardship Allowance
- Industrial Disablement Pension

PLUS
(if your income is still low)

**D**
- Family Income Supplement
- Housing Benefit
- Concessions on Health and Education Benefits eg free prescriptions, school meals etc
- Childminders can claim Supplementary Benefit

---

**If you are aged under 65 and are working less than 30 hours per week**

**A**
- Earnings
- Income from savings, insurance

PLUS
(if you are separated or divorced)

**B**
- Maintenance

PLUS
(if you qualify)

**C**
- Widow's Benefit
- Child Benefit and One Parent Benefit
- **Attendance Allowance**
- **Mobility Allowance**
- Special Hardship Allowance
- Industrial Disablement Pension

PLUS
(if your income is still low)

**E**
- Housing Benefit
- Family Income Supplement (if working at least 24 hours per week)
- Concessions on Health Benefits and Education Benefits

Or

**F**
- Supplementary Benefit

**Chart 4**

**If you are a woman aged 65 or over and are working**

Each box represents a possible source of income. These incomes can be combined together to give your total income. However, in this chart, your income from A and B, and possibly your retirement and industrial disablement pensions, will affect how much maintenance (C) you can get. Also your total income from A, B, C and D together will affect the amount of benefit paid if you claim any of the benefits in boxes E or F. But free prescriptions, attendance allowance, and mobility allowance (emphasised in Box D) are exempt from this totting-up; they won't affect your claim from Boxes E or F.

So, follow the version which applies to you:

---

If you are aged 65 or over and working 30 hours or more per week

**A**
- Earnings and income from savings and insurance policies

PLUS
(if you have one)

**B**
- Occupational Pension

PLUS
(if you are separated or divorced)

**C**
- Maintenance

PLUS

**D**
- Free prescriptions
- Retirement pensions (see p. 101) and if you qualify
- **Attendance Allowance**
- Child Benefit
- Industrial Disablement Pension
- Special Hardship Allowance
- **Mobility Allowance\***
  **(if you applied for it before your 66th birthday)**
  \*only payable up to your 75th birthday

PLUS
(if your income is still low)

**E**
- Family Income Supplement
- Housing Benefit
- Concessions on spectacles and dentistry

---

If you are aged 65 or over and are working less than 30 hours per week

**A**
- Earnings and income from savings and insurance policies

PLUS
(if you have one)

**B**
- Occupational Pension

PLUS
(if you are separated or divorced)

**C**
- Maintenance

PLUS

**D**
- Free prescriptions
- Retirement pensions and if you qualify
- **Attendance Allowance**
- Child Benefit
- Industrial Disablement Pension
- Special Hardship Allowance
- **Mobility Allowance\***
  **(if you applied for it before your 66th birthday)**
  \*only payable up to your 75th birthday.

PLUS
(if your income is still low)

**F**
- Supplementary Benefit
- Housing Benefit
- Family Income Supplement
  (if you are working at least 24 hours a week)

---

So if you are a lone parent working between 24 and 30 hours per week you can choose whichever would pay you the most:

*If you are working more than 24 hours per week* it is always worth making a claim for *Family Income Supplement* unless you have very high earnings. Your savings are not taken into account and will not affect your entitlement to this benefit. Your entitlement to this benefit is calculated by adding together all your weekly income (except child benefit, housing benefit and attendance and mobility allowances). This total income is then compared with a set weekly amount called 'the prescribed amount' for your family. This amount is fixed each year by Parliament and depends on the number of children in the family. The DHSS leaflet FIS 1, called *Family Income Supplement*, sets out the different 'prescribed amounts'. If your income is less than the prescribed amount for your family you will qualify for some family income supplement.

*If you are working less than 30 hours per week* you need to find out whether you would be better off getting Supplementary Benefit or Family Income Supplement. First check if you meet the basic conditions for each benefit. For example, your savings must come to less than £3,000 (1984 level) to be able to claim Supplementary Benefit.

*If you are already getting Supplementary Benefit,* fill in a claim form for *Family Income Supplement* (see DHSS leaflet 'Family Income Supplement', FIS 1). The FIS Unit in Blackpool will let you know how much FIS you are entitled to. If it is more than your Supplementary Benefit, tell your Supplementary Benefit Office that you are going to get FIS and want your Supplementary Benefit claim to stop. If it is less than your Supplementary Benefit, you *must* write to the FIS Unit within 10 days, telling them that you don't want to claim FIS.

*If you are already getting Family Income Supplement* you may not be able to claim Supplementary Benefit until you have had your full year on FIS, but you should ask the DHSS to assess you. Your local Supplementary Benefit Office will be able to tell you whether you would be better off on Supplementary Benefit and when you can begin to be paid Supplementary Benefit.

*If you get neither benefit at the moment* ask the Supplementary Benefit Office to work out how much Supplementary Benefit you would be entitled to and send a completed FIS form (see above) to the FIS unit. When the FIS unit write back giving you the amount of FIS they will pay you, you will know which benefit to take.

*The advantage of claiming FIS*: The DHSS calculates your weekly entitlement based on the evidence you give them (for example, pay slips), of your income on the day of the claim. However, once your entitlement is calculated you will continue to receive that amount for 52 weeks regardless of what happens to your financial circumstances during that period. If you think your earnings may go up significantly in the next six to nine months it is worth claiming FIS rather than Supplementary Benefit, if you have the choice. This is because Supplementary Benefit will go down week by week as your earnings increase, but the FIS will stay the same for 52 weeks.

*Family Income Supplement and Supplementary Benefit will both act as 'passports' to other benefits and concessions. So if you receive either of them you will automatically qualify for free prescriptions, free school meals, free optical and dental charges.*

**If you're not working** or have had to give up work since your separation or bereavement, you need to know how earnings will affect other income. For example, you need to check whether the amount you will lose in Social Security benefits is more or less than your potential net earnings, that is, after tax and National Insurance have been deducted.

It may be that you have reached a point where you can confidently go back to work and be economically self-sufficient. But it's more likely that you don't know what your earning power is going to be. Perhaps you'd like to do a job for a trial period, or just do a few hours' work a week. You're not at all certain that you can manage to do it or earn enough. It is really important to grasp any opportunity that will increase your independence and sense of achievement. But earnings, however small, can affect both your benefits and your maintenance. You may be prepared to take a small drop in income by going back to work either because you need the challenge or you believe that you will gradually be able to increase your earnings significantly. But you can't make these choices until you know to what extent an attempt to work is likely to jeopardise your other income.

Here are a few guidelines to help you weigh up the choices and decide what would be in your best interests:

• **You can feel free to go ahead and try working** if your income consists of any of the following: child benefit; widow's benefit; industrial disablement or death benefit or war disablement pension, interest from savings and investments or a private insurance policy.

None of these will be affected by earnings and you do not have to notify the DHSS or other relevant authority of your intention to find work.

*If you are getting widow's benefit* you may have to earn quite a lot before you see any increase in your income. This is because your widow's benefit is taxable and any earnings, however small, will probably increase the amount of income tax you will have to pay.

• **You must plan very carefully before taking paid work** if you get any of the following: regular maintenance payments; Housing Benefit; occupational pensions or other benefits; retirement pension; Supplementary Benefit.

**Maintenance**: If you have already been awarded a lump sum payment this should not be affected by your potential earnings, and the maintenance you receive for the children, however it is paid, should not be affected by your earnings. But if you are getting regular maintenance payments for yourself or you and your partner have not yet agreed an amount of maintenance for you, then your ability to earn money could be taken into account and reduce the amount of maintenance awarded.

**Housing Benefit**: If you are getting Housing Benefit but not Supplementary Benefit, your earnings will be taken into account. You must tell the local authority and let them know exactly how much you are earning. In 1984–5, the first £20 wouldn't affect your Housing Benefit, but after that your benefit would reduce on a sliding scale as your earnings go up.

**Occupational pension or other payments through an occupational scheme**: If you receive regular payments from any superannuation or private pension or insurance scheme provided by your or your husband's employer, you must check whether your earnings will affect the payments. Every scheme is different so find out the terms and conditions *before* you take work.

**Retirement pension**: If you are over 65, your retirement pension will not be affected by any work you do. But if you are between 60 and 65 both the hours you work and the money you earn will be taken into account. You may be prevented from claiming any retirement pension or you may get a reduced rate. Check with the DHSS before you take work. It could pay you to take part-time rather than full-time work.

**Supplementary Benefit**: This is primarily for people who aren't working, so if you do more than 30 hours' paid work per week, your Supplementary Benefit will stop even if your earnings are small. Even if you continue to claim Supplementary Benefit, your earnings will be taken into account and will affect how much benefit you can have. However, lone parents are allowed to earn more than other claimants before their benefit is reduced. Roughly speaking if you earn less than £20 per week after deducting necessary expenses, you will be able to keep well over half of it on top of your Supplementary Benefit. However, if you are earning more than a few pounds a week, particularly if you have other income, (for example, maintenance or a widow's pension), your earnings could make your income too high for supplementary benefit. When your Supplementary Benefit stops you will be able to claim other benefits, such as Housing Benefit and Family Income Supplement, to boost your earnings. Single parents beware, however, because if you return to Supplementary Benefit you may temporarily lose your right to the long-term rate. Check with the DHSS.

**Any paid work will seriously affect your right to benefit if you are getting any of the following:** Invalidity Benefit; Sickness Benefit; Unemployment Benefit; Maternity Allowance; Invalid Care Allowance or Severe Disablement Allowance. You must find out exactly what paid work the DHSS would permit you to do. Strict rules apply to all these benefits and if you take work without the DHSS's permission you could lose your benefit altogether. So make absolutely sure by checking with the local DHSS office.

### Letting the DHSS know about earnings

If you are getting any Social Security Benefits, it is advisable to let the DHSS know in advance that you intend to take paid work, even though earnings cannot affect certain benefits such as widow's benefit. But this will ensure that the DHSS does notify you if there are special conditions relating to a particular benefit, and you cannot then be accused in the future of deliberately withholding information.

## Which benefit?

If you intend to claim any kind of state benefit you should consult the booklet 'Which Benefit?', obtainable from your local Social Security Office or Citizens' Advice Bureau. This outlines in general terms all the pensions, allowances and other payments payable by the state, and tells you which leaflets to get for more detailed information.

Ask for FB2 'Which benefit?' and make sure it is the latest edition. It is published each November.

If you would like further information or advice about how your income would be affected by claiming benefit, or if you are not satisfied with the information the DHSS has given you, seek advice from a CAB or from one of the organizations, such as One-Parent Families, who are there to help. Their addresses are listed at the end of this book.

# Claiming Social Security benefits

Most women picking up the pieces after bereavement or separation will find themselves claiming Social Security benefits, perhaps for the first time. You may feel reluctant to do so; feel unable to cope with the bureaucracy, confusion or the sometimes offhand and brusque manner of officials. It's also very difficult to find out what you should be claiming and whether your benefit is correctly worked out. Don't be put off – millions of pounds go unclaimed every year because people do not know what to claim, don't like to make a claim or claim for the wrong benefit. It doesn't matter whether you are claiming benefits because you are on a low income, or benefits where your entitlement is due to you because of National Insurance contributions that have been paid, or benefits paid because of your particular circumstances, for example, Child Benefit – they are yours, *as of right* if you meet the conditions for claiming. Perhaps you feel put off by the stories of 'scrounging', or feel that claiming benefits is like asking for 'charity'. But it isn't scrounging to claim a benefit to which you are entitled. It doesn't feel like 'scrounging' or asking for charity when you visit your GP, or if you have your appendix removed. Yet the principle is the same. You and your partner have over the years made an enormous contribution to society and the treasury. When you were working you paid tax and National Insurance. You pay indirect taxes such as VAT every day. If you've brought up children, you've also made an enormous contribution to society's future. In the same way that those taxes and National Insurance go towards paying for the National Health Service they also pay for Social Security. And you have the right to take what health care, and which benefits, you need – and to which you are entitled.

Having said all this, it is perfectly true that when you claim benefits it can be very distressing to have to give so many details about your personal life. Before making a claim, whether in writing or by visiting the local office, it is important to be well prepared. You should make sure that you have read the relevant leaflet and know exactly what you want to claim and what information to provide. You can also get very detailed information on benefits and claiming from a number of excellent publications, some of which are listed at the end of this book. It is important to be psychologically prepared too. Overworked and harassed DHSS staff do not always treat claimants with the consideration and respect they should. Officials can be very overbearing but there is no good reason why you should be intimidated. The best tactic – if you can – is to remain calm, polite, and if possible, friendly! You, at least, will then emerge from the interview with your self-respect and dignity intact and able to face such people fearlessly in the future.

If you feel you need some support before making a claim, or are not satisfied with the way you were treated or your claim has been decided, don't hesitate to ask for help. Your local CAB, Law Centre or other advice centre, or one of the helpful organisations listed at the end of this book, will be able to advise you and may take up your case direct with the DHSS, if you want them to.

### The 'advantages' of being a woman on your own

We talked a lot earlier about the way that society disadvantages women who find themselves living alone after years of marriage. But the Social Security system has also always been unfair to married women and women living with a man as his wife. These women have been deliberately excluded from claiming certain benefits precisely because they have been considered as their husband's financial responsibility. This means that now you are on your own, there may be benefits that you can claim that you couldn't have before.

**Invalid Care Allowance (ICA)**: This is paid if you are looking after a severely disabled person for at least 35 hours per week. Women living with their husbands, or living with a man as husband and wife, are not allowed to claim. If you are caring for someone, check whether you can claim invalid care allowance

**Supplementary Benefit**: This has special rules for couples which mean they have to make a joint claim and benefit is paid to one of them. It may be that you were getting Supplementary Benefit when you were with your partner, but the benefit was paid to him. Or you were prevented from making a claim either because of your partner's income or because the special rules didn't allow you to be the partner who could claim. You can now claim in your own right as a woman on your own. Check pp. 93–7 and the box on p. 94 to see if you qualify.

**Allowances for children who live with you**: Were you getting any of the following benefits while you lived with your partner: Invalidity Benefit; Severe Disablement Allowance; retirement pension; Industrial Disablement Pension?

If you were, you probably didn't get an allowance for each child with your basic benefit. If you are still getting any of these benefits, or if you make a claim in the future, make sure you claim an extra allowance for each child. Write to the DHSS office which sends you your order book and ask for a claim form for the children.

**Family Income Supplement (FIS)**: This can only be claimed by couples if one partner is working at least 30 hours per week. However, as a lone parent you only have to be working 24 hours or more to qualify. So you may be able to claim for the first time. For example, if you work 24 hours per week, you are now eligible.

**Severe Disablement Allowance (SDA)**: This is a new benefit which replaced non-contributory invalidity pension (both NCIP and the benefit for married women – HNCIP) in November 1984. As a disabled married woman you had to prove you couldn't do housework to claim HNCIP. You don't have to pass the housework test to claim SDA, so you should ask the DHSS for the new leaflet which describes severe disablement allowance to see if you meet the conditions for the new benefit.

**How to claim**

Once you have worked out which benefits might apply to you, you need to make a claim to find out if you do qualify. You should make a claim as soon as possible because it is difficult to get benefit backdated before the date of the claim, even if you met the conditions for some time before you claimed. The procedures are different for each benefit and are explained in the relevant DHSS leaflet. Ask the CAB if the leaflet seems unclear.

Many benefits can be claimed by post, by filling in a claim form or writing a letter. The DHSS usually notifies you of your entitlement to widow's benefit, retirement pension and child benefit and explains how to claim. With other benefits you have to work out for yourself which ones to claim. It is always worth making the claim in writing, either on the form or by letter. This is true even if you visit the local office. If the claim was in writing and you kept a copy of the application, there cannot be a dispute about the date of the claim and the information you provided. It may be necessary with certain benefits (for example, Supplementary Benefit) to give all the information again during an interview once they receive the written claim.

**How to appeal**

If you are not satisfied with a decision that has been made about your entitlement to benefit, for example, if you are refused or not happy with the amount awarded, you can appeal. You must write to the DHSS within 28 days of receiving the decision and say why you are not satisfied, and that you wish to appeal. An independent appeal tribunal will then hear all the facts and evidence and decide whether the DHSS's decision was correct. You have the right to attend the hearing and give evidence. If you want to appeal you should get advice from an advice centre, such as a CAB.

The Secretary of State makes certain Social Security decisions, for example, about your contribution record for entitlement to retirement pension. You cannot appeal against a Secretary of State's decision but you can ask him to review the decision, to reconsider the facts and make a new decision.

## How are you paid?

You will get an order book for most benefits that you claim. It will provide fortnightly, monthly or quarterly orders which can be cashed at the post office. In the first few weeks or months, while the DHSS is deciding your correct entitlement, you won't get an order book; instead you will be sent money in the form of a Girocheque through the post. The cheque will usually arrive on the same day of the week. Giros sometimes get lost. If yours is delayed or lost let the DHSS know immediately. If you have no money, the Supplementary Benefit Office should give you some money over the counter to keep you going. You may have to pay this money back once the Giro comes through.

Some benefits, such as Unemployment Benefit and in certain circumstances, Supplementary Benefit, are never paid by order book. They are always paid by Girocheque usually fortnightly. You do not have any choice about whether you are paid by Giro or order book nor at what interval. The DHSS decides, and there is no right of appeal.

However, there are now some benefits, such as retirement pension, Mobility and Attendance Allowance, and Child Benefit, where you can choose to be paid direct into your bank account. You may find this more convenient for budgeting, or if you are saving the benefit to pay for something in particular. However, it is sometimes difficult to spot when errors have occurred if benefits are paid direct. Like all large institutions, the DHSS is not infallible and errors occur. If benefit is incorrectly overpaid you will have to pay it back even if it isn't your fault. This is one of the rather unfair aspects of the benefit system and there is nothing you can do about it. If you have an order book it is relatively easy to look through it in advance and see if orders appear to be paid at a different rate to the others. You can then check with the DHSS whether this is a mistake and get it changed. When benefit goes direct into your bank account, you won't spot any errors until they have happened and you may not spot them even then unless you read your bank statements very closely.

## What is Supplementary Benefit and can it help you?

Supplementary Benefit is intended for people who aren't working full time (that is, less than 30 hours per week) or at all, to make sure their income does not fall below a certain level. Every year, Parliament decides the level of Supplementary Benefit. It is based on weekly set amounts for the claimant and her or his dependants, which are supposed to reflect the minimum amount of money the family needs for bare essentials each week. There are also extra weekly additions if you have special costs – for example, arising out of old age, disability or an expensive form of heating. The set amounts are based on the rates of inflation and the retail price index for the previous twelve months, and they are increased each November.

You can claim Supplementary Benefit if you have no other income, or if your other income is below your 'Supplementary Benefit level'. It will be paid on top of your

## Benefits for people on low incomes

If you are having difficulty making ends meet or have found your income has been significantly reduced, you should check to see if you qualify for any of the following. You will have to show that your income, and in some cases, your capital, is low enough to qualify.

### Supplementary Benefit
*A cash benefit from the DHSS.* If you are not working, or working less than 30 hours a week, you can claim this benefit on top of your other income from benefits or earnings. You will also have to show that your savings and capital are less than £3,000 (1984–85 level) see pp. 93–7 for more details.

### Family Income Supplement
*A cash benefit from the DHSS.* If you are working more than 24 hours a week and have at least one child, you can claim this benefit on top of your other income. Your savings and capital will be ignored. See pp. 82–6 for more details.

### Housing Benefit
*Help with your rent and rates – you will get a rate rebate; and either a rebate or cash allowance towards your rent from the local authority.* If you are getting Supplementary Benefit you will automatically get most of your housing costs met from Housing Benefit. You do not have to apply because the DHSS will tell the local authority to pay housing benefit to you.

If you are not getting Supplementary Benefit you can apply to the local authority for this benefit. Your capital and savings will not be taken into account but you will be paid Housing Benefit if your income is low. You should always check whether you can claim Supplementary Benefit from the DHSS first. If you can't apply to the local authority for housing benefit see pp. 98–101 for details.

### Health Benefits
*Payment of prescription charges, optical and dental charges, milk and vitamins.* If you are on Supplementary Benefit or Family Income Supplement, you and your children will automatically qualify for free health benefits.

If you are on a low income you can apply for help with these items. You may qualify for a reduced rate or free treatment. Ask for leaflet.

### Education Benefits
*School meals, clothing grants and travel, provided by the local education authority.* If you are on Supplementary Benefit or Family Income Supplement your children are automatically entitled to free school meals.

If you are on a low income ask the authority what help it offers.

If you have children, see also box on p. 97, 'Help with the costs of bringing up children'.

other income to bring your total income up to Supplementary Benefit level. When you make a claim, the DHSS will work out your 'Supplementary Benefit level' depending on your personal circumstances. They will then add up your weekly income. Some of your income isn't taken into account and will be ignored for the purpose of this calculation. If your real income is less than your assigned 'Supplementary Benefit level', you will get Supplementary Benefit to make up the difference. Once you get Supplementary Benefit, however small the amount, you are entitled to other concessions, such as free prescriptions, free school meals and lump sum payments for unexpected needs.

Once you are getting Supplementary Benefit, most increases in your income from other sources will simply reduce your Supplementary Benefit, unless it is income which is ignored in the assessment.

---

*When Margaret and Ian separated, he agreed to pay her £20 per week maintenance. She claimed Supplementary Benefit for herself and the two children; she got £13.50p per week Supplementary Benefit on top of her child benefit and maintenance. After six months on her own, Margaret heard about One-Parent Benefit, so she made a claim. But she found that when her Child Benefit was increased, this counted as income for Supplementary Benefit purposes, so her Supplementary Benefit was reduced by the amount of the One-Parent Benefit. For the same reason, when Ian started paying her an extra £5 per week maintenance this just reduced her Supplementary Benefit by £5, so she wasn't any better off. But then Margaret got a part-time job in the local day centre which paid her £10 per week. She found that the 'special earning rule' for lone parents meant that the first £7 of her earnings was ignored, so her Supplementary Benefit went down by £3 but she had £7 a week on top of her benefit.*

---

If you are struggling to increase your income, it may seem as though Supplementary Benefit just works as a powerful disincentive. But for many women who are separated and divorced it can provide an essential safety net – a secure, stable income instead of dependence on the vagaries of irregular maintenance payments.

---

Brian and Cynthia sorted out their own financial arrangement when they separated. Cynthia has a part-time job which pays her £50 per week. They owned their own home and had a mortgage with monthly interest of £60 per month. Brian agreed to sign over his share in the home to Cynthia because her parents had lent them the deposit. He also agreed to pay her £18 per week maintenance. Cynthia knew money would be tight but she thought she could just manage. She coped quite well for the first six months, then Brian's firm ran into difficulties and he was put on short time. He began paying Cynthia very irregularly, some weeks no money at all, and then £50 all at once. She found it very difficult to budget her tiny income; and then she had six weeks with no money from Brian. The final straw was a big winter electricity bill. In despair she visited the local electricity showroom to see if there was some way she could pay it off in instalments. Luckily, the person she saw there told her she should be claiming Supplementary Benefit. When Cynthia visited the Supplementary Benefit Office they found that even with the maintenance her income was just below Supplementary Benefit level. The DHSS asked Cynthia to agree to a court order requiring Brian to pay £18 per week maintenance and have the money paid direct to the DHSS. This meant that the DHSS could pay her the full weekly income, whether or not Brian paid, and then the DHSS would pursue Brian for the debt.

---

If you are in Cynthia's position, you have the choice. The DHSS can't make you take out a court order nor even reveal the name and address of your ex-partner if you don't want to. If you aren't getting maintenance and don't want to force your ex-partner to pay, the DHSS can't make you do so. They must pay you Supplementary Benefit based on your income and if you can show you have no maintenance payments, then they must give you the benefit to which you are entitled. If you have a maintenance order, the DHSS will assume you are being paid and will reduce your Supplementary Benefit by the amount of the maintenance. So if you are fed up with having a fluctuating income, or are tired of putting pressure on your ex-partner, you can do what Cynthia did. But the choice is yours. If you feel that the DHSS are putting a lot of pressure on you to pursue the maintenance payments and you are unhappy about it, get help and advice from a CAB, Law Centre or other advice agency.

It is very important to claim Supplementary Benefit if you can, even if it only increases your weekly income by a small amount. This is because there are a number of concessions and special payments that you will be entitled to as a Supplementary Benefit claimant which you would not otherwise get:

**Long-Term Rate of Benefit:** Most people have to be available for work to claim Supplementary Benefit. However if you are disabled or have to stay at home to look after children, disabled or elderly dependants you can get a higher rate of benefit.

Women over 60 and some disabled people are assessed at the higher long-term rate from the day of the claim. But lone parents and carers of disabled or elderly people will get the long-term rate after twelve months on the basic rate of Supplementary Benefit.

**Housing Costs:**
   *Mortgage Interest payments:* Supplementary Benefit will pay you the interest payments on your mortgage and a weekly amount towards insurance and repairs.
   *Rent and Rates:* Supplementary Benefit claimants automatically get their full rent and rates met through housing benefit (see p. 98).

**Lump Sum Payments/Single Payments for Special Needs:** Weekly benefit is intended to cover day-to-day expenses, but if you have a sudden need for essential items, such as new beds or clothes during pregnancy and for the new baby, you can get a payment towards the cost of certain essential items.

**Free Health and Education Benefits and Fares to Hospital:** You are automatically entitled to the following for you and your children: prescriptions; optical and dental treatment; fares to hospital appointments; school meals.

**Extra Weekly Expenses:** When you are assessed for Supplementary Benefit your extra weekly costs should be taken into consideration and added to your 'requirements'. But if your circumstances change, for example, you have extra costs arising out of your own ill health or your children's, or you move to a centrally heated home, you will be able to claim weekly additions towards meeting these and other extra costs.

# Help with the costs of bringing up children

## Social Security Benefits

The following benefits are all non-taxable and paid whether or not you are working and regardless of your other income:

**Child Benefit** is paid if you are looking after a child who is under 16; or aged 16–19 and in full time secondary education (up to A-level or OND).

It is paid for each child. The child does not have to be your child, for example, your niece or granddaughter; nor even related to you, she could be a friend's child. But you must be responsible for her physical and financial welfare.

Special rules apply if the child doesn't always live with you or if someone else is contributing to the child's keep. See: DHSS leaflet Child Benefit CH1 for more information.

**Child Benefit Increase (one-parent benefit)** is paid *on top of* your child benefit if you are a lone parent or a single person bringing up a child. It is paid as a fixed weekly amount regardless of the number of children you have.

You cannot have one-parent benefit if you are already getting any of the following: Child's Special Allowance; Guardian's Allowance; an allowance for the child with your widow's pension; retirement pension or Invalid Care Allowance.

You will be no better off claiming one-parent benefit if you are already getting any of the following: Supplementary Benefit; Housing Benefit; an amount for the child with your invalidity benefit; industrial or war disablement pension. The amount of the one-parent benefit will simply reduce the amount you get from the other benefit.

**Child's Special Allowance** is paid on top of child benefit for each child of your ex-husband if he has died.

Special rules apply so check DHSS leaflet Child's Special Allowance HI93 to find out if you qualify.

**Guardian's Allowance** is paid on top of Child Benefit for each child who is defined as an 'orphan'. You do not have to be the child's relative or legal guardian to claim, but either both parents must have died or one must be dead and the other missing or in legal custody.

If you do not qualify for Guardian's Allowance you should ask your Social Services department to see if you are eligible for a fostering allowance. For more information on Guardian's Allowance see DHSS leaflet Guardian's Allowance HI 14.

The following benefits are paid if you are on a low income:
**Supplementary Benefit** See pp. 93–7, the box on p. 94 and DHSS leaflet SB 7 to see if you qualify.

## Housing Benefit

This benefit is paid by the local authority to people on Supplementary Benefit and other low incomes to help with their housing costs:
**Rates:** If you qualify you will get a reduction, called a rebate, on the rates you have to pay. Some people will not have to pay rates at all.

**Family Income Supplement** See pp. 82–6 and 94 and DHSS leaflet FIS I, 'Family Income Supplement' to see if you qualify.

**Housing Benefit** See below or ask your local authority for information about whether you should claim.

*If you are pregnant* you may also qualify for:

**Maternity Grant:** a lump sum payment which you must claim either within 14 weeks of your expected date of confinement or within 3 months of the birth.

**Maternity Allowance** This is a weekly benefit paid for a maximum of 18 weeks – 11 weeks before the birth and 6 weeks after. You should claim 14 weeks before your expected delivery date. You must satisfy the National Insurance contribution conditions for this benefit, but if you do you can have it as well as Maternity Grant. See DHSS leaflet NI 17A, 'Maternity Allowance and Maternity Grant', for more details on both benefits.

**Supplementary Benefit Single Payments** If you claim Supplementary Benefit you can have a lump sum payment for maternity clothes and for the things you need for the baby. If you get maternity grant you will be expected to use this for these items; but you will get a lump sum if you need to spend more than this amount. The Maternity Allowance will count as income and will reduce your Supplementary Benefit.

*Help from the local authority.* The Social Services Department has money – called 'Section I Payments' which can be used for *any* purpose that helps to keep a family together or benefits the children. It can be used to clear fuel debts, buy essential furniture, pay for a holiday. The Social Services can also offer practical help, such as day care, home helps, etc. Check with your local Social Services office to see what is available.

The Education Department often has special concessions for low income and single parent families; for example, they can provide help with the costs of travelling, school uniforms. Most of these concessions are discretionary and you will have to ask your local education department what help they provide. However, if you are on supplementary benefit or family income supplement, the local authority *must* provide your children with free school meals. The local authority must also provide transport if your child lives more than three miles from the school (two miles for under 8's).

**Rent:** If you qualify and you are a council tenant, you will get a rebate on the rent you have to pay. Some people will not have to pay any rent at all. If you are not a council tenant, the local authority will give you a cash allowance towards your rent. It can be paid directly to you or to your landlord.

Owner-occupiers cannot get help with their mortgages from the local authority because housing benefit only helps with rent and rates. You should check whether you can qualify for Supplementary Benefit, as you can get help with mortgage repayments from Supplementary Benefit.

**1 Housing Benefit for people on Supplementary Benefit:** If you claim Supplementary Benefit, you will automatically qualify for Housing Benefit. The DHSS will tell the local authority to pay you the full cost of your rent and rates. You may have to pay a small amount if there are any service charges included with your rent, or if other adults live with you. You do not have to apply, but the local authority will send you forms to fill in and will tell you how much housing benefit you can have.

**2 Housing Benefit for people who are not on Supplementary Benefit:** If you have not claimed Supplementary Benefit, always check whether you can get Supplementary Benefit *before* you apply to the local authority for Housing Benefit. This is because some people can get more help from Supplementary Benefit than they can from Housing Benefit on its own. Also if you claim Supplementary Benefit first, this can help you qualify for a special payment called Housing Benefit Supplement on top of your Housing Benefit (see p. 101).

If you don't qualify for Supplementary Benefit, apply to the local authority. The Housing Benefit Department will calculate how much Housing Benefit you can have. The Housing Benefit calculation is similar to the calculation for Supplementary Benefit. You and your children are given an allowance, based on your circumstances, called a 'needs allowance'. You get a higher needs allowance if you are a lone parent, disabled, or over 60.

The amount of Housing Benefit you receive will depend on whether your income is above or below your needs allowance. If you want details of how Housing Benefit is worked out you should ask the local authority for an explanatory leaflet. The *National Welfare Benefits Handbook* (see Child Poverty Action Group in 'Directory') will also describe the calculation. You can ask for help at your local Citizens' Advice Bureau or other advice centre.

*You can claim Housing Benefit whether or not you are working. Your savings and capital will not be taken into consideration when calculating your entitlement to Housing Benefit.*

**3 Housing Benefit Supplement (HBS):** This is a special payment for people who fail to qualify for Supplementary Benefit because their income is a little too high. You can only get Housing Benefit Supplement if you apply for Supplementary Benefit. You must meet all the other conditions for claiming, for example, have capital and savings below Supplementary Benefit level; be working less than 30 hours a week, (see list on p. 97). When the DHSS notifies you that your income is too high for Supplementary Benefit, they will send you a letter which will include something called your 'excess income figure'. You must take this letter to the Housing Benefit Department. They will then calculate your entitlement to Housing Benefit Supplement using your 'excess income figure'.

If you qualify, your Housing Benefit Supplement will be paid as an increase in your Housing Benefit. So, for example, if you have an 80 per cent rate rebate of £5, and qualify for £2 per week HBS your rebate will be increased by £2. The Housing Benefit Department will send you notification of the amount of Housing Benefit Supplement you are receiving. Keep this carefully – it is a very important piece of paper. It will act as a 'passport' to all the payments and concessions that a Supplementary Benefit claimant can have, (see table on p. 97), such as free prescriptions, school meals and single payments. If you are a lone parent, after a year on HBS you may qualify for Supplementary Benefit at the long-term rate.

# Will I get a retirement pension when I reach 60?

### How is retirement pension calculated?

The state retirement pension is based on the National Insurance contributions paid during your 'working life'. Married and divorced women can usually use part or all of their husband's contribution record as well as their own to help them qualify for a pension. The retirement pension scheme has been modified and enhanced at different times and now consists of three components (see table). Entitlement depends not only on the level of contributions paid but also in which years.

The method of calculating entitlement is extremely complicated; even the DHSS depends on a computer in Newcastle. It is in fact very rare for someone to need to work out precisely their National Insurance record. All you probably need to do is to work out how to protect your

## Benefits for women over 60

### Retirement Pension

**Basic Retirement Pension.** A taxable weekly cash benefit from the DHSS. You can qualify if you or your husband paid enough National Insurance contributions during your 'working life', (see p. 101).

If you are aged 60–65 you can only have this benefit if you have retired from full-time work and earn less than a certain amount. Special rules apply to widows.

You will receive a basic pension plus additions for any children who live with you and who are supported by you.

**Graduated Retirement Pension.** A weekly taxable cash benefit from the DHSS. This is a small weekly pension based on NI contributions paid between 1961 and 1975. Widows can add half their husband's entitlement to their own.

**'Additional' Pension.** A weekly taxable cash benefit from the DHSS. This weekly pension is based on earnings and NI contributions since April 1978. Years when the contributor was 'contracted out' (see p. 106) do not count.

This pension (SERPS) is paid with widow's benefits, invalidity pension, and retirement pension.

**Invalidity Allowance.** This is paid on top of a retirement pension when people transfer from invalidity benefit (see p. 103).

Retirement pension, graduated retirement pension and additional pension can all be paid at the same time, or you may have entitlement to one and not another. For example, if you only started working in 1980, by the time you retire you may not have enough contributions for a retirement pension but you may have had enough earnings for an additional pension.

## Other benefits

**Supplementary Benefit.** *A cash benefit from the DHSS.* You can qualify if you have a low income from benefits or are working less than 35 hours a week. Your savings must be less than £3,000 (1984/85 rate).

If you qualify for Supplementary Benefit you will receive:

Automatic assessment for the higher long-term rate from the day of the claim;

Lower heating addition if you are aged 65 or over; or the higher heating addition if you are aged 85 or over.

You will also qualify for the benefits and concessions listed on p. 97.

**Mobility Allowance.** *A cash benefit from the DHSS.* You can claim this benefit if you have walking difficulties. It is paid whether or not you are working and regardless of your income or capital.

You must claim before your *66th* birthday but benefit will be paid until you reach the age of 75 once you have made a claim.

See DHSS leaflet 'Mobility Allowance'.

**Attendance Allowance.** *A cash benefit from the DHSS.* You can claim this benefit if you need help with personal care, such as washing and dressing, or if you suffer from a condition where you could be a danger to yourself or others. There is no age limit on claiming this allowance and it will be paid as long as you need help.

See DHSS leaflet 'Attendance Allowance'.

**Widows' Benefits.** You can continue to receive widow's pension or widowed mother's allowance until you are 65 if you have not retired, or you are not entitled to a retirement pension.

*If you were over 60* when your husband died you can only get a widow's allowance if your husband was not entitled to a 'Category A' retirement pension.

**Invalidity Benefit.** *A cash benefit from the DHSS.* If you were receiving this benefit on your 60th birthday you can choose whether to transfer to retirement pension or stay on invalidity pension until you reach 65.

If you have other taxable income you may be better off staying on invalidity benefit which isn't taxable. Otherwise change to retirement pension which is taxable but paid at a higher rate than invalidity benefit.

Any invalidity allowance which is paid with your invalidity pension will continue to be paid when you transfer to retirement pension but it will become taxable.

Special rules apply to women who are over 60 and who only qualify for a reduced rate of retirement pension.

**Invalid Care Allowance (ICA) or Severe Disablement Allowance (SDA).** *Cash benefit from the DHSS.* If you have no

entitlement to retirement pension and you were receiving either of these benefits on your 60th birthday, you will continue to receive it for the rest of your life. If your entitlement to retirement pension is *less* than the amount of ICA or SDA, your SDA or ICA will be paid to top up your retirement pension.

**Free Prescriptions.** You automatically become exempt from prescription charges on your 60th birthday. Just fill in the back of the prescription form.

**Housing Benefit.** A cash benefit from the local authority. You can claim this to help with your rates and rent if your income is fairly low. You will qualify for an extra allowance once you are 60 and a more generous calculation which will increase your entitlement to Housing Benefit.

**Deferred Retirement.** A way of increasing your retirement pension. If you are still working when you reach 60, this is a special provision which allows you to increase the value of your retirement pension. If you decide not to take your retirement pension, and continue working, you will stop paying National Insurance contributions. But special rules mean you will go on 'earning' increases to your retirement pension for each year you work between the ages of 60 and 65.

## If you are on a low income.

If you claim the benefits listed in this table and your income is still low check the table on p. 94 to see if there is anything else you should be getting.

contribution record in the future, to make sure you can get the best pension you can (see p. 102). But if you do want full details of how retirement pensions are calculated you should read a good Social Security handbook such as *Your Rights* (see Age Concern in 'Directory') or the *Rights Guide to Non-Means-Tested Benefits* (see Child Poverty Action Group in 'Directory').

Broadly speaking, in order to qualify for a full retirement pension you must have paid or been credited with enough National Insurance contributions in nine out of every ten years of your working life – this means age 16–60 for a woman. 'Credited contributions' are a way of protecting your contribution record during weeks or years when you are not paying insurance contributions. You will get a reduced pension if you or your husband's contribution record is adequate for at least a quarter of your working life. For example, if you worked for ten years before you got married and paid full National Insurance contributions, and then took another job when you were 55, you would have 15 years of contributions to count towards your retirement pension. Your working life was 44 years. You needed 40 years for a full retirement pension, but you have 15, which is 37 percent of 40, so you get 37 percent of the full retirement pension.

Most women will have paid some contributions before they got married. Whatever your age, whether you are married, divorced or widowed, you need to find out if there is anything you can do now to protect your future retirement pension, or to juggle your own and your husband's contribution record to your advantage. Particularly if you are under 45 there is a lot you can do to ensure you get an adequate retirement pension.

### How to protect your retirement pension
*If you have been working* and paying a full National Insurance contribution either as an employed or a self-employed person, you will qualify for a full retirement pension in your own right as long as there are not more than four years during which you were not paying or being credited with contributions.

*If there are several years when you weren't paying NI contributions* you need to take steps to protect the rest of your 'working life'. If you are *divorced* you can use your ex-husband's contribution record for the years you were married as if it were your own. So any years when he was paying contributions, and you weren't, can be added to the years when you were paying. If you are *widowed*, the contributions your husband paid will count towards a pension for you, but you may get a bigger pension if you can use your own contribution record.

Whatever your status, if you're not paying NI contributions you need to check whether you can get *credited contributions* (see below) or *home responsibilities protection*.

**What are credited contributions?** This is a way of protecting your NI contribution record when you are not working. You can qualify for a weekly credited contribution which counts towards your retirement pension in exactly the same way as if you had paid the contribution.

You will automatically qualify for a 'credit' for each week in which you are getting one of the following benefits: Invalid Care Allowance; Sickness Benefit, (or Statutory Sick Pay); Invalidity Benefit; or Unemployment Benefit.

Otherwise, you can only get a credit if you are signing on at the Unemployment Benefit Office; sending medical certificates to the DHSS showing you are unfit for work; or you are on an MSC or another approved training course.

If you do not come into any of these categories, you should check whether you qualify for *home responsibilities protection*.

**What is home responsibilities protection (see DHSS leaflet NP27)?** This is a way of reducing the number of years of your 'working life'. We said earlier that this means from age 16–60 for a woman for the purpose of calculating retirement pension. However, you can knock off up to twenty years if there are tax years (April to April) since 1978 when you were either receiving Child Benefit or getting Supplementary Benefit because you were looking after an invalid. You don't have to apply. Each year when you were not working will automatically be removed from the record of your working life. So if you have been getting child benefit for the last 6 years, your working life is 44 years (16–60) minus 6 years – i.e. 38 years; if you go on getting Child Benefit for another 5 years, your working life will reduce to 31 years.

You can also get home responsibilities protection for any year you were caring for someone who gets Attendance Allowance, but you must apply for the year to be removed from your record. Use the application form on leaflet NP27. *Married women who have chosen to pay reduced NI contributions cannot get home responsibilities protection, or credited contributions.*

**How does the married women's reduced National Insurance contribution affect your pension?** If you are working and have chosen to pay the married women's reduced contribution, there is nothing you can do to protect your right to a retirement pension, unless you write to the DHSS asking to give up your 'married women's option'. It is in your interests to do so even if you have to pay more National Insurance each week. Apart from your retirement pension, you need to start paying a full NI contribution to build up a future right to Sickness and Unemployment Benefits.

Many women get caught because they do not know that the day that they become divorced they must pay a full NI contribution if they are earning more than £34 per week (1984/85 figure).

If you are not working and it is less than 2 years since you last paid a reduced NI contribution, write to the DHSS immediately and ask to give up your option. If it is more than 2 years, your option has automatically finished so you don't need to do anything.

**How to find out if you have enough National Insurance contributions** You can at any time write to the local DHSS office and ask them to tell you how many years of contributions you already have towards your retirement pension. If you do not get a satisfactory answer or don't understand the answer you get, you should go and see your local CAB, advice centre or write to Age Concern for advice. They will be able to tell you how many more years of paid or credited contributions you need, and whether it is in your interests to claim credited contributions. For example, if you are a widow who is not working, you are automatically protected by home responsibilities protection if you get Child Benefit. But once Child Benefit stops, you will have to 'sign on' at the Unemployment Office in order to get credited contributions.

**What is contracting out and how does it affect retirement pension?** Since 1978, certain employees have been allowed to 'contract out' of the additional pension (see table on p. 102). If you are paying towards an occupational pension scheme which will provide as good a pension as the additional pension, your employer can 'contract out': this means you don't pay towards the additional pension. Years when you are 'contracted out' don't affect your right to a basic pension because you still pay a NI contribution, but they don't count towards your additional pension.

If you change jobs and get a refund of your superannuation or occupational pension payments, you are automatically 'contracted back in' for the period covered by the refund.

**How to claim your retirement pension** The DHSS normally writes to women about four months before their sixtieth birthday. If you have not received a letter three months before that birthday, contact the local DHSS office. They should then send you a claim form to fill in. The DHSS has numerous leaflets intended to help you sort out your rights to retirement pension. These are the leaflets you should ask for:

NI 32 'Your Retirement Pension'
NI 32A 'Your Retirement Pension if you are Widowed or Divorced'
NI 32B 'Retirement Benefits for Married Women'
NI 92 'Earning Extra Pension by Cancelling Your Retirement'
NI 184 'Retirement Pensions for People over Eighty'
These are all obtainable from your local DHSS office. Ask for help there, from the Citizens' Advice Bureau or Age Concern if you don't understand how the rules apply to you.

### Occupational and private pensions

Most people who are in full-time employment will be making contributions to a private pension scheme organised by their employer. In local authorities this is known as 'superannuation'. There are many different kinds of schemes offering lump sums on retirement as well as, or instead of, a regular pension.

*If you are working* you should find out exactly what scheme, if any, you are paying into, and what the benefits and conditions of the scheme are. For example, you should find out what would happen if you decided to get a job with another employer. Most schemes give you the option of freezing your pension rights or transferring them to your new pension scheme. Both these options mean you would lose out. Because of the complex actuarial calculation, you can never transfer the full value of what you have paid in; freezing your pension means you just get paid on the years you have paid. This will be a poor deal unless it is extremely generously index-linked. If maintaining the value of your pension is important to you, it may be worth staying where you are rather than changing jobs.

*If you are widowed* you should find out exactly what sort of occupational pension scheme your husband was paying into and what money is coming to you. You should also find out whether there are special conditions attached to it. For example, whether it will continue if you were to remarry, retire, or get an occupational pension or other income in your own right.

**Private pension schemes.** Only employees can participate in occupational pensions. If you are self-employed or not working you may want to take out a private pension policy to ensure you have an adequate income in retirement. Over the past two years, a wide range of these sorts of insurance scheme have been set up. If you want to take out a policy, get information on as many different schemes as possible and take expert advice. Find out which one meets your needs and gives you the best return on your investment.

# Maintenance

Here we look briefly at how maintenance payments can affect, and be affected by your other income, and the implications of accepting one kind of financial settlement rather than another. Most of what is described here applies only to maintenance orders made through the courts. If you are agreeing a voluntary arrangement it is up to you and your ex-partner to decide what is reasonable, both in the short term and in the long run.

It may not be possible for you to choose a particular form of maintenance or financial arrangement because of your own or your ex-partner's circumstances. For example, if you were not married to your partner you can only get a maintenance order for your children; you cannot get one for yourself. The following may help you decide what would be the best option for you.

### Maintenance for children

There are advantages in having maintenance orders, whether as a lump sum or regular payments, paid direct to the children. This is because regular payments are treated as taxed income; this means that if the maintenance is paid direct to you and you have other taxable income, you may end up paying income tax on the maintenance. However, if the money is paid to the child you will not have to pay income tax unless the annual total is more than the single person's tax allowance (see p. 114). Also the father can claim tax relief on maintenance payments for children, so is able to make the payment out of income *before* tax.

Special rules apply if maintenance is being used to pay school fees, and such an arrangement is not so taxably advantageous. Also, if the maintenance is being used to create a trust fund for the child then it is treated as the payer's, not the child's income.

If you decide to ask for maintenance paid directly to the children, the money can still be administered by you on their behalf; and if it is paid periodically you keep the right to go back to court and ask for the order to be changed if circumstances alter.

Maintenance paid to, or on behalf of, children should not be affected by any improvement in your financial circumstances, or by your remarriage.

**Lump sum maintenance orders**
It is sometimes possible to choose a lump sum payment as well as, or instead of, regular maintenance. The advantage of a lump sum order, whether paid all at once or in instalments, is that the total amount, once agreed, cannot be varied; although your ex-partner can negotiate on the size and timing of any instalments. This means that even if your finances improve in the future, or you remarry, your total maintenance is guaranteed. The other advantage is that you are not liable to pay income tax on a lump sum; although you may have to pay capital gains tax (see p. 117) if you were not married to your partner or if you get a lump sum after you divorce.

The disadvantage of a lump sum payment is that it can never be reassessed in the future if your financial circumstances deteriorate. It would also be treated as capital and could prevent you from claiming Supplementary Benefit (see p. 94) – although it would be ignored when assessing for Family Income Supplement and Housing Benefit.

If your ex-partner has left you with a lot of debts or there are large overheads that need paying, it might be worthwhile trying to negotiate a lump sum payment to clear these bills, which would be separate from your need for regular maintenance payments.

**Periodic (regular) maintenance orders**
This means that the court decides a set amount which your ex-partner must pay at regular intervals. The amount is based on both your financial circumstances at the time of

the assessment. But the order can be varied at any time if either you or your ex-partner applies to the court because of a change in either of your circumstances. For example, if you lose your job, you could ask for more money; but if he becomes unemployed he can ask the court to reduce the amount of the payments. If you remarry the maintenance for you (but not for the children) stops immediately.

One disadvantage of regular maintenance payments under a court order is that they count as taxable income, so you may have to pay income tax on them; your ex-partner can get tax relief on any payments made to you.

The amount of maintenance you can get will be affected by any other income you have, for example, from employment, occupational pensions or investments. Equally, any maintenance payment you receive will be taken into account as income when assessing you for Supplementary Benefit (see p. 94), Family Income Supplement (see p. 94), or Housing Benefit (see p. 98).

### Voluntary maintenance

If you agree a voluntary arrangement with your ex-partner, any regular payments for you or the children will *not* count as taxable income. This is because they are treated as *his* income. This means he cannot claim tax relief on them; but if you already pay income tax on your other income a voluntary arrangement may help you avoid increasing your income tax. However, a voluntary arrangement is *not enforceable* and it can prejudice your chances of getting maintenance through the courts in the future. So only do it if you feel really confident that he will pay you regularly.

### Maintenance in kind

Your ex-partner may agree to pay certain of your overheads directly instead of paying you maintenance, for example, the rates, house insurance, school fees or even the mortgage. There are few financial advantages to either of you in doing this. You can never be sure if and for how long he will continue paying. He cannot claim tax relief on these payments so he would be making them out of taxed income, whereas if he paid you direct he could claim tax relief. He could of course get tax relief if he was paying off your mortgage, but only if his total mortgages (on any property he currently owns as well as your home) were less than £30,000. You also need to check very carefully what happens to your right to stay in the home if you decide to let him pay the mortgage (see below).

*Financial arrangements for joint belongings.* The court can decide how to apportion any joint belongings, for example, the family home, furniture, etc., in any way that it sees fit. It can ask either of you to transfer property to the other, or share it in specific ways. Obviously, if you and your ex-partner can come to some agreement before going to court about how you want to divide things up, the court is likely to follow this if it seems reasonable. The settlement of property on divorce is based on a number of factors. The most important consideration in relation to the marital home is that neither partner is made homeless, and as far as possible is not financially disadvantaged by the separation. Another guideline which is not rigidly applied is that the wife should be entitled to a third of the marital property and belongings. If you and your partner were not married, or are sorting out your finances without getting divorced, you will have to prove your legal rights. In any case you will need expert legal advice to come to an advantageous settlement.

There are, however, one or two points to bear in mind regarding what happens to the family home if one stays put but the other has the right to part of the proceeds when the home is eventually sold. The first point is that however financially beneficial such an arrangement may be to you both now and in the future, you should check to see what your liability for capital gains tax will be and if you can avoid it (see pp. 117–121).

A common arrangement where there are children is for the wife to stay in the home and for the home to be sold after the children have grown up. This arrangement may involve the husband in paying either some or all of the costs of the mortgage. This may be the only way that you can continue to have a secure home while your children are young. You may be confident of being financially independent by the time they have grown up, for example, because you plan to return to work full-time. However, before entering into such an arrangement, you need to be certain of exactly what you will be left with at the end of the day. For example, if he has continued to pay the overheads, you could be entitled to nothing from the proceeds of the sale of the home; or you may have difficulty establishing what proportion of its market value on sale should be paid to you. Even if you do have a precise financial arrangement to give you a fair share on the sale of the home, you may find that it is not sufficient to enable you to buy anything else, and unless you have a good income you will not be able to raise a mortgage. You should also check which of you has the right to decide when the home must be sold, and try to make sure you retain some control over when and how.

If you have had any legal aid to help with the financial costs of the divorce or separation, you should also check whether you will have to pay anything when the property is finally sold. If your legal expenses are very high you could find that a substantial sum will have to be paid back once you get the capital from the sale of the property.

Financial settlements regarding property are separate from any arrangements regarding maintenance. However, you can sometimes come to an agreement to accept the transfer of the property instead of a maintenance payment. One advantage of doing this, is that your home does not count as a resource in any way if you need to claim benefits, such as Supplementary Benefit or Family Income Supplement, whereas weekly or lump sum maintenance would be taken into account.

## Taxation

There are two different kinds of taxes which we all have to pay – direct and indirect. Indirect taxes are charged on goods and services before we acquire them, so everyone pays them regardless of their financial circumstances. Two obvious indirect taxes are stamp duty when we buy property and value added tax which is added to most goods and services.

There are also direct taxes on income and wealth, which individuals have to pay depending on their financial circumstances. You may believe that you have so little income or capital that you won't be liable for any tax. This may be so, but in order to plan your financial future you need to know how your potential income and capital are going to be affected by taxation. There are three main taxes which could affect you now and in the future and could reduce the money available to you. These are: income tax, capital gains tax, and capital transfer tax. You need to know how much tax you are likely to have to pay and whether there are ways of increasing your money without increasing your tax burden.

There are a number of publications which can help you sort out your liability for income tax and other taxation. *Money Which* is part of *Which* magazine (produced by the Consumers' Association) and carries a lot of articles and

| | | | **Income which is exempt from income tax** |
|---|---|---|---|
| • Mobility Allowance<br>• Attendance Allowance<br>• Invalidity Benefit<br>• Sickness Benefit<br>• War and Industrial Disablement Benefits<br>• Child Benefit and Child Benefit increases<br>• Family Income Supplement | • Housing Benefit<br>• Maternity Allowance<br>• Maintenance for *children*<br>• Expenses and fringe benefits from your work (if you earn less than £8,500)<br>• Interest from national savings bank certificates | • Income from a scholarship<br>• Redundancy payments<br>• Any increase or allowances paid for *children* for example, with widow's or retirement pension<br>• Supplementary Benefit (but only if you are not required to 'sign on' for work)<br>• Death grant | |

This includes income from lodgers, tenants; and honorarium or lump sum payment for services; interest or income from investments or shares; regular maintenance payment. In particular, remember that the following Social Security benefits are taxable:

**All other income is taxable.**

| | | |
|---|---|---|
| • Widow's benefit<br>• Invalid Care Allowance<br>• Statutory Sick Pay<br>• Unemployment Benefit | • Retirement Pension<br>• Industrial Death Benefit | • Supplementary Benefit paid to unemployed people |

The following income has tax deducted before you receive it. It is therefore not added to your taxable income when assessing your liability for income tax for the year:

| | | |
|---|---|---|
| • Interest from building society accounts | • Interest from bank deposit accounts | • Income from annuities |

information about making tax returns. If you want more detailed and technical information and can cope with the jargon and legal language, there is a very thorough text-book on all aspects of taxation – *Tolley's Practical Tax Guide*. It is available in most public reference libraries.

### How much income tax will you have to pay?

You only have to pay income tax on certain kinds of income. The box (see above) shows income which is not taxable. All other income is taxable and you will have to pay income tax once your total taxable income for the year goes above a certain level.

The Inland Revenue is responsible for calculating your income tax liability for the tax year. The tax year runs from 6th April of one year to 5th April of the next. Everybody is given a personal tax allowance for the tax year based on their personal circumstances. This is the amount of taxable income you can have before you have to pay any income tax. Once your taxable income is greater than your personal tax allowance you will have to pay a fixed percentage of it as income tax. Both the level of personal tax allowances and the percentage rates of income tax are reviewed by the Chancellor of the Exchequer each year in the April budget. Tax allowances usually increase each year in line with inflation. The rate of income tax depends on your total annual income: the basic rate is 30 per cent, but if your total income is above £15,400 (1984/85) you will be charged at a higher percentage on a sliding scale. The percentage rates have not changed for a number of years, although the income bands are increased in line with inflation; but either could be increased or decreased in the next budget.

Everyone, including children, except married men, gets the same tax allowance, known as the single person's tax allowance (£2,005 in 1984/85). But you can also have extra allowances if you have particular expenses or fall into certain categories: for example, everyone aged 65 or over gets an extra allowance. There are extra allowances if you are blind, if you are bringing up a child on your own. It is to your benefit to know your own tax allowance. Find out from the Inland Revenue what allowances you can claim.

The tax allowance means that even if all your income is taxable, you will not have to pay income tax if your income for the year is less than your personal allowance. For example, many Social Security benefits are taxable but it is usually the case that if your *only* income is from benefits, you won't pay income tax because your income will be just below your tax allowance. This will also be the case if you are in low-paid, or part-time work. Your liability for income tax is worked out by adding together all your taxable income for the year, deducting all relevant tax reliefs and expenses. You then pay a percentage of the amount by which your income is greater than your tax allowance as income tax.

*If you are self-employed* you can deduct certain work expenses from your total taxable income for the year. Such things as the cost of your office space, if you have any; stationery, necessary books and periodicals, travelling costs are all deductable. You will have to keep very clear accounts which show how much you have earned; when you received payment and lists of all your expenses and when they were incurred. You should keep all receipts so that at the end of the year you can prove to the Inland Revenue exactly how much income and expenditure you have had.

Once you are handling a substantial amount of money each year, say, more than £3,000, you may find advice from an accountant helpful, (see p. 116).

### How is income tax paid?
Most people who are working have their income tax deducted weekly or monthly, together with a National Insurance contribution, from their earnings by their employer. This is called the PAYE scheme. You are entitled to an itemised pay slip with every payment from your employer which will show how much you have paid in income tax. If you do not get one you should make sure that your employer provides one, as it may be difficult to prove in the future whether or not income tax was paid.

*If you are self-employed,* you will have to submit regular tax returns and the Inland Revenue will notify you of what income tax you have to pay. They will usually do this at the end of the tax year, so you should put money aside to anticipate your income tax bill. Put into a Building Society account, it will earn interest. Around 25% of your gross earnings should be adequate.

*If you are not working, or you have periods out of work,* the Inland Revenue will usually send you a tax return form to complete in February or March, on which to list all the income you have had during the previous year. They will then calculate whether you have paid too little or too much tax during the year. You will get a refund of any overpayment, but will have to pay any underpayment. You can either do this by paying a lump sum, or if you are working it can be deducted weekly or monthly through PAYE scheme from your future earnings.

*If you have income in addition to any earnings* you may have to pay income tax at the end of the year as well as weekly or monthly. For example, you may have some employment where your tax is deducted by your employer; some income from self-employment; some income from investments and rent from tenants. All these different kinds of income are taxable and the Inland Revenue will probably assess your liability for tax at the end of the year for all your income except that from your employer. So you may pay some income through the PAYE scheme and the rest at the end of the year.

115

*If you have more than one job* your different employers may all be deducting income tax. Or if you have one or two or three part-time jobs you need to be very careful. Your total taxable income for the year will probably be above your tax allowance, so you will be liable to income tax. But your individual employers are not deducting income tax because your income from each of them is below your tax allowance, so you end up at the end of the tax year owing money to the Inland Revenue. This shouldn't happen if you make sure in advance that both employers and the Inland Revenue know about your jobs. It will be a problem if you take several short-term jobs during the year. In any case, you should make sure at the end of the tax year that no mistake has happened and that you have paid the right amount of tax. If you think you have paid too much tax, ask the Inland Revenue for a tax refund.

The Inland Revenue publish a lot of leaflets on tax allowances and income tax for particular people, for example, on tax and pensioners. Ask at your local Inland Revenue office for leaflets or ask for a personal interview if you would like some advice. They are always very willing to be helpful.

**Can an accountant help?**

If you are in full-time employment, as long as you are not self-employed or if your income consists of Social Security benefits, your assessment for income tax will be straightforward. You will not need advice from an accountant unless you have substantial savings and capital, or expect to acquire fairly large sums of money in the near future.

Accountants can offer two different kinds of advice. They can help you sort out a particular problem you are having, for example, a dispute with the Inland Revenue about how much tax you should have paid last year. Or they can advise you on how to handle your money. This can include managing your income and capital for you, both to maximise your income and deal with your liability for tax. It is up to you to decide how you want to use an accountant. Accountants do charge very high fees. However, you can arrange an initial interview with an accountant for a small charge, to discuss your particular problem and what the accountant can do to help. You may find this interview provides sufficient advice and information to you to go and deal with the matter yourself. Or you may want the accountant to sort it out for you. The accountant should give you an idea of what has to be done, what the firm would charge for sorting the matter out, and how you would have to pay. In many cases, where you ask an accountant to sort out one problem, – for example, getting you a tax rebate for a previous year or reducing the tax you have to pay on income or capital, – you won't be charged until the work is completed. If, for example, they get you a tax refund, the accountant would just deduct the fees and expenses from the refund before paying you the balance. Before deciding whether to use an accountant or deal with the matter yourself, find out what it will cost and whether you are going to have to pay anything in advance or during the course of the work. If you decide to use an accountant, remember she or he will charge you for every letter and telephone call made and received on your behalf. So you can keep the costs down by using their services carefully and only contacting them and asking them to deal with something when it is essential.

Accountants, like other professionals and anyone providing a service, vary enormously in their particular skills and areas of expertise. It is always worth using one who has been recommended to you: find out if anyone you know has used an accountant; or your bank manager or solicitor may be able to recommend someone.

*If you are self-employed,* working free-lance or have fluctuating earnings and periods in and out of work, you may need help to sort out your income tax and make sure that the Inland Revenue doesn't charge you too much. You probably will not need advice until your work starts to produce substantial amounts of money – say, at least £3,000 each year. An accountant can offer advice on book-keeping, on setting expenses against your income, and what rate to charge for the job. You can also use an accountant to sort out your books at the end of the year and deal with the Inland Revenue on your behalf. But again, always check in advance what the accountant is likely to charge; if your overheads are small and your income is fairly regular you may not benefit from anything the accountant can offer. You could do the paperwork yourself.

### Capital transfer tax and capital gains tax
These are two taxes which are intended as taxes on wealth and profits. The rules which govern these taxes are very complicated and if, after reading this section, you think you may have to pay either now or in the future, you should get expert advice. This section looks briefly at what sort of transactions can be liable.

*Capital Transfer Tax (CTT)* This tax replaced estate duty, and affects not only a person's estate on death but certain transfers of assets during lifetime. You may have to pay CTT if you dispose of any of your valuables or capital (but not income) during your lifetime, either by giving them away or selling them for less than their real value. Where you do not reduce your assets but either sell them or transfer them for their real value, you are not liable for CTT; but you may be assessed for capital gains tax (see p.119) if you could be thought to have made a profit. For example, you may decide that now your husband has died, you have no use for the holiday flat you bought on the coast. So you give it to your closest friend in exchange for some furniture of hers that you have always admired. If the flat is worth less than the furniture, you or your friend may have to pay CTT on it. You won't have to pay CTT if the furniture is worth as much as the flat – for example, if rather remarkably, your friend has just given you a unique piece of Queen Anne furniture or a Charles I table and chairs. But you will have to prove to the Inland Revenue that you haven't made a 'profit'; otherwise you will have to pay capital gains tax (see below).

CTT is also charged on a dead person's estate, both on items that were given away during the deceased's lifetime, and items given on death to someone other than the spouse. So CTT could be charged on your husband's estate if he gave away belongings or other assets before he died, or in his will, and the CTT has not already been paid.

Many transactions, particularly those of small value, are exempt from CTT; the more important ones are listed below. When CTT is charged on a transaction there are two different rates of tax: the higher one for transfers or disposals which occur on death or within three years of death; and a lower rate for disposals that occurred earlier.

## Capital Transfer Tax

The following transfers are not usually liable for capital transfer tax:

• Transfers from husband and wife during the marriage or on his death if you were still married at that time.

• Small gifts (up to £250 each year) to any one person.

• The first £3,000 transferred to one person during your lifetime.

• Gifts or financial settlements on marriage.

• Gifts to charities.

• Gifts to political parties.

Special rules and limits apply to most transactions which could make all or part of the transfer liable for CTT. If you are planning to dispose of any assets get expert advice first.

*How is CTT paid?* You can choose who pays the CTT, either the person who is giving away the asset or the person who receives it. The rate of CTT depends on a number of complicated factors – for example, it will depend which person pays and whether there have been other transfers within the last ten years. It is worth taking advice to find the most beneficial way of transferring the asset.

## Capital gains tax (CGT)

This tax was introduced to make sure profits from sales or from increased value of capital or possessions should be taxed in the same way as profits in the form of income are liable for income tax. It means that if you sell possessions, or, for example, shares, and make a profit, you will have to pay CGT on the 'profit'. This is calculated by looking at what you originally paid for the item and comparing it with what you sold it for. You can also deduct any costs you incurred in selling the item – advertisements, auctioneer's commission. But if the net amount you get is more than your original costs, you may be liable for CGT.

---

*Elizabeth, a divorced woman in her fifties, had been in a highly paid job for a number of years. Her hobby was collecting antiques. When her marriage broke up she needed to 'buy out' her husband from his share of their house so she could continue living there. When she sold some of her most valuable furniture to raise money, she was shocked at the amount of CGT she had to pay. She said, 'I found I'd bought well over the years and some of the pieces fetched very good sums compared with what I'd bought them for. Much of my pleasure at having been able to raise so much money so quickly vanished when I realised how much CGT I had to pay. Eventually, I had to sell more furniture to meet the tax bill and pay my ex-husband for his share of the house'.*

---

Again, not all transactions are liable for CGT and it's worth finding out in advance. The box on p. 121 lists the most important transactions which are exempt from CGT. Women who separate from their partners should be particularly careful. Any property which transfers from one partner to the other is exempt from CGT if the transfer occurs while a married couple are living together. But if you wait until you are separated to decide who gets Auntie Mabel's Chinese carpet or the Chippendale table and chairs, one of you could end up paying a lot of CGT (see *gifts,* below). Also you have to pay CGT on any money you make from the sale of property which is not your home. If you and your partner need to sort out the ownership of your mutual home, you need to do it within two years of one of you leaving that home. This is because for CGT purposes the property will be treated as your home for up to two years after you stop living there. So if you sell it and divide the proceeds, or if one of you buys the other out, one of you could end up paying CGT on this money if you haven't lived in the home during the previous two years.

---

*Arthur and Sheila decided to separate after living together for twenty years. Sheila had been offered a challenging new job in the North of England, their children were both away from home and it seemed a good time to go their separate ways. Arthur stayed in the family home, Sheila was in no hurry to sort out their financial affairs. She didn't want a divorce, the mortgage was paid off on their home and her new job paid her enough to rent a flat where she was going. Time drifted on and she and Arthur met from time to time, at birthdays and Christmas. After three years, Sheila felt settled in her new job and found a small house she wanted to buy. She knew her share of the family home was worth a lot of money and would be sufficient to purchase the property in the North. She wrote to Arthur and found that he too was ready to move, as their home was too big for him on his own, and so he put it on the market. When they found a buyer, Sheila was horrified to find that while Arthur didn't have to pay capital gains tax on his half because he was selling his 'home', she did have to pay CGT on her share because it no longer counted as her home since she hadn't lived there in the last two years.*

---

*Capital Gains Tax and Gifts* CGT is often confused with CTT because of the way gifts are treated for capital gains purposes. If you give something away then, clearly, you don't make a profit. However, there is a special provision that makes sure that if you give things away to close family or partners in a way that avoids capital transfer tax, you will have to pay capital gains tax. So if you give possessions or investments to a member of your family, the transaction is treated as a sale and you are treated as acquiring the market value of the goods from the transaction. Here is a case in point: When Mary's husband died, her niece came and lived with her for a few months until Mary felt more

## Capital gains tax

If you dispose of assets, you may have to pay capital gains tax, but the following are exempt:

- Your main or only residence and one other dwelling if it is occupied by a dependent relative.
- Winnings, for example from football pools.
- Any private car, including vintage car.
- Money – sterling or foreign money intended for your personal use.
- Personal injury compensation payments.
- Gifts to charities or any gift of historical or scientific interest.
- Gifts of less than £100 in value each year to a particular individual.
- Any item worth less than £3,000 (or transfers of up to £5,000 (1985/86 rate) in a year.

Transfers between husband and wife are exempt while the couple are living together.

secure and able to cope on her own. Mary's husband left her some valuable silver which she never used, and she decided to give it to her niece who was very fond of it. The silver was now worth a great deal of money and Mary discovered that she would have to pay capital gains tax when she handed the silver over. She would be treated as having 'gained' the market value of the silver when she disposed of it. However, because Mary took advice she also found that there was a way of delaying the payment of CGT.

This method of delaying payment is called 'rolling over' or 'holding over'. Most women will not be in a position to make valuable gifts to their close relatives, but if you are, you should take advice from an accountant.

# Insurance

As a woman on your own, you are unlikely to have a great deal of money to spare for hefty insurance premiums. There are now many different kinds of policies for different risks and it is important to differentiate between them and work out which ones are useful or necessary for you.

Broadly speaking, there are two different kinds of insurance:

1 Policies which protect you from costs and replace possessions after accident or loss
2 Pension and life assurance schemes which provide you or your dependants with a lump sum and sometimes a regular pension when the policy reaches maturity or when you die.

**Protecting yourself against accidents and loss of possessions**

Insurance policies aren't cheap but if you can afford it, it does make sense to cover yourself against costs arising out of accident, burglary or losing valuable items. Of course it is usually open to you to choose whether to take the risk or take out insurance, and which sort of policy to have. However, if you own a vehicle, you are obliged to have motor insurance, although you can choose which sort of policy you want. If you are buying a property on a mortgage, the building society will insist that you have insurance to cover the full cost of replacing the property if it were destroyed. The building society may also tell you which insurance policy they wish you to have. If you own or are buying a leasehold property, you will have to pay a share of the house insurance, but it will be up to the freeholder to decide which policy and which insurance company to use.

If money is very tight, insurance often seems like a 'luxury' but you need to weigh up in your own mind whether the weekly or monthly cost of an insurance policy

## Car and house and contents insurance

### Car insurance

**Third party.** You must by law be covered by 'third party' insurance. It covers the driver against damage to other people, including passengers. It will cover you for any liability from an accident including damage to other vehicles or property as well as personal injury to others.

It does not cover you for damage to your own vehicle, and would not cover you for loss or theft of your vehicle. Third party is the cheapest form of motor insurance.

**Third party, fire and theft.** This covers you for the above and would also give you the market value of the vehicle if it were stolen or destroyed in a fire.

**Comprehensive.** This means the car is insured for third party but the policy will also pay for damage to your own

and any other vehicle in the event of an accident. Some policies cover personal possessions as well. Comprehensive policies can be expensive and vary in the cover they offer.

**No claims bonus.** This is a way of encouraging you not to make claims. The insurance company give you a discount, usually up to a maximum of 60 per cent. Again different companies operate different rules and concessions, and it is worth shopping around. Broadly speaking, the longer you have been driving and the fewer claims, the higher the discount. But some insurers will take into account years when you were driving but did not have insurance in your name. They vary, for example, in the way they treat women who have been driving vehicles insured by their partners who now want insurance in their own name.

is easier to meet than the costs of replacing items, or the building and repair work necessary if you were unexpectedly flooded or had a fire. Even if you decide you do want to take out insurance, it is often very difficult to decide which sort of insurance to go for and which company to use. There are so many different policies around offering very different sorts of cover at very varied prices. It is always worth shopping around, and finding out as much as you can about all the different policies offered by different insurance companies.

Some policies only meet the costs of replacing items in very limited circumstances and others provide wider cover: find out exactly what will be covered. For example, if you lose something outside your home, will the policy cover you or not? Will you get the full replacement value, or will the age of the item be taken into consideration? You can also find policies that will insure you against the risk of someone suing you for loss or injury. If, for instance, you own a horse this kind of insurance may be worth having to protect against the possibility of the animal getting out of control and causing damage, or possibly injuring someone.

### House and contents insurance

You can choose whether to have a joint policy or to take out separate property and contents insurance. Find out which would give you the best deal.

If you are a leaseholder, get a copy of the property insurance policy from the freeholder or the managing agents. Find out exactly what you are covered for and if you are treated as an 'interested party'. This means whether you can make claims directly to the insurers or whether only the freeholder can do so.

It is essential with both house and contents insurance that you do not under-insure. When you take out the insurance you have to specify the full value of the items being insured. The higher the value, the higher the cost of the policy. However, if you underestimate the total value of your property or possessions, the insurers can refuse to pay if you have to make a claim. It is therefore essential to make realistic estimate of their value, and to recalculate it each year to check their current market value and increase the insurance if necessary.

**Contents**. Find out exactly what risks are covered; policies vary but usually cover fire, theft, flood and other 'acts of God'. Find out which are 'contents' and which are 'fabric'.

**All risks**. This is a special clause which allows items such as jewellery to be covered in all circumstances. Basic contents insurance may only replace items which are lost, stolen or damaged in particular circumstances. But 'all risks' will replace them even if they are lost because of your own carelessness. It usually covers you when you are travelling as well as in your own home. Again, check which items will be covered.

Once you decide which sort of policy would meet your needs, get as many quotations as possible before deciding which insurance company to use. You will be amazed by the variation in price from one company to another. *And always read the policy and the small print thoroughly before deciding to sign.*

### Taking out life assurance and pension policies

The first thing to say is that, unless you are very comfortably off and want to find a way of saving and protecting your financial future, taking out life insurance in middle age probably doesn't make financial sense. You should find out to what extent you can still benefit from any life insurance your ex-partner took out while you were together.

The broad principle behind these policies is that you pay a fixed amount over a number of years, and at the end of this fixed period, you receive either a lump sum or a pension which reflects the amount you have paid in and the interest it has earned. The financial advantages from investing in this way are: you qualify for tax relief on the instalments; and the final sum is tax free – that is, no capital gains or transfer tax. This is also a reliable method of guaranteeing financial security for your dependants in the case of your death. There are three sorts of life assurance:

1 **Whole Life:** This is usually the cheapest form of life insurance and provides a lump sum on your death, whenever it occurs.

2 **Term Insurance:** This is a way of protecting your dependants for a particular period against the risk of you dying. The policy pays a lump sum to your dependants if you die before a given date. So, for example, if you are 40, working, and have 'school' age children, you could take out term insurance to pay them a lump sum if you were to die before the youngest was, say, 25. If you hadn't died by that date, the policy would end; you get nothing, because the risk you insured against hasn't happened – you are still alive.

**Mortgage Protection:** This is the most common form of term insurance. It means that if you die before the mortgage is paid off, the insurance covers the outstanding debt.

Whole life and term benefit your dependants, but don't help you.

3 **Endowment Insurance:** These policies provide a lump sum and sometimes a regular pension at the end of a fixed period or on the policy-holder's death, whichever happens first.

You need to find out which ones are index-linked – some policies offer a very poor rate of return over a long period if inflation is high.

*Endowment for children*: these policies, often taken out by grandparents, are a way of paying for the child's education or training. They usually run for about fifteen years, paying a lump sum at the end of the period.

There is no tax relief on endowments taken out by an adult on a child's life.

## Proposed Changes to Social Security Benefits (1985)

In June 1985, the government announced that there would be major changes to some social security benefits in April 1987. The Appendix, at the back of this book, gives a brief outline of the government's proposals. However, until the new legislation is passed, we cannot say definitely what changes will take place or predict, with any certainty, how the benefits described in this chapter will be affected. It will be very important, in the autumn of 1986 or early 1987, to check how the proposed changes listed in the Appendix could affect your rights to claim. The new rules will mean that there are some benefits you could claim now that you may be unable to claim after April 1987. However, you can protect your rights by claiming now, as the government has promised that no-one who is already getting a benefit will be adversely affected by the changes. Equally, it may be that the changes will create new entitlements for you – you should check to see if there are benefits which you will be able to claim after April 1987 which you can't get now.

# CHAPTER 7

# WHERE TO LIVE

**Now we look at the problems and possibilities connected with your choice of housing, and at the ways some women on their own have chosen to keep a roof over their heads.**

Second only to worries about money must come the question of deciding where to live. Even if your partner has left you your house or flat, with a reduced income you may feel quite unable to maintain it. If you're divorced, you may find yourself without anywhere to live, because your former dwelling has to be sold, or because you can't keep it up. Even if you have been allowed to remain in the marital home, this may be only for a limited period, until your children are grown up; eventually you may have to move.

Earlier in this book the point was made that vital decisions like moving house should be deferred for as long as possible after the shock of bereavement or divorce. It's well known that when a person is distressed she is likely to make wrong choices about important matters. It's very easy when things have gone badly wrong to believe that a change of surroundings may help and that action – any action – aimed at achieving this may be therapeutic. This is often far from true: the added upheaval can turn out to be just one more factor in prolonging the effects of the trauma you've been through. So, if you can – wait.

## Assessing your situation

A few months spent in assessing your situation can help enormously in deciding just what your next step should be. You'll be thinking about just why you feel the need to move: is it because it's financially quite impossible to stay where you are; or because you are lonely? Because you would be happier living nearer to family or friends, or because the situation of your house is such that, lacking a car and with poor public transport, you can't get to the nearest town for shopping and social life? Because the garden is too big to manage by yourself; or because the house needs constant repairs you just can't tackle? These are all good reasons for thinking of a move – and all good points to consider seriously when you start to take action and find somewhere else to live. But they're also problems which it may be possible to solve without taking such a drastic step. Much of this chapter – and this book – is aimed at helping you cope well with your situation wherever you live, and at this point it's a good idea to think of the advantages of staying put and possible solutions to existing problems as well as weighing up the likely benefits you would derive from a move.

## Moving is costly

The first thing to remember about moving house is that it generally costs a lot of money. Even if your move is from one local-authority owned property to another you will have removal expenses (nowadays very costly unless you are able to do it yourself), plus a considerable outlay for new furnishings – old floor coverings and curtains very seldom fit. A lower rent could be offset for many months by the expenses involved in your move. If you would be moving from a house or flat of your own, the expenses would be very much greater. Relinquishing your present mortgage and taking out another involves some expense: estate agents, surveyors and solicitors have to be paid, and, like the tenant of rented property, you have to face an outlay connected with the move which can run into several hundred pounds. Since the whole cost of a move may run into *thousands*, you have to take this into account when selling and buying. Unless you are to be out of pocket your new dwelling has to cost several thousand pounds less than the sum you finally get for your old one. If you hope to actually raise capital from the move, you have to plan for a very considerable difference between the selling and buying prices. This could mean a drop in amenities and standard of living that you would do almost anything to avoid. You have to be very sure that there is no alternative before committing yourself and your family to that.

If you have children still at school, it may be important not to move away from your present neighbourhood even if you do have to move within it. It can be very disrupting to a young person to be moved to a new school when she is not at the point of a 'natural break' between schools or courses. When there's more than one child involved it's unlikely that all will be at the best point for a move. Some teenage children appear to be little affected by changing schools, but a shy adolescent who finds making new friends difficult can become withdrawn and alienated. Younger children, too, can be very upset by the loss of neighbourhood friends and the familiar environment.

When a move is inevitable, and if you are to remain in the same district but not in the 'catchment area' of your children's schools, the school and the Local Education Authority will generally permit them to remain where they are to complete their school education. Make sure to discuss this with the head teacher before you move.

# Making the move: 1 Council housing

## Council housing

If you want to move from council property to other council accommodation:

Go to the Housing Department.
Explain your reasons for wanting a transfer.
Explain carefully the kind of accommodation you want.
Ask to be put on the list for a transfer.
Inspect any property you are offered. Refuse it if it does not meet most of the needs you have already explained.

If you agree to accept it ask about any repairs and redecoration you think necessary.
Make firm arrangements about moving-in date.
Organise transport of your furniture etc.
*Remember*: if you repeatedly refuse accommodation that the Housing Department officials think is reasonable, you can considerably delay any further offer.

The steps you have to take if you decide to ask for a change of council house or flat are outlined above. If you're considering moving house from one owner-occupation to another, the problem may be greater – partly because the timing of your move is very difficult to plan for.

## Housing Associations

The Housing Association movement has expanded in recent years. They're organised in different ways, and often work in conjunction with local authority housing departments. Public libraries' reference sections normally include several directories of Housing Associations, or you can enquire at the local council offices for local information.

# 2 Buying and selling your home

The big question is: should you look first for the house you want to move to, then sell your present one? Or should you first get a buyer for your present house and then look for another? Unfortunately a definite answer is almost impossible to give – there are possible snags with both courses of action. The experience of two women make the point.

---

*'Having had the experience in the past of moving house before selling our previous one, I was determined this time to try to sell first, and I avoided the temptation of getting agents' descriptions of houses for sale and possibly falling for a house before I was ready. So I put my house on the market. After a few false starts a couple came along who had just returned from overseas and were living in a furnished flat while they looked for a house. They were desperate to get away from the expensive flat and made a good offer for my house on condition that the sale was completed within a few weeks. I felt sure I wouldn't get a better offer, so I accepted and signed the contract. But it put me in a terrible spot. I had to find something at once, and that had to be somewhere where the owners would be ready to move out in double-quick time. I did find somewhere – but it wasn't ideal; and by the time the solicitors got round to doing all the 'searches' and the building society could arrange the mortgage, the agreed date for the people to move into my house was past. I had to move out, store my furniture – very expensive – and inconvenience a friend by staying with her for several weeks until I could take possession of the new house. All that wouldn't have been so bad. But because I was so rushed I found that I'd been pressured into buying a house that had a lot of defects that are going to cost more than I can afford to put right.'*

---

*'I'd been thinking of moving for a year or more. But every house or flat I looked at had something badly wrong with it. Then one day I got the agent's particulars about a ground-floor flat in an old house that had been recently converted to a very high standard with a terrace and garden attached to it. It was exactly what I'd been looking for. I rushed back to the agent and made an offer. He told me someone else had offered the same amount, so I added a bit more, and the offer was accepted. I was really excited. The next thing was to sell my own house. That's when my troubles started. It seemed impossible! No one showed any real interest. After a month I reduced the asking price, then after a few more weeks I agreed*

*to reduce it again. Meanwhile the owners of the flat were pressing me to exchange contracts. I felt certain that someone would want my house at the much-reduced price, so I did agree to the exchange of contracts. I was right – someone did offer to buy my house, and I was terribly relieved. It seemed I would just make it in time. But the nightmare was only beginning. The buyer of my house had to sell his to raise the money to buy mine, and the people buying his had to get a buyer for theirs . . . the chain stretched back to infinity, it seemed.*

*It's a long story, but what happened in the end was that I had to get a 'bridging loan' which cost me a lot of money in interest. I'd already paid more for the flat than I'd intended, and I'd got much less than expected for my house. And to think that my original idea in moving from my large house to a small flat was to* make *money! All that is nearly a year ago, and it will take several more years to recover my losses.'*

These two stories illustrate very graphically the snags you can meet, whichever sequence you decide to follow when selling and buying a house or flat. Perhaps the only advice to offer is to suggest that you adopt a very cautious attitude when you start to house-hunt. Decide that you won't commit yourself too far, however attractive the property. If you haven't got a very long way towards selling your present dwelling, don't sign anything binding in connection with the new one. You may have to face the possibility of losing the house or flat you want because someone else beats you to it. Unless you can afford to lose a lot of money in order to secure it, it may be wise to let it go and hope that something else equally attractive will appear. A lot will depend on how easy you think your present dwelling will be to sell. If the asking price is sensible, if it's in a convenient neighbourhood and in a good state of repair it's obviously going to attract more possible buyers than a run-down house far from transport and amenities and overlooking a smoky factory or a cemetery. If you're stuck with a house like that it's only realistic to expect to have to sell for a low price and wait some time for a buyer; and you would be very unwise to hope to get a better house in a pleasanter area without having to pay a great deal more for it.

**Legal formalities**
Recently the monopoly of solicitors in doing conveyancing work was criticized. But the next thing to decide when

you're planning to move is whether or not you can manage without a professional to do the legal work connected with selling and buying. Be warned. It *is* possible to arrange everything yourself. But first you should read up about the whole process – books which take you step-by-step through the maze are listed below – and when you've done that you may very well decide that the whole business is too time-consuming and complicated to undertake. Of course you can save quite a lot of money doing it yourself – solicitors, and perhaps other professionals in the future charge high to medium fees – but in this, as in everything else connected with buying and selling a house, you really must consider your personal position. If you are in full-time work, perhaps with family responsibilities as well, you can't possibly devote the amount of time and energy needed to go through the complicated procedures without being overstretched and overstressed. The aim of this book is to help you cope with the ordinary business of life – not to encourage you to aim at Superwoman status, able to tackle everything that could possibly come your way.

## Books to consult

Before deciding to buy or sell property without the help of a professional you should buy or borrow:
 *Which? Way to Buy, Sell and Move House*
 *The Legal Side of Buying a House*
 *Raising the Money to Buy your Home*
All the above are published by the Consumers' Association and should be in your public library, or can be ordered from a bookshop. Just be sure you get a recent edition.

### Raising the money

Most women embarking upon buying a house or flat will need to take out a mortgage. Once again, there are books that can help you understand what is involved. In most cases, the first step will be to find a building society or other source of a loan, and it's as well to make enquiries about sources of finance as soon as you've decided to look for a new home, and before you've actually found something you want to buy. The first port of call should be the local office of any building society in which you have savings. Priority is normally given to people who are already savers with the particular society. If you haven't a share account with a building society, or if yours turn you down for some reason, you could try other High Street building society branches. Make an appointment with the manager, and be prepared to produce evidence of your financial position. The aim of this preliminary discussion is to find out what the limit of an advance is likely to be – for example, you may be given a figure of £18,000 and this means that unless you have a very valuable property to sell, or a considerable capital sum, you will have to select a house or flat in the range £25,000 to £30,000. You have to bear in mind that the building society is likely to offer you only 80 per cent to 90 per cent of *their* valuation of the property. So you must be able to find, from whatever source, a few thousands of your own to add to the sum advanced by the society.

Other possible sources of finance are listed on p. 133. If the estate agent, your solicitor or bank can't suggest any company or group likely to be able to offer a mortgage, work through this list, and if you still draw a blank, consider consulting a mortgage broker. Make sure that you select someone on the lists of the British Insurance Brokers' Association or the Corporation of Mortgage, Finance and Life Assurance Brokers (you will find their address in the 'directory of useful organisations' at the end of the book). These organisations have codes of conduct for their members whose names are available from the head offices.

Discrimination against women when offering a mortgage is illegal, so a single woman should be treated exactly the same as a man in similar financial circumstances. Older people of both sexes, however, may find it more difficult to get a mortgage. If you are over forty-five you may have to accept a shorter mortgage term, and of course this means that your monthly payments will be higher. If you are older still – at or beyond retirement age – you may find it very difficult to get a mortgage from a building society, and if you do, it could be for a short term – say ten or fifteen years – and you might have to provide additional security. If you are in very good health as well as in a secure financial position you might be offered an insurance-linked mortgage after a medical examination, but you would have to repay the loan over a short period and with a high rate of interest.

Whatever your age or circumstances, the chances of getting a mortgage at any particular time depend on the state of the economy in general. The 'money' pages of the daily and Sunday newspapers are worth studying to get an idea of how the mortgage scene is affected by the current

# Getting a mortgage

These are possible sources of a loan:
• Building Society
• Bank
• Insurance company (for 'endowment mortgage')
• Local authority (especially if you are a council tenant)
• Your employer (big companies only, and generally for younger borrowers)
• A private person (a rich relative, or someone suggested by your solicitor who wants to invest in property)
• A 'finance house' or moneylender – last resort only, as interest rates are exorbitant

**What kind of mortgage ?**
There are two kinds of mortgage normally available:
**A repayment mortgage.** You borrow a specified sum of money, and the amount you repay each month depends on the amount of the loan, the current rate of interest and the length of the mortgage term. Although the amount you repay every month is the same (except for fluctuations in the interest rate) in the early days of the mortgage term you'll be paying more in interest

and less in capital repayment. As time goes on and the capital sum is reduced, the interest is less.
**An endowment mortgage.** You take out a life insurance policy for a sum equal to the amount of the loan at the end of the mortgage term, or if you die before that. You have to make two separate payments: (a) premiums on the life assurance policy for the length of the mortgage term and (b) interest on the whole sum of the loan for the length of the mortgage term. Building societies normally charge a higher rate of interest on endowment mortgages than on repayment mortgages.

**Tax relief on mortgage interest**
You get tax relief on both kinds of mortgage – on the interest you pay. With a *repayment mortgage* your tax relief will decrease over the years, as you pay less in interest. With an *endowment mortgage*, the tax relief will fluctuate only as the rate of interest and the rate of income tax change, and you will get tax relief right through the period of the mortgage. For some people this will offset the higher interest rate charged.

market. If people are investing heavily in the building societies, obviously they have more to lend. When investments are going elsewhere, or people in general aren't saving, there are waiting lists for borrowers, and your chances of getting a loan may be badly affected.

On p. 134 there's a summary of the procedures most people have to go through when selling and buying, assuming that a professional is employed. If you plan to do it yourself, consult the books listed earlier in this chapter (p. 131.)

Moving can seem daunting, but like many of the changes this book covers, if you take it step by step and work through the process gradually you should be able to keep on top of the inevitable disruption. Bear in mind that leaving a home full of memories is always emotionally stressful, too, and try particularly to care for yourself during this time.

# Buying and selling your home

## Buying a house or flat

This is the usual sequence of events:

• Make preliminary 'in principle' enquiries about a mortgage.

• Find a suitable property through an estate agent or an advertisement.

• Make an offer to the vendor (seller) or to him through the estate agent. Make sure that this offer is made 'subject to contract and survey'.

• Arrange finance

• Arrange for an independent survey or ask the building society's surveyor to do a thorough survey for you while he is doing the survey for the society. *The building society's survey alone is not adequate* to uncover serious defects which could be impossible or expensive to remedy.

• Inform your solicitor (or other professional see col. 2.) Through the agent, or from you, they will get the name of the vendor's solicitor or other professional adviser and handle paperwork from now on.

• Finalise mortgage arrangements and insurance of the house you are buying. Pay a deposit – normally 10 per cent of purchase price. You may need to borrow.

• Exchange contracts. You are now committed to buy and to hand over the necessary sum on a specified date.

• Make moving-in arrangements.

• Arrange a 'bridging loan' with your bank if there is to be a gap between buying the new home and selling the former one.

• Arrange with your solicitor or professional adviser how the sale is to be completed on the specified date – i.e. what arrangements they are making to hand over the money to the vendor or the vendor's representative, which must be done before you can move in and take possession.

## Selling

This is the usual sequence of events:

• Advertise your property or put the sale into the hands of an estate agent. Price it realistically, by comparing with prices of similar property or taking estate agent's advice. If you deal with a well-established agent he should not under-price for a quick sale.

• Await potential buyers.

• Accept a reasonable offer (through the agent if you are working through her or him).

• Inform your solicitor or (after a law change) other professional you plan to use in connection with the legal work. They will now take over, contacting the buyer's solicitor, doing the necessary paperwork, and coming back to you with any questions.

• Exchange contracts. You are now committed to the sale and there will be penalties if you fail to vacate your property at the specified time.

• Arrange your removal.

• Pay the professional charges which will include any sums disbursed on your account – e.g. stamp duty. (A solicitor normally deducts his or her fees etc. and estate agent's commission from the sum received from the buyer of your house.)

*You can check with the books listed in this chapter, p. 131, to make sure your advisers are acting correctly.*

## Check list for the move

Here are some points to remember when you move house:

• Arrange with the occupier of your new house to let you in to measure up for curtains, carpets etc. in advance.

• Get estimates from several removal firms for moving your furniture, etc. to the new address. Or hire a van and enlist the help of friends.

• Make sure your goods will be insured in transit and transfer your household effects insurance so that you are covered at the new address.

• Inform the Gas and Electricity Boards concerned (a) that you are leaving your present address on a specified time and date and (b) that you wish to be connected to supplies at the new address on a specified time and date.

• Inform British Telecom similarly.

• Unless the removal firm undertakes to pack everything (costly), arrange with them to hire tea-chests or other containers to pack breakables yourself.

Get a supply of boxes from grocer or supermarket to pack up other goods.

• Unless you are moving into a very small flat, label each container with the description of the room into which the contents are to go – e.g. 'Bedroom 1', 'Front room'. This saves a lot of time in unpacking.

• Don't pack away kettle, teapot, cups etc. – you and removers will need refreshment.

• Inform friends and relatives, organisations you belong to and other people with whom you need to keep contact of your new address and telephone number if applicable.

• As soon as the move is completed check that gas and electricity are connected; that you can prepare a simple meal with equipment and ingredients to hand; that the necessary number of beds are made up, with curtains at bedroom windows. Then relax – everything else can wait!

# Must you move?

As we've seen, a move can be a very costly business and it's nearly always worth looking at the options. Of course you could be in a position where you have few choices, or where the only solution seems to be to move in with relatives, for instance. If you're thinking of doing this, though, read again Elizabeth's story earlier in this book, p. 48. Unless you can be offered a room or rooms quite separate from your relatives' and some minimal separate cooking facilities, it's going to be very hard on both sides to live amicably together. A few women do manage it, but these are usually people who previously had a close and loving relationship with the daughter, son or other relative concerned – and with her or his partner. Even in those circumstances you should discuss the way you want to live together beforehand, how much contact and privacy each party wants, what your responsibilities and obligations are. Try to anticipate possible areas of conflict and establish some 'ground rules' to deal with them. This isn't paranoid or unfeeling: by now life will have taught you that just about the hardest thing in the world is to live in close contact with another person, and family is no exception.

Margaret and her daughter have found that they can live under the same roof, but they had their ups and downs.

*'When my husband died I was horrified to find that instead of the comfortable income I'd expected, his business had been heavily in debt and I had nothing but the state pension to live on. The house was sold to pay off some debts, and with the sale of most of our furniture I was left with so little that there was no question of being able to get a mortgage, and, as I hadn't worked since I was 18, and then only in a 'little job' before marriage, I couldn't earn anything. We had a family discussion about what I was to do, and Lesley was very pressing about my moving in with her. I was reluctant, but it seemed the only solution.*

*'She had a spare room, and I was able to furnish it as a bed-sitter with some of my own furniture. Lesley wanted me to have all my meals with her and her family, and at first I did. But I think that was quite a mistake. Naturally I wanted to pay my way, but we both found keeping accounts of who ate what and how much it cost terribly irksome. If we didn't, then I think we both felt uncomfortable. She probably felt at times that I was eating more than I paid for, and I sometimes felt that a meal of baked beans on toast wasn't worth what I'd arranged to pay for it!*

*'Then there were difficulties about who cooked and who washed up – silly things, but they can cause friction. Worst of all, I'm used to a tidy house and I couldn't stand the clutter and mess. Lesley lives in a bit of a muddle. I suppose I should have been more tolerant, but I did find it hard not to keep attempting to tidy up after the children or clean the kitchen or hoover the stairs! It's understandable that Lesley saw this as interfering, a criticism of her housekeeping, and 'spoiling' the children as well.*

*'We never had a bad row, but there was this friction. So one day I thought about what the main problems were, and I realised that the whole trouble was really connected with meals. If I didn't have to eat with them, which often meant hanging about until they were all there for the meal, and staying around afterwards because of the washing up, I'd need to spend much less time downstairs. I could choose when to visit and be visited. Neither Lesley nor I could afford to make my room self-contained. But we did two things that have improved our*

*situation enormously. We had a large walk-in cupboard next to the bathroom made into a little shower-room; and best of all, we got a Baby Belling-type electric cooker. I can make perfectly adequate meals for one on it, and even invite the children up for tea with Granny's special drop scones! I still have Sunday dinner with the family, but that's the sort of thing lots of grandmothers do. I feel far more independent. I pay rent for my room and a share of the fuel bills – we estimate these quarterly and I believe I pay a fair share. Life is a lot easier.'*

# Other solutions

## Sharing with friends

Margaret's solution was comparatively simple and not too costly. If you are considering sharing someone's home this is the kind of arrangement you could make *before* trouble starts. And if sharing with a much-loved daughter can be difficult, how much more adaptable you may have to be if you try to move in with a friend. You may believe yourself to be tolerant and flexible, but the most adaptable of people can find themselves irritated by small things which can mount up to ridiculous, but very real, grievances.

Differences in lifestyle stretching right back to the way you were brought up can make it very difficult to adjust. Even people in a couple-relationship have to make allowances for each other's peculiarities and foibles. If you've been in such a relationship you'll remember having to accept habits that you might find intolerable in someone with whom you were not so close; or you may have experienced total inability to accept behaviour that was so irritating and impossible that it drove you away, physically or emotionally. But then you were probably motivated, because of the relationship, to try to maintain it; if your partner could not or would not modify his or her behaviour you did your best to put up with it. With someone less close, that motivation isn't there. Being aware of the possibility of some incompatability should enable you to guard against its developing; and an important part of sharing a home with *anyone* is being able to be independent of her a lot of the time. Small adaptations, as we've seen, can help to facilitate this. And a willingness to communicate dissatisfactions and disagreements is just as important. Bottling up your grievances and then exploding is a recipe for disaster.

So – talk about how you're to live with your friend before you even consider moving in. Admit to certain prejudices – such as liking open windows or doing the washing up

137

as soon as the meal is over – and be willing to admit that they may be unreasonable from your friend's point of view, and to suggest compromises. Work out finances so that neither has grounds for feeling exploited or exploiting and agree to review the situation after, say, six months, to keep pace with inflation or to adjust your contribution because experience has proved that it's too little or too much.

Similar ground rules are necessary if you plan to join some form of communal living. A group of women belonging to the Older Feminists' Network has been exploring possibilities of joining together to buy a large house and adapt it for occupation by group members. There are organisations that have experience in setting up communes of this kind, and if you would consider starting some form of group living or joining an existing setup, contact *Communes Network*, a magazine that lists communes in the UK (subscription £4.00 for 10 issues, from Redfield, Winslow, Bucks MK18 3LZ – it should be in large libraries). *A Directory of Christian Communities and Groups* (£1.75 including postage) can be obtained from the Community Resources Centre, Mary Burnie House, Westhill College, Birmingham B29 6LL. For communes outside the UK contact the *International Communes Network*, Laurieston Hall, Castle Douglas, Kirkudbrightshire, Scotland, with s.a.e.

Anyone considering communal living obviously has to consider very carefully not only what her obligations and commitment are likely to be, but whether she is willing to give up some degree of independence in favour of the togetherness and constructive sense of purpose offered in a well-established commune.

**Ways to stay put**
Of course if your house is too big for you you can do the reverse – find someone to move in with you. Obviously the compromises and adaptations necessary will be similar to those needed when you move in with someone else. As the original occupant and therefore a sort of 'landlady' you'll want to be extra sensitive to the possibility that she'll feel embarrassed to raise difficulties or inhibited about making criticisms because she feels she ought to be grateful to you for offering her a home.

Another possibility is to become a real landlady and let one or more of your rooms. You should be wary, of course, if you plan to do this, that you select someone with whom you're likely to be reasonably compatible, and to put the arrangement on a completely businesslike footing. The room you offer should be furnished as a bedsitter with comfortable and adequate furniture, and, if you're not going to instal a separate meter, you must make sure that the rent you charge is adequate to cover the cost of heating, water heating and light. You should provide at least an electric kettle and ideally a gas or electric cooking ring, especially if you're not offering to provide any meals or snacks. Make sure that the general conditions of the letting are put in writing, and that there's an understanding about the use of bathroom and toilet, if you can't provide these separately. You should provide your tenant with a rent book. If you're unsure about what constitutes a fair rent you can apply to the Rent Tribunal to fix the appropriate sum. Look into the tax position, too. Any income you get as a 'landlady' may be taxable. But with allowance for expenses you could benefit. Ask at the local Inland Revenue office for advice, and consult *Which? Tax Guide* at your local library.

This solution was one that met the needs of Daphne, a divorced teacher and a grandmother. She decided to let a room to a student.

*'I knew there was a great need for accommodation in my area, because there's a polytechnic and a university in the city, and neither has enough hostel accommodation for their students.*

*'And too, I have grandchildren in London who stay with me quite regularly for part of their school holidays, as both their parents are working. So I didn't want to have a permanent lodger who would occupy the spare room and prevent the children from coming. The arrangement I made when I offered the Students' Accommodation officer my room was that it would be available for term-time occupation only. I undertook to store the student's belongings during the vacations and to accept a very nominal rent to hold the room for the student while she was away. As university vacations are longer than school holidays I was able to have the children staying as usual. It's worked out perfectly. I've had two women students in succession, and although we don't live in each other's pockets, I've enjoyed the contact with them and their friends. I don't make a huge amount of money, of course, but it's made it just possible for me to stay in the house I love and to pay the rates and some other outgoings, which my salary could barely meet.'*

If you're in Daphne's position and there's a university or college in your area, this could be something that would be worth exploring. Daphne was lucky – she got on well with her students. But even if you do meet problems with an individual, the arrangement you make need last for only a year, and if things become quite intolerable before the year has elapsed, you can contact the accommodation officer again and put the problem to her. If your objections are reasonable you'll meet with sympathy and under-standing and your student will either have to go or her behaviour will be discussed with a view to improving it.

### Home repairs

Perhaps your problem is not so much having too much room, or lack of money for basic expenses connected with the house, but that quite major repairs are needed and you don't have the means to pay for them. In the year or so before the 1983 General Election the Government extended the existing system of Improvement Grants, which then covered the installation of basic amenities to homes that lacked them, to include a 90 per cent grant for people needing major repairs to old houses, called the mainten-ance grant. This system enabled many owner-occupiers to have leaking roofs repaired, damp courses put in, and so on. The money was advanced by local authorities who were partially reimbursed by central government.

By the middle of 1983 however, because of cuts affecting local government, this successful scheme began to grind to a halt. Waiting lists were closed and people who had applied for grants were told they would have to wait months or years before their applications could be considered. The 90 per cent advance was reduced to 75 per cent and this meant that many people could not afford to have the repairs done, even if the local authority would accept their application. It's not possible to forecast what will happen in the future, but if you think you might qualify for a grant, contact your local Housing Department, and ask for information about 'Staying Put' schemes from your Citizens' Advice Bureau or Age Concern.

### Improvement loans

Some of the building societies can provide 'interest only' loans to elderly people to improve their property. If you make this arrangement and you are on Supplementary Benefit, or might qualify for it, the DHSS may undertake to pay the whole amount of the interest to the society. This means that the society secures a 'reversionary interest' in the property (i.e. it gets its money back when you die) but you can get the benefit of the improvements while you live in the house, without extra outlay. Ask about the scheme at the offices of the high street building societies. If you are not on Supplementary Benefit you will still be able to get essential major house repairs done under this scheme without using up all or part of your savings.

Some building societies and insurance companies have special schemes, similar to these, which enable you to raise capital on your home which then reverts to the building society on your death. If you have a substantial property and no one dependent on you to whom you would wish to leave your money or house, these schemes may be worth considering. Don't rush into the first scheme that offers, though. The National Association of Widows can advise about sheltered housing schemes – particularly worth considering if you are an older woman whose infirmities may be making it difficult to run your house.

**Local authority help**
The amount of help given by local councils to older people varies from place to place, and even the most caring of councils is constrained by lack of central government funds. However, some local authorities – like the London Borough of Camden – issue leaflets and booklets explaining the sort of help they can give, whether it's advice on raising a mortgage on an old property, or how to get a Senior Citizen's pass for local amenities or a home help.

Housing Benefits are now organised on a local authority basis, so if you think you qualify for rent or rates rebate, contact the housing department. Recent government cuts have raised the 'ceiling'.

Finally, in some of the inner cities you'll find Housing Aid Centres. Staff there will help you sort out any problems you may have with the council, your landlord, your building society or anyone else involved in your housing, and many of the organisations mentioned in this book see it as part of their job to help people in your position – the National Council for One-Parent Families, the National Association of Widows, Gingerbread, Age Concern (see the 'Directory of useful organisations') and, of course, the Citizens' Advice Bureau, among them. By reading all the literature available from such organisations you may solve your immediate problems, and, just as important, plan for a future in which you can be as independent and self-sufficient as circumstances allow. Part of your strategy should be aimed at providing for a dignified old age, and where you live is a crucial factor in this.

# CHAPTER 8
# WORLD OF WORK

**If you're already in a job, you'll probably want to stay. If not, there are still opportunities for retraining, rethinking, and starting up on your own. We look at the options.**

In Chapters 4 and 5 we suggested that no one who is suddenly widowed or is in the immediate aftermath of divorce should rush into hasty decisions about re-ordering her life. At this time of upheaval, you're fortunate if you have work outside the home, because it does give a sense of continuity and is a distraction from the pain and problems of adjustment. And most women in your position, too, need the income it brings.

If you haven't a job, and don't feel confident about getting one, don't underestimate yourself or the abilities you've been developing all this time. Running a home is a managerial job. Whether or not you started out as a good organiser, you've had to become one. You met all sorts of demands every day of your life – the regular meals, the clean house and everything moving like clockwork were just the background for the skill at handling people that you also developed. You arbitrated in quarrels, comforted in distress, encouraged, sorted out problems, helped with school-work, nursed the sick, paid bills . . . the list of things you did almost as second nature is virtually endless. Look back and remember how daunting all these varied jobs would have seemed to you when you first undertook them. Remember how, if you 'allowed' yourself to be ill, everything began to fall apart. That's how important your work was. If you could do all that, the challenge of moving out of the home and into something new should seem much less frightening.

Of course a pressing need to earn may force you to go *back* to work if your job up till now has been caring for children and your home. If you left a skilled job to have children there may not be any great problem. But the vast majority of women never have had well-paid work and if it's a time of high unemployment and a shortage of part-time jobs it may be unrealistic to suggest a wait-and-see policy at this point. To supplement a pension or because maintenance payments are inadequate or are failing to arrive you may simply have to take what work you can get. However, before taking on something really ill-paid or distressful, you should look at the possibility of qualifying for Supplementary Benefit. It could be that if you got your full entitlement you would be better off than you would be working. Check the information in Chapter 6 and get information and advice from the Citizens' Advice Bureau or the local DHSS office.

If your need to earn is not so urgent, in this chapter we're going to look at the possibilities for retraining, or updating your old skills, or getting an education you missed out on in earlier in life or setting up a small business of your own. Some women in your position have done one or more of these things. Perhaps you think such plans, such enterprise, are not for you. You could be quite wrong, though it's very understandable that after years at home the prospect of anything beyond your four walls, anything that demands study, learning new skills, and above all, confidence, is a great challenge.

# Build on your skills

If you already have a training behind you, no matter how far back, it's always sensible to consider looking for work which will make use of past education and experience.

Gillian was a secretary, but left her job to get married and start a family. 'I must be the last of a generation that stopped work on marriage,' she says. 'But my husband thought it reflected on him if his wife had to work. In those days we did what our husbands wanted! So I was several years at home before having the children. That means I've been even longer away from outside work than many women. Once on my own I had to get a job, and I'd had good speeds years ago, so I thought I'd try temping, hoping that practice would bring them back.

'At first I just took on copy-typing. It was terribly boring, but no one seemed to notice how slow I was, that was the main thing. To get the work done I worked through the lunch hour, and after a couple of weeks I found I could copy-type quite adequately, so I did take time off for lunch. The next step was to practise my shorthand and I got my son to give me dictation in the evenings until I thought it was good enough. The agency tested me and I passed, so

I went to a big company as a shorthand typist all through that summer. When a department head's secretary was on holiday, I stepped into her job for a couple of weeks. I must have done the job all right, because when a proper permanent secretary's job came up in another department, they offered it to me. The woman I work for seems very happy with me. She says I think of things she'd never think of and take a lot more responsibility than most secretaries would, so she's put me up for promotion to an executive job. Not bad for a 50-year-old, "out-of-work" for half her lifetime!'

Another woman, a shop assistant, found her part-time job with a small self-service grocer. Her past experience was with a stationer, but she felt that 'once a sales person, always a sales person', and the transition wasn't at all difficult. Her customers find her much more helpful than the average shelf-filler or cashier, with the result that when her employer opens another shop she's moving there to become a full-time manager.

Both these women have found that despite initial 'rustiness' they had real skills to offer, and that once some initial resistance on the part of the employers is overcome, an older person has actually some advantages. She's often more willing to stay in a job, more adaptable and even *healthier* than some younger women; and quite quickly becomes someone the firm can rely upon.

# Training opportunities, further and higher education

**Confidence-building**

It's all very well for them, you may think, but what have *I* got to offer in the job market? If you need help in restoring confidence and assessing your potential, you should consider one of the courses offered to 'returners'. There are numerous, but not very well publicised, courses available, under such titles as 'New Opportunities for Women', 'Wider Opportunities for Women', 'Fresh Start', 'New Horizons'. The idea behind these courses is to help women decide what they're best at, what their aims are, and how to achieve them either through further education or in work. Some not only help you assess yourself but offer help in learning how to study again after years without practice. The courses vary in length from one day a week for a short period to five days a week for a year, and some also offer an introduction to the new technology.

To find out what's available locally, enquire at a college of further education or polytechnic, or from the *Educational Guidance Service for Adults* – see 'Directory' at the end of this book.

## TOPS

The Manpower Services Commision runs TOPS – the Training Opportunities Scheme. It's intended for people over nineteen who have been out of full-time education for at least two years. In theory, at least, a full-time course lasting up to a year which is geared to the employment market can qualify for a TOPS grant, and the training given is in either a completely new skill or aimed at brushing-up an old one. Thus you can choose a catering, crafts, or technical course – as long as it's likely to lead to a job afterwards. Most women still seem to want to do clerical courses, but TOPS organisers welcome more adventurous types. You have to make a good case for following your chosen training, and in the first instance you should enquire at your local Employment Office or Job Centre (if it hasn't disappeared). While following the course you are paid a wage somewhat higher than a student's grant, sometimes with allowances for travel expenses and for dependants.

Exceptionally, TOPS grants are given to people who want to 'up' existing professional qualifications, and they are sometimes offered to those wanting to do a year's management course.

## The Open University

The original idea of the Open University was to provide 'second chance' higher education, and their degree courses are still a major part of their work. There are no formal entrance qualifications such as GCEs. If you have already followed a further education course you may be credited for any qualification you may have, and thus cut perhaps a year off the length of time it normally takes to work for an OU degree – six years. Although there is individual tuition by correspondence or telephone, with attendance at local centres and at summer schools being part of the courses, you have to be prepared to give up a great deal of time to the necessary study, making use of books, television and radio programmes, often at 'unsocial' hours. Someone in full-time work will inevitably have to sacrifice her social life to some extent, but if you're working part-time or can devote yourself to study for several hours a day, less single-minded dedication is needed. When the OU was founded, it was expected that its graduates would compete in the job market on equal terms with graduates from other universities and in the 1970s this did happen. However, in a time of recession, the majority of OU under-graduates intend either to improve existing qualifications – trained teachers without degrees, for example – or from pure interest and love of learning.

Partly as a result of the recession and partly because of drastic financial restrictions imposed by the Government, in recent times the OU is increasingly offering non-degree courses which can involve anything from a few weeks' study to a whole year's. These courses, covering a huge range of subjects, are very largely concerned with scientific and technical and management up-date options – ideal for someone who has been out of the job scene for some years and needs to get familiar with the new technology. If you're in that position you should explore what's on offer. (Look in the 'Directory of useful organisations' at the end of this book.)

**Open Colleges**
In some places adult education centres, further education colleges, polytechnics and occasionally universities have joined together to provide alternative paths into higher education. They offer ways of building on existing skills, enabling people to get the qualifications necessary to go on more advanced courses. Although they're called Open Colleges, the buildings, as such, don't yet exist, though in about ten areas the scheme is now operational, based in one or more of the institutions that are working together.

**Universities, polytechnics, colleges and education**
'Mature' students are welcomed on most degree courses. The usual entrance qualifications – relevant A levels – are waived for older people, as long as they can convince admissions officers that they are capable of benefiting from higher education. This vetting may be by examination or by interview, or require the production of evidence that she carried out some relevant study. Not surprisingly, once a mature student is accepted, she tends to stick: the drop-out level is low, and examination results often above average.

You can take the Diploma of Higher Education at poly-technics or colleges of higher education, spending two years full-time or three years part-time. The course is recognised as equivalent to the first two years of a normal degree course, and can be 'converted' to a degree with two further years' study, or sometimes only one.

Business, technology, industrial relations: all these are possible subjects of study for diplomas and degrees and are much more likely to lead to good jobs in the modern world than the subjects that have hitherto been most popular with women – the arts or social science subjects which have been unkindly and unjustly called 'soft options'. What is clear is that, in spite of the shrinkage of opportunities for study of conventional subjects at conventional universities – and the attendant lack of highly-qualified scientists, engineers and technologists brought about by the cuts imposed on the universities – the swing to education for middle management and the less exalted ranks of science and technology has resulted in more opportunities for mature students, second-chancers and others wanting to improve or brush-up their knowledge. Women, 41 per cent of the workforce in Britain, but mainly in the low-paid jobs, should be the first to seize these opportunities to improve their position.

Since it's impossible to cover in just part of one chapter of this book the whole range of possibilities for further education and training, you should make enquiries from the organisations listed in the 'Directory', and look out for a publication from the National Extension College *Second Chances*, published in Autumn 1984. This should be in your public library.

## Cost of training

If you're accepted on a TOPS course, you will be paid a modest wage and possibly certain expenses. Full information is given in the TOPS leaflets, and any further enquiries should be made when you are accepted for the course.

The situation when you undertake other forms of education and training may be less clear-cut. For a degree course taken as a 'mature' student you will be eligible for a grant from the Local Education Authority – provided you haven't received a grant from an LEA before (for example, if you 'dropped out' of university before completing your degree). Before the stringencies of the last few years LEAs often gave 'discretionary' grants for approved courses. Now these are virtually non-existent in most authorities'

You may choose to train in a new skill, or to update your old skills so that you have more to offer today's competitive job market.

areas. However, it's always worth trying – ask at the Local Education Offices. The Open University is fighting a battle with the Government for increased funding. The result of Government policy towards the OU – a 'freeze' in recent years – has meant that OU fees have become too high for many students. Unlike full-time university students they aren't eligible for LEA grants. Again, however, you should enquire early at the Education Office about the possibility of a discretionary grant. In the event of your being given one for an 'associate student' (non-degree) course you may be required to pay your OU fee yourself, and on proof of this, the LEA will reimburse you. For a degree course, in cases of need the OU has established a 'Financial Assistance Fund' to provide help with course fees. There's also an arrangement with the Department of Education and Science which may offer free remission of fees to unemployed students. You should get full information about these schemes from the OU when you are offered a place. Finally, there are loan schemes operated by the National Westminster Bank and the Leicester Building Society – details should be sent you when you have registered.

# Starting your own business

A government elected in 1983 and dedicated to 'free enterprise' and an 'on your bike' philosophy encouraged various schemes to help people in small businesses, rather than tackling in any significant way the real problems of unemployment as they affect the millions rather than the few. This does mean, however, that for an individual with some particular skill or expertise to sell there may be opportunities, advice and money available, and if you're wondering how to make use of your talents and experiences without going into paid employment, it's worth exploring the possibilities of official help.

Some women simply fall into their own business in an unexpected and unplanned way. Betty has always enjoyed making clothes for her children. She created her own designs and used patchwork, embroidery and appliqué decoration in striking and original style. 'Lots of friends admired the things I made,' she says, 'but of course when the children were little I didn't have time to do more than clothe my own family with designs I thought up. Once they were older, though – into jeans and tee-shirts or school clothes – I did start to make a few jackets and pinafore dresses for friends' children. I just charged them for the materials. They got some bargains – they'd have paid pounds and pounds for similar styles from craft shops!

'When the marriage broke up, of course one of the first things I thought of was making some money, and I realised that I had something to offer that people would pay for. I was rather diffident about telling my friends I'd have to charge them in future, but of course they understood, and what's more, told other people about my clothes. I got a lot of orders, and soon I found that I'd have to confine myself to just two or three designs. I just couldn't spend the time on the variety of different garments and decorations I'd enjoyed before, mainly for my own pleasure. It was no longer a hobby, I was in business. Within months it became clear that I needed someone to help me – and a friend put me in touch with a woman who was a good dressmaker. She came into partnership with me – she does the cutting and making while I concentrate on the decoration. And having someone else working with me has meant that we've been able to spare the time for one of us to take a stall at the occasional craft fair, and we've got orders through that. We find direct selling much more profitable than selling to shops, with their huge mark-up. We charge quite a bit less than the posh shops but we still manage to do quite well. Keeping accounts was a bit of a headache, but once again a friend came to the rescue – she'd been an accountant and was glad to take on the 'books' as a part-time job.'

Betty and her partner haven't spent a penny on advertising. Other women selling home-crafted goods have found that a one-off advertisement in a Sunday newspaper or women's magazine, if they've got a simple illustrated catalogue to back it, brings in floods of orders. The danger, in fact, is that if you're too successful with your publicity you'll get more orders than you can cope with; so anyone trying this method of mail-order selling must be quite sure that she's got adequate stocks of her product and someone to see to her packing, posting and book-keeping. (A little-known concession by the Post Office, out to encourage mail-order, is an arrangement whereby they allow a proportion of the *first* mailing of publicity material to go post-free. One woman sent out 2,000 catalogues as a result of an advertisement, and the postage on 1,500 didn't cost her anything.)

If you're a good cook you might start up a business in the same way as Betty started her very different one – cooking for friends. Plenty of busy people would be glad to have a main course or special pudding cooked for them, ready to be heated up or taken out of the fridge at the last moment when they're entertaining. You could do the whole meal, buying ingredients, cooking and serving in the customer's home. Or you could offer to deliver single dishes. Find out prices from local take-aways and restaurants and aim to produce something better for less money.

Constance, who had had catering experience when she was young, got the idea of starting up a shop selling home-made pâtés, quiches and other foods. She took a short lease on a rather decrepit shop, did it up herself, found out about local regulations (mainly concerned with hygiene) and opened up on a local market day in her small provincial town. She was content to remain small to start with, but the shop became so popular that she started to buy from local cooks who baked in their own homes, and employed a retired woman to drive the van to collect their products every morning. Her teenage daughter now serves in the shop. Soon they'll be looking for larger premises.

The point to bear in mind – these women did – is that if you want to make use of your skills and start any kind of business, you must identify a gap in the market. It's no use starting up something in a town or village where there's already someone doing exactly the same thing, and no use producing something indistinguishable from similar products that are mass-produced and consequently cheaper. Inevitably where women are concerned, the sort of business they think of is something involving traditional 'female' skills – if you've got something more unusual to offer there will be less competition; though, as in Betty's case, if you can do something superlatively well you could be successful against any kind of competition.

If you're not the entrepreneurial type you may prefer to consider to set up a co-operative. This can be structured either as a partnership or a company. You can read about setting up co-operatives in the *Be Your Own Boss Starter Kit* (see 'Useful books'; p. 152).

**Getting started**
One of the best ways to find out about the nuts and bolts of setting up a business is to read the relevant trade papers and periodicals. If you don't know which to consult, a large public library usually has quite a good selection; or in the reference section you should find the directory *British Rate and Data* which lists them all and tells you how to get them. The *Exhibition Bulletin*, also in your public library, lists the trade exhibitions and shows where you can meet manufacturers (e.g. of textiles). Your local council should also be able to provide you with information about the chosen area, and advise you about any plans for development that might affect you: the Industrial Development Officer is the person to approach, and the same official should be able to offer other kinds of help and advice.

*Starting Your Own Business* and *How to Make Your Business Grow* are two useful publications which you can get free from the Small Firms Service. Dial 100 and ask for Freephone 2444 to get the name of your nearest Centre. And if you need finance to start things going, high street banks will usually give you a loan, provided you can show that your business is likely to be viable, and that you can offer some form of security against the loan.

You will almost certainly need advice not only from the bank manager but from a solicitor and accountant – *Choosing and Using Professional Advisers* and the *Small Business Guide* explain how to get advice and financial help; and *Starting Your Own Business* tells you how to deal with tax questions. The Small Firms Service can supply a free Customs and Excise leaflet *'Should I be Registered for VAT'*? Your turnover has to fairly considerable before VAT is payable, but it's worth checking your position.

To start with you probably won't be employing anybody else, but like Betty you might find that eventually you need help. In this case, ask for leaflets from the local DHSS office. 'Guide for the Self Employed' and 'People with Small Earnings from Self Employment' are the two free leaflets you should consult right at the beginning of your venture, so that you know about the National Insurance regulations that affect you.

You may also need to consult the local planning office to make sure that you have permission to start a business in your own premises or in a shop or office, and, if you do, to find out how to apply. You must also be sure that, if you're running a business from home, you're not breaking a tenancy agreement or doing something that's prohibited under the legal title to your home. You should also look into the question of insurance – household insurance wouldn't normally cover a business run from the premises.

All this may sound too off-putting to someone who hasn't any experience of running a business. It needn't be – most of the books listed on p. 152 give full information

## Useful books

*Be your own Boss Starter Kit*, £5.95, from the National Extension College, Cambridge CB2 2HN.
*Earning Money at Home*, £4.95, from the Consumers Association Castlemead, Gascoyne Way, Hertford SG14 1LH.
*Starting Your Own Business* and *How to Make Your Business Grow* (free from branches of Small Firms Service. Freephone 2444).
*Choosing and Using Professional Advisers*

edited by Paul Chapin, £4.95 + 50p postage, from Enterprise Books, PO Box 81, Hemel Hempstead, Herts HP1 1AA.
*The Small Business Guide* by Colin Barrow, £4.50 + £1.25 postage, (from BBC Publications) PO Box 234, London SE1 3TH.)
*Good Housekeeping Guide to Starting Your Own Business*, 35p and large s.a.e. from 'Family Matters', Good Housekeeping, 72 Broadwick Street, London W1V 2BP.

and advice about the formalities, and the Good House-keeping booklet *Guide to Starting Your Own Business* is an excellent introduction to the whole subject: it's a signpost telling you where to go, what to do and whom to consult and includes a very comprehensive booklist.

## Who will help?

As we have seen, the Government has really concentrated a lot of effort into promoting its ideal – 'the small businessman' (sic). You can take full advantage of the various advisory services on offer. Some of the advice agencies deal with preliminary enquiries completely free of charge, and offer later counselling for very moderate fees. Like every other service, the amount of help and useful advice they offer can vary from centre to centre, depending to some extent on the competence and enthusiasm of their staffs. But it's always worth contacting the appropriate one with your questions and problems.

There isn't space here to list them all – the *Good House-keeping Guide* does that – but these are some of the more important agencies: The Small Firms' Service is the Government agency which provides free information and runs a low-cost consultancy service. It has a number of Small Firms Centres attached to it, and there are over fifty Area Counselling Offices. (See the 'Directory of useful organisations' at the end of the book.)

If you live in the country, or in a small town (not a suburb), the Council for Small Industries in Rural Areas (CoSIRA) is the body you should contact. There are thirty area offices: find your local one in the telephone directory. In addition to the services offered by the small Firms Service, CoSIRA offers training, help in finding premises, and loan and grant schemes to help set up small businesses in rural areas.

If you live in Wales, Scotland or Northern Ireland, contact the Welsh Development Agency, the Scottish Development Agency or the Local Enterprise Development Unit, Belfast, for similar services (see the 'Directory').

There are also Enterprise Agencies which offer help and advice to local businesses. Funded mainly by local business people, with managers seconded from industry, they usually provide similar services to those detailed above, and sometimes offer management training courses geared to specific types of business or industry as well. Business in the Community (see 'Directory') will tell you where to find your nearest Enterprise Agency.

I'ts always worth finding out, too, what, if anything, your local authority has to offer in the way of grant and loan schemes.

There are special arrangements for people who have been registered as unemployed for more than 13 weeks – enquire at the Job Centre. Instead of the normal unemployment benefit, anyone showing that she's setting up a *new* business is entitled to a weekly payment (£40 at the time of writing) for 52 weeks, provided she can put up £1000 of her own money. The scheme may be phased out in 1985 – but you could enquire anyway.

| | |
|---|---|
| Free publicity | *Maggie decided to start in a small way making the rather unusual type of tiny dolls that her children had enjoyed. Her first customer was a local craft shop. But the shop could sell only a few dolls, and Maggie wasn't too satisfied with the price they gave her – which they paid only after they, in turn, had found buyers. She wrote to a women's magazine for advice, sending a colour photograph showing two of her dolls. The magazine was interested, and asked to see samples. By appointment Maggie went to the magazine's office and one of the editorial staff was so impressed with the originality of her work that she asked Maggie to leave the dolls for illustration and a write-up as a small item in the magazine. She impressed upon Maggie that she must be able to fulfil any orders that came in as a result of this news item: but naturally she couldn't guarantee how many these would be. In the event there were several hundred orders from the magazine's readers, and by working overtime Maggie was able to get all orders into the post within 28 days. After that there was a steady trickle of orders and repeat orders, and Maggie found that she didn't need to pay for any publicity or advertising.* |

*'If you have a really good product and it's something that's likely to appeal to the readers of a particular magazine this seems like the best way of getting free publicity,' Maggie says. 'Try just one magazine at a time. They don't like it if they find that rival magazines have also featured your product at the same time. If you find that customers are running out after a few months, that's the time to try another medium. But be honest – tell the person you see that the other magazine has featured you a while back.'*

# CHAPTER 9

# HOUSE MAINTENANCE FOR BEGINNERS

Your partner may have carried out basic repairs around the house himself, or he may have been the one who took major responsibility for arranging professional repairs, maintenance and improvements. This chapter aims to provide you with a basic knowledge of tools and techniques, so that you can deal swiftly with household emergencies like burst pipes. It will also help you to forestall unnecessary expense in the future, by spotting potential problems early on and doing simple maintenance tasks yourself.

## How your home functions

Vital to every modern home are the services: water, sewerage, electricity and often gas as well. It's as well to have some idea how all these things work so that you can spot any trouble early, and take the right emergency action if necessary.

### Water and sewerage

The water supply enters your house via an underground pipe, connected to the Water Board's main which runs down the street. It is delivered at sufficient pressure to enable it to travel up a pipe called the rising main, into a cold-water storage tank, usually in the loft. From here water is drawn off as required to supply cold taps, lavatory cistern, and the hot water cylinder, if there is one, which feeds the hot taps. One tap, usually at the kitchen sink, is fed directly from the rising main, in order to supply fresh water for drinking.

When the water has been used it is discharged into the public sewer running under the street via a separate network of pipes called the waste system. Metal-covered inspection chambers are provided at various points in the ground outside to give access in case of trouble. These can be concealed but must always remain accessible.

The most important thing to know about your water supply system is the location of the various stop taps or stop cocks, so that you can turn it off quickly if necessary. There is one outside the house, below the soil surface and covered with a protective box. This is turned with a special long-handled key, and is mainly for use in case the Water Board has to turn the supply off from outside. But the main one to locate is that fitted to the rising main, close to the point where it enters the house; it's usually under the kitchen sink. Check that this turns freely and turn it occasionally to ensure that it has not seized up. Other stop taps are fitted to the cold and hot water cisterns so that they can be isolated if necessary.

The most likely problem to arise with the water supply is a freeze-up, although these are much less common nowadays with modern systems using copper pipes and well insulated. If you have an old installation with lead pipes, keep a pipe repair kit in the house for peace of mind. These consist of special adhesive tape and mastic used to make a rapid temporary repair to a burst pipe. With either type it's a good insurance to keep central heating on all night at a low setting in very cold weather.

Avoid blockages in the waste system by using the lavatory only for the purpose intended, and if you put tea leaves or cooking oil down the sink accompany with plenty of cold water or hot detergent solution respectively. Keep the gullies outside clean; they should have covers to keep out autumn leaves.

If you have to send for a plumber be extremely careful. Many people have been badly ripped off by unqualified, incompetent, unscrupulous 'plumbers'. Be prepared with phone numbers of local plumbers who have done satisfactory work for friends or neighbours. Never pay for anything in advance, and get a second estimate.

## Emergency action: water

**Frozen pipes**. Wrap in cloths and pour over hot water. Or play a hairdryer on the spot.

**Burst pipes**. Turn off the stop cock to prevent further water coming from the cistern. If it is a hot water one also turn off or put out the heat source – boiler, fire or immersion heater. If no stop cock is fitted, plug the outlet and tie up the ball-valve arm. If you can't get to the cistern turn off the stop cock fitted to the rising main (usually under sink) and turn on bathroom taps and the kitchen hot tap to drain it. Also flush the lavatory repeatedly, if it's the cold water cistern.

**Water dripping through the ceiling**. Pierce ceiling in several places with drill or bradawl to prevent it from collapsing as a heavy weight of water accumulates on top. Place large receptacles such as refuse bins below to catch the water.

# Electricity

Electric power enters your house from the electricity supply cable under the street (or in country districts it may come in overhead) via a sealed fuse box, and the meter which registers how much you use. Both these items belong to the Electricity Board and should never be tampered with. Next comes the fuse box, correctly called the consumer unit, which is a built-in weak link to protect you: if too many appliances are plugged in a fuse blows. An additional safety precaution is the earthing system. A terminal from the consumer unit goes directly into the ground, and links up with all the earth wires around the house and in appliances. In the event of a short circuit, electricity is conducted safely to earth via this system. (Some modern installations have a more sophisticated device called an

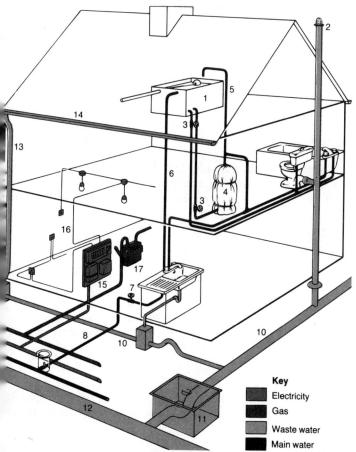

**How your house works**
1 Cold water storage cistern
2 Ventilated soil pipe
3 Stop taps or wheel valves
4 Hot water cylinder
5 Vent pipe
6 Rising main
7 Main water stopcock
8 Main water supply pipe
9 Waste water gulley
10 Waste water pipes
11 Inspection chamber
12 Sewer
13 Rainwater downpipe
14 Rainwater gutter
15 Electricity: consumer unit, main on/off switch, Board's sealed fuse and meter. Cable to main supply.
16 Ground floor ring circuits for electric power and light (incomplete)
17 Gas: meter, on/off tap and pipe to main supply.

**Key**
■ Electricity
■ Gas
□ Waste water
■ Main water

157

Mending a fuse: no problems here, but the rating of the new fuse wire *must* be the same as the one marked on the fuse.

earth leakage circuit breaker, which trips automatically if there are any faults and cuts the electricity off.)

In modern installations the consumer unit also contains the main on/off switch controlling the supply to the whole house. Each fuse (or a miniature circuit breaker in a very up-to-date one) controls a separate ring circuit and is marked or colour-coded. The number of ring circuits depends on the size of the house: a typical set-up is two power circuits, one downstairs and one upstairs; one or two lighting circuits; and separate ones for an electric cooker and any water heating appliances. The ring circuit wiring travels round the house, hidden under floorboards and in conduits in the walls, and is tapped into by means of sockets, ceiling roses and switches.

If your electrical wiring system has any of these features: a mains switch separate from the consumer unit; a multitude of chaotic-looking fuse boxes; cable sheathed in anything but grey pvc; round-pin plugs of different sizes; it is dangerously old and needs replacing.

Blown main fuses are rare unless you overload a circuit, but keep a card of fuse wire by the consumer unit just in case. A torch in a safe place is also handy in case it is dark when disaster strikes; or if the trouble proves to be a power cut. Also stock spare light bulbs, and 3amp and 13amp cartridge fuses. (Some consumer units also take cartridge fuses.)

Electricity is potentially lethal, so be safety-conscious about using it. Never touch appliances, plugs or switches with wet hands, or take appliances into the bathroom.

## Emergency action: electricity

If all the lights go out and plunge you into darkness:

1 Fetch alternative light source (torch, lantern or candles) kept in safe place ready for such emergencies.
2 Check street: it might be a power cut. If not fetch tool kit.
3 Switch off electricity at main switch.
4 Pull out fuses to find one with a broken wire. The fuse will be stamped to show what type of wire it takes; cut a length of this type from the card of fuse wire. Undo the screws in the fuse,

remove broken wire and fit a new piece. Replace fuse.
5 Switch electricity back on. If the fuse blows again there is a fault somewhere and you should find out what it is before trying again. When a power fuse blows, the fault may simply be that too many appliances have been plugged in at once.

*Note*: Some consumer units need cartridge fuses instead of wire; others have circuit breakers which only need resetting.

Replace or repair frayed flex, damaged plugs and faulty appliances *promptly*. Warning signs; fishy smells, crackling noises, sparks, intermittent working. If you have any doubts about the safety of the electrical installation as a whole, get it checked. Your local Electricity Board may do this free of charge.

Reading an electricity meter presents no problems with the modern digital type of meter. But if you still have one of the old clock dial types, and find it confusing, your local Electricity Board showroom has a leaflet explaining all.

To make sure that any electrical work you have done for you is sound, look for the NICEIC symbol. This identifies electricians on the roll of the National Inspection Council for Electrical Installation Contracting.

## Gas

If your house is connected to the gas main there will be an incoming pipe, with a large tap to switch on and off, and a meter. A network of pipes takes the supply round the house, fitted with smaller taps to turn off the supply to fires. In some modern installations the meter and on/off tap may be in a white box outside, enabling the meter to be read even if you are out.

The UK supply is now all natural gas from the North Sea, which is not poisonous in the way that the old manufactured town gas was. But a build-up of escaping gas can still cause an explosion, if ignited by a flame or spark. So always make sure that gas taps are properly turned off; and do not delay between turning a tap on and lighting the burner. An artificial smell is put into natural gas to help detect leaks quickly.

Another risk from gas (also from any other fuel that requires air to burn) is asphyxiation, if it is burnt in a badly flued or badly ventilated appliance. Regular servicing is the main key to safety. But if you have a bathroom water heater which is not of the balanced-flue or room-sealed type, make sure that there is a permanently open ventilator in the room, and switch off the heater before getting into the bath.

No DIY repairs should be attempted on gas appliances. Fires, central heating boilers, warm air units and water heaters should all be serviced annually by a qualified gas fitter. Look for a firm using the CORGI symbol (Confederation for the Registration of Gas Installers). A list is available at Gas Board showrooms. Elderly or handicapped people living alone can obtain a free safety check of their appliances and fittings.

Your main gas tap (usually located near the gas meter) is OFF when the notched line on the spindle of the tap points across the pipe. Make sure you turn off all appliances and pilot lights before you turn the main supply off.

## Emergency action: gas

If you smell gas:

**1** Put out cigarettes. Do not use matches or naked flames, or operate electrical switches (this is because they could cause a spark).

**2** Check quickly for blown-out pilot lights or left-on gas taps on cooker or gas fires. Turn off; open window to disperse gas.

**3** If you cannot locate the source turn off the gas supply at the main tap close to the meter. It is *off* when the notched line in the spindle of the tap points across the pipe.

**4** Phone the free 24-hour emergency service listed under 'GAS' in the phone book.

# Maintaining your house

**Watch out for problems**

The old saying 'A stitch in time saves nine' goes double for house maintenance. Small faults, unspotted and unre-paired, soon become expensive major problems. So it's a good idea to make at least an annual check-up of the exterior and structure of your home. Autumn is a good time to do it, in time to get everything snug and watertight against the winter.

**The roof**

A pair of binoculars makes checking this much easier. Look for out-of-place or missing slates or tiles; have them fixed promptly. A watertight roof is top priority, as water getting in anywhere eventually causes all sorts of serious prob-lems. If the roof looks very uneven, complete re-roofing may be necessary, as eventually the nails holding the slates or tiles in place rust through, and patching up is no longer sufficient. But check with your local authority before having the work done. Although Government cuts have made this more difficult, you *may* be able to get a grant, which will be quite substantial if you are aged 60-plus, to help with the cost.

Also check the chimney stacks. The pots should be intact and firmly based in their cement flaunching; if not in use they should be capped to stop rain or birds getting in. Check brick stacks for crumbling mortar, which could make them unsafe. The flashing which covers the join between chimney stack and roof should be firmly in place and there-fore watertight. Finally check that any TV aerial is firmly anchored and not just about to topple off. If telephone wiring is loose contact British Telecom; outside the house it is their responsibility.

## Gutters and downpipes

Check these during or immediately after rain so that you can see if they are carrying rainwater away swiftly as they should, and drips from cracks, holes or failed joints will show up. Gutters should be clean, not choked with debris or supporting plant life, and should slope evenly towards the downpipes. Sagging spots indicate loose support brackets. The ends of each run of guttering should be closed with a stop-end piece. The tops of downpipes should also be clear of debris, let alone bird's nests, so that water gushes freely through and runs quickly away through the gully at the bottom (some gutters discharge into a soakaway in the ground).

If you can reach damaged guttering, cracks and leaks can be repaired quite simply with sealing tape or mastic sold for the purpose.

Also check that all external pipes, both rainwater and waste ones, are firmly fixed to the wall. The tall vertical pipe that ventilates the soil pipe should have a 'bonnet' fixed on top to keep it permanently free of obstructions. A dripping overflow pipe means that a cold water or lavatory cistern is overflowing.

## Walls

The vulnerable part of a brick wall is the mortar, or pointing, in between the bricks themselves. Age and driving rain eventually cause it to break down, allowing moisture to penetrate and bricks to work loose. It should look solid and even, and not crumble away if poked. Repointing small accessible areas is easy to do with a bag of ready-mixed mortar. Rendering or pebble dashing which has 'blown' – come loose from the structure beneath – or already fallen off is a job for the builder. The new patches will not match unless the wall is then redecorated.

Areas of wall that get little sunlight may show green lichen or moss growth or cause black mould growth inside the house. This is caused by damp and rain penetration, and with any luck can be cured by brushing the wall with one of the colourless silicone waterproofing solutions. White patches (efflorescence) on brickwork are not serious, just unsightly. Treat by brushing with a stiff *dry* brush.

Cracks in a wall can look alarming, but are usually just the result of the house having settled many years before. If you are worried about a large vertical crack, stick a strip of glass across it (if it's inside, paper will do). If the patch remains intact after 9 months or so all is well; no further movement is taking place.

The builder's terms for the parts of your house. The picture shows two types of pitched roof – a traditional roof built *in situ* and a modern factory-built section.

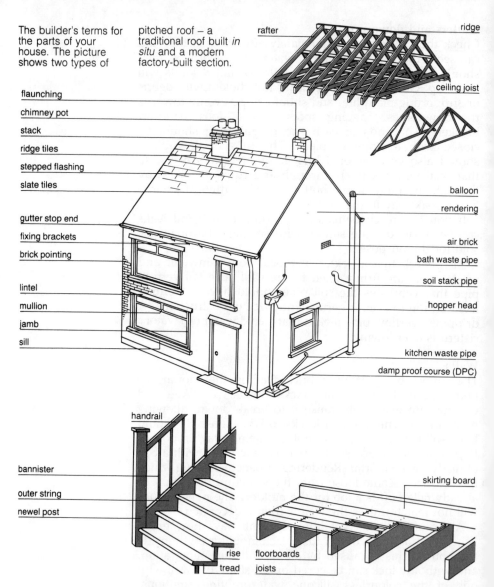

rafter

ridge

ceiling joist

flaunching

chimney pot

stack

ridge tiles

stepped flashing

slate tiles

balloon

rendering

gutter stop end

fixing brackets

air brick

brick pointing

bath waste pipe

soil stack pipe

lintel

mullion

hopper head

jamb

sill

kitchen waste pipe

damp proof course (DPC)

handrail

bannister

outer string

newel post

skirting board

rise

floorboards

tread

joists

Ivy or virginia creeper growing on a sound wall does no harm, but can pull out already loose mortar. But keep it cut well back away from gutters, window and door frames.

The most important part of any wall is the damp-proof course, which stops damp rising up the wall from the ground beneath. This can be seen from the outside either as a black line, which is the edge of a plastic vapour barrier, about 6ins/15cm above ground; or in old houses, by a row of holes where a chemical dpc has been inserted. It is vital that the dpc is not bridged at any point by piled-up soil, compost heaps or rubble. If there is no sign of a dpc you need one if the house is not to be permanently damp, cold and expensive to heat. Get a free survey and estimate from one of the firms specialising in dpc installations (look in the Yellow Pages under 'Damp-proofing'). Also phone your local authority to see if a grant might be forthcoming.

Air bricks or metal grids let into the walls at low level are to ventilate a suspended timber floor, and must also be kept clear.

### Doors and windows

All exterior woodwork needs regular painting, not for decorative reasons, but to protect it from rot. Metal windows need protection from rust. Look for flaking or blistering paint; every point where the paint film has broken allows water to penetrate and cause further deterioration.

Exterior painting should always be done in fine weather. If it is done on damp, rainy or frosty days it will not last, because moisture trapped under the new paint causes it to break down rapidly.

Some modern houses have exterior woodwork finished with coloured timber preservative. This should not be painted, but occasionally re-treated with preservative. Replacement doors and windows with aluminium frames need no maintenance; neither do any plastic components.

Also check that all doors and windows are functioning smoothly (oil hinges and bolts) and are proofed against weather and draughts.

### Structural timbers

The softwood timber used in house construction is vulnerable to attack by the common furniture beetle, or more precisely its larva, the woodworm. If it is damp it may also be attacked by dry or wet rot.

Woodworm is easy to spot on exposed timbers such as rafters. In the early stages it shows up as a scattering of neat round holes; there may be little piles of sawdust lying underneath. Later, as the timber inside has been eaten by generations of worms, it becomes severely weakened and eventually disintegrates. Many older houses have already been treated for woodworm. Check the house documents to see if they include a guarantee form, and what areas it covers. Otherwise keep an eye open for the tell-tale holes, and for small blunt-headed beetles appearing in the late spring. Check all the timbers that you can see, especially in the roof space and under the stairs. While you are in the roof space also check for any dead birds or old nests as they can be a source of pests such as carpet beetles. Remember to walk on the joists only; the plasterboard or laths in between will not support your weight. You might also take the opportunity to check over the insulation in the roof space – see the section on roof insulation on p. 186. If a roof space has not been treated do not use it to store old furniture, wood or wickerwork items, which might be harbouring unsuspected woodworm.

Where a timber floor is covered by fitted carpet it is worth lifting it up in the corners every year or so to make sure that all is well below.

Small outbreaks of woodworm can be treated by applying a proprietary woodworm killer. But for anything widespread contact a timber treatment company; they all give free surveys and estimates.

Rot, either the wet or dry type, is only found in timber with a relatively high moisture content, so it should not arise unless damp or water are getting in somewhere. Wet rot on the backs of skirting boards is a common occurrence in houses with no dpc, or a faulty one. Rot reveals its presence by slowly breaking down the timber, which will have soft spots and criss-cross cracking; there may be cobwebby growths on the back, and a musty, mushroomy smell. If it has spread into floor joists, and weakened them, the floor may give when walked on. Dry rot is much more serious than wet, as it can spread through masonry to reach other timber. As it is hard to tell the two apart, a timber treatment survey is always advisable. Treatment for rot involves curing the reason for its outbreak, removing unsound timber and treating with fungicide.

## Tools for the job

Being able to do DIY jobs depends on having a set of basic tools. If yours have seen a lot of wear, check them over to see what needs replacing. Experienced DIY enthusiasts and professionals can manage with battered old wrecks, but for the beginner a new, 100-per-cent-efficient tool can make all the difference between success and failure.

**Measuring and marking**

Dressmakers' tapes and old folding wooden rules are not accurate enough, or long enough. You need a steel tape at least 10ft/3 metres long. Old ones are fine if they are unkinked, legible and show metric measurements. A steel rule is also handy for small-scale work and to use as a straight edge to cut against.

Measuring that a shelf or hanging fitment is perfectly horizontal requires a spirit level. To find out whether an old one is working properly put it on a marked spot, then turn it round. The bubble in the centre should be in the same position.

Cutting a piece of wood so that the end is 'square' (at right angles to the long edges) calls for a try-square, a piece of metal set at right angles to a wooden stock or handle. If you need to buy one consider getting a combination square instead. These are not necessarily more expensive, and measure not only right angles but mitres; they also function as a spirit level and incorporate a steel rule.

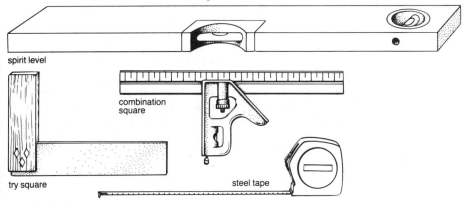

spirit level

combination square

try square

steel tape

**Nailing and screwing**

A medium-sized hammer will cope with most jobs, but a very small light one is only good for putting in tiny panel pins or tacks; it will not do for nailing down floorboards! Some hammers have a claw opposite the hammer head, used for pulling out large nails; others have a tapered part for starting small nails or working in awkward spots. Check that old hammer heads are firmly fixed to the handle.

A handy little tool used with hammers is the nail punch, or nail set. This is placed on top of an oval nail or panel and struck to drive its small head below the surface, leaving a hole to be concealed with filler.

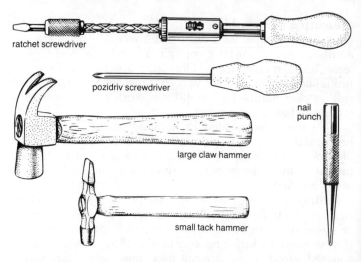

ratchet screwdriver

pozidriv screwdriver

nail punch

large claw hammer

small tack hammer

Screwdrivers are the most likely tools to need replacement, as one with a nicked, round-cornered blade and bent shaft can do no good. For general purposes a medium-sized one with a ¼in./6mm blade will suffice, plus a small one for electrical work. But you can never have too many. Ratchet screwdrivers are easier to use than ordinary plain-handled ones as they only have to be turned half round, not all the way; but they are more expensive. If you are starting from scratch, a wallet containing a handle plus five or six different blades is a good buy. This will include a Pozidriv (star) driver which is needed occasionally.

If you have a weak grip pick screwdrivers with big round handles rather than slim straight ones. Or treat yourself to an Easydriver, which has a large ball-shaped handle.

**Cutting**
Blunt blades are more likely to cause accidents than sharp ones, because the extra force needed leads to error. New blades can be obtained for even the oldest Stanley trimming knife, which is an indispensable tool for general cutting work. It also takes saw blades for both wood and metal, which are useful if you have no saws. But for accurate sawing you need a small panel saw. An old rusty one is useless; discard it and get a new one with a replaceable blade.

Another saw that may be in a tool kit is a tenon saw, fine-toothed and with a rigid back, which is for small-scale accurate work like cutting joints in wood. More specialised ones are the hacksaw, for metal and plastic; the padsaw or

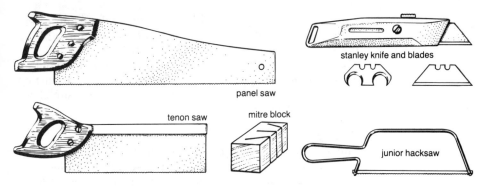

panel saw

stanley knife and blades

tenon saw

mitre block

junior hacksaw

keyhole saw, for cutting openings inside a piece of wood (e.g. a cat flap); and the coping saw, a larger but more precise tool for similar work. Enclosed cuts are started by drilling a hole or holes large enough to get the saw blade into.

For sawing firewood use a bow saw, a big coarse-toothed affair; for making kindling an axe or wood splitter.

To do any but the most coarse sawing work some kind of holding device is necessary. For straight cuts use a bench hook; for 45° cuts a mitre box or block. A vice can also be used to some extent; or one of the patent portable workbenches (Workmates).

### Hole boring

The standard hand tool for this is a hand drill, or wheelbrace, so called because it works like an egg beater by turning the wheel on one side. A larger one, with a big loop in the handle, is a carpenter's brace, only needed for making very big holes. Old drill bits will almost certainly be blunt and need replacing. A box of 7 high-speed twist drills will do most DIY jobs. In addition have a counter-

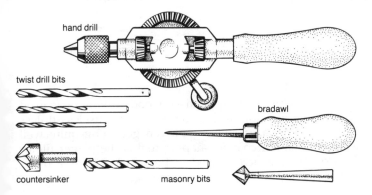

hand drill

twist drill bits

bradawl

countersinker

masonry bits

sinker, a cone-shaped drill bit used for making the recess which the head of a countersunk screw sits in; and a No.12 masonry bit for making holes in walls.

Another essential hole-boring tool is the bradawl, a simple spike on a handle used for marking and starting screw holes; or you can use the corkscrew-like gimlet for the same purpose.

### Pulling and gripping

The serrated jaws of pliers can grip both round and flat objects, and also incorporate wire-cutting blades (for expanding curtain wire and electric flex). A large blunt-nosed pair is more powerful; a small pair with long pointed jaws is good for reaching into confined spaces and is worth having.

The best tool for pulling out unwanted nails is a pair of pincers. A tack lifter, with small forked blade, is excellent for getting up very small nails, and for the tacks encountered in upholstery work.

Wrenches and spanners are mainly for plumbing and car maintenance. For general purposes an adjustable spanner should suffice.

A vice is another kind of gripping tool; not essential but very useful if you have one.

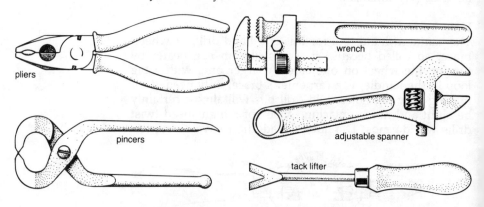

pliers

wrench

pincers

adjustable spanner

tack lifter

### Shaping tools

Planes and chisels are specialised woodworking tools used for shaping and for cutting joints, and are useless unless they are kept razor sharp. You can get along quite well without them. A coarser shaping tool is the planer file or Surform tool, which is used in the same way as a plane but needs less skill and no sharpening.

**Electric drill**
This is by no means essential, but very labour saving. Use it to drill holes fast and easily (particularly in hard walls) and, with attachments, for sanding and paint stripping. Hold the drill firmly in both hands, one on the main pistol grip handle and the other on the side handle (this is reversible to allow for working in corners). Keep it absolutely straight to ensure that screws go in straight, and to avoid any risk of snapping the drill bit.

Some drills have two speeds, or an infinitely variable speed; a slow speed is recommended for drilling into masonry. Others have an alternative hammer action which makes short work of drilling into hard masonry, but creates the most horrendous noise.

The drill should have a rubber disc attachment which, covered with suitable abrasive paper, fits into the chuck and is used for coarse sanding or stripping work. It can also be fitted with wire brushes, for removing rust and paint from metal; and lambswool pads for polishing.

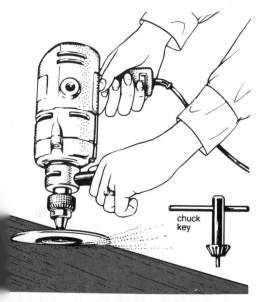

When using a sanding disc attachment, tilt it slightly as you sweep over the surface with broad strokes. If you use the disc flat it can gouge circular marks which are hard to remove.

chuck key

Another vital accessory is a key that locks the chuck on to the drill bit or attachment in use. Replacements should be available if it has gone missing.

If an old electric drill makes excessive noise, or sparks appear inside, take it to an agent for the brand who will advise whether it is worth repairing.

# Decorating

Most women have a pretty good idea how to tackle decorating, and if you haven't there's plenty of advice around, ranging from books to magazine features to manufacturers' leaflets. But new tools and materials come on to the market all the time, so now might be a good time to re-assess your methods, with a view to getting future decorating done more quickly and easily, while ensuring that it's going to last as long as possible.

### Decorating tools

Fortunately basic decorating tools are fairly cheap, so that if what you've got is worn to death, a replacement won't cost a fortune. Expensive items like big ladders, steam wallpaper strippers or pasting tables can be hired if and when you need them. Look in the Yellow Pages under 'Hire Services'. But it's essential to have your own pair of steps, for regular domestic work such as cleaning windows or rehanging curtains, as well as for decorating. Courting the risk of a fall by balancing on chairs and tables is just stupid; and the older you get the more serious a fall can be.

### Woodwork

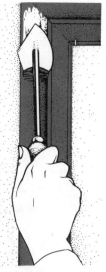

Scraping fancy moulding with a combination shave hook.

Ignore any advice to strip old paint off completely. This is strictly for masochists. Only strip paint that is badly flaking off and/or chipped over most of its surface; or so thick that another coat would prevent doors or windows from closing. Usually just a few vulnerable spots like window ledges need stripping; this can often be done dry with a sharp new shave hook. All the rest needs is a good rub down with medium, then fine abrasive paper to remove loose paint, roughness and bumps, and give a 'key' for new paint. Paintwork in good condition, just getting a colour change, can simply be washed down with one of the new liquid sanders, which clean and key in one go.

If you do have to do any stripping there are plenty of products and tools to help. Liquid chemical strippers are fine if there are only one or two layers of paint to remove. The new peel-off paste strippers will remove ten layers in one go, but are expensive for large-scale work (ideal for furniture renovation). A coarse sanding disc in an electric drill will remove paint on flat surfaces, but use it very carefully or it leaves circular marks behind. Blow lamps work fast, but watch out for singed wood, and never use near windows as the heat will crack the glass.

The new hot air blowers work at much lower temperatures than conventional blow lamps and are safe anywhere.

When wood has been stripped bare it must be primed before repainting. Use one of the new acrylic primer/undercoats, which are water-based and dry rapidly. (Indoors you can get away with emulsion paint if you've got some of a suitable colour left over.) For the actual finishing coat go for cans of gloss marked 'Easy Brush Clean'. With these paints brushes can be washed out in hot water and detergent, which is far less trouble than messing about with white spirit. If the new paint is a very different colour an undercoat is advisable. If it's the same or similar a single top coat, particularly if you pick a jelly paint (the ones you don't stir), may be all that's needed.

# Decorating

### Preparation
Household bucket and sponge for washing down (sugar soap is better than detergent; less foamy)
Cork sanding block and plenty of abrasive paper for smoothing and keying
Stripping knife for removing wallpaper
Shave hook for scraping off flaking paint (plus combination shave hook, with curved edges, if there are fancy mouldings)
Filling knife for applying cellulose filler

### Painting
Large, medium and small brushes for woodwork (or try paint pads – good for large flat areas like flush doors)
Roller and tray for emulsion paint

### Paperhanging
**All types of wallcoverings**: Steel tape, wallpaper shears (or use old dressmaking shears), plumbline (or key on a string), Stanley knife, smoothing brush (a sponge is OK for vinyls)
**Ready-pasted wallcoverings**: Add water trough
**Standard wallcoverings**: Add large brush to apply paste, and a long work surface (cover a polished table with decorator's polythene sheet)
**Hessian**: Smooth on with a clean paint roller instead of brush

## Walls

If you intend to hang a new wallcovering it's always best to strip off anything already on the wall, as if it is left it soaks up the paste and makes hanging much more difficult, since the lengths of paper won't slide around freely. But if you intend to paint, a single layer of good-quality paper, well hung and still adhering firmly to the wall, can made a good foundation for emulsion, especially if it has an interesting texture. But beware any gold in the pattern – this will eventually make a ghostly reappearance. A very thin paper will bubble up when wetted by paint, and multi-layers may start to detach from the wall.

Stripping off a wallcovering may actually be a quick and easy job, if it is a dry-strippable type. Check by lifting a corner to see if the top decorative layer can be peeled away leaving a paper backing behind which will make a good foundation for either paint or new wallcovering.

Sometimes stripping off old paper has the disastrous effect of taking lumps of plaster away with it. If this only happens in a few spots ordinary cellulose filler will put things right. But for big patches use one of the new ready-mixed plasters sold in large plastic tubs. They are designed especially for the amateur plasterer, as unlike ordinary pink builder's plaster they take a long while to dry, so that it doesn't matter how long it takes you to get the surface smooth and level. A plastic float is supplied for doing this.

When stripped or previously painted walls are in poor condition, covered in lumps and bumps and flaking paint, don't knock yourself out trying to smooth them enough to take a coat of emulsion. Scrape and sand off the worst,

Using one of the new Paintmate machines takes much of the mess and bother out of decorating, and speeds up the process too.

then hang a lining paper; *not* the thin, flat, cheapest type, but woodchip or one of the white relief papers, which cover a multitude of sins. Alternatively use one of the new textured paints. Those designed for walls are not prickly to the touch like the ceiling ones, but have a ripple effect. The snag is that if you don't want white the colour range is very limited.

For a full choice of colour pick either silk or matt emulsion. Silk finish is slightly more durable, and better in the steamy conditions of a bathroom or kitchen. Matt is best for disguising flaws in old plaster. Ignore any advice to use gloss paint on kitchen or bathroom walls (or ceilings). It's more expensive, hard to do and looks terrible. If the walls have been previously gloss-painted, sand them thoroughly before painting or papering to 'key' the surface and enable the new finish to get a grip. If you want an extra-hardwearing finish, Dulux Silthane Silk is a paint somewhere in between gloss and emulsion which can be used on both walls and woodwork.

### Ceilings

Paint these the quick and easy way with a new type of solid emulsion paint from Dulux. This comes in its own tray all ready to roller on, and is guaranteed not to drip. So far it is available in white only. If you want a coloured ceiling, and especially if you are having to buy new decorating tools, consider investing in a Paintmate. This is a simple form of spray painting machine, powered by a soda syphon bulb, which makes painting unbelievably clean and easy, and is ideal for use on ceilings. It is designed for use with special litre cans of Berger emulsion and gloss, but other manufacturers' emulsion paints can also be used by means of an adaptor kit supplied with the machine. Paint can be applied with a roller or a large paint pad, as preferred. Smaller pads and brushes are supplied for painting woodwork.

Papering a ceiling to hide flaws is a neck-breaking job which, fortunately, is out of date. Nowadays textured ceiling paints will do the same job but much more quickly and easily. One or two coats will satisfactorily disguise the average old ceiling covered in patches of partially-removed paint and lots of hairline cracks. But if it's already been papered, you will have to strip that off first.

If a ceiling is really uneven the best answer is to put up polystyrene ceiling tiles. As they are small and light they are much easier to handle than lengths of paper.

# Techniques

Having a set of tools is one thing. Knowing how to use them is another. If you haven't previously had much to do with handling saws, drills, hammers and so forth, here are a few tips to help you do jobs efficiently and safely.

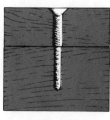

Joining wood: to join two pieces of wood with screws, drill a clearance hole in the top one and countersink its top to recess the screw head, then drill a slender pilot hole in the second one.

## Working with screws

The diagram shows how two pieces of wood are joined with a screw. The clearance hole in the top piece is drilled large enough for the screw to be pushed clean through. Its top is countersunk, if necessary, to enable the common countersunk screw to sit flush with the surface, or be recessed and hidden with filler. The pilot hole in the second piece is done with a fine drill bit so that when the screw is driven home with firm pressure its thread bites into the wood and gets a good grip.

If you are putting up a fitting – say, a curtain rail – the principle is the same, but the pre-drilled holes in the brackets take the place of the first piece of wood. The pilot holes drilled into the window frame must be very fine, so that the load-bearing brackets are firmly fixed, and it may be better just to spike them with a bradawl. Indeed, you may have to use the bradawl; if the top of the window frame is very close to the ceiling using a hand drill may be awkward or impossible. If you overdrill a pilot hole and a screw fails to grip (this is easily done with the tiny screw eyes used to fix expanding curtain wire) just fill the hole with plastic wood and start again. Also do this if the wood is peppered with holes from previous fixings.

Putting screws into masonry to hang cupboards, fitments such as a plate rack, or to fix shelf supports, requires a slightly different technique. Instead of a pilot hole, you make a screw-sized hole in the masonry, then fill it with a plug which the screw thread can bite into. Modern plastic plugs are very efficient and easy to use. Get a bundle of brown general-purpose ones: they will take a range of different screw sizes (Nos.6–12) and fit the hole made by

A countersunk
B roundhead
C Pozidriv
D chipboard
  (Twinfast)
E mirror

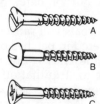

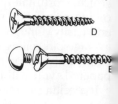

your No.12 masonry bit. The screw number indicates its gauge, or thickness. The length should be sufficient to go through the fitment or timber batten, through the plaster covering on the wall (allow ½in./1cm) and well into the masonry. If screws are not supplied a No.8 2in./5cm screw is usually a safe choice.

In some types of wall it is hard to drill neat holes as the masonry crumbles away. Plugging compound used to be the answer, but unfortunately at present this is off the market because it contained asbestos. Try the special cellular block plugs, which are sold for use in modern houses with aerated concrete block walls. Another problem is the partition wall (outside walls too, some of the new timber-framed houses) which consists of plasterboard on a timber framing. For lightweight fixtures use the special plugs designed for use on plasterboard; otherwise find the timber studding by test-drilling with a fine drill and fix to that only.

Some types of concrete wall prove totally impenetrable, even to an electric drill. A hammer drill may solve the problem, but otherwise you will have to keep to free-standing shelves, and make use of the various patent stick-on alternatives to conventional hooks sold for securing things to walls.

When removing old, stubborn screws, go carefully. If the slot in the top of the screw gets mangled all is lost. Clean the slot of paint first, and if it looks rusty squirt on some penetrating and easing oil. Get a screwdriver that fits the slot width exactly and *push hard* while making the first turn (anti-clockwise). Once the screw's grip is broken it will turn the rest of the way without difficulty until it comes out.

### Working with nails
To avoid bruised fingers and bent nails start with gentle taps to place the nail in the wood. If it is really tiny, grip it in a pair of long-nosed pliers. Hold the hammer near the end of the handle, *not* half-way down, and swing it by pivoting straight forward from your wrist. Do not try to put ordinary nails into walls: use masonry nails (hard to get in) or picture hangers.

Remove unwanted nails with a claw hammer or pincers, putting a scrap of wood or hardboard underneath the tool to prevent the wood being marked – if this matters. Pulling in short sharp jerks will leave a smaller hole than one long pull which could leave an unsightly mark.

plastic toggle plug
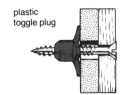

moulded nylon rawlplug
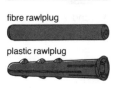

fibre rawlplug

plastic rawlplug

extruded plastic rawlplug

Joining wood: to join wood with nails, angle them as shown for greater grip. These are wire nails, with heads, for rough work. When appearance matters use headless nails (panel pins) and punch them below the surface; angle the nail punch in the same direction as the nail was driven in.

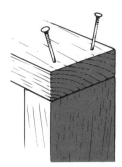

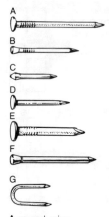

A round wire
B panel pin
C hardboard pin
D tack
E clout nail
F masonry nail
G staple

If your nails split the wood they are either too large, or placed too near its ends or edges. Oval nails are less likely to cause splits than round ones, but must be placed with the long part of the oval head in line with the grain of the wood.

### Using saws

To cut wood accurately you must not only keep the saw on the cutting line, and prevent it from wavering about, but make the cut perfectly upright: the end of the wood must not slope like a badly cut loaf. Always mark the line to be cut with a try-square so that the cut end will be at a perfect right angle. Support the wood firmly while sawing (see fig.). Start the cut by drawing the saw *backwards* a few times, guiding it against the thumb of your free hand. Do not try to force it; apply light pressure on the down stroke only. Saw just on the waste side of the line, as the thickness of the blade will remove a little wood. Use a panel saw at a slight downward angle. A tenon saw is used flat, preferably in a mitre box.

Hold the saw at an angle, and draw it backwards several times to start a cut. Apply pressure on the forward stroke only.

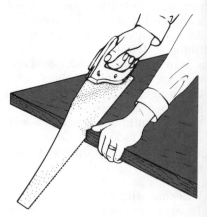

### Using knives

There's no need to be afraid of sharp knives. Properly handled they are less likely to cause you injury than a corned beef tin! To cut straight lines, say when cutting a floor tile to size, mark the cutting line and place a steel rule on it. Press the rule down firmly, keeping fingers well away from the line, and stroke the knife gently towards you until the cut is complete. In all other cases stroke the knife *away* from your body, so that if it should slip no harm is done.

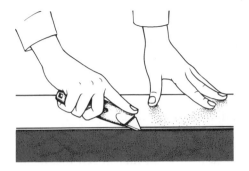

Cutting against a straightedge. Sharp blades are essential for safety and accuracy when cutting.

## Using abrasive paper

When using this in decorating work, to smooth and key surfaces, it doesn't matter how you do it, except that you shouldn't rub straight over the edges of square-section timber, or over mouldings, as you will blur their shapes. But on new or stripped wood basic rules must be observed or you will get ineradicable scratches, and fail to get a smooth finish. On the flat and edges of a board, work up and down in the direction of the grain; never across or round and round. Use a sanding block on the flat. Fold the paper into strips or wrap it round pieces of dowel rod to deal with corners, curves, ledges and mouldings (steel wool can also be useful for getting into crevices). Or you can buy some useful little plastic gadgets for tricky sanding jobs, which take stick-on sheets of abrasive paper in various grades.

Always wear work gloves when sanding as the dust is very drying to the hands. If possible do power-sanding out of doors to avoid getting a film of dust everywhere.

Sanding wood: always work in the direction of the grain – up and down it on the top, bottom and long edges of a board, but only one way on the short edges (end grain). Never go across or round and round or scratches will appear, and stay.

## Adhesives

Modern adhesives are remarkably strong, but very special-ised, so it's important to use the right one for the job, and to follow the manufacturer's instructions exactly. The main types for DIY work are:

*PVA (polyvinyl acetate) woodworking adhesive.* A white, water-based adhesive for all interior woodwork. It makes very strong joints, but the pieces must be cramped together while it dries (around 30 minutes) with a vice, G-clamp, tourniquet, sticky tape, or with weights.

*Contact adhesive.* A thick, jelly-like adhesive which comes in tins, complete with plastic spreader. Use when it is impossible to cramp pieces of work together. It is left to get tacky, when it makes an almost instantaneous bond, so there's not much room for manoeuvre, and a mistake is there for good. Its main use is for sticking sheets of laminated plastic onto worktops. It's highly inflammable, so first turn off all nearby pilot lights. Also handy for sticking back loose pieces of moulding or veneer on furniture.

*Waterproof wood glue.* Tins of powdered resin to be mixed with water immediately before use. Use it for repairing garden furniture or other outdoor items. It also has some gap-filling properties and is good for badly fitting joints on old furniture. Several hours cramping required.

*Epoxy resins.* Two-part adhesives in tubes used for mending china, glass and metal. Very strong, hot-water proof.

*Super-glues (cyanoacrylates).* These work all the miracles claimed, bonding almost anything to anything, almost instantaneously, but as this can include your fingers handle with extreme caution. They are also very expensive; save for small tricky jobs.

*Latex adhesive.* A thick white type mainly used for fabrics and carpets. Also handy for sticking down overlapping pieces of vinyl wallcovering, where ordinary wallpaper paste will not work; and for sealing large pruning cuts.

*Wallcovering adhesives.* Modern wallpaper adhesives based on cellulose are strong, clean and easy to use (plenty of 'slippability'). There are several different ones designed for different types and weights of wallcovering; make sure that you match paste to paper, or buy an all-purpose type. Vinyl wallcoverings must always be hung with a paste containing fungicide; otherwise, as they are impermeable, mould growth can develop underneath them.

*Flooring adhesives.* Vinyl tiles which are not self-stick, and cork ones, should always be fixed with the flooring adhesive recommended by the manufacturer. Sheet vinyl and carpet tiles are normally laid loose and secured with double-sided adhesive tape at strategic points.

# When things go wrong: simple repairs

However well-decorated and equipped your home may be, the passage of time means that things deteriorate and sometimes break down altogether. Knowing how to do simple repairs can save a lot of aggravation, not to mention money, particularly where electrical appliances are concerned. All the following jobs should be well within the capabilities even of those who have never had to tackle DIY before.

## Plumbing

**Blocked sink.** Underneath every sink there is a bend or trap in the waste pipe which is permanently filled with water in order to stop drain smells backing up into the house. Unfortunately, as we all know, it is prone to get blocked. With modern plastic plumbing undoing the trap to free a blockage should present no problems as the plastic locknut, or nuts, can be turned by hand. Don't forget to put a bucket underneath first. Poke around inside the trap with a bit of stiff wire to free any lodged debris, run a little water through and replace the nut(s). If it leaks when tested, get a roll of PTFE tape from a hardware shop, undo the trap and wrap a few layers round the threads before reassembling.

Old-fashioned metal traps are much harder to undo, even if you have a large enough wrench. So it's worth trying to clear the blockage with washing soda or proprietary drain cleaner; or use a sink plunger.

To open a metal trap, place a length of wood in the U-bend and tighten a wrench on the nut at the bottom. As you turn the wrench anti-clockwise, counteract its force with the wood, otherwise the soft lead pipe may bend. Some metal traps are opened by placing a piece of wood between two metal lugs and turning.

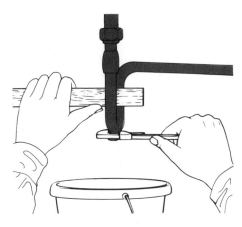

When undoing the nut at the base of the old fashioned metal U-bend, put a piece of wood in the bend to counteract the turning force of the wrench, otherwise the pipe may get bent.

**Dripping taps.** These require new washers. Unless it is a Supatap, the slender type where the tap nozzle and cross-head are combined, fitting a new washer involves turning off the water at the main stop cock. This is simple if the affected tap is the cold water one at the kitchen sink, but more complicated with others. Any basic plumbing book explains how to proceed with the various kinds of tap. There is nothing difficult or strenuous in it.

**Overflowing cistern.** Remove the lid and gently bend the arm of the ball float downwards. This lowers the ball so that it shuts the water off sooner. Modern ball floats are plastic and virtually indestructible, but an old metal one can rust into holes, fill with water and therefore cease to function. To repair it all you have to do is get a new one and screw it on. But as trouble invariably occurs when shops are shut, temporary measures may be required. Tie the ball arm to a piece of wood placed over the cistern, to shut off the flow of water from the storage tank above. Then either use buckets of water to flush the lavatory, or remove the float, drain it, tie up in a plastic bag and replace.

If water continues to flow in when the ball arm is lifted up there is a defective washer in the valve. Repairing this involves dismantling the valve and fitting a new one, first turning off the water at the appropriate cock. There are now rather a lot of different types of ball valve, but if you can recognise what you have from a drawing in a basic plumbing book, following the instructions should enable you to do the repair without too much trouble.

**WC pan faults.** A blockage should not occur here if the WC is used only for its intended purpose, but if it does, you need a large WC plunger; a small sink one will not do.

A more common fault is a slight drip at the back, caused by the perishing of the black rubber seal between cistern pipe and WC pan. If you have fairly modern plumbing and a large wrench, experiment to see if you can undo the nut holding this pipe at the top. (There is no need to turn off the water.) If you can, a replacement rubber seal can be obtained at any hardward shop. Take the old one in to make sure that you get the right size.

**Central heating systems.** Don't wait for problems – have the system serviced annually. If you find a radiator fails to heat up properly, you can effect a dramatic cure by 'bleeding' it – removing air inside which is blocking the flow of hot water. All you need is a radiator key (from hardware shops). Put this into the hole it fits at the top of one end, turn anti-clockwise until a little water dribbles out, then tighten up again.

### Electrical appliances

When any appliance goes dead, the first thing to do is carry out a fault-chasing routine, as the problem may be something quite elementary which is stopping electricity getting through to it.

## Checklist for electrical faults

Check for:

- Power cut, disconnection or hungry coin meter
- Plug not properly engaged in socket
- Fuse in plug blown
- Faulty plug wiring (see diagram below)
- Socket outlet not working

- Blown fuse in consumer unit (to mend, see p. 158)
- Flex pulled loose from appliance, or cut
- Faulty connector or switch in flex
- Controls not properly set (e.g. oven accidentally set on auto-timer)

## Wiring up a plug

**1** Open the plug by undoing the large central screw on the back. Loosen off the two smaller screws securing the cord grip, if present; some plugs now have plastic grippers inside instead.

**2** Slit the outer layer of insulation at the end of the flex and cut gently round to remove enough so that when it is pushed under the cord grip the inner coloured wires reach their respective terminals with about ⅜in./1cm to spare. (You may have to cut the wires to different lengths.) The brown one *must* go to the terminal marked 'Live', the blue one to 'Neutral' and the green/yellow one, if present, to 'Earth'. (On an old appliance the wiring colours are red to 'Live', black to 'Neutral' and green to 'Earth'.) Strip ⅜in./1cm of coloured insulation off each wire and twist the exposed strands together.

**3** Push the flex under the cord grip and partially tighten it. Fit the exposed wire ends into or round their respective terminals and tighten up the screws (on some plugs you may have to remove the cartridge fuse to get the live wire in). Screw on the back cover and finish tightening the cord grip.

*Warning: Properly wired plugs are vital for electrical safety. Never neglect to connect up an earth wire, and make sure that the cord grip is present and securely gripping the outer insulation.*

**Electricity can kill: always unplug appliance before inspection or repair**

**Vacuum cleaners.** A chock-full dustbag can cause a cleaner to cease functioning. With the upright type it could be a thread wrapped round the impeller blades. Unplug the cleaner and pull off the cover-plate at the front of the motor to find out. Or it might be that the drive belt has broken; buy and fit a replacement. Poor functioning can be caused by a dust-choked felt filter; split hose; or partial blockage anywhere along the line.

**Kettles.** A kettle which has boiled dry may go dead because the safety cut-out has tripped. To reset this put the empty kettle between your knees and you should see the cut-out sticking up inside the flex coupler plug on the back. Push it hard back with the end of a wooden spoon.

Otherwise you probably need a new element. These are simple to fit provided that it is not the automatic type of kettle that switches itself on and off. Unplug the kettle and remove the flex from coupler plug. Unscrew the plastic cover and manoeuvre the element out. Obtain a new one of the same size and rating. Fit the rubber washer supplied on to the element, replace in kettle, fit fibre washer to the outside and replace the coupler plug cover.

To fit a new kettle element, unplug the kettle and unscrew the coupler plug (*right*). This frees the element. Buy and fit a new one of the same type and size, complete with rubber and fibre washers.

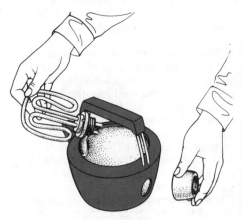

**Toasters.** Can fail if packed solid with crumbs. Unplug, turn upside down, remove the crumb tray and clean.

---

**Electricity can kill: always unplug appliance before inspection or repair**

---

**Electric fires.** Dead elements can be removed and replaced with new ones if you are neat-fingered and patient. New elements can be obtained for even quite old fires if they are well-known brands. Make a careful note of how all the connections are made before removing the dud element, and wire the new one up *exactly* the same way.

### Floors and floorcoverings

**Creaking boards.** Lift the floorcovering and look for the lines of nails fixing the boards to the joists below. If the offending board has nails missing at one end, renail with large round-headed nails (wire nails). Sometimes, when a board has been cut, there is nothing to fix into, and you will have to nail a piece of wood to the side of a joist and then nail the board to that. If the timber is full of enlarged holes, or splits, large screws may do the trick. If nails are present but not holding, try punching them deeper in; or better, replace them with larger ones. Do not nail anywhere except into joists or added timber, and keep to the edges; there may be electric cable and/or pipes running across the centres of some joists.

With creaking stairtreads, prise up the tread, brush a bit of wood glue underneath and fix down with a couple of large wire nails driven in at an angle. If this fails, and the underside of the stair is accessible, fix small metal brackets in the angle underneath the creaking stair.

**Worn carpet.** Holes and splits in carpet should be mended at once, as catching a foot in them could lead to a nasty fall. Rejoin gaping seams with a length of carpet-seaming tape glued underneath. Fitted carpets can be patched from above. Steal a piece from somewhere hidden, larger than

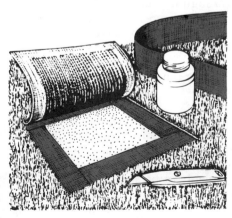

Patching a carpet: modern non-fraying types of carpet are easy to repair as shown.

the damage, matching the pattern and pile direction. Tack the patch over the damage and cut through both layers with a sharp Stanley knife. Seal the cut edges of the patch with latex adhesive. Discard the damaged piece. Stick carpet-seaming tape under the cut edges as shown. Brush the underside edges of the patch with adhesive, position and tap the joins with a hammer.

**Vinyl sheet and tiles.** Old sheet vinyl which is curling up at the edges can be secured with double-sided adhesive tape. With lifting vinyl tiles, use a bit of contact adhesive. Clean the floor below thoroughly first in both cases.

**Loose ceramic or quarry tiles.** Lever up the tile and chip away all the sand and cement or adhesive underneath. Refix with a small bag of ready-mixed sand and cement, or tile adhesive, as appropriate. If some are cracked, broken or missing, replacements for white or standard-colour ceramic tiles, and most quarry tiles, can be obtained from DIY stores or builders' merchants.

### Doors and windows

**Sticking and jamming.** Missing or loose screws in a hinge often cause a door or window to drop and fail to close. Tighten up or replace them. If the holes are enlarged plug with matchsticks or plastic wood. Jamming can sometimes be caused simply by multiple coats of paint that need scraping off. Windows may stick because rain has caused the timber to swell; it helps to open them now and then in winter to get some air in to the wood and stop them 'freezing' shut.

**Door knobs.** If a door knob comes away in your hand, the reason is usually that the small grub screw securing it to the spindle running through the door has dropped out on to the floor. Find it! They are almost impossible to replace, and the alternative is a new knob set costing several pounds. Refix with the door knob positioned so that the hole for the screw is on top, not underneath, and tighten the screw up routinely from time to time.

**Sash windows.** Never leave a broken cord unrepaired. Although the window still works, the remaining cord is over-stressed and could break at any time, possibly causing a nasty accident by trapping someone under the sash. Replacing sash cords is not all that difficult, provided you have detailed instructions in a good DIY manual, but it takes two people with plenty of patience.

Replacing cords can also cure a sash window of rattling or being hard to operate. This is because the positioning of the upright beading at each side which holds the sashes in place is critical: too tight and they stick, too loose and they rattle. The outermost pair of beadings can be levered off (start in the middle) and repositioned without otherwise disturbing the window, but this will damage the paintwork. The easy way out is to cure rattles with a pair of rubber wedges from a hardware shop, and make a tight window easier to open by fitting a pair of handles to the bottom rail.

Do not leave sash windows with the catch holding the two sashes together either undone or missing. Apart from giving some protection against burglars, the catch takes the strain off the upper sash cords.

**Broken window panes.** Mending these is perfectly straightforward provided that the window is on a ground floor, as fitting the new glass must be done from outside. The diagram shows how the glass is kept in place. Wear stout work gloves and knock the glass *gently* out from inside. Chip away all the old putty from the rebate. Measure up for the new glass, deducting ¼in./6mm from both height and width of the opening to give sufficient tolerance to accommodate any distortion in the frame; also seasonal movement. Bed the new pane on a layer of putty and tap in a few glazing sprigs to hold it in temporarily. Then fill the angle between glass and frame with more putty, shaping it with a putty knife or old chisel – copy adjacent windows. Leave to dry for a few weeks before painting.

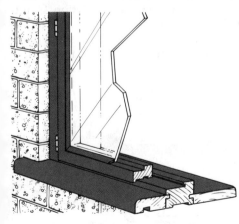

The glass pane rests on a thin bed of putty on a rebate (ledge) in the frame. An outer layer of putty, smoothed off at a 40° angle, makes a weather proof joint. New glass can be obtained from a glass merchant: most will cut your pane while you wait.

# Keeping warm in winter

Being able to keep comfortably warm in winter without incurring uncomfortably large fuel bills is vital to those living on a single income, especially if that income is a pension. Good insulation and draught-proofing are the answer, and fortunately most of it can be done by simple and often inexpensive DIY methods.

The warmth that you pay such high prices to acquire is only too anxious to make its escape through the roof, walls, windows, doors and even the floor. Frustrating it takes two forms: insulating the materials the house is built from so as to slow down the inevitable heat transfer to the cold outdoors; draught-proofing tiny gaps around doors, windows, etc, which, although individually insignificant, can add up to the equivalent of a dirty great hole in your front door.

### Insulation

The full importance of insulation has not been fully realised in the UK until quite recently, so it's a good idea to check over your home to see whether it comes up to modern standards.

**Roof.** This is the most important area of all. If it is completely uninsulated, as much as a quarter of your heat could be escaping through it. Take a look in the loft, armed with a steel tape. If there is nothing in the way of thick 'blanketing' or plastic granules to be seen contact your local authority at once to apply for a Home Insulation Grant. This will cover insulating the floor area of the loft to the current standard of 4in./10cm thick, also all tanks and pipes in it, and an uninsulated hot water cylinder wherever it is

Working with fibre glass you must wear rubber gloves. A mask (obtainable from D-I-Y shops) may help you feel more comfortable in a dusty atmosphere. Lay a board between the joists to take your weight.

located. If you find *some* insulation, but it is less than
4in./10cm thick, it needs topping up. Unfortunately grants
are not available for this. But it is not an expensive operation, even if you don't fancy scrambling about in the roof
yourself. The materials used are cheap: rolls of glass-fibre
mat or bags of loose-fill material such as vermiculite. Both
are light and clean to handle. If you do carry out the work
yourself, remember that you must work kneeling on a
board placed over the joists – a foot placed in between will
go straight through the bedroom ceiling.

A useful booklet available free from the Energy Efficiency
Office, 'Make the Most of your Heating', explains the techniques of DIY roof insulation, plus other associated work
such as pipe and tank lagging. It also outlines the cost and
comfort benefits to be expected from all forms of insulation
and draught-proofing, including double glazing. The
booklet is available from branches of Her Majesty's
Stationery Office, or direct from the Publications Division,
Department of Energy, Thames House South, Millbank,
London SW1 P4QJ.

**Walls.** These can be insulated to a very limited extent by
lining with rolls of polystyrene sheet, but this is too thin
to do very much (though it can be effective in reducing
condensation). The major method for walls applies only to
those constructed of two leaves of masonry with a cavity
in between which can be filled with polystyrene beads or
mineral wool fibres. But it is not a DIY method, and not
cheap. Post-war houses are likely to have cavity walls;
before that this type of construction was less common, and
very old houses never had cavity walls.

One thing that you can do is apply aluminium foil to
the walls behind radiators sited on external walls. This is
claimed to reduce the heat lost through this area by more
than half. Use ordinary kitchen foil, or a thicker type sold
for the purpose, and stick on with double-sided tape.
Shelves fitted above radiators sited under windows will
help to deflect heat into the room.

**Windows.** The simplest and very effective form of insu-
ating windows is to have thick curtains, well-lined (preferably with Milium aluminium-backed lining), and to draw
them each day as soon as darkness begins to fall.

Double glazing both insulates and draught-proofs
windows, but is relatively expensive, even if you do it
yourself. Consider it if you've already taken all the measures suggested here and/or if your house is in an exposed
position. A conventional DIY double glazing system

consists of pvc track which is cut to size and screwed to the window frames to hold the interior panes of glass, set in frames which slide in the pvc track. But there are now several cheaper alternatives on the market.

One system uses acrylic sheet instead of glass, set in self-adhesive plastic frame sections. This can be supplied as a kit containing all the necessary tools to do the job, and full instructions. The sheet is easily cut to size by scoring with a sharp blade and snapping, and it can be removed and stored in summer.

Insulating a hot water cylinder is simplicity itself with a strap-on lagging jacket.

Even cheaper are the 'seasonal' double glazing systems using plastic film secured with double-sided tape. Wrinkles are removed from the film by heating it with a hair dryer. But once the film is removed in order to open the window it is of no further use.

**Ceilings.** If it is impossible to insulate the roof, upper floor ceilings can be insulated instead, but this can never be anything like as effective. Polystyrene tiles or sheet will help a little if very thick. More expensive, but much better, are fibre insulating board tiles (from some builders' merchants).

**Hot water cylinder.** Unless you have the instantaneous type of water heaters there will be a hot water cylinder around somewhere, which should be insulated with a padded jacket. If this is less than 2in./5cm thick it's worth buying a second one (they are not expensive) and fitting it over the top. They are simply strapped and tied in place.

## Draught-proofing

As well as reducing direct heat losses, efficient draught-proofing can make you feel more comfortable at lower temperatures, thus making further fuel savings. But don't go too far and completely seal up the house. Some venti-lation is essential, particularly if you have heating appliances which need air to burn: solid fuel, oil, paraffin, and gas heaters – unless these are the balanced flue types which draw air from outside. Air bricks or ventilators should never be blocked.

**Doors and windows.** Test for draughts by wetting the palm of your hand and holding it close against their edges. The cheapest draught excluder is the familiar self-adhesive foam rubber strip applied to the frame. A more durable version of the same thing is a roll of transparent hard plastic which is nailed on. To draught-proof ill-fitting sash windows, fit foam strip to the frame at top and bottom, and cover the join where the two sashes meet with a strip of wide flexible rubber tacked to one of them. If you don't want to open a window during the winter draught-proof it with almost any kind of adhesive tape, or with clear liquid draught seal. Another type of re-usable seal is tubular weather strip – ideal for sliding patio doors – which is pressed in to fill gaps up to ⅛in./3mm wide.

Any door with a gap underneath needs a draught excluder fitted across the bottom. The simplest and cheapest are the stick-on plastic ones, but for a permanent job fit a patent screw-on type incorporating a rubber or brush seal. A front door needs something more solid to exclude driving rain as well. These are called door thresholds or weatherseals, and a number of proprietary brands are available. And don't forget to fit one of the draught excluders designed to cover the inside of the letter box.

Sometimes draughts get in round the frame of a door or window, where it has shrunk away from the surrounding masonry. Seal such gaps with a flexible waterproof sealant sold for the purpose.

Lastly don't forget to check the ceiling hatch. If this fits badly warm air is constantly escaping into the roof.

**Floors.** Unless a boarded floor is covered with thick fitted carpet, cold air is likely to come up through gaps between the boards. A few narrow gaps can be filled with a flexible wood filler; with wide ones hammer in strips of small-section wood. But if a floor is gappy overall cover it with sheets of hardboard. This will not only keep out all draughts but improve the insulation value of the floor. Also check for gaps underneath skirting boards, and either seal with cellulose filler, or pin on lengths of quarter-round moulding.

**Fireplaces.** An unused fireplace is a big hole to the outside and should always be sealed off. This can be done quite simply by pinning or gluing on a sheet of hardboard. But some ventilation should be provided to avoid condensation forming in the chimney: fit a plastic ventilator into the panel at low level, or use perforated hardboard.

## A useful book

*Handywoman* by Sonya Mills (Corgi Books) is a paperback full of advice for the amateur, covering in more detail the information given in this chapter. A useful guide to a large number of DIY jobs which you can tackle on your own.

# Trouble-free gardening

If you already have a garden, you'll probably have had some experience of looking after it. You or your partner will have built up a store of tools, and, probably, a knowledge of how to use them. The only addition you might need, if you've a lawn and only a hand-mower, is some form of powered mower, but even this won't be necessary if there is only a little grass and you're reasonably active.

But if you haven't a garden, and you're planning to move, do consider the pros and cons of taking on a garden. Even the smallest needs some time-consuming attention for about eight months of the year. Now that you're on your own, can you spare the time – perhaps at least two hours a week? On the other hand, many women find gardening very relaxing and a good way to get fresh air and exercise while taking their minds off their problems.

Perhaps you now find yourself for the first time in charge of a very large garden which it would be quite impossible to maintain single-handed. A good solution might be to find a keen gardener – perhaps an active pensioner – who is him- or herself without a garden and would take over your plot, partially or wholly, and keep it tidy, at the same time providing both of you with some garden produce. In at least one London borough, there's a scheme to put people in this situation in touch with each other. If there's no such organisation in your area – ask at the Social Services Department – try a notice in a shop or library.

Any public library carries a large selection of gardening books with such titles as 'Gardening in Two Hours a Week' and most garden centres supply booklets on various aspects of gardening. If you're a complete novice you can learn quite a bit by studying these publications, or one of the gardening magazines. In most garden centres – now to be found all over the country – there's at least one horticultural expert who will answer questions, discuss problems and make useful suggestions. It's worth going to the centre on a weekday when you can expect the horticulturalist to have time to talk to you.

## Should you replant?

In the long term there's no doubt that replanting a garden which has hitherto needed a lot of attention can pay dividends in time and money saved. At a nursery or garden centre you should find a variety of shrubs that will provide a certain amount of colour and interest throughout the year, together with other perennial plants to provide ground cover and thus keep down weeds. Unfortunately, shrubs can be quite expensive, compared with the cost of seeds and bedding plants. But with minimum care they can be relied on to last for years, spreading satisfactorily to cover bare spots and thus cut down on the weeding. After a few years the only problem you could encounter would be overcrowding and hence the need to cut back drastically (good for most shrubs, anyway) or the sacrifice of some of the less attractive plants. Modern methods of growing in garden centres mean that most shrubs will be in containers and can be planted out at almost any time of the year except when the ground is hard through frost, or snow-covered.

Take some thought about the eventual heights of any shrubs you buy – this information is usually to be found at the point of sale – so that potentially large shrubs are placed at the back of a bed or border and the smaller ones at the front. Dig a hole large enough for the roots with their surrounding compost plus a sprinkling of bone meal and peat or whatever the expert suggests, cut away the container and put its contents into the hole, surrounding it with a peat, compost or garden soil mixture, and firm down thoroughly with your feet. You should then give the shrub a good watering, which must be repeated if the weather is very dry.

Spaces between shrubs can be filled with bedding plants for the first year or two, or bulbs such as daffodils which can remain in position for years with minimal attention.

### Crops from the garden

The idea of providing yourself with fresh fruit and vegetables from your garden is a very attractive one. But unless you are really a very keen gardener, it may not be feasible. It's been reckoned that the average family saves very little money by growing their own produce, and the cost in terms of work is quite considerable. All crops are subject to attack by various pests which means an expenditure of time and money on pesticides – and great care in their selection and use if you are to avoid danger to animals or people. Weeds in the flower garden are unsightly; in the vegetable patch they will smother your crops unless you hoe or handweed regularly.

Fruit bushes or trees need pruning annually: if you already have some in your garden you probably will want to keep them, so consult a good gardening book which will show you just where and how to make your cuts.

**Indoor gardening**

For the last twenty years or so there's been such a boom in houseplants that most women will be familiar with them and their foibles. Even chain stores and supermarkets are now selling the more popular plants and almost invariably there are instructions on their labels indicating whether they are easy or difficult to grow, whether they are suitable for sunny or shaded positions, and so on. Two points that some beginners forget are that the majority of house plants appreciate a couple of weeks or so out-of-doors in summer (make sure to keep them adequately watered) and that plants grown on a windowsill should never be left over-night in cold weather next to the window with curtains drawn between them and the room. More houseplants die through overwatering than from any other cause – and most need a little dose of Baby Bio or similar fertiliser during their growing season. Finally, house plants should normally be repotted, with a little fresh compost once a year, in a pot just one size larger than the existing one.

# CHAPTER 10

# CAR MAINTENANCE FOR BEGINNERS

This chapter is intended to give you a basic understanding of how your car works, and to enable you to carry out certain simple maintenance and diagnostic tasks. Even if you don't, in the end, choose to do these yourself, you will have gained enough knowledge and confidence through reading this chapter to hold your own with the garage mechanic and his technical jargon. And who knows – you may get hooked . . .

*This chapter has been prepared by engineer Sheila MacDonnell.*

## What makes a car go?

To make a car move, power must first be developed in the engine and transferred to the car wheels. Pistons, in cylinders, are each attached by a rod to the *crankshaft*. Each piston, consecutively, is forced in a downward power stroke, and this power stroke turns the crankshaft, rather like the effect of pushing pedals up and down to turn the wheels of a bicycle. The piston is forced down by the quick burning of a mixture of petrol and air above its head.

The up-and-down movement of the pistons and, in turn, the crankshaft's rotary movement are all done at very high speed. The power is then conveyed to the car wheels.

In the case of a front-wheel drive car, it is carried from the engine through the clutch and then the gear box directly to the front wheels. The front axle, known as *two half shafts*, joins across from wheel to wheel. At the centre of this axle is the *differential*, a geared connection between the two halves. If the axle were a solid bar, the car would not turn corners efficiently. The wheel on the inside of the curve would be dragging the other wheel through a greater curve and this would result in scuffing and sliding. With the introduction of the differential, each wheel on its own half shaft is able to turn at different speeds when turning a corner. When on the straight, their speed will be identical.

This is a front-wheel drive car. The parts will be located differently in different makes of car, but you should be able to identify the main components from this diagram. In a rear-wheel drive car, a propellor shaft extends the length of the car from the engine to the rear axle – it's that 'hump' along the floor of the passenger compartment. In a rear-wheel drive car the gearbox is usually located further back, behind the engine. See also pages 198–9.

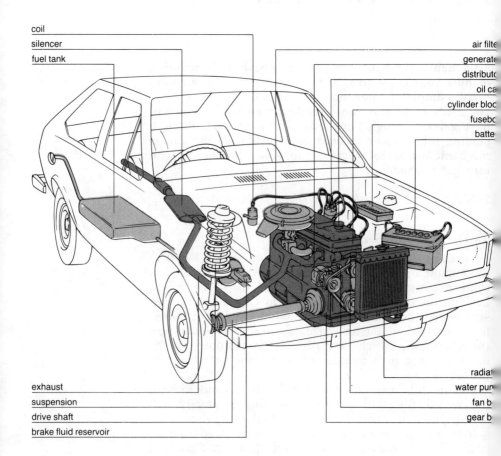

coil

silencer

fuel tank

air filte

generat

distribut

oil ca

cylinder bloc

fusebo

batte

radia

water pur

fan b

gear b

exhaust

suspension

drive shaft

brake fluid reservoir

With the rear-wheel drive car the engine lies fore and aft under the bonnet. The power is taken through the clutch, gear box and via a *propeller shaft* to the rear axle, which is connected to the rear wheels. With four-wheel drive (as in a Jeep, Land Rover or Range Rover) the power is taken to all four wheels of the car. (The Range Rover is permanently in four-wheel-drive but with the Land Rover it can be changed from rear-wheel to four-wheel drive as required.) Most cars nowadays are front-wheel drive. The advantage of front wheel drive is that the weight of the engine is directly over the driving wheels, giving them greater purchase on the road and lessening the tendency to skid. It also gives more room in the passenger compartment and boot because the transmission doesn't run the length of the car. With four-wheel drive, the power is transmitted equally to all four wheels and the car is even more able to find grip in slippery conditions.

If minor maintenance is going to be carried out by the owner, the simpler the engine is to work on the better (e.g. it helps to have plenty of space around the engine's layout). So, consider this point if you're buying a new or second-hand car.

# Buyer beware

When buying a car, either new or secondhand, the two most important facts to be considered are its cost and suitability for the driver's purpose. If the car is a used one, unless you are sure it has been given regular first class maintenance, and you have been accustomed already to the kind of basic servicing described in this chapter, then it is wise to take with you a friend who has had experience in car buying when deciding on your purchase. Better still, money invested in an AA inspection is never wasted, since it will be extremely thorough and they have no axe to grind. Since while the car is being examined you may well hear engineering phrases with which you are not familiar it is as well to brush up on a few of these so you can understand the proceedings.

If, for instance, your adviser and the seller use the phrase *engine capacity* they are referring to the total volume of air and petrol mixture used in the engine to create the power; it is measured in litres or cubic centimetres. This amount of mixture is worked out by the manufacturer by measuring the working capacity of the piston in a cylinder and then multiplying it by the number of cylinders in the engine. The greater the engine capacity, the more powerful it is.

For example, a Jaguar may have a 4.2 litre engine (1000 cubic centimetres equals one litre), a Mini or a Fiesta most often has a 1.0 litre engine, while a Ford might have a 1.3, 1.6, 2 or 3 litre engine, depending on the model. The most suitable size for an engine will, of course, depend on the size and weight of the car and performance required.

Another phrase you may hear is *power steering*. This is most useful when parking or manoeuvring a large, heavy car or when driving it at slow speeds. It works by means of a pump that drives a light oil under pressure to increase the effect of the effort you put into turning the steering wheel; it is worth remembering that it only works when the engine is running.

*Power brakes* (servo assisted) work in much the same way, a light pressure of your foot being increased to have a very much greater effect on the brakes and giving greatly increased stopping power. Once again, it is most useful with heavy cars, and does not work if the engine has stopped.

*Automatic gears* also allow easier and more relaxed driving, especially in traffic. A gearbox is needed on every car to adjust the power of the engine to the load; if you are starting from rest or climbing a steep hill you need maximum pulling power. This means you must use a low gear. In other words, though the engine is turning over fast, the wheels are moving slowly but powerfully.

## Check list for buying a secondhand car

*Always* inspect the car in daylight.
*Never* buy a car more than three years old without a current MOT certificate.

**1 Outside the car**. Check the body for rust and accident damage. A handy trick is to run a magnet over any parts of the bodywork which look as if they have been repainted; body filler and glass fibre used to repair damage are non-magnetic. Look under wings for evidence of rust or damage and inspect the whole length of the exhaust pipe. Check that doors, boot and bonnet all fit properly. Wobble the wheels with your hands to look for play in the wheel bearings, suspension or steering although these can only be fully checked if the vehicle is jacked up. Check the condition of the tyres, feeling them for splits and bumps and checking the tread depth. Don't forget the spare tyre. Check that the car is supplied with a jack and wheelbrace. Bounce each corner of the car. If the bouncing doesn't quickly subside, new shock absorbers may be needed.

**2 Inside the car**. Check the mileage. If the mileage indicator (odometer) shows a low recorded mileage yet the upholstery and the pedal rubbers are worn, be suspicious; the odometer may have been tampered with. Check that all the windows and door locks work properly. Check the seat belts, and try out all the controls (lights, wipers, horn, etc). Check that the carpets are not wet and the floor is not rusty. Check that the steering wheel only moves slightly before the front wheels begin to turn, to check for too much play in the linkage.

**3 Under the bonnet**. Inspect the engine. If it is dirty, or the oil (check with dipstick) is black, this is evidence that

If you have a manual (hand operated) gearbox you will have pressed the clutch pedal and manually pushed the gear lever into the position that will give you the gear you require (the lower the number of the gear the greater the pulling power). An automatic gear box will do this for you. There is no clutch pedal to press, the only foot controls being the brake and accelerator, and you will always be in the most suitable gear for the load.

# Routine maintenance

It is important for the car owner to be familiar with the services and inspections that have to be carried out, either by herself or by a garage, and which are necessary for the upkeep of the car. Whenever the bonnet is raised it is a good idea to take a general look around the engine. Do this with the engine *off*. A spinning fan is invisible, and even experienced mechanics have been injured by forgetting this. Plug leads and all wire connections can be quickly checked for security and for freedom from chafing or wear;

the car has not been properly maintained. Look for oil leaks. Check the brake fluid level; if it is low it may indicate a leak. Start the engine and listen carefully for knocks and rattles. Walk round the car and look for blue smoke from the exhaust pipe, which could indicate worn valve guides, piston rings and/or cylinder bores. These require major repairs. Ask your friend or the vendor to rev the engine and look again. Black smoke means a faulty choke, a blocked air filter or a malfunctioning carburettor.

4 **On the road**. *Always* go for a test drive. While still stationary, but with the engine running, apply the handbrake and put the car into third gear. Then slowly take your foot off the clutch. The engine should stall; if it doesn't, the clutch is slipping. Note whether there is any tendency for the car to veer to one side either as you drive along or when you brake. Make sure the gears change smoothly and don't slip into neutral.

If you discover faults or accident damage you can use them to negotiate with the vendor for a reduction in price. If you feel uncertain, ask the vendor if he or she is willing to allow an independent assessment by an engineer from one of the motoring organisations (see Directory of useful organisations). Their *vehicle inspection service* costs about £34 (1985 price) for most cars and can be arranged within a few days. The engineer can recommend what you should be paying for the car in the light of necessary repairs.

197

usually this can happen where they bend and possibly touch some other component. Check also that the short ribbon-like earth lead on the battery is making a good connection between the battery and the car body. Make sure the two hoses connecting the radiator to the cylinder block are in good condition, and that the clips holding them in place are tight. The fan belt should also be correctly tensioned as, with the amount of play recommended in the instruction book; some of the large cars have more than one belt to drive various components, and if so, they should all be checked at the same time. Look out for any oil or water leaks, and if you spot them attend to them without delay. All this only takes a few minutes but can save you a great deal of trouble in the future.

**The fan belt**
Your car's handbook will tell you how tight the fan belt should be. The generator pivots towards or away from the engine along an adjusting strap. To tighten the fan belt, shorten the bolts on the mounting brackets and the bolt on the slotted strap, and move the generator away from the engine till the fan belt is tight enough. Then tighten the bolts again. Reverse the procedure to loosen the belt. To remove the fan belt push the generator in towards the engine as far as it will go.

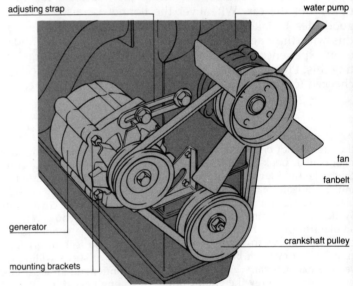

adjusting strap — water pump — fan — fanbelt — crankshaft pulley — generator — mounting brackets

## General maintenance checks

A maintenance check on the engine is advisable once a week and certainly before any long journey. *Petrol level* should, of course, be checked continually – the level shown on the gauge may be slightly inaccurate, and often shows a lower reading than the amount actually in the tank. This is a wise precaution on the part of the manufacturer, making you look for a filling station before you actually run out of fuel.

The *oil level* is checked by examining the oil dipstick which goes down into the sump with the engine switched off. You have probably noticed, when asking for oil at a garage, that the mechanic pulls out the dipstick, wipes it clean on a rag and then inserts it again. The reason for this is that the engine has just stopped running, and consequently the oil has been swilling around in the sump and has splashed up on to the dipstick; the reading would therefore probably be incorrect. By wiping the dipstick clean and reinserting it the correct oil level in the sump is registered.

It is important for the *battery* to receive the necessary regular maintenance unless it is of the 'sealed' type; if it is, it will probably last for the life of the car and no acid or distilled water can be added – it's not needed.

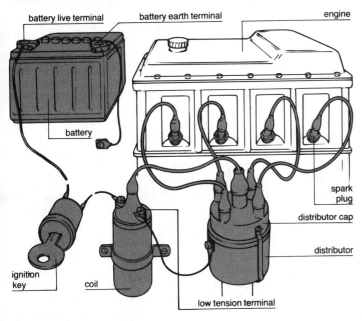

The electrical system. Check the high tension (HT) leads frequently to make sure they are secure and free form wear. If the engine won't start on a damp day, try spraying the leads, distributor cap and coil top with a moisture repellant like WD40 or Damp Start.

If the battery is not a sealed one it must be checked periodically, making sure the mixture of acid and distilled water just covers the tops of the lead plates in the cells. Each cell has a removeable plug to let you see inside. Add distilled water if necessary until the correct level has been reached. The easiest way to do this is to use one of the patent battery fillers available (the Lucas one is a good example). When the spout of this is pressed down on top of the plates, bubbles can be seen rising inside the filler, and a 'glug-glug' noise is heard. As soon as the correct level has been reached, the filler turns itself off. If instead

Check that the earth lead is making a good connection between the battery and the car body. It is important to know the *polarity* of your car (see p. 213).

you top up by pouring from the plastic bottle the water comes in, you have to stop at frequent intervals to check the level and the water is liable to be spilled. If so it must be carefully mopped up.

The electrolite in the battery (the liquid) is a mixture of sulphuric acid and distilled water (*tap water should never be added*) and is very corrosive, so if it comes into contact with your skin or clothes wash it off immediately. If it should come into contact with your eyes, again wash off and seek medical guidance. Make sure the two battery terminals (+ and −) are well greased to avoid corrosion.

Check that the *water container* for the windscreen washer is topped up to the correct level. Check also the *hydraulic fluid* which operates the brakes and often the clutch. It is usually contained in transparent plastic containers lying to one side of the engine and the level can be seen through the plastic without unscrewing the plug at the top. If topping up is necessary, it is essential to use the correct hydraulic fluid.

The *cooling system* normally operates on a mixture of water and anti-freeze, but the engines in some cars are air-cooled, a fan driving the air over metal fins (as in the Volkswagen Beetle and some Citroens for example); a system similar to that used in most motor cycles and light aircraft engines. The advantages are a quick warm-up and no radiator or anti-freeze problems. However, your car is probably water-cooled, and a check must be kept on the water level in the radiator. Some systems, like the Renault, are completely sealed. You should keep an eye on the level in the coolant bottle. If the level goes down in a sealed system there is certainly a leak, and you should take the car to a garage at once.

*Anti-freeze* is necessary to prevent the water from freezing in cold weather, when there would be a very real danger of cracking the engine block, shattering the water pump or bursting the radiator, all very costly to replace. It also contains a corrosion inhibitor, so should be used all year round. When topping up the radiator, use a mixture of water and anti-freeze in the correct proportion (see the instruction book) otherwise the mixture will become gradually weakened and when winter comes may have lost its efficiency. The anti-freeze should be renewed every second year. This is done by opening the drain taps (or nuts) at the bottom of the radiator and cylinder block and allowing the water to drain away; their position will be shown in the handbook. On some cars it will also be necessary to remove the bottom hose connection. Then let the engine tick over while you keep flushing out the system with clean water – if you have a garden hose, place the nozzle in the filling aperture on top of the radiator and let the water run, while at the same time it drains away. Alternatively, keep filling the radiator from a bucket until the drain water looks clean. Let all the water drain away, close both taps, and mix the correct amount of anti-freeze with water in a container. Pour this into the radiator, top up with plain water until the correct level is reached set the heater controls to HOT, and run the engine for a while to make sure the mixture has circulated before refitting the radiator cap.

A tyre pressure gauge

Check the *tyres* with a gauge for correct pressures (these will be given in the handbook) and examine them for signs of wear. If this is obviously taking place in the middle of the tread the tyre has been over-inflated; if at the outside edges, it is under-inflated. The latter condition can cause dangerous stress to the tyre walls, while the former leaves too little tyre-surface in contact with the road. The law does not give much leeway for the depth of the tread – the minimum is one millimetre or the depth of the rim round a 10p piece (a proper tread gauge is inexpensive and more accurate). Check the pressures once a week and before a long journey, and at least once a month remove stones, flints, etc, with a slim screwdriver, taking care not to damage the tyre as you do so. Keep an eye on the Schräder valve through which the tyre is inflated. If grit gets into it, the valve may not function properly and will allow the pressure to drop slowly. This is why it is essential to screw the caps on to each valve tightly. Don't forget that the *spare* tyre must also be in good condition.

A tyre tread gauge

*Keeping the car as rust free* as possible is very important. If rust has occurred in a spot on the paintwork, it should be attended to as soon as possible, otherwise it will spread over the metal. Though some anti-rust liquids can be applied directly to the rust patch, it is best first of all to get rid of it by rubbing down with fine emery paper, applying zinc or red-lead paint that will prevent rust from forming again, and when it is dry painting with matching cellulose (available in the form of an aerosol or 'touch up' stick).

Most modern cars are 'undersealed' against rust when they are initially made. If you have any metal parts made from aluminium, rust cannot occur; however, aluminium is very susceptible to sea spray and road salt.

# Changing the wheel

If you are unlucky enough to have a puncture, or find your tyre has gone flat through a faulty valve, the wheel is changed as follows.

1 Try if possible to get the car on to a level surface and apply the handbrake. If you can, chock the undamaged tyres with bricks or blocks to minimise the risk of the car moving while it is being jacked up. Remove the hub cap. You may have to use a screwdriver as a lever. Place the wheelbrace on the nuts of the faulty wheel and loosen each one half a turn. This may be difficult if the nuts have been put on previously at a garage by mechanical means, making them extremely tight and stiff to move, but it may be possible to increase the leverage on the brace by means of another spanner or a metal tube; or you could try standing on it. Do not loosen the nuts too much, or the wheel may fall off before the car is jacked, causing it to crash down and injure you. When the nuts are loose, double check that the handbrake is on. Now place the jack under the jacking point of the car (see handbook) and jack up the wheel until it is well clear of the ground. Next loosen the nuts completely and remove them, together with the wheel. (Place the nuts inside the hub cap so you don't lose them.)

2 Remove the spare wheel from the boot and place it in position on the bolts.

Replace the nuts and tighten them as much as you can with your fingers. The nuts are rounded off (bevelled) at one end and it is vital that the rounded side of the nut is placed *against* the wheel.

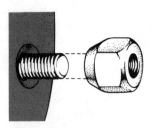

3 Lower the wheel until it just touches the ground – enough to prevent it from turning – and tighten the nuts with the brace, doing each one in turn diagonally since this gives even pressure and distributes the stress on the nuts. Make sure all the nuts are fully tightened.

4 Finally lower the wheel completely, and again check the nuts, then remove the jack and replace it, together with the punctured wheel, in the boot, and check the pressure on all four tyres. Have the puncture mended as soon as possible.

Changing the wheel is a job that is worth practising at home, before you really need to do it in the course of a journey.

### Cleaning the car
It is important to clean the car and wash the metalwork at regular intervals, perhaps once a week, since this will not only help to preserve the finish but will give you the chance to detect scratches and paintwork damaged by flying stones that might develop into rust spots unless quickly dealt with. The secrets of successful car washing are: (1) stand the car in the shade, never in the sun; (2) try to work on

a day with high humidity or a fine drizzle – what is known in Ireland as a 'soft day'; (3) use a lot of water. The dirt is loosened on a damp day and comes off easily, but on a dry day there is a danger of rubbing grit into the paintwork and scratching it badly.

A gentle flow of water or a spray from a hose should first be used to get rid of as much of the dirt as possible (if you don't mind working in the rain, a really wet day is the ideal time for washing). Then use a car shampoo with a good wax content – never use household detergent since it will cause streaking and will eventually harm the paint and metal work. A soft sponge should be used to apply the shampoo, which should then be rinsed off with clean water, and the surface should finally be dried thoroughly with a chamois leather. If you have a hose, clean the under-surface of the car and remove mud from behind the wings and from the wheels.

Never remove dirt or rust from the metal parts with anything that will scratch. Washing with the shampoo, lots of water and plenty of elbow grease should be sufficient, but in the case of really dirty and neglected metal work a 'chrome cleaner' will work wonders. However, this does contain a mild abrasive and should only be used very occasionally.

If you try to clean the car with a single bucket of water it will soon become full of dirt and grit, as will the sponge or chamois, and damage to the finish is inevitable. Plenty of fresh, clean water must be available, even if it means refilling the bucket many times. For the same reason the sponge must be kept clean and rinsed frequently.

Once washed, the car should be 'leathered' with a chamois to remove all drops of water and any water lodged behind components that might start corrosion. Finally, don't forget the inside of the car, the windows, the windscreen and the components, especially the windscreen wipers. Safety demands that these should all be kept as clean as possible and if the windscreen develops a traffic film, a waxy layer that smears in the rain, it can usually be removed with wet newspaper (also useful on metal work) or by putting a small amount of toothpaste on a clean, damp cloth, using it to polish the glass and finally washing off any traces. Alternately you may use a little methylated spirits on a cloth.

The best way to clean the interior is undoubtedly by using a vacuum cleaner, either a domestic one or a small one plugged into the car's cigar lighter socket or connected to the battery terminals. If you use a brush you often simply spread the dust around. Cloth upholstery can best be cleaned with one of the commercial 'upholstery shampoos' available at most accessory shops.

# Diagnosing common problems

Here is a list of tips and troubles with which to familiarise yourself. They will make it a lot easier to understand the various possible engine faults.

### Failure to start

A great many drivers who cannot start their car engine immediately, 'flood' the carburettor. They know that the engine needs a rich mixture when starting from cold and (unless it has an automatic choke) they pull out the choke control and keep depressing the accelerator pedal. With a *warm* engine this results in *flooding* or making the mixture too rich. If the engine will not start because it has been over-choked, or starts and then stops, clear the carburettor as follows: make sure the choke control is pushed back 'in' so that it is not operating. Operate the starter motor, whilst holding down the accelerator pedal. This should clear the excess petrol out of the carburettor and the engine will start once more. Take your foot off the accelerator and the engine should tick over normally. You may have to repeat this procedure a second time, but the engine should soon return to normal running.

If you have managed to start the car, but have forgotten to push the choke control back, the engine may start to stall about a mile from base. If so, carry out the procedure above.

When an engine *stops unexpectedly* and the petrol system is suspected, first check that there is sufficient petrol in the tank. The breather pipe into the petrol tank may be blocked up, causing a partial vacuum which prevents fuel flow. This can be caused by mud slung up from the ground. The only way to overcome this is to remove the filler cap on the tank, regaining normal air pressure inside if this is the problem you will normally hear the air rush in. If it is inconvenient to clear the breather pipe by the roadside, the cap can be removed at intervals during the journey until the trouble can be dealt with properly.

Trying to *start the engine on a cold, damp morning* can be very frustrating; difficulty is normally caused either by wet spark plug leads, which allow the electrical current to pass down the exterior of the wires instead of getting to the plug, or else through the petrol not vapourising quickly enough to make a satisfactory mixture for burning. The first step is to thoroughly dry the plug leads, the lead from the distributor, and the distributor cap, using a dry cloth and at the same time cleaning away any dirt or grease from them and from the plug tops (dirt can also cause short-circuiting). If the engine still will not start, there are products on the market called 'Quick Start', 'Damp Start', etc. which, when sprayed on the leads and distributor cap, will remove the dampness and usually cure this trouble.

If the car will not start because the battery is flat, the trouble can be overcome by means of *jump leads* (long thick wires with crocodile clips at either end). You can buy these quite cheaply from a car accessory shop, and keep them handy. You will also need the aid of someone who has a car with a battery in good order. People are usually very willing to help: it doesn't take long. The procedure is to position the two cars with their batteries as close together as possible and then to connect the negative (−) terminal of the *good* battery (it should be marked on the battery) to the negative terminal of the *bad* battery by means of the black jump lead. Next you clip the second (red) jump lead to the positive (+) terminal of the *good* battery and clip the other end to the positive terminal of the flat one. The engine of the car with the satisfactory battery is then started and run at a brisk rate; it should now be easy to start the second car. Keep it running while you let the speed of the first car drop to a tick over; then unclip the jump leads. After five or ten minutes a charge should have built up in the flat battery, but it is wise to take the car on a long run so that the battery is eventually fully charged.

Provided the battery is not completely flat, the car can often be started, provided it has a manual and not an automatic gearbox, by means of a 'push start'. If possible, this should be done with the car facing downhill. The ignition is switched on, the handbrake released, the clutch depressed and the gear lever is put into second gear. Then with the clutch still depressed the car is pushed or allowed to roll downhill until a moderate speed has been reached, when the clutch is released. This has the effect of turning the engine over fast and powerfully, and the car should start. This can be done on the flat, too, if your car is pushed by a couple of energetic helpers.

If the car still will not start check that (1) there is enough petrol and (2) that the ignition system is operating as below.

## Electrical faults

If a fault is suspected in the electrical system all wires should be checked, *especially* the one leading from the coil to the distributor head since this has a habit of coming loose. (This is the thick *high tension* wire, part of the system that carries the power to the spark plugs, so take care not to examine it while the engine is running or the ignition switched on). Check also that all other wires are properly connected, especially the thin low tension one also leading from the coil to the distributor since this can vibrate loose at the distributor end.

*If one of the spark plugs is 'dud'* or not firing correctly (you may notice this by the unrhythmic sound and feel of the engine) the faulty plug can be found by switching off the engine and feeling them. If the engine has been running for some time the good plugs will be hot (take care not to burn your fingers) while the dud plug will be cold.

*If a light bulb has gone* the glass may be clear and this will indicate that there is a broken filament. If the bulb glass is cloudy or dark, suspect a dirty contact. If more than one bulb isn't working, suspect a blown fuse or a break in the circuit.

## Overheating

If the temperature gauge shows the engine is overheating and the weather is hot, it has possibly been driven too hard or (more common) driven slowly for long periods in heavy traffic. The car should be stopped immediately, or serious damage may be caused. Alternatively, the fan belt may be slack, causing both the fan and the water pump that circulates the water to revolve too slowly. If the radiator cap is loose, the coolant will eventually boil. A sticking thermostat in a watercooled engine can cause the water to become very hot. When the engine is cool the thermostat keeps the water circulating round and round the cylinder block, but when a certain temperature is reached, it should open and allow the water to get to the radiator for cooling. If it fails to open, overheating is bound to happen.

*If the front grill of the radiator* has become gummed up with foreign matter overheating can result because the air cannot pass through it; if so it should be cleaned with water and a detergent. Do not scrape the radiator or grill.

*If the radiator is leaking* the engine will soon overheat as the coolant drains away but this can be mended temporarily by pouring a patent 'Leak Stopper' into the radiator and running the engine. The sealer reaches the leak and swells to fill the crack, but the only real cure is to have the radiator replaced.

Occasionally a water pump develops a leak, but this cannot be mended even temporarily in this way, and the only solution is to have it replaced.

## Gaskets

If the metal components of the engine were bolted directly together, the join would not be water- or gas-proof. To make sure that it is, a 'gasket' has to be positioned between the two metal surfaces to take up any unevenness or irregularity. They look rather as though they were made from card but are in fact composed of an asbestos/copper mixture which is proof against heat and pressure. They have to be cut with great accuracy so that they conform exactly to the apertures in the engine through which the gases and liquids pass.

Most of them rarely give any trouble, except for two that are subject to constant vibration and stress; even these usually last for the life of the car but it is as well to be able to detect a failure in either. These are the 'head gasket' which lies between the cylinder head and the main block, which could be damaged on a water cooled engine; this will allow water to leak out when circulating round the water jacket. It will fall down into the oil sump and the oil will appear sludgy and grey/green when you are looking at the dipstick. You may also notice bubbling in the radiator along with a loss of liquid from the cooling system, or constant steam from the exhaust pipe.

The other gasket is the one joining the exhaust manifold to the exhaust and silencer assembly, which may 'blow' or become damaged. This will result in a 'put-put' sound but it can be replaced and tightened by a garage mechanic in minutes.

## Wheels and suspension

If you notice a vibration from the steering at certain speeds it is a sign that the wheels may need *balancing*. This is done at the garage or at a tyre centre by clipping small lead weights to the rim.

The *suspension* works as follows. If you are driving along a rough road the wheels will bump up and down so the axle is connected to the car body by springs which smooth out the ride. However, springs are bouncy in themselves and after a bump has been hit the car might develop a fore-

## Emergency spares

Carry as many as possible of the spares listed below because they can be invaluable in an emergency.

Before stocking the car with the really essential spares, first of all get rid of the rubbish – toffee papers, dirty rags, dog biscuits, spanners that do not fit anything on your car, and so on.

*Jack for wheel changing* (should be supplied with the car).

*Set of spanners* which fit the nuts on the car; screw drivers, large and small; pliers.

*Insulating tape* – handy for repairing a wire when the insulation has broken. It can also be used to anchor anything loose.

*Towing rope* and string.

*Torch.*

*Spare lamp bulbs.* These are best changed by a garage, but in an emergency consult your handbook. Check that the spares carried are of the correct type and wattage: kits for your type of car are usually available from the dealers.

*Spare fuses.* These are usually either in the lid of the fuse box or standing upright with the other fuses. Fuses are either made of glass through which the fused wire can be seen, or of porcelain with the wire running along the side (continental type). Alternatively, your handbook will tell you the circuit into which each fuse is wired.

*Spare fan belt.* If the belt has broken it can be replaced as explained in the text (see p. 209).

*Spare spark plugs.*

*Clean rags and wet chamois* or sponge. A bottle of water will supply the wetness when needed.

*Petrol container.* Invaluable if you run out of petrol and have to collect some from a garage.

---

and-aft rocking motion, like a small boat in a choppy sea, unless some form of controlling the bounce was introduced. This is provided in the form of a 'shock absorber', a vital part of the car's suspension.

Most cars have a 'rear suspension' formed by two long, laminated, curved leaf springs connecting the axle and rear wheels to the body ('cart-wheel springing'). The front wheels have 'independent suspension' (known as IFS), each of the front wheels moving up and down without affecting the other. Some cars have this type of suspension on all four wheels ('all-round independent suspension'). Details of the suspension system vary considerably from car to car, some using torsion bars, some rubber springing, others 'hydrolastic' suspension.

Generally speaking the suspension system is pretty reliable and major faults are rare. Modern cars have nylon or rubber bearings which do not need attention but if not, the swivelling parts must be regularly lubricated with oil or grease when the car is serviced. However, shock absorbers do sometimes wear out and if one, or one of the car's springs, has gone, the car will appear one-sided and awkward – you can sometimes notice the effect in another car when you are driving behind it. A worn or leaking shock absorber can affect the road-holding, and should be replaced as soon as possible; modern types are 'sealed units' so the entire thing has to be replaced by the garage – it is not a major undertaking. Trouble can also occur if rubber bushes holding the springs have deteriorated but once again this is a job for the expert.

# Understanding warning signals

### Red ignition light

It is important for the car owner to know why the red ignition light goes 'on' and 'off'. When the car is stationary and the engine is off the red light doesn't come on. When it *does* come on (e.g. when the engine is switched on) it means that there is current coming from the battery. This current is not generated by the battery, since all the battery does is to store current. When the generator (dynamo or alternator) is running it makes the electricity, and some of this is sent to the battery to be stored, ready to supply current to turn the starter motor and hence the engine. Once the engine is going, the generator also turns, and current is no longer required from the battery, so the red light goes out.

In other words the battery is the generator's right-hand mate and supplies current for the engine when the generator can't – either because it is not turning, is faulty, or because the fan belt that drives it is slack or broken. But whenever the battery is called upon by the engine to supply current the red ignition light comes on. In an emergency it can supply enough power to the plugs for the car to be driven to a garage, provided the distance is short and the battery is fully charged. But if the problem is due to a broken fan belt, the engine will overheat in a short space of time as the water pump is also driven by this. At the garage the faulty fan belt or generator will be attended to, but the battery will need recharging, since the amount of current it holds will have become very low because it has been used to supply the engine.

Actually, if you carry a spare fan belt you can fit it yourself. The three nuts holding the generator in position are loosened off, and the generator is pushed in towards the engine. If the belt has broken it may have fallen to the ground or it may be caught up and will have to be removed. If it is badly worn it should be replaced, and if merely loose it should be tightened, the correct amount of tension being described in the handbook. If a new belt is being fitted, it is placed in position over the engine drive pulley, the waterpump drive and the generator drive. The generator is then pulled back into position and the amount of play adjusted on the longest run of the belt. When this is satisfactory the three nuts are retightened. You should carry an 'emergency fan belt' with you in any case. This is a temporary belt which can be fitted without tools, and will get you home or to the garage.

Incidentally, the type of generator known as an 'alternator' is much more common these days than a 'dynamo'. An alternator generates a large amount of power at much lower revs than a dynamo, so it helps the engine to start more easily, cutting out the battery more quickly. Even when idling in traffic the alternator is still able to charge the battery. It generates alternating current (which must be changed to DC or direct current before entering the battery), but there is no need for drivers to worry about this unless they are interested in the study of electricity. It is enough to know that an alternator is a bonus, one to be appreciated.

### Oil pressure

When about to start the car we switch on the ignition, and, as we have mentioned, the red ignition light comes on. In addition an 'oil pressure warning light', usually of a different colour, also glows to show that there is not enough pressure in the oil in the sump to drive it into the cylinders and bearings. As soon as the engine starts the pressure builds up almost at once, and the light goes out.

If, when you are driving, the oil pressure warning light comes on, *stop at once* and turn the engine off immediately, because it tells you that the oil is not reaching the engine, which will either 'seize up' (the pistons sticking in the cylinders) or else the bearings will over-heat and melt. The most common cause of the trouble is a failure to check the oil level at regular intervals, but it can also be caused by an oil filter which has been incorrectly fitted by the garage when servicing your car or, much more unusual, by a faulty oil pump or blockage in the system.

Don't let your oil level run down to 'minimum' before topping it up with more; the less oil there is in the sump the hotter it becomes, and the less efficiently it works. On the other hand, there is no point in filling the sump until the oil rises above the 'maximum' level on the dipstick. Excess oil will only be thrown out on to the road and in extreme cases could damage the engine.

## Noises – critical and not so critical

**1** If there is a *knocking sound*, especially noticeable when you accelerate, STOP AT ONCE and seek expert guidance. It may mean a *big end* has worn. The big end is the part of the piston's connecting rod which couples to the crankshaft (the 'small end' of the connecting rod attaches the rod to the piston).

**2** If there is a *rumbling sound* from the engine when it is under strain – e.g. climbing a hill in too high a gear – this is also serious. It may mean that a 'main bearing' has worn. Damage to one of these, or to a big end, may result in particles of their white metal linings ending up in the oil and causing serious damage.

**3** If there is a *juddering or squealing* sound when the brakes are applied it may simply mean that asbestos dust has built up, but it can also mean that the linings or pads are badly worn and must be renewed as soon as possible. Alternatively the pads, drums or discs may have become distorted.

**4** If there is a *clanking sound* when moving slowly forward it may be due to a loose propeller shaft or rear half-shaft (axle).

If you hear clanking when cornering in a front-wheel drive car, the drive-shaft joints may be worn out.

**5** *Rhythmic thuds from one wheel* could come from a soft tyre or, more important, from loose wheel nuts, which could result in an accident. Retighten the wheel nuts and check that they are on the correct way round, i.e. rounded side nearest to the wheel.

**6** *Clutch makes a grinding noise* when depressed. Drive the car slowly to the nearest garage for examination.

**7** *Noises from the silencer* are usually due to a loose or broken baffle, but could be caused by a hole. Either way the silencer will have to be replaced without delay as it may allow poisonous exhaust gases to leak into the car.

**8** If when driving, usually when climbing a hill, you hear the *engine starting to rev up* but the car does not increase in speed, it means either the clutch is worn and slipping or else there is oil on the surfaces. Either way it must be attended to as soon as possible.

# Glossary of terms

Here is a glossary of auto-engineering terms and the names of the various components you may come across, with a brief description of their purpose and function.

*Flash point*. This is the point at which the mixture of petrol and air, *when under compression*, will self-ignite. This is undesirable, since to get maximum power from the piston being forced downwards to turn the crankshaft, everything must be timed so that the mixture is fully compressed and is ignited by the spark from the *plug* at exactly the right moment, forcing the piston down on the 'power stroke'. If self-ignition of the mixture occurs *before* the piston has compressed it fully, the igniting mixture will not burn uniformly and will explode in all directions against the cylinder walls, instead of giving full power by burning on the piston head.

*Pinking.* The sound of the explosion when the mixture detonates on the cylinder walls is commonly called 'pinking' because it sounds like a metallic 'pink-pink-pink-pink'. It is not good for the engine and you are most certainly not getting full power from it. The trouble can occur through: (a) the mixture being ignited by a hot spot in the cylinder head; (2) the ignition being too far 'advanced' so that the plug ignites the mixture before it has been completely compressed; or (3) by the flash point occurring before the mixture has been fired by the spark plug. This would happen if a '2-star' (low octane) petrol was used in an engine designed to work on '4-star' (high octane) fuel. Always use petrol of the star value recommended by the car's manufacturer. If the engine is meant to use 2-star petrol there is no point in purchasing the more expensive 4-star type; the higher the compression ratio of the engine the greater the need for high octane fuel.

*Compression ratio.* When the piston is at the bottom of its 'induction' stroke, the space above it is filled with the mixture that has been sucked in (let's assume the volume of this is 280 c.c.s). When the piston reaches the top of the stroke and the mixture is fully compressed, the space above the piston might be reduced to 40 c.c.s. The total space divided by the compressed space, in this case 280/40, is then 7 to 1; this is the 'compression ratio' of the engine.

*Fail safe.* Some components are made so that should they fail in their function they will be safe from causing harm to other components or systems.

*Battery electrolite.* This is the mixture of sulphuric acid and distilled water in the battery. Without it the lead plates could not hold the current that is charged into the battery from the generator.

*Condenser.* This is the small tube-like component (correct name 'electric capacitor') which is fitted to the contact breakers in the distributor. Its function is to capture the excess flow of electricity when the contact breakers open, and to hold the electricity until they close again. If the condenser was not fitted the residual current would arc across from point to point, eventually pitting and burning out the points, and the engine would run in an irregular manner. Condensers fail occasionally, but are easily replaced.

*Specific gravity.* The 'SG' of any liquid is the weight of 1 c.c. compared to that of 1 c.c. of water. Water is said to have a specific gravity of *one.*

*A solenoid* consists of a metal plunger inside a coil of wire. When a current passes through the coil the plunger becomes magnetised and moves quickly down into the coil of wire. It is normally used to open and close a heavy-duty switch such as that on the cable connecting the starter motor to the battery. The solenoid requires little current to operate, but allows the maximum current to reach the starter.

*Polarity check.* As we've seen the signs used on electrical components are + (positive) and − (negative). The metal chassis of the car is used as a common conductor, a 'return' for various electrical circuits, thus completing them. Until the 1970s British cars had the positive side of the electrical system connected to the chassis ('earth return') since this was done in order to reduce corrosion on the battery terminals and wear on the central electrodes of the plugs. But it was found to increase corrosion on the chassis, so nowadays most recent models connect the negative side of the electrical system to 'earth'. If an electrical repair is being undertaken, or a new electrical component is being fitted, it is important to find out if the car has a positive or negative earth, that is to say if the + or − terminal of the battery is connected by the earth wire to the chassis. Damage to components can be caused if they are fitted incorrectly (polarity-wise) into the electrical system.

An excellent handbook for those of you who have found this chapter interesting, is *The Car Owner's Manual* by Joss Joselyn and Ian Ward (Orbis Publishing). It is clearly illustrated and easy to read, and doesn't assume the reader is a man.

# PART III
# RELATIONSHIPS

*Relationships aren't just with husbands or lovers. Don't underestimate the importance of relationships with friends, the people you work with, your children, your grandchildren.*

# CHAPTER 11

# LONELINESS – OR FREEDOM?

*'Loneliness is a word to express the pain of being alone . . . and solitude is a word to express the glory of being alone.'*

P<small>AUL</small> T<small>ILLICH</small>

**In this chapter we look at the advantages and disadvantages of living alone and see how some women have come to terms with the problem of isolation.**

## Living alone

Alison is a divorced woman in her fifties. A few years ago she left her husband after many years of unsatisfactory marriage. Later they were divorced. He has married again; she lives by herself in a small flat.

'Straight after the breakup it was so new, for nine months or so it was really exciting,' Alison says. 'It was exciting that I could do just what I wanted to do, see who I wanted to, be what I wanted to be and live where I wanted to live. But then I think I went up and down. It had taken me seven years to leave. I kept a diary, and in it I was writing "I'm not getting anything out of this relationship, and when the children are a bit older and I can be self-supporting, I don't want to be here any more." So by the time I left I'd worked things out and I knew that I needed to be alone.

'Now I do have to say that sometimes I'm lonely, very lonely at times. But in a way it doesn't feel unacceptable – I can live with it. It doesn't throw me into deep depression or anything. It's just a state I'm in sometimes. There's a sort of yearning in it.'

The 'yearning', Alison says, is for a 'special person' with whom to share her experiences. 'I do have friends to go out with,' she says. 'But the freedom I enjoy most of the time does mean that I can be lonely, too. If I have some time on my own it's often very good, a day passes very quickly. But at other times I do feel the need of someone, and the days go so slowly. At times like that I feel apathetic, and it needs a big effort to go out and make the contact. I think to myself that no one ever rings me. I'm always the one who makes the effort.'

Rita remembers the loneliness of her marriage, which broke up some years ago. On a touring holiday with her husband, for instance, it was she who initiated every conversation. He would reply in monosyllables. In the end she gave up and kept her thoughts to herself. Yet she, too, has been lonely at times, in a different way, since her divorce.

'It's not so much being alone that I felt,' Rita says. 'It was the break-up of a long relationship, with the crushing sense of having been abandoned. For me it was a kind of obliteration of myself when I was left. When you're on your own those feelings come into sharp relief. I'm not exactly clear whether that's loneliness or a by-product of having been walked out on.'

---

*'When I was married I seemed to spend my time waiting, waiting. He was away a lot, and I was always waiting for him to come home. Then when he left, I had nothing to wait for. I used to go out night after night, to the cinema, the theatre, anywhere. I'd miss the whole performance because I fell asleep – I was getting only three or four hours' sleep each night. No one has slept through so much of a film as I have. I had to invent things to do.'* RITA

---

These two women had not been happy in their marriages and both now agree that despite the feelings of desolation they've suffered at times, on balance they are far more relaxed and contented than they were. They know that most of the time they positively enjoy their independence. For Lindsey it's a different story. Her husband suffered a massive heart attack and died while she was out shopping one day. She was left with two teenage children.

'We were always a close family and my husband and I really had no interests outside the home and the children. My first reaction when I found my husband dead was terrible guilt. If only I'd been there I might have been able to do something. People, including doctors, have tried to talk me out of it, but that feeling is really still with me. Whatever they say, I feel I was to blame. So I've had that to contend with as well as everything else.

'It's more than two years since it happened, and goodness knows I've had enough worries with the children, the house, getting a job, managing on much less money. In a way we've come through. The children seem happy enough, I quite like my work and the people I meet there. But along with those 'if only' feelings there's a terrible ache. Some people would say I couldn't be lonely, with the children and their friends in the house at weekends, and my job to occupy me. I'm hardly ever actually *alone* except when I'm in bed. And I suppose that's what I miss most, the warmth, the cuddling up, the private conversations – they mattered to me more than sex. I feel I've lost someone and something quite irreplaceable. They say you get over a bereavement in two years or so. I don't agree. I can't imagine ever getting over this kind of loneliness.'

### Lonely – you're not alone

A Market and Opinion Research poll commissioned by the *Sunday Times* and published in December 1983 showed that:
- One quarter of British adults feel lonely sometimes
- Four per cent always feel lonely
- Twice as many women (32 per cent) as men feel lonely sometimes
- Single parents, the widowed, single old people, the divorced and unemployed are most likely to feel lonely.

# Looking to the future

Even women who have come to terms with living alone and are actively enjoying the experience admit that they see a problem looming up in the future.

Alison again: 'Loneliness for me is more a fear of being alone in old age. Sometimes if I'm ill and there's no one there to do anything for me I realise that this is what it could be like later on. I could be alone for days, helpless perhaps, and no one would know. That – and being taken off into some dreadful old people's home – is what I dread.'

Rita has grown-up children. They have their own lives to lead, she says, and although she would like to believe that they would help out if she needed them in the future, she doesn't hold out much hope of this happening. If they don't take much interest in her now, she thinks, they're not likely to do so when she's old, frail and 'unappealing'.

'To me,' Rita says, 'loneliness often comes down to our feeling that we haven't been successful as parents. If we'd had better relationships when they were younger they wouldn't be so apparently detached and uncaring now.'

Rita admits that part of the reason for her children's lack of concern for her may be that she's always been seen as such a capable person, someone they and others could always depend on, and this image has been reinforced by the way she has coped since her divorce. Despite periods of depression and despair she's carried on with her job and only her closest friends know how helpless and bereft she has felt behind the facade of self-sufficiency.

Rita has been hard on herself in her attempt to preserve this image. To test herself, she says, she once went on holiday alone. 'I wanted to see how it would be to be completely out on my own. It was a disaster. Once I'd spent a morning with a guide book in hand looking at the sights, had a meal alone, read a book, the days just seemed endless. No doubt about it, I had a bad time. I failed my test.' But should she have set herself such a difficult one?

If these three women, and thousands like them, had developed independent interests while they were still married, perhaps they would feel less isolated now. But this is a lot easier said than done. As most divorced, separated and widowed women find, when they lose their partner they also lose their former status in society. The better and closer the relationship, the more a woman is seen as part of a couple, and, as in Lindsey's case, the isolation of a happy marriage can mean that there is no relationship at all with others outside their own four walls. It's asking a lot of a woman like this to restructure her life, and be someone quite other than she's been for many years. And it's easy to become depressed and self-pitying. – depression and self-pity.

# Making contact

Every 'agony aunt' gets a stream of letters from isolated women crying out for help. Very often the writer pre-empts the reply by asking the columnist not to tell her to go to evening classes, join a club, take up voluntary work. She's tried all that, she says, and feels as lonely as ever.

'Everyone in the group seemed to know everyone else,' one woman wrote. 'They weren't unfriendly, just caught up in their own little circle. They kept on talking about people they knew and their doings, and I couldn't join in. How could I have made contact? What did I do wrong?'

Yet neither the agony aunt nor anyone else can do more than suggest organisations and activities in which a lonely, isolated person may become involved and meet compatible people. Of course it's important to choose a group with which you are likely to have interests in common. 'Voluntary work' for instance, is a blanket term that covers everything from driving infirm people to an outpatients' clinic to helping with a toddlers' group. If you're interested in older people you could enjoy the former, if you're good with children you would get a lot of pleasure from the latter voluntary job. Many lonely women have found friends through joining a local group of MIND (the National Association for Mental Health). In some areas these groups run clubs where there's no distinction made between former psychiatric patients and the helpers: they're essentially self-help groups where all benefit equally from the various activities; there are also 'befriending' arrangements by which volunteers – some ex-patients themselves – visit people at home or in hospital who for one reason or another need this kind of support.

Below we list some suggestions for anyone interested in the idea of voluntary work of this kind.

## Voluntary work

To find out about possibilities:
• Ask at your public library for a list of local voluntary organisations *or* write or telephone your local Voluntary Work Information Service, Volunteer Bureau, Council of Social Service – titles vary in different areas.
• Choose to volunteer help to an organisation with whose aims you sympathise – the work will be more satisfying and you're likely to meet people who have something in common with you.
• Don't undertake too much at first – two hours a week done regularly will be welcomed much more than a promise of a whole day a week which can't be honoured.

If you are unable to get information locally, write with s.a.e. to The Volunteer Centre, 29 Lower King's Road, Berkhamsted, Herts HP24 2AB.

Miriam lives on a large housing estate on the outskirts of a Midland city. She's involved in voluntary work in a different way.

'My husband and I were members of the tenants' association, and we went to meetings occasionally and I helped with jumble sales sometimes, but you couldn't say we were active members,' she says. 'But when he died in a road accident some of the women committee members were wonderful. It was just like my Mum used to talk about – in the old days when there was trouble in the street the neighbours all helped out, with money and looking after the kids and so on. I used to think she was exaggerating, looking at the past through rose-coloured spectacles. I thought everybody was too busy, too wrapped up in themselves these days to help a neighbour in trouble. When Fred died I found out how wrong I was. The women who came to my flat were people I didn't know all that well; they didn't push in and take over or anything, but they let me know they'd be *there* if I needed anything. When I'd got over the shock one of them suggested I might like to go on the committee – and it was the best thing that ever happened to me. I've done all sorts of things I never thought I could – like picketing the Town Hall when we were demanding that they did something about a dangerous road that the kids had to cross going to school. I was never interested in politics, but through the tenants' association I joined a women's peace group and went to Greenham Common on one of those demos. And I've done my share giving support to other women in trouble on the estate.'

When the Older Feminists' Network was formed in 1982 dozens of women from as far afield as Cornwall and the North of England came to London for the first meeting. Almost without exception their reason for making the effort was a desperate need to overcome their feelings of loneliness, and isolation from other like-minded women. In Chapter 10 we'll be looking at some of the results of these early meetings and seeing how other more local groups have developed alongside the national Network.

Brenda was widowed after many years of marriage. She has two grown-up children, but only one of them, her daughter, lives in this country. For a long time Brenda thought she ought to get out and meet people, but she'd always been shy, and it seemed almost impossible for her to go out and 'join something' as her magazine aunties always seemed to advise. Finally, she did decide to make enquiries about a local club she'd read about in the paper. But, as she says: 'I was too embarrassed to ask the librarian for the address I wanted. It was only because I was talking

## Women only

Many women's organisations welcome new members. Your public library has a list of local branches.

For information about the Older Feminists' Network write with s.a.e. to A Woman's Place – see the 'Directory of useful organisations' at the end of the book for their address.

The National Housewives Register has local groups for 'lively-minded' women. Membership tends to attract younger women at home with children, but there is no age barrier. (see 'Directory'—write with s.a.e.)
See Chapter 12 for further discussion on women's organisations.

to my daughter one day and told her what the problem was that this paralysing feeling was overcome. She took me in hand. I felt very foolish when she made the enquiries on my behalf and actually took me along to the first meeting of the group I am now part of. She even made sure I talked to the woman next to me, and from that first meeting onwards I have become more confident. Perhaps it was a piece of luck that this lady was a really nice person who suggested calling for me on the way to the next meeting, where she introduced me to other people. I might have been cold-shouldered, but I wasn't. I have my daughter to thank for getting me out of my shell.'

If, like this woman, you feel paralysed and unable to take initiatives, perhaps there's a lesson to be learned from her experience. Because it was her daughter to whom she 'confessed' her difficulty she was less ashamed of it than she would have been with a stranger. But is there anything to be ashamed of if, because of the isolated life you've led and the demands made upon you by your family, you've reacted by clamming up and actually being frightened at breaking out of your shell? After all, what you've been doing over the years is exactly what was currently expected of women. In devoting yourself to others, never taking any independent action, you've been obeying a lot of unwritten rules. Who is to blame for that? Certainly not you.

So, if to start with you have to take advantage of the sort of prop the daughter and the other woman provided in this case, this is understandable and acceptable. The main thing now is to react positively to offers of help, to take as much as you need, and to make it your aim to free yourself, however gradually, from the hampering habits of a lifetime. If you accept the help of a daughter, a son, a neighbour or a friend you will be half-way towards solving the main problem of loneliness and isolation – the chilling sense of lack of that human contact that every one of us needs and the feeling of purposelessness and waste that descends on so many older women once they believe that their useful lives are over. It's to help you break down such barriers that this book has been written.

**Adult Education**
Although it's a standard 'remedy' that doesn't always work, some women have found that day-time or evening Adult Education classes provide the contacts they need to get out of the rut of loneliness. Even with the lack of money for such activities that the Government has imposed on

local education authorities, in most areas some of these classes are carrying on, providing there's sufficient demand for them.

Some older women, in particular, find interest and stimulation at daytime classes run by the local education authorities. We have discussed adult education and training in more detail in the *Work* chapter (see pages 142–54). But it's well worth looking into the programme – normally available in late summer for the following session; you can find a copy in your local library. You might find it very advantageous to get away from the domestic subjects – which most Centres offer – and into something more novel and challenging. And the chances of meeting like-minded people are increased if you choose something you're really interested in.

## Enrolment in Adult Education

According to the *Sunday Times*/MORI poll quoted earlier, 79 per cent of lonely people attending evening classes found it very easy to start a conversation with a complete stranger.

Enrolment for most evening or daytime Adult Education classes takes place in September for the following 'academic year'.

The programme for your local Centre or Institute is normally published in mid- to late summer, and you can get a copy at the public library or on application to the office of the Local Education Authority (see telephone directory for this, under the name of your borough or county).

Enrol for your chosen class(es) at the time stated on the programme. Sometimes latecomers can be accommodated, but not if classes are already full. Watch for shorter courses, listed in the programme but sometimes advertised in local papers. Enrolment for these will be at a different time if they start in January, for instance.

## Too much to bear?

If this chapter hasn't helped you to find a way to overcome loneliness at least part of the time, you may need more than any book can give.

For those who feel trapped at home, unable to go out and meet people, contact The Phobics Society, 4 Cheltenham Road, Chorlton-cum-Hardy, Manchester, M21 1QN *or* Action on Phobias, 17 Burlington Place, Eastbourne, Sussex BN21 4AR.

Widows can get practical help and support from CRUSE or the National Association of Widows (see 'Directory'). Gingerbread has local groups for single parents.

Ring the Samaritans (number in your telephone book) for help if loneliness and depression are overwhelming you. Talk to your GP if s/he is a sympathetic person.

For a discussion of steps to take if you feel you need psychiatric help see Chapter 17.

*Always send s.a.e. when contacting voluntary groups.*

# CHAPTER 12
# FRIENDSHIPS

**Here we discuss what friendship means to different women at different stages of their lives, and suggest ways of broadening the horizons of women whose friendships have suffered during years of isolation at home.**

When the first industrial revolution began to break up the traditional patterns of family and neighbourhood relationships it was the social lives of women that suffered most severely. The middle-class and more affluent working-class woman might have found herself mistress of her own small domestic domain but the price she had to pay was isolation, which could soon become suspicion of, or competition with, other women – 'outsiders'. 'Working' women found themselves burdened with two demanding jobs, one in the family and one at the workplace, which gave them little time for friends outside the acquaintances developed with workmates in working hours; though until the Second World War, friendships between women in inner-city streets and in the villages, mutually supportive groups of neighbours, did survive.

With rehousing in satellite towns, suburban estates and high-rise flats, most of these neighbourly relationships broke down, and it was mainly the middle-aged or older women who lost these lifelines. Younger women, at home with small children, could sometimes break out of the pattern of isolation through meeting others in the same situation at clinics, playgroups, and by the school gates. There was no such point of contact for older women.

'At first I was delighted with the new house', says Betty. 'I couldn't believe my luck, after years of living in really bad conditions in a Victorian block that's now been pulled down. People had gradually moved away and it was getting me down, on my nerves. When we finally moved out we all said we'd keep in touch, and for a while we did see each other occasionally. But now it's down to Christmas cards. Some of my old friends from the flats have gone to other towns and some are on other estates, but they're on the far side of the city and the buses are impossible.

'I thought I'd make new friends here, but really I haven't. I'm at an age when I'm in-between – I haven't got small children so I don't see the young mums but I'm not exactly an OAP either. It wasn't so bad when the children were younger and my husband was alive. I was too busy to miss my friends much. But since he died and the kids don't need me so much and I can't get a job, I could do with some really good friends to talk to, to hear their troubles and moan about mine.'

With the development of the women's movement there's been quite a lot of research – mainly in the United States – on women's friendships. Surveys have shown that whereas men tend to have different sets of friends and acquaintances for different activities (one set for their preferred sport, another to drink with, another for political or community activities), women's friends are usually 'all-purpose'. They're people who have similar life styles and similar interests and they do things together. They're more willing to reveal themselves and more open to receiving confidences of a personal kind than their male counterparts. But researchers have, on the whole, tended to investigate the attitudes of younger women, those who, so far, have been most influenced by feminism, with its emphasis on 'sisterhood'. They may be setting a pattern for the future – but what about today's older women?

# Questioning some common attitudes

### Competitive attitudes

Women who were young in the 1940s and 1950s remember the competitive attitudes and suspicion that were part of teenage life at a time when every girl's chief ambition was to find someone to marry her. Girl friends would be let down without a second thought if a boy asked for a date and it clashed with something prearranged between friends. 'Pretty' girls would form alliances with those considered less attractive, to act as foils in the competition for male attention. Sadly, widowed and divorced women today still experience something similar. Their married contemporaries can see them as predatory, a threat to the marriage relationship. This may be why so many women on their own find that former friends melt away.

'Bill and I were friendly with a lot of other couples. The

men were people he worked with, mostly. We used to meet for drinks on a Sunday or go out for a meal occasionally, and visited each other quite a lot. When he left, I suppose they sort of took sides, or the men were embarrassed to be friendly with him at work and with me at home. I suppose I expected this, really. What hurt me more was that women who had been my friends and who had been very sympathetic about my difficulties with Bill just didn't want to know when the divorce was through. One or two of them have been quite nice about it, saying they'd love to have me to tea or something, but of course I'm working during the day so I can't go. They don't invite me when their husbands are around. I did have a little party but several couples made excuses not to come and the others haven't invited me back.'

Alison doesn't think that sexual jealousy or anxiety were the reasons why her former friends didn't invite her as they had before her divorce. 'I think it's because the wife is 'protecting' her husband from boredom. She thinks he'd get bored if the women wanted to talk. So she gets invited when the husband isn't there – in the afternoon, or when he happens to be out for the evening.'

Other women report that they do, quite unwittingly, seem to threaten their friends' marriages, and some American research reports that it's very common indeed for a friend's husband to make advances to a woman on her own. Even when such advances are firmly rejected, it's often difficult to maintain a friendship with the man's wife. Unreasonably, but understandably, the victim of the advance feels embarrassed and guilty – and that's not a good basis for a close friendship.

---

*'When my children were little I was very friendly with some other mothers – there were four of us. We used to do a lot of things together, with the children. I really thought at the time that we'd be friends for life. But of course we're not. I don't know any of them now. I look back at that stage in my life and I think of it as when I was a mother.'*

ALISON

---

### Old friends – no friends?
What about friends made before a marriage? It's many women's experience that they, too, fade away as partnerships shift. This may be due to the exclusive nature of so many marriages, the possessiveness that makes it imposs-

ible to maintain a friendship if the husband happens not to like a friend or feels threatened by her.

A more assertive woman is likely to see that she does provide some time and space in her life to keep up with *her* friends, whether or not her husband happens to get on with them. If this has been the pattern of a marriage, when a woman finds herself alone she has a supportive network of friends which can make all the difference.

One woman says that she'd kept in touch over the years with an old school friend and when the friend came to live in a neighbouring suburb they managed to pick up where they'd left off so many years before. Shared experiences and shared memories of their schooldays, she says, have made them feel close again – better than sisters – and they're still on the same wavelength. They meet weekly to do something enjoyable, and despite the fact that one is widowed and the other happily married their interests are remarkably similar.

Alison's experience is a little different. She has a very old friend – they knew each other when they were little girls – and they still keep in touch. 'We meet twice a year and it's really very pleasant to hear each other's news about our children and so on. One time we enjoyed it so much that my friend got quite enthusiastic and suggested meeting 'in between'. Strangely enough, it didn't work. Actually we have very little in common, and we found that at this extra meeting we hadn't anything to say to each other. So it's back to twice a year now.'

---

*'I'm quite ashamed to confess it – I've never told anyone before – but once I got over the shock of my husband's death and began to pick up the pieces I began to realise that in some ways it was a relief. For the first time for more than twenty years I could please myself what I did and who I did it with. If I was having a good time I didn't have to rush back to make anyone's tea. If I didn't feel like cleaning the house I could leave it until I did, without anyone to criticise. I could wear what I liked. Most important of all I could choose my friends, and those I have now are people he wouldn't have approved of – and if he had been alive that would mean that I'd never have made friends with them. I'd always thought of myself as happily married – now I realise that the price I paid for so-called contentment was a sacrifice of many of the things I need. This seems a terrible thing to say – but it's true.'*

WIDOW, FORTY-SEVEN

---

Alison doesn't agree that women tend to have 'all-purpose' friends. Hers, she says, are people she likes to do different things with – she much prefers to be with one friend at a concert, to go for a country walk with another – and she'd hate to go out in a group.

### The marriage trap

There are many divorced women who realise, after the separation, that they just have no friends of their own.

'I lost the art of friendship when I was married', says Pamela. 'I only learned again how to be friends with women when we split up.'

Rita agrees. Soon after her marriage she came to live in Britain. She had had a lot of good friends in her own country, but she knew no one in the city where her husband worked. '"Who will be my friend?" I asked him. "You don't need a friend," he said, "you're married now." So I buckled down, gritted my teeth and tried to make friends with his friends. They didn't like me. I soon got caught up with child care, acting the hostess. There was no sense of the close sharing I'd had before. I swallowed the whole package – it's a betrayal of your husband if you actually share with outsiders! And when the split came, I didn't tell anyone what was happening. I felt ashamed, it was my fault. Talking to anyone else about it would have been a betrayal of my husband.'

Pamela is another woman who came to Britain quite friendless. 'My husband wanted to keep me to himself. I was actually flattered! I met other women through my children, and we did things together with the children. But we never got close. Men can make prisoners of us: we're in a prison and we feel we're betraying them if we want to have friends outside the marriage. When I got married I thought that 'forsaking all others' in the marriage service meant not having sexual relationships with anyone but your husband. I soon realised that he thought it meant much more than that. So when things began to go wrong I had no one to talk to.'

Almost every woman quoted in this chapter has experienced the excluding atmosphere that makes social life so difficult for the 'unattached' woman. They complain that their married friends don't want to see so much of them as they did, and that, since to the single person all the world appears to be in couples, making new friends across this barrier is very difficult.

*'Friends mean more to me than lovers. Lovers come and go, but friends stay on. Lovers put strains on you, but friends are supporting. Friendship is a far more sustaining relationship.'*

AN 'OLDER FEMINIST'

But are we too ready to accept these barriers as a social norm? Should we be questioning the 'rules' of social behaviour that make it embarrassing to some of us to go out and about with another woman, and make us slip into the old habit of not inviting women friends to a meal or a concert or a film because these sorts of activity are associated in our minds with 'dating' behaviour? Can we only enjoy a quiet evening at home or an outing with another person if these social occasions are seen as somehow leading up to some kind of relationship – just as, in our teens, being 'taken out' for an evening was one of the accepted forms of courtship?

If we can rid ourselves of this attitude and take the initiative in asking other women to join us in some kind of social activity, we may feel strange at first. But the other women – 'attached' or 'unattached' – once they've experienced the relaxed pleasure of such an occasion and the opportunity to talk without the inhibiting or dominating presence of the usual 'obligatory' male will probably want to repeat the experience. From such beginnings friendships can develop. But, just as in earlier years not every 'date' turned out successfully, so, too, it's possible that after all, once we know the other woman better, we find we don't have much in common. How else are we to discover this, though? And how else to discover the opposite – that the woman met casually at the school gates or walking her dog is someone whose friendship we would value, and who, in turn, would gain a great deal from knowing us?

*I think one of the reasons why it's so difficult for housewives to make real friends isn't just the marriage relationship. That's part of it, but the thing is that one of the ways you make friends is performing some function together – through a school or through work or taking kids out together. I don't think I can remember a close friend that I haven't met through things like that. Of course at parties you're supposed to meet people but in fact you don't. It's all too superficial.'*

PAMELA

Although Rita was on quite good terms with her neighbour, while her marriage lasted she didn't see her as a particularly good friend. 'The first real contact we had was when we met one day and she asked me where I was going for my holiday. When I told her that we always went where my husband could do what *he* wanted, she seemed most surprised. 'Don't *you* ever get a choice?' she asked. Then I realised that this was what I always did – followed my husband's wishes. She made me think.

'When I was in trouble with my husband planning to leave me, I didn't say a word to her about it. I just couldn't. It was only when he'd gone that I turned to her. She was wonderful. She'd sit up all night with me, if necessary, discussing my situation and hers – she too had been divorced though she was in another relationship by then. We talked about what had gone wrong and why, she didn't mind how much time she gave me, how often we seemed to go over the same ground. Other friends were supportive, too, but the total openness and honesty that developed between me and this friend was what really gave the greatest support. I actually don't know what would have happened to me if I hadn't had her as a neighbour.'

### Friendships with men

American research points up the difficulty most women experience in forming friendships with men. Response to questionnaires shows that women are more likely than men to discuss their emotions and feelings, and that this applies in a male/female relationship. As Helen Mayer Hacker writes in the journal *Psychology of Women* (Spring 1981): '. . . women may be predisposed to self-disclosure, but they are also trained to please men. Consequently, the amount and kinds of self-disclosure that take place may depend on the needs and wishes of the man. If he wants her to speak, she is willing to comply. If he prefers to talk, she will be a receptive audience or sounding board . . . it may be hypothesised that he will listen only to her problems and failures, but that she will listen both to his problems and his triumphs.'

There are many women who would like to form friendships with men, with or without sexual involvement.

'It would be ideal to combine the two,' says Pamela, 'to be able to have a lover who was a dear, dear friend, and who would last, whatever the vicissitudes of the sexual relationship. But it doesn't seem to work out like that.'

## Marriage and friendship bureaux

Marriage bureaux and dating agencies have been investigated by journalists and others. Generally speaking, their services are not satisfactory – despite claims of 'computer matching', clients may be put in touch with completely incompatible people. The better agencies (those subscribing to the Code of Practice (see below)) are unlikely to accept women over fifty. Beware the agency that charges a very large 'registration fee' and a much smaller fee for a satisfactory introduction. Such an agency may rely for its profits on the initial fee and make no attempt to find a suitable partner. Agencies whose registration fees are lower than their 'satisfaction' fees are more likely to make the effort to introduce a suitable partner.

The Association of British Introduction Agencies is an organisation of agencies that comply with the Code of Practice and most reputable firms belong to this.

## Lonely hearts

Some local newspapers and weekly magazines carry individuals' advertisements for friends and marriage partners. Anyone contacting someone as a result of an advertisement should make sure that the meeting is arranged in a public place where retreat is possible if necessary. Don't invite anyone to your home until you feel confident that s/he can be trusted, or make sure that someone else is present.

## Friendship and support

There are organisations whose prime aim is to enable divorced and separated people to make new friends. Reports from women who have been to their meetings are often critical, though some say they do serve a need. The chief criticism is that those attending tend to be women on the lookout for a new male partner and that the activities of the clubs are limited to dances, and other social activities. But if you're interested, there's nothing to be lost by sampling. Contact the National Council for the Divorced and Separated or the National Federation of Solo Clubs (see 'Directory' for addresses).

Since her marriage broke up she has attempted to form relationships with several men, but it hasn't been a success. She thinks that friendships with women are more satisfactory. She's found that possessiveness creeps in to men/women relationships. 'When it's a sexual thing, you're more vulnerable to feelings of rejection. You think that if someone else is getting attention, then I'm not. Somehow friendship between women is not so scarce – it's more generous, there's more of it.'

Rita agrees. 'There's an open-handedness to friendship between women that keeps it going. Possessiveness is limiting, a closing in.'

# The meaning of friendship

Rita recognises her good fortune in having a great friend living so close. Other women find that – especially after a marriage break-up – work colleagues are a source of friendship. 'There's a sort of *esprit de corps* that can develop when you're working together. It's quite likely that some of you, at least, are the same sort of people. You already have a lot in common, whether it's because you find yourselves protecting your mates from the boss or because you've got some aim in view that others share.'

Busy women – and this applies particularly to mothers in single-parent families – often find it difficult to make time to foster friendships outside working hours. In the canteen or café or over a teabreak there *is* time for contact. The initial barriers are broken down. Then the friends know and like enough about each other to decide to make the effort to meet outside work, and this can be the beginning of a really strong relationship. Although finding any kind of job, let alone a compatible one, may be difficult, if there is any choice it would seem to be a good idea to choose one where you aren't working alone or with only a few other people. If you don't you could find yourself as isolated at work as you are at home.

As we saw in Chapter 11, women attending the same evening class or who are members of the same women's, political or other organisation are likely to make friends. Hundreds of women have found lasting friendships through the women's and peace movements, particularly in the small groups that form on a neighbourhood basis.

'I quite like my own company,' says Joan. 'But I do know that I need other people sometimes. I have no friends at work, really, and I'm not into the neighbourhood network, chiefly because I don't have small children and I'm out all day. But this doesn't matter. Two years ago I heard of the Older Feminists' Network. I went to a few of the London meetings, but I couldn't afford to go every time. However, one day I met there another woman from my town who had been a few times, too, and she knew another woman who lived near her but couldn't get to the London meetings. So we all got together one evening and decided to meet fortnightly. Soon there were seven women in the group. We talked a lot about ourselves at first, until we got to know each other. Then we started to choose a different topic for discussion at each meeting – such as 'Children', or 'Mothers', or what marriage meant to us – a sort of 'consciousness-raising' group is what it turned out

to be. We worked out some ground rules, giving everybody who wanted to talk time and attention. Now we feel very close. We don't just talk – some of us are active in politics or the peace movement – but the meetings every other week have provided me with the friends I needed. Most of us couldn't spare the time to see these people individually, but keeping to the fortnightly date is manageable. We're committed to it, and we look forward to it.'

On p. 235 there's a list of organisations, most of which have local branches or groups, and your public library can tell you about others in your area.

> Friendships, especially those based on a common interest, can often span the generations.

# Getting out and making new friends

Some women find it very difficult to define friendship. They know that they need friends, but years of isolation and inhibition may make it very difficult to develop the closeness and openness that must be part of the relationship. Of the women whose stories are included in this chapter, perhaps Rita comes closest to describing what a close friendship has meant to her.

'You get to know each other inside out. I don't have to

pretend anything to her, nor she to me. We're both brutally frank about our husbands, children, our expectations and so on. I have another friend, someone I got to know when I was at college. Because we live in different countries there have been ten or fifteen years' gaps between our meetings. But when we're together it's as though we hadn't seen each other for about ten minutes. We just pick up where we left off. We've both been through marriage and divorce, our kids have exchanged visits. We're terrible correspondents, but it doesn't seem to matter.'

Some of the women quoted in this chapter have come to realise that the patterns that developed during their years of marriage, with the attitudes of placating and humouring of husbands and children that they accepted without question, were in fact stultifying to them as people with social needs outside the family. However painful the break-up of the marriage – and all of them knew grief and bewilderment when it happened – they have come to understand that in many ways it was a liberating experience. Now, despite all the difficulties they face in daily living, they have found in new friendships a strength and joy that seemed barred to them when they were enclosed in the small domestic world. Of course it takes some courage to admit, even to yourself, that a marriage that seemed reasonably happy had within it some element of lack or frustration. It may seem disloyal to a dead partner to question, now, whether you missed out on some positive aspect of life. But whatever the past, you now have to look to the future.

If you have been a wife and mother, giving all your energies to filling that role to the best of your ability, it isn't easy to re-shape your life, to take initiatives, to seek out the friends you've never had. You have to be prepared for false starts and for disappointments. But, just as you need people, people need you, and perhaps this chapter will have shown you how to take the first steps, and what the rewards can be.

Shyness, inhibition, a belief that you're not interesting enough for anyone to bother with – yes, these are common feelings, and especially common among women. Does it help to know that these feelings are shared – and if you can overcome them, just a little, that you'll be meeting others more than half-way? Since your partnership broke up you've achieved a great deal on your own: but nothing more rewarding than the ability to make and keep new friends.

If getting out and meeting people is a problem to you, this checklist of possible activities to tie in with your interests may help. Your local public library is often the best source of information about clubs and societies – the main branch is most likely to have an up-to-date list. The Citizens' Advice Bureau may have lists, too. Where there is no local organisation, the national office of the association you're interested in may help. The addresses of national organisations can be obtained from your local library. Always send a stamped self-addressed envelope when writing.

## What's your interest?

| Interest | Organisation | Where to find out |
|---|---|---|
| Bee-keeping | Local association | British Bee Keepers Association |
| Birdwatching | Local groups | Royal Society for the Protection of Birds |
| Brass rubbing | Local centre | Public library |
| Children | Pre-school playgroups | Pre-School Playgroups Association |
| | Mother and Toddler groups | Clinic, health visitor, church, public library |
| | Parent-Teacher Association | School |
| | Brownies, Cub Scouts | Public library |
| Cycling | Local club | Cyclists Touring Club |
| Drama | Dramatic society | Public library |
| Films | Local film society | Public library |
| Folk dancing | Local clubs | English Folk Dance and Song Society |
| Music | Music appreciation class | Adult Education Centre |
| | Jazz club | Public library, National Jazz Centre Ltd |
| | Musical society | Public library |
| Old people | Clubs, groups | Public library, British Red Cross Society Age Concern |
| Outdoors | Rambling clubs | Public library, Ramblers Association |
| Peace | Peace groups | Public library, Campaign for Nuclear Disarmament |
| Photography | Photographic societies | Public library |
| Politics | Political parties | Public library |
| Sport | Sports clubs | Public library, Sports Council |
| Swimming | Local public baths | Amateur Swimming Association |
| Tenants | Tenants' associations | Public library, National Tenants' Organisation |
| Toy libraries | Local toy libraries | Toy Libraries Association |

For daytime and evening classes in leisure subjects contact your local Adult Education Centre, College of Further Education or Workers' Education Association. Lists of Local Education Authority adult education classes are available in public libraries; the new programme is generally issued in July/August for September enrolment.

# CHAPTER 13
# NEW RELATIONSHIPS

**Re-marriage may be the last thing you are considering. But people need people, and even though you may never enter into a permanent partnership again you have social and sexual needs. Here we look at ways in which some women have met them.**

It's been calculated that by the year 2000 one person in five will have married twice. In 1980, 11 per cent of marriages were between partners who had been through the divorce courts. There are fewer marriages between people who have been widowed, because widowhood tends to happen later in life, when the chances of re-marriage – especially for women – are greatly reduced.

It seems that despite some possibly very bitter experience many women who have been married before are willing to try again. Their motives may be the need for financial support; the belief that their children need a father-figure; inability to tolerate loneliness; desire for a loving relationship; the need for sex.

Any or all of these reasons for entering into another partnership may be valid. But, as we saw in Chapter 4, it's possible to slip too early into a situation from which it's difficult to extricate yourself. Fortunately in a social climate where co-habitation among young unmarried people is so common, it's a great deal easier now than it was twenty or so years ago to avoid making this sort of mistake. Nevertheless any kind of commitment to live together can lead to the same sort of misery and bitterness as a marriage break-up causes, if later one or both partners decides that the relationship must come to an end. If your first marriage was less than happy, it would seem very sensible to be cautious about committing yourself too far to another relationship, and perhaps to consider whether, now that you have had a taste of independence, this isn't something too precious to give up. Many of the women quoted in this book are glad that they didn't succumb to the undoubted pressure to form new relationships.

# Needs – social and emotional
## Need for security

When a woman on her own is having a hard struggle to keep her head above water financially it can be very tempting to give up the fight and return to the security she knew in her marriage. Milly, whose husband died leaving her with three school-age children, no independent career and very little money, got a job as a waitress in a local café. After a while one of her customers, a middle-aged bachelor, asked her out, introduced her to his mother, with whom he was living, and eventually suggested marriage.

Milly's debts were piling up and she saw no way of extricating herself from the poverty trap. Long hours on her feet, problems with the children – everything conspired to make her feel drained, exhausted, and anxious about the future. She accepted the offer and retreated thankfully from her job. The man seemed pleasant and attentive, and above all he had money: he wasn't rich, but he did seem able to offer her a more comfortable life.

It didn't work out. Once they were married her husband showed himself to be mean, close and secretive about his money. He kept comparing her housekeeping abilities with his mother's, consulting the mother at every turn about the family budget and complaining that Milly was extravagant and wasteful. Worst of all, he was domineering towards her children and appeared to resent every expenditure concerned with them. In the end, Milly realised that the very reason for which she had married him in the first place – his relative affluence – must have been the result of miserly, obsessive 'saving'. The couple eventually split up, and Milly found herself once more on the poverty line.

Of course not every 'marriage of convenience' of this kind ends so badly. Rachel and Brian met at a club for divorced and separated people. She liked him from the first and went through a lot of mental conflict when she discovered that with a good job and no ties he was very comfortably off, while she was failing to make ends meet. Would others – as well as she herself – see her motivation in teaming up with Brian as possibly a completely mercenary one? She had had a bad experience in her marriage, and was very wary of committing herself again.

It took many months – some of the time spent living together – for both Brian and Rachel to decide that the relationship would be a permanent one. Although at first the attachment had been brought about by liking and respect for each other, in the end they decided that the partnership meant even more than that – it fulfilled the needs of both for a warm, loving relationship in which Brian's wealth was simply an almost irrelevant bonus.

### A father-substitute?

In Chapter 14 we'll be looking at some of the problems that can arise with the children of women on their own, and particularly at the relationships between children and their 'own' parents and with step-parents.

It is very natural that a woman trying to bring up children by herself finds life a very hard struggle. She may believe that the children are missing out, not only in terms of treats and a comfortable life, but because they lack the male role-model that popular psychology suggests is needed to produce well-balanced individuals. Before accepting this idea totally, it might help if we asked ourselves what kind of 'model' of maleness we want our children to have put before them? Women who are trying to bring up their children, both boys and girls, in such a way that they don't accept sex-stereotypes – the strong, outgoing, dominating, active man and the passive, submissive, 'unselfish' woman – may not want their children to identify too closely with either stereotype. If a new man in their lives is likely to reinforce the very ideas we're trying to combat – will it really help the children?

When a woman feels that her children need a man about the house, it is often her own need that she's thinking about. No doubt about it – there's a lot of wear and tear on the emotions when a woman has to cope on her own with difficult children, adolescents who are going through the pains of adjusting to adult life and are behaving in a hostile way towards their lone parent. In these circumstances she desperately needs someone with whom to share her thoughts, support her in making decisions, and generally take the heat out of fraught situations.

But does she have to re-marry, or form another sexual relationship, to get this kind of help? Other women – perhaps those who have been through similar experiences and have emerged relatively unscathed – can prove valuable as sounding-boards and confidants. There are support groups – not only those specifically for lone parents, but a number of self-help networks that have developed in recent years (see Chapter 14). Relatives and friends may be just sufficiently detached to be able to offer help and advice but close and concerned enough to care about the one-parent family and its problems. And women who have joined up with others in some form of co-operative housing find that living with other women provides a relief from 100 per cent involvement with their children – to the benefit of all.

### Loneliness – and love
In Chapter 11 feelings about loneliness and the need for a close relationship are discussed. Most of the women quoted felt that this was indeed a problem to them – but no one interviewed for this book felt that this alone was a good enough reason for forming a new, permanent relationship. Most who continue to live alone get great satisfaction from their work, leisure, feminist or other political activity. They recognise that they do experience painful loneliness at times, but that the freedom they may have found for the first time in their lives is worth the occasional heartache.

*Yes, I get very lonely at times. But nothing, nothing at all could persuade me to get involved with someone merely to 'cure' my loneliness. I feel I've had freedom to grow as a person over the last few years. I can tackle things I never believed I could cope with on my own. I'm more confident, more at peace with myself than I've ever been. A new man would have to offer something very special indeed before I'd consider giving all this up – in fact he'd have to be the sort of person who respected my freedom and saw it as part of me. In my experience a man like that is rare!*

(AN OLDER FEMINIST)

### Sexual needs
In today's more relaxed climate it is possible for a woman to recognise her sexual needs and to want to do something about meeting them. For some, past experience of sex has been unsatisfactory and has distorted their perception of themselves and their needs. Others have led happy sex lives and the loss through divorce or widowhood has been one of the most painful deprivations they have had to bear. Whether the individual's experience of sex has been frustrating and inadequate or whether she fully understands what she is missing and yearns for a renewed outlet for her sexual feeling, the time will come when she may be overwhelmed by the desire to express her needs in a relationship with another person.

Sandra found her need for sex so compelling that she entered into a series of one-night-stands. 'Some of the men were the sort I wouldn't have considered for a moment before I was married,' she says. 'But they were available, and interested in me that way, and it's very easy to drift into a sort of "why not?" attitude. Maybe I had to get it out of my system and actually no harm has been done. But in the end I began to feel disgusted with myself and to become a bit more choosy. I didn't want to be like a man and get into this casual "scoring" way of life. I knew I needed something different – and luckily I've found it. My present boyfriend is someone I took a while to get to know; we've got a lot in common apart from bed. We can talk as well as fuck.'

## Middle age and beyond

If they are honest with themselves, of all the reasons women give for forming a new relationship, their sexual needs seem to be the most important. And, surprising as it may seem to some younger people, this applies with equal force to many women in their forties, fifties and sixties.

'I think sex gets better as you get older,' says Rita. 'When you are older you feel that you've got the choice – you may want it more, or less. You may want it or not. It's up to you. When you're younger – or this applied when I was young anyway – the attitude was that *men* needed sexual satisfaction, and you were there to help them satisfy their needs. That wasn't necessarily meeting your own needs.'

'Before I was married I knew nothing about contraception,' says Alison, 'and I didn't really know much about sex either. I didn't know what I was missing. Now I do. I became much more bodily aware when I was about fifty – after my marriage ended. I have a great need for sexual contact, and that's something that's completely missing from my life at present.'

Pamela agrees that as a divorced woman in her forties she can be 'a lot more choosy. I know what sexual experiences have been good for me and what have been a bit empty. I don't want to repeat those. I think I know the signs now, so I don't get involved with someone with whom I could be emotionally ill-fitted. I may have turned down some good times, but I don't think so. It's a bit sad, though, that you get fewer offers when in fact you're more open and able to enjoy sex.'

These two women – and many others – see that their decreasing 'attractiveness' is their biggest disadvantage as older women. This, of course, begs the question 'what is attractiveness?' Television jokes about battleaxe mothers-in-law, series like the popular 'Sweet Sixteen' of 1983 with its 'cradle-snatching' theme of the older woman and the younger man, as well as the images of older women as granny-figures in advertising and the media generally tend to dismiss the older woman as a non-sexual being. Isn't accepting all this accepting a male view of women? One woman in her sixties who took part in a TV documentary was congratulated by her boss on her 'glamorous' appearance. He had no comment to make on the content of what she said, believing, presumably, that to her what she looked like would be much more important, as it was to him.

In recent years many books on sex have stressed that sexual activity doesn't end with middle age. There's every reason, the writers say, to continue your sex life into your seventies or eighties. This has prompted former *Guardian* Women's Page editor Mary Stott to comment that this is all very well – but for the majority of older women such exhortations are a cruel joke. 'Nobody loves you when you're old and grey' may not be true in a literal sense; but when 'love' is interpreted more narrowly to mean sexual love it's all too near the mark.

This is a dilemma that has to be faced, and even women totally committed to feminism admit that 'ageing' is something they dread, not only because of the lack of opportunity for continuing an active working life. They meet double – and in the case of Black women, triple – discrimination: as women they are inferior; as older women they are invisible; and if they're Black they meet racism as well. And in a man's world they see themselves as sexually

---

*'What are older women doing to break down the attitude that they aren't interested in sex? When we discussed the menopause with a group of younger women hardly anyone mentioned sex. By not talking about it we're colluding with the notion that we don't "do it".'*

*'It's more difficult for us to talk about sex than it is for younger women for whom it's been much more natural to have sexual relationships at a much earlier age. They've always talked about it among themselves, whereas it's only in recent years that it's been something I've felt I could talk about at all. Even now it's not easy.'*

(MEMBERS OF A NW LONDON OLDER WOMEN'S GROUP)

---

disadvantaged. This happens just at a time when for many the liberating experience of freedom from domesticity, child care and from the fear of pregnancy, added to a flowering of their sexuality makes it possible – in theory – to enjoy a good sex life. It's very easy to reject the male view of female attractiveness; less easy to live with this view expressing itself in every aspect of life.

'I hate my lumps and bumps.'

'It's the sags I can't stand. Sagging breasts, sagging jowls – it's disgusting.'

'My neck shows my age. I have to wear high-necked clothes all the time.'

'I never wear short sleeves. My arms are a giveaway.'

'I always thought dyed hair was ridiculous. Now I dye mine, even though I think grey would suit me better. I just feel it would be so ageing.'

These remarks don't come from advertisements for cosmetics or 'figure-trimming' clinics. They were made by 'older feminists'. Ought they to know better? Actually, they do. But so powerful is the 'keep young and beautiful' culture in which they live that they go along with it, well aware that they are accepting and colluding with the hostile climate that sees women of middle-age or beyond as 'old bags', 'past it', of no interest to men, and not very interesting anyway, except as the butt of cruel jokes.

If committed feminists are affected in this way, how do they come to terms? Feminist or not, it's something every woman has to solve for herself if she is to continue to lead the full, active, satisfying life she knows she is capable of.

## A new life

'My answer to depression, sexual deprivation and loneliness has been to get involved in something completely new. When I left my husband I started training in a completely different field from the work I'd done before. This has brought me new interests, and new friends. I work as part of a team – all women – and we get on so well together it's been a revelation to me. We've got all sorts of plans for developing the work in future. Something to absorb me, something to look forward to – and I've got a feeling of achievement and self-respect that fully compensates for the lack of sex in my life. I can just forget it most of the time – maybe there's something wrong with me, but to be honest I don't care!' This is how one social worker sees her life in her late forties.

'When I look at my divorced friends – and there are a lot of them about – it's the ones who are *doing* things, especially new things, who seem less bothered about lack of sex. Are they compensating, sublimating or whatever the psychologists would call it? Maybe they are, but does it matter? Right through your life you have to make compromises. Surely it's better to be busy, active and alive than to sit around moaning about something you probably can't do anything about, anyway,' says another divorced woman.

In a discussion about a publication on the menopause, which they had been asked to comment upon, a group of older women looked round the room and realised that every woman present had started on some new project, some new phase in her life round about the time of the menopause. This, they felt, gave the lie to the rather negative tone of so many books and articles about older women and the dire effects of the 'change of life'. The change in *their* lives, they thought, had been for the better. (In Chapter 16 we look at the physical and emotional effects of the menopause in more detail.)

# Love of women

One of the changes possible for women at any age is a recognition that a relationship with another woman can bring satisfaction of their sexual needs and the comfort of a stable involvement in a loving atmosphere that they may never have experienced in a heterosexual relationship. Younger women now find it less difficult to be open about the way their sexuality finds expression. 'Coming out' as a lesbian is not now such a rare situation as it was twenty years ago, though many young women go through painful scenes with parents and friends when they decide that sex with a woman is right for them. An older woman who, despite her feelings for other women, has been forced by the weight of custom and convention to deny these feelings and get married, can experience a great sense of release when she recognises the reality of her needs and is able to free herself from a marriage that has never been right for her. Other women, who have repressed and denied their sexual feelings may, some time after the break-up of their marriage, come to a gradual or a sudden recognition that the resolution of their sexual needs does not, as they have always believed, lie in a new relationship with another man, but that the caring, understanding, loving partnership they need must be with a woman. Yet others recognise that they can form relationships with either sex. It's the *person*, not the genitalia, the way she or he gives and receives love, that's important.

Entering into a lesbian relationship in middle age, of course, can be fraught with problems, especially if there are children of a marriage. Whether or not adolescent children accept and understand their mother's new relationship depends not only on individual personalities and the sort of relationship they have had with her over the years, but on what they have been able to observe in their parents' marriage.

---

*My friendship with Linda developed when we met at a group we both belonged to. I was about to split up with my husband, and when I realised that a relationship with Linda could be very important to me I decided to move in with her. Neither of us has had a lesbian lover before. We were shy about it at first but it's been marvellous for both of us. We fit together in a way I think few heterosexual couples do. We're sure it's going to last. It's the friendship and the love – much more important to us than sex alone.*

(JENNY)

---

'My son and my daughter take totally different attitudes towards me,' says a woman who left her husband in order to join her woman lover. 'My son has cut me out of his life completely. All he could say when I told him was that it was disgusting and incomprehensible. My daughter did find it hard to take at first. She didn't know how to explain things to her friends. But she didn't refuse to visit me, and once she met the two of us together and saw how right it all was for me she accepted the situation. Although she's the younger of the two, I think she had a lot more under-

---

## Information about lesbian relationships

**Further Reading**

*So You Think You're Attracted to the Same Sex* by John Hart (Penguin).
*Rocking the Cradle: Lesbian Mothers, a Challenge in Family Living* by Gillian Hanscombe and Jackie Forster (Sheba Feminist Publication).

**Lesbian Line**

There are telephone help lines throughout the country. They give all kinds of help and information and will also tell you how to find your nearest bookshop with a gay or feminist section. Look in the 'Directory' at the end of the book for the help line nearest you.

standing of my needs and had observed the marriage with a much more critical eye. Now she has a boyfriend and they seem very relaxed and happy together. I don't think there'll be any problems there. But it's still a grief to me to be without any contact with her brother, especially as his wife is pregnant and I won't be able to enjoy a grandchild. Maybe he'll loosen up in time . . .'

There are several support groups and advice services that are available to lesbian women of any age, including a group attached to the Older Feminists' Network (see p. 221) and a group – Gemma – for disabled lesbian women. The box opposite lists helpful books.

## What have you missed?

So far we've been looking at the lives of women who, because of their age, have found it difficult to form new sexual relationships; who have preferred to remain celibate; or who have chosen other women with whom to share their lives and their sexuality. But there is another group – women who have had a heterosexual partnership in the past, feel they have missed out on the positive aspects of it, and believe that they want, and can find, a way to express their needs in a loving sexual relationship.

Surprising as it may be to women who read magazines or listen to radio phone-ins, there are still many women who don't understand the workings of their own bodies, and are made to feel inadequate, 'frigid', because their men expect an instant sexual response and it seldom, or never, happens. Such men never ask themselves whether there isn't something about *their* lovemaking that leaves something to be desired; or they may be content to relieve their own tensions with a quick 'poke' and not expect their partners to respond at all.

If this has been your experience it may be hard to rid yourself of the belief either that there's something wrong with you or that the joyful experience that sex is supposed to be is something of a myth. You may never have explored your own body – you accepted that touching yourself 'down there' was dirty, or wicked.

'I'd had three children and had been married for fifteen years before I read a book that explained what masturbation was and that it was something most people did and was nothing to be ashamed of,' says a fifty-year-old widow. 'That made a huge difference to me. For the first time I was able to tell my husband what I needed in bed, and show him how to bring me to orgasm. It was a revelation to us both. I am so glad that we had that experience together for the last few years of his life. We could have had it earlier if we hadn't both been ignorant.'

Recent textbooks on sex have emphasised the role of masturbation in teaching a woman – and her partner – what brings her to orgasm. But there is a danger here that because she knows that stimulation of her clitoris is likely to bring her to climax, and communicates this to her partner, he is going to see this 'push-button' sex as a way of getting the preliminaries over with before he gets on with the 'real business' of intercourse – penetration and ejaculation. He can congratulate himself on the consideration he shows in giving her sexual pleasure, but he doesn't ask, and isn't told, that for a large majority of women there are more 'erogenous zones' than one. Lovemaking isn't just sex in the narrowest sense of the term. Women need stroking, touching, caressing all over their bodies and to be brought to orgasm by the short route – direct stimulation of the clitoris – can cause a feeling of loss. Something is missing and it's probably sensing this that in the end can leave a woman feeling bored, let down: 'If this is all it's about, it's hardly worth the trouble.'

If your past experience has made you believe that the odds are heavily against your finding a man who will 'let' you lead the kind of life you want, who will be a partner in every sense as well as a lover, you are right to be cautious about committing yourself to another sexual relationship. It is doubtful in the absence of deep friendship, respect and love that sex alone will meet your needs. This is not to say that no female/male sexual relationship can be everything the textbooks describe – and more. Rarely, but not impossibly, a couple can come together, love together, have happy sex together, wipe out the pain of past experiences and grow separately and individually, in the relationship and as people. Together they can make the great leap forward from the patriarchal attitudes that stultify the lives of so many women and men.

### It's your choice

But you are realistic, and you do ask yourself whether you can afford to embark upon another relationship when the odds are really against its ever being satisfying. If we look at the incidence of second divorces the figures aren't too encouraging. Clearly, this is something every individual has to work out for herself, in the light of her own circumstances. But if you have found any compensation, and satisfaction, in the life you've been living since you were on your own, maybe you should face the fact that your happiness, or at least your contentment, may depend more from now on on what you make of yourself as a person than on dependence on another.

# CHAPTER 14
# CHILDREN

How are children affected by bereavement, divorce or separation? How does the mother on her own cope with the problems of adolescence? We look at these questions and at the relationship between a mother and her adult children and with her grandchildren.

In times of crisis or when they are facing difficult decisions, parents have an additional dilemma. How much should their young children be involved? Should they be shielded, told half-truths, kept in the dark until presented with a *fait accompli*, or allowed to participate in family discussions and face the full truth and import of traumatic events?

The standard child-rearing books offer little help with this problem, though they sometimes have something to say about dealing with the major crises of death or divorce. And it is in these extreme situations that adults feel most at a loss, floundering for the right answer to their children's questions, for ways to ease the obvious pain. In a state of confusion it's all too easy to handle things in a way that is ultimately not helpful to the children concerned.

## A parent's death

Dr Sula Wolff in her book *Children Under Stress* (see 'Directory') quotes a survey which found that 'most mothers thought it was best to shield their children from the rituals surrounding death. No child under sixteen wore mourning and only about one in ten attended the funeral. Many had never seen their father's grave. Some mothers even avoided telling the children that their father had died.'

These women may have thought that they were protecting their children from pain, but the same survey showed that when the father's death *was* acknowledged, it was the widows themselves who were more affected by grief. It may be that in avoiding involving the children the mothers were, in fact, trying to protect themselves from having to cope with the painful reactions of the family

while trying to come to terms with their own loss.

The famous child care guru, Dr Spock (see 'Directory') believes that children must be given a chance to mourn – whether it's by attending the funeral of a close family member (he thinks it unwise to take a young child to the funeral of someone she didn't know well), or by handling sensitively her distress at losing a pet. Obviously the loss of a parent is far more traumatic and its effects are long-lasting, but grief at any loss, says Spock, 'must be coped with bit by bit, usually in the company of other sympathetic family members. Parents can set an example for the children by speaking of their recollections and sadness when these come over them.'

How you actually explain the facts of death to your child must of course depend on your own beliefs, religious or otherwise. Some atheist or agnostic mothers find themselves in a dilemma, and may decide that it would be letting their child down lightly if they adopted the formula 'some people believe . . .', going on to describe the way many religions perceive an afterlife. This may satisfy a young child for a while, but the question 'What do *you* believe?' almost inevitably follows sooner or later, and the answer to that has to be decided in advance. Others will concentrate on the relief from suffering experienced by the dead person, and on the contribution that person made to her/his family and the wider community during her or his lifetime. Another approach is to draw an analogy with the rest of nature and concentrate on birth, death, and rebirth in another form – perhaps the remembrance in the minds of those surviving. It's a difficult problem, something that may be easier to resolve if you've clarified your thoughts in discussion with someone you respect and trust.

## Divorce and separation

Although death of a parent is fortunately not very likely nowadays to affect very young children, divorce is a different story. It might seem that by its very prevalence the children involved are more likely to take it in their stride. But research shows that children are slow to accept a broken marriage, even when the evidence of unhappiness, incompatibility and actual physical violence seems inescapable. Several studies have concluded that the conditions under which the divorce takes place affect a child's ultimate emotional stability: if there were many rows and scenes, heard or witnessed by the child, she is likely to be more disturbed, and for longer, than she would be if the break was a reasonable, amicable one – much more disturbed, in the long term, than she would have been by a parent's death. The children of widows, in fact, seem to be more resilient than those of 'messy' divorces. But in both cases, the provision of a stable, reasonably happy environment after the event is the best base for recovery from the original trauma.

However, even if the child knows that the separation was necessary, she can be slow to accept it emotionally. A few days after her divorce was finalised, the mother of eight- and nine-year-old children said: 'Although the separation was a very gradual affair – for a year before we moved away their father had not been living with us, but nearby, and he saw the children every day – they were surprised and upset when I finally took them away. They were too young to really understand. Even now – three years later – they still have a childish hankering after an ideal world. When we split up we told them that we no longer loved each other in the way we had. In a way they accepted that – but they still often ask whether I still love their father. It's difficult – because I don't. I must admit I'm not completely honest. I have to hedge, which I wouldn't do with an adult. And so I think of the last time we saw him when we had a good time together, and say "I'm very fond of him". It's an approximation to the truth: I think it would be damaging if I actually said I didn't love him.'

Judith Wallerstein and Joan Berlin Kelly in an American study of 60 divorcing families found that although many of the children 'had lived for years in an unhappy home, they did not experience the divorce as a solution to their unhappiness, nor did they greet it with relief at the time, or for several years thereafter'.

If, as this study shows, the effects of a break-up can last for a very long time, how can you best handle the impact of divorce on your children? The answer seems to lie in the way you tell them what has been happening, and why the separation was necessary. 'When he understands the divorce is a serious and carefully considered remedy for an important problem, when the divorce seems purposefully and rationally undertaken, and indeed succeeds in bringing relief and a happier outcome to one or both parents,' say Wallerstein and Kelly, '. . . though the transition period may be difficult, the child's overall sense of coherence and order is not undermined.'

This study also underlines the need for parents to remain in close touch and, however bitter the recriminations have been when the family was together, to avoid involving the children in quarrels and, above all, not use them as tools in a prolonged struggle over rights and duties. Once the divorce is a fact, it should be accepted, and all efforts directed at rebuilding relationships in the new situation of one-parent family'.

This ideal can be difficult to attain, of course, if situations arise such as those described earlier in this book, when an ex-husband may refuse to pay maintenance for his children and the only redress their mother can find is to refuse him access to the children until he pays up.

'I was driven to desperate measures,' says Catherine. He demanded his right to see the children. I didn't see why he should take them out, spend a lot of money on treats and presents, and then dump them back on me without a penny for their keep. I was angry that the children could see him as kind, jolly, generous Dad while I was always nagging at them if they wore their shoes out too quickly, and didn't give them money for sweets. I'm ashamed now of the doorstep struggles we had when he called. It was only much later, when I was settled in a job and he'd actually faded out of the picture, that the children were able to appreciate what the real situation had been. They're bitter about him now – they've gone to the other extreme. I did try to avoid that, but I suppose they're only reacting to what they now understand.'

**Lack of money**
Most widowed or divorced women are faced by a much reduced standard of living, and like one mother, find that this leads to problems with their children. She says that her children have found it difficult to adjust to lack of money, especially while she was unemployed, and especially when their father on their visits to him was able to spend more lavishly on them.

'I think that like many people in my position I'm a bit inconsistent about money. We're very hard up, but sometimes I just feel like taking them out and not worrying about spending £5. The next day I find it hard to explain that we have to walk to school rather than catch a bus.'

All the same, the children are beginning to understand the reasons for the difference between their father's relative affluence and their mother's shortage of money. 'I do less explaining now. And although my daughter sometimes finds it hard to accept that she can't have something she wants and seems to see my refusal as a sort of rejection, her brother sees that he doesn't need, and simply can't have, a third ice cream.'

This change is part of this mother's policy of gradually taking her children into her confidence, explaining as much to them as she thinks they are able to absorb at the time. She has had to go through some difficult experiences and careful thought before she reached her present attitude. 'When they were tiny I thought we should be totally truthful. I had a very idealised view of a relationship of complete honesty. I tried to carry this out, but I've realised since that to be completely honest with people there needs to be a basis of equality, and equality of understanding. So I've had to modify this rather extreme view of how you should involve children because there are certain things they can't grasp. Apart from that, I've always tried to tell them the truth as far as I thought they could understand it at their particular age.'

As this mother is finding every day, children can be capable of facing more than we often expect of them. Just how much will depend on your knowledge and empathic understanding of your individual child.

# The child who's upset

All the same, we can't ignore the fact that many women's experience does confirm the research findings: children can be disturbed by the disruption of their lives caused by the break-up of their parents' relationship. If you are clearly upset and disorientated by what has happened to you, it would demand a superhuman effort to conceal this from your children, and every mother has the experience of finding her moods reflected in the behaviour of even the youngest baby. Sadness, anxiety, tension are communicated without your being aware of it. Just at a time when you need the maximum support and help in sorting out your own feelings and actions you can find yourself isolated with children who are reacting with grief, hostility, school refusal and disruptive behaviour at home and outside it. And you have no partner with whom to share this extra burden. Even if in your marriage you felt you had little support in dealing with problems connected with the children, you could at least sound off about them. Now there's no one to listen.

Before you consider getting professional help, it would be worthwhile thinking about the network of friends and relatives with whom you might discuss the problems. Any one of them who is a parent will have met at least some of the difficulties with which you are now faced, and most women are only too glad to share their ideas and experiences. If they're wise, they won't offer hard advice: if *you're* wise, you won't take it uncritically. After all, the child is yours and you know her/him best. But what you really want is a sounding board, someone with whom to try out ideas, to listen while you sort them out. Throughout this book you'll find suggestions about different kinds of support groups. If you have no close friends, you could find help and friendship in one of these.

If the main problem seems to be concerning the child at school, try talking to the Head or the class teacher. Not all will be understanding or sympathetic, but some will be. The school should have been informed, and be kept informed, about the major change that's happened at home, and in crisis situations a good teacher will make allowances, provide an outlet for turbulent emotions and be someone outside the immediate situation to whom the child can turn as a friend. If the problem at school seems insoluble the child may be referred for child guidance, and perhaps the whole family for family therapy – but this won't, and shouldn't, be considered until every other resource available to you and the child has been tried.

If the difficulties are mainly connected with the home, you may prefer not to involve the school directly, but to ask your doctor or the Samaritans (telephone number in local directory) for help. Should the child be referred on for psychiatric assessment and help, you should give your consent for the school to be informed, unless you are quite sure of a stigmatising or hostile reception there.

### Don't push!

One of the problems quite often met by lone parents is caused by their need to be both mother and father to their children, to make sure they are not disadvantaged by the loss of one parent, in fact to prove to themselves and the world that their child is a perfect specimen and they haven't done the wrong thing in agreeing to the divorce or separation. Many parents are prone to attempting to fulfil themselves through their children. The temptation to do so may be greater if you are on your own.

'My daughter is academically brilliant but she just won't work,' wrote one mother. 'Of course she was upset when her father left home, and over the divorce three years later. But she's older now – ten – and surely she can't still be disturbed about it. I do everything I can to encourage her. I make sure she sits down at a regular time every day to do some homework, even when it hasn't been set. I take her to ballet lessons, she learns both piano and violin. I take her to the library regularly – but I'm appalled at the babyish books she would like to choose. Every time I see her teacher or read a school report, it's the same thing. She doesn't try, she's got a good brain but doesn't use it, she daydreams in class, she's untidy and feckless.'

To some readers this quotation from the letter written to a woman's magazine may seem like a caricature. The mother in question, however, may be only a rather extreme example of someone who for her own reasons is so ambitious for her daughter that she can't see how the child is using the only weapon available to her in her need for personal space – non-co-operation. She's ready to dismiss as unimportant the child's upset over the family situation, believing that by doing all that she does for her daughter, pushing her on to live up to her 'academic' potential, she is compensating for the loss of a parent.

Not all lone parents act in such an extreme way – and of course there are still-married parents who are just as over-ambitious and controlling of their children – but there is a potential danger when there is no other counter-influence in the home. If your child could even remotely match the picture presented in that letter, could you, too, be 'compensating' her in a similar way? Everyone, not least children, needs to be allowed to develop at their own pace and in their own way and parents who have tried to force the pace have lived to regret it in later years. A child who is anxious to please her mother and compensate *her* for all the trouble she's gone through may fall in with the mother's aims, be a 'good' girl and pass all the examinations at the right time and with high grades, only to break down or break out in late adolescence when she is finally able to react to all the pressure of earlier years. Many of the so-called teenage problems can be traced to a history of parental over-ambition. No child can live up to an image of 'perfection' set before her by a loved parent and failure to do so is one potent cause of depression, which may not manifest itself until many years later.

# Adolescent agonies

Few adults can look back with pleasure and satisfaction at their teen years. Many parents, even if they have had very happy relationships with their children, dread the problems and conflicts that so often arise with adolescents. When they do, parents sometimes hardly know what has hit them. Once more it's a question of having to cope alone; and once more, talking to friends and counsellors can help. The growing girl or boy may feel the need for counselling, too, if teachers, youth leaders and friends aren't able to help. But the desire for counselling must come from the young person her- or himself. Parental pressure to 'get help' is a sure way to put the teenager off trying to find it.

'My son was a terrible problem to me. Looking back, I don't know that his behaviour was any worse than that of lots of fifteen- or sixteen-year-olds. But although I had felt that I was managing very well on my own up till then, I suddenly found myself longing for a man – even his father

# A helpful book

. . . for anyone trying to cope with an adolescent and her or his problems is *Help! I've got a Teenager!* by Robert T. Bayard, PhD, and Jean Bayard, PhD. These American clinical psychologists, who have brought up five children and see many hundreds of adolescents and parents in their California practice, offer sensible advice to help readers change their own attitudes towards their 'difficult' children. They show how the most helpful thing a parent can do to preserve her own sanity and allow her children to grow towards responsibility and independence is to stand back and not attempt to impose her own will and her own standards on the rebellious teenager. Although the authors are American, editing for a British market has been well done and the advice and information given apply fully to this side of the Atlantic.

– to put him right. Peter was terribly aggressive and rude to me and my friends, wouldn't do anything to help in the house, stayed out all night without telling me where he was, or else came home drunk. He and his friends took over the flat, playing loud pop music and preventing his sister from studying and actually using physical violence on her when she protested. I know he was part of a group that stole things from shops, though he never got caught. It was particularly worrying as I had to go out to work and I never knew what he was up to during the day – I had a pretty good idea he was bunking off from school.

'Then things changed. The school started working with computers and that really grabbed Peter. He must have decided that if he bunked off he'd miss out on the computer. He decided to get a Saturday job and saved up for a home computer. He put birthday and Christmas money towards it, and his grandmother – my mother-in-law, who'd always been interested in the children and kept fully in touch – gave him £50. After nearly a year he had his computer and became quite involved with it. He decided that he wanted to work with computers as a career – and if he was to do that, he'd have to get qualified. This meant O levels for a start. Rather late in the day he began to really work at school, and although his teachers had thought he'd never be able to sit any kind of exams he took seven subjects and passed all of them – with four very good grades. Now he's in the sixth form, doing A level work and intending to go on to university or polytechnic. Just as important, he's a different boy at home.'

This woman's story underlines what many parents have found – that aimless or destructive behaviour in an adolescent is often a matter of lack of interest and incentive

# Drug problems

If your child is taking drugs or you suspect that s/he might be, contact The Lifeline Project (pamphlets and reading list, comprehensive service for drug-users) or Release (see 'Directory').

---

in school work. Once a real interest is aroused – whether it's by an inspired teacher or by a new subject – the girl or boy is motivated and sees that earlier activities are a waste of time. Things are much more difficult for the adolescent who fails to find himself or herself in this way, and who like so many hundreds of thousands in the 1980s has no prospect of a training or a job. The hopelessness that this situation breeds is not, of course, anything to do with being the child of a 'one-parent family' – and the solution is a social and political one which is more than the purely personal concern of the individual mother. But anyone at the end of her tether trying to cope with a difficult adolescent could think how she would have felt and behaved in a similar situation in her own youth, and, insupportable as the behaviour may seem to her, she will realise that to be *in* that situation is even more insupportable for her daughter or son. It certainly isn't a problem that affects the victims alone and if adults don't take action in whatever way they think appropriate they can't blame the victims for taking action of which they disapprove.

Many women with adolescent children will be forming new relationships and these can be a cause of family problems. A new 'father figure' doesn't necessarily mean that the situation with children is any easier – being a stepparent can be fraught with difficulties. If the new relationship is with a woman other, different problems may arise. We'll be looking at some of these in Chapter 17, along with the stories of some women who have managed to cope successfully with long- or short-term lovers' relationships with their children.

---

# Counselling services

The National Association of Young People's Counselling and Advisory Services, National Youth Bureau (see 'Directory') co-ordinates various youth counselling agencies throughout the UK. Send s.a.e. for a list of local projects if you can't find one under the name of 'Off the Record', 'Open Door', 'Contact', 'Link', 'Under 21', 'Chat' etc., or through your council's Social Services Department.

---

# Grown-up children

There can be few mothers who would prefer to keep their children dependent. Research in the United States has shown that, far from wanting to keep the nest full, a majority of mothers are only too delighted when their offspring have flown. The 'empty nest' syndrome, so often blamed for 'menopausal' women's depression, is, in fact, a myth. Most mothers look forward to the transformation of their dependent young people into independent, loving friends. There may be problems along the way, while the adolescent daughter or son launches out alone, but if the relationship has basically been a good one, the happy day will come when past conflicts will be seen as trivial, and the common background of experience and outlook asserts itself. The day when you find yourself asking your daughter's advice about some problem marks the beginning of a relationship of equality that can be one of the most satisfying to you both.

It's when this happens that you can find that your daughter or son is the best possible support to you if you are lonely or upset. While keeping your own independence – so hard-won, perhaps, over the years – you will respect theirs.

'I am very anxious not to interfere in my adult children's lives,' says Penny. 'I brought them up to be independent – they had to be, at a very early age, because I had to work hard to keep the family going. I've always asked myself – and I still do – whether I'm offering gratuitous advice when I feel like intervening in their lives. If they ask my advice – fine, I'll give it, even though they may not take it. If they don't ask, I don't offer it. I've sometimes seen them making what I thought were bad mistakes. If they didn't consult me, I didn't say anything. Sometimes I was right, sometimes they were. I try to see them as close friends. I wouldn't muscle in on a friend's marital problems, for instance, so I don't with theirs, and there have been some. In the end they may consult me, just as any good friend might do, and then I say what I think. They treat me in the same way.'

# Grandchildren

Similar self-imposed rules apply to a successful relationship with grandchildren and their parents. We all want to get away from the stereotype of interfering grandparents, and most manage to do so without trouble. Yet there are still some 'baby books' around that advise young parents to ignore, or even keep away from, the 'interfering' mother or mother-in-law. Not only is this hurtful to an older woman who believes in the autonomy and independence of her adult children, but it can be damaging if it deprives the baby's parents of her wisdom and support. The baby or older child, too, will miss out on what can be a very joyful and rewarding relationship.

Child care practice changes as society changes. An older woman knows this – after all, she has lived through the various shifts of opinion handed down as gospel by the 'experts'. She expects that her daughter or daughter-in-law will follow the most recent trend, just as she did with her own children. Each generation believes it is doing the best thing for its offspring, reads the most recent literature and consults the currently fashionable 'authority'. A grand-mother may feel that the baby isn't being handled in the way *she* would choose. But that baby isn't hers; it's the parents (mainly the mother) who have to care for it 24 hours a day, and in general they choose to do it their way. Where a grandmother can be of enormous help is in taking the anxiety out of the young mother's situation, helping her to take a more relaxed attitude towards any problems she is encountering. Anyone who has successfully reared her own children knows that with each successive child the panics and worries lessen and 'doing what comes naturally' becomes easier. That is wisdom that can be passed on – a generalisation that can be applied without in any way telling the younger woman what to do.

'By the time my daughter's first baby was born I had been divorced for many years,' says Joan. 'I was about to retire. When my own children were growing up I was much too busy to do more than give them a reasonably comfortable home and some attention at weekends. In some ways I felt I'd missed out on their childhood. I had to be very careful not to try to compensate for this by involving myself too closely with Carol's family. When she went back to work I could have offered to look after the toddler – but I didn't. I was too afraid of "taking over". So Carol made her own arrangements with a child minder, and I provided a back-up service when the minder was ill, or in an emergency I came in to look after the child in her home. As a retired person with no one but myself to bother about this was easy to arrange, and Carol was very grateful. I don't think it would have worked if I'd had the child every day.'

Now that Carol has two children Joan's friendship with them is very precious to her, to Carol and the children. They see as much of each other as the children want, Joan still steps in in an emergency and if *she's* ill the grandchildren are solicitous and helpful. Like many grandmothers she's experiencing all over again the more positive aspects of caring for children. But she's involved herself in a voluntary job so that her daughter's family isn't the sole focus of her otherwise solitary life.

# PART IV

# YOUR HEALTH AND WELL-BEING

*Learn to take pleasure in your responsibility for your own health. You will reap the benefits as you find you can keep physically and socially active on into your later years.*

# CHAPTER 15
# FIT AND WELL

**In this section we look at the ways in which a woman of any age can maintain her health and fitness, and discuss the role of stress in the development of illness and disabling conditions.**

If good general health is important for everybody who wants to function at top capacity and to enjoy life as far as possible, it is even more vital for the woman on her own to do everything she can to keep well or to regain past fitness. She is perhaps more likely than most to be affected by the strains of daily living; and ill health can be particularly difficult to tolerate when there's no one else at home to offer help and support.

The media pour out a wealth of information on health matters, so in theory it ought to be possible for all of us to keep to some basic health rules. But so much material that appears in print is confusing and contradictory, and there are so many changing fashions in diet, exercise and other aspects of body maintenance that some of us simply give up and carry on as before, hoping for the best. We know that too much stress is bad for us – but how can it be avoided if we have to earn a living, care for a family, cope with the emotional problems of ourselves and others?

## Are there health rules?

A healthy body depends to some extent on heredity – and we can't do anything about that. Well-being depends, too, on a good environment, and that is only to a limited extent within our control. Two vital aspects of health are, however, influenced by factors that most people *can* control – diet and exercise. And – perhaps with difficulty – we can avoid taking into our bodies substances that are known to have harmful potential – cigarette smoke and too much alcohol.

You may not want to turn into a health freak, obsessed with weight control, dietary fibre, vitamin intake and daily

## Healthline

A telephone information service is run by the College of Health, 18 Victoria Park Square, London E2 9PF, in collaboration with the Exeter Health Authority and with assistance from the Gloucester Health Education Services.

You can dial (01) 980 4848 any day between 6p.m. and 9p.m. for recorded information lasting 2–6 minutes on a range of health topics and approved by a panel of medical experts. The service is free except for the cost of the telephone call. A directory of the topics covered by the service costs £1.00 from the College of Health. Ask for the tape you want by number (if you have the directory) or tell the Healthline operator the topic you want to know about. Have pencil and paper handy to note down information.

jogging. But there are some basic rules and simple measures that can be adopted by almost anyone, and if they are followed consistently for a while they become so much part of daily life that they are second nature. And if they *are* followed consistently the benefits will be so obvious that no one would willingly revert to her former state of half-health. None of the rules is difficult to understand, or too expensive to adopt; and even taking more exercise, which *does* often involve setting aside some time in the day which many will believe they can't afford, need not involve as much as they may think.

In later chapters we'll be looking at the special problems that may be faced at the time of the menopause and in old age. But it's true to say that in the absence of specific and life-threatening disease most women can get a good deal fitter than they are, no matter what their age. So now we'll look at how this can be done.

## Well Women Clinics

In many areas there are Well Women Clinics. A few of them offer Family Planning services only but most offer some form of screening as well. You can get the address of your nearest one from the Community Health Council, whose address and telephone number are in the local telephone directory.

## Organise for Health

There are a number of organisations which both campaign for health and provide information about health issues in general and women's health in particular. They are listed in the 'Directory' at the end of this book under the general heading "Health".

# A guide to healthy eating

## A good diet

The saying that 'we are what we eat' is very largely true. In recent years a wealth of research confirms that diet plays a crucial role in the development of a number of disease processes, and its importance as an influence on our general health is becoming increasingly obvious. A good diet doesn't necessarily mean 'dieting' in the sense of losing or gaining weight through what is eaten or avoided. In fact, much of the information on slimming diets has been misinformation and has caused health problems that didn't exist before as well as failure to achieve the desired weight.

Moreover, much of the received wisdom about the 'right' proportions of protein, fats and carbohydrates has also come under strong criticism. Ten years ago an overweight woman would avoid bread, potatoes and other carbohydrates in the belief that these foods were making her fat. She might adopt a 'high protein' diet, or one high in fat, which was somehow credited with the ability to burn up the calories in the carbohydrates. Now it seems to be very clear that a healthy diet is also a slimming diet – and that means that the balance of nutrients recommended for health as well as for appearance has shifted from the high-protein 'reduce-carbohydrates-and-the-fats-will-take-care-of-themselves' diet to one in which fat intake is reduced to a maximum of 30 per cent of the energy-producing foods with the major calorie content provided by various forms of carbohydrates and proteins – the latter not necessarily animal in origin.

The 'fattening' and unhealthy element in so many carbohydrate-rich foods is not so much in the carbohydrate content itself as in the fats and sugar that so often seem disguised within them. Potatoes in themselves aren't high in calories; but serve them as chips, crisps or roast and they've soaked up the fat that is. Cakes and pastries and puddings whose main ingredient might appear to be flour (carbohydrate) also contain sizeable proportions of fat, and probably some sugar as well. The sugar, of course, is an empty-calorie 'food' – a form of carbohydrate that has no real nutritional value except as a provider of instant, short-term, and probably unnecessary energy.

The woman on her own may be fully aware of what constitutes a healthy diet; but because it's difficult to take much interest in food when eating alone – especially if she's been used to preparing meals for the enjoyment of others – and because she may be short of money, she can

## Guide to healthy eating

| Eat more: | Eat less: | Avoid – or eat sparingly and very occasionally: |
|---|---|---|
| Fruit, fresh, or dried without added sugar | Butter | Cream |
| Vegetables, fresh, uncooked or lightly cooked, root or green | Margarine (use polyunsaturated) | Pork meat, including ham |
| | Whole milk (substitute skimmed) | Sausages |
| Beans, dried, all varieties | Meat (remove visible fat before cooking; do not fry) | Continental sausage |
| Lentils and pulses | | Meat pâtés |
| Sprouted beans | Cheese (use low-fat varieties – Edam, and of course cottage cheese) | Cream cheese, stilton, Danish blue, parmesan and processed |
| Wholemeal bread | | Condensed milk |
| Wholemeal flour | Eggs (not more than three whole eggs a week) | Ice cream |
| Wheat germ | | Cakes, pastries, sweet biscuits |
| Bran (but avoid processed bran which has added sugar, and see p. 291) | Cooking oil (use corn oil, sunflower or safflower) | Sugar, including 'brown' |
| | Nuts | Honey |
| Natural yogurt, sugarless | | Jam, marmalade, pickles |
| Fish, white (cod, plaice etc.) or oily (herrings, sardines, mackerel) | | Chocolate and sweets |
| | | Salt |
| Brown rice | | Crisps |
| Wholemeal pasta | | Processed peanuts |
| | | Convenience foods, including hamburgers, fish and chips and other 'fast foods' |
| | | Lard |
| | | Suet |
| | | Non-polyunsaturated margarine |
| | | Canned fruit in syrup |

**Alcohol**
Medical opinion is divided – some say 1–2 glasses of wine a day is beneficial, others suggest avoiding all alcohol. Alcohol in pregnancy should be avoided, and sufferers from high blood pressure or heart conditions should be very moderate drinkers. Alcohol and tranquillisers and some other drugs don't mix.

find herself living on snacks, convenience foods, tea and coffee both during the working day and when she gets home in the evening. If this is the pattern you've fallen into, you should consider how to change your diet to a healthier one that won't be too troublesome to prepare or too costly. It can be done.

If we look first at the typical diet of many people who live alone we can see how this change can be brought about. The table on the next page shows this.

Note that an adult needs far less of the body-building protein foods than most of us eat – and if meat is cut to about three servings a week this will also mean a consider-able reduction in fat intake. For anyone with a heart

| Breakfast | change to |
|---|---|
| Tea or coffee, with or without toast and butter | Tea or coffee, low-fat milk, sugarless muesli |

| Mid-morning | change to |
|---|---|
| Tea or coffee | Tea or coffee only – muesli breakfast still |
| Biscuits or bun and butter | satisfies |

| Lunch | change to |
|---|---|
| Cheese or ham sandwiches | uncooked salad with nuts and raisins or low- |
| Cake or chocolate biscuits | fat cheese, wholemeal roll |
| or fried foods with chips and ice cream | Natural yogurt and a piece of fresh fruit |

| Mid-afternoon | change to |
|---|---|
| Tea | Tea |
| Cake or bun and butter | Fresh fruit or bran biscuit |

| Dinner | change to |
|---|---|
| Chop and two vegetables or | Meat with visible fat removed, grilled or roast |
| Omelette or egg and bacon or | or |
| Sausage and tomato or | Fish (not fried) or |
| Meat pie or other convenience food with or | Pasta dish with non-meat sauce or |
| without vegetables | Beans with rice and low-fat sauce or |
| Tinned fruit and cream or biscuits and cake or | other vegetarian dish |
| biscuits and cheese | Vegetables and/or salad to accompany above |
| Coffee with whole milk | Fresh fruit and/or low-fat cheese with |
| | wholemeal bread |
| | Coffee – black or with skimmed milk |

condition, not more than three eggs per week are recommended (egg yolks are high in cholesterol, which is possibly implicated in heart disease) and this is a reasonable rule to follow for everyone. Spreading fat should be mainly 'high in polyunsaturates' margarine, and with bread and cheese it's quite possible to do without butter or margarine altogether.

The modified diet suggested above meets all the criteria for a healthy diet, and it is not expensive. Just cutting down on meat, or cutting it out altogether, can save a lot of money which, if you have it, is better spent on fresh fruit. However, before adopting a completely vegetarian diet you should consult some of the books listed on p. 268. It's quite possible to keep healthy on a non-meat diet, as well as making good ecological sense – but a little more care is needed in planning the menus so that all nutritional requirements are met. The recipe books suggested in this chapter offer a huge selection of vegetarian dishes, many of them simple to prepare and with easily obtained ingredients. Watch, too, for magazine recipes – there's an increasing interest in the media in vegetarian food – and for Colin Spencer's regular articles in the *Guardian*. Many women, bored with a lifetime of 'meat and two veg' meals, have found a new interest in cooking as a result of going vegetarian. It's no longer the 'nut cutlets' type of diet that used to be seen as typical vegetarian fare: in countries where meat is scarce, or forbidden for religious reasons, a wealth of dishes have been devised which can easily be adopted by Western cooks.

That said, there's no need to be fanatical or puritanical about what you eat. An occasional treat for a special meal when you don't bother about calories or high-fat content or too much sugar is neither going to make you fat or kill you. Just don't make a habit of it!

### What about supplements?

Medical opinion in general is quite firm – an adult on 'a normal, balanced diet' doesn't need vitamin or mineral supplements. The 'health food' industry, on the other hand, derives much of its profit from the sale of capsules and tablets containing various vitamins and supplementary minerals, and sundry enthusiasts propagandise on behalf of their particular pet vitamin or mineral.

The whole subject is full of ifs and buts. The first 'if' involves the question 'what is a normal, balanced diet?' And furthermore, 'do most people get it?' For many, the answer has to be a qualified 'no'.

Vitamin C, for instance, is mainly supplied by fresh fruit and (preferably uncooked) vegetables. Many people, even when they can afford to buy these items, some of which are quite expensive, do not get them in a really 'fresh' condition. Vitamin C content decreases as harvested vegetables age, quite apart from the loss involved in common cooking methods. So it may be that people unable to pick their own vegetables straight from garden or allotment either have to eat more of them and more fruit, or take some form of supplementary Vitamin C, for their diet to provide enough for health.

The next question we have to ask – and this also applies to Vitamin C requirements as well as those for certain other vitamins and minerals – is: what exactly are the daily

---

## Why you should cut down on . . .

**Sugar**. It causes a build-up of plaque on the teeth which leads to tooth decay and gum troubles; it is linked with obesity and diabetes.

**Fats**. They are implicated in heart disease and overweight, in itself a cause of many other health problems.

**Salt**. This has been linked with high blood pressure and kidney disease.

---

requirements? Again taking Vitamin C as an example, the recommended daily intake – 45 mg per day in the United States – is believed by many American researchers to be sufficient only to keep ill-health (scurvy and other skin disorders) at bay. They believe that a diet that promotes health would include an intake of not less than 200 mg a day. The British recommended intake is even lower.

Finally there is the question of special needs for special groups of people, and here there is a certain amount of agreement. Children, pregnant women and lactating mothers have long been prescribed extra Vitamins A and D. Smokers and those who drink more than a very moderate amount of alcohol need extra Vitamin C. The elderly probably need some form of supplementation of certain vitamins and minerals – not least because their diet may be inadequate. Those people who for various reasons don't get enough sunshine on their skins may be deficient in Vitamin D. And recent research has made a strong case for supplementation of Vitamin B6 (50–100 mg a day or more) for women suffering from 'pre-menstrual tension', while for the same group some success has been claimed for supplementation of the diet by Evening Primrose oil in capsule form.

One of the reasons advanced for the avoidance of vitamin supplements is the possibility of overdose by cranks and other enthusiasts. Very large quantities of Vitamins A and D have certainly caused problems – a classic, often-quoted case is of the man who lived and died on carrot-juice, of which he drank enormous quantities daily; and a few babies whose intake of Vitamin D was far beyond normal requirements have developed bone and skull abnormalities. A simple rule to follow is to differentiate between the 'fat-soluble' and 'water-soluble' vitamins. The former – A, D, and E; also K, not usually provided in supplement form – are stored in the body and therefore overdoses are theoretically possible if large quantities are taken. Vitamins in the B group – there are many – and Vitamin C are water-

## Vegetarian eating

Major bookshops and health food shops stock numerous cook books on meatless eating. Three suggested titles are:
*Gail Duff's Vegetarian Cookbook* (Pan)
*Middle Eastern Vegetarian Cookery* by David Scott (Rider)

*Eastern Vegetarian Cooking* by Madhur Jaffrey (Cape)
The Vegetarian Society and the Vegan Society can provide information and produce various publications, including cook books.

soluble, which means that normally any excess is excreted; because they are not stored in the body small quantities (mainly or entirely derived from food) need to be consumed daily. Huge doses of *any* vitamin, however, can be too much for the body to cope with.

A comprehensive handbook on nutrition particularly as it affects the ability of the body to heal itself is *Health on Your Plate* by Janet Pleshette (Hamlyn Paperbacks). The sections on vitamins and minerals, their effect on health, and in which foodstuffs they are to be found, are well worth reading, even if you don't completely go along with the nutritional approach to natural therapies.

### What about food additives?
Not least of the advantages of living on the sort of diet suggested earlier in this chapter is the fact that, by cutting out junk foods, bought snacks and 'fast' meals you'll almost completely avoid the doubtful additives that industry is now pumping into these items to 'enhance flavour' or 'prolong shelf-life'. Almost completely – because unfortunately it isn't possible to eat the proverbial apple-a-day, unless it's extremely well washed, without consuming a small dose of pesticide or even some form of coating designed to preserve the fruit or improve its appearance. The fibre in the apple's skin should be a useful addition to your diet – but unless you've grown your own, have bought it from an impeccable source or really scrubbed it clean you may decide to sacrifice the fibre along with the chemicals. The same may apply to vegetables – even cooking, which can destroy Vitamin C, *won't* necessarily affect the residue of pesticides and weedkillers that may have been applied to the growing vegetables. And many people are worried about the growth hormones and anti-biotics used on animals in intensive rearing conditions – traces can remain in carcasses sold as fresh meat or meat products: another reason why you might decide to cut down on meat in your diet or cut it out altogether.

### Good food – summed up
On p. 265 you'll find lists of foods divided into three groups: those you should eat more of, those you'd do well to cut down on, and those to be generally avoided. As a woman on your own, or in charge of a growing family, it may seem too complicated to change the style of eating that's been your pattern for many years. Your children may be particularly resistant, even if you aren't. But most of us,

## Food additives

Many foods are now packaged with labels showing 'E' numbers, as required by EEC regulations. These numbers indicate what additives are included in the food, and a booklet listing the numbers and what they mean can be obtained free from the Ministry of Agriculture, Fisheries and Food.

Write to the Ministry at Whitehall Place, London SW1, for this booklet called 'Look for the Label'.

Considerably more informative, however, is *E for Additives* by Maurice Hansen (Thorsons) because it decodes the EEC numbers and shows which foods contain which additives, along with their possibly adverse effects. It's particularly useful if you are considering possible allergy in yourself or a child.

adults or children, can be gradually persuaded to change our eating habits. Some years ago, when wholemeal bread was a rarity eaten mainly by 'health freaks', a London doctor introduced it into a ward of men suffering from various 'diseases of civilisation'. Most of them, like the rest of the population at the time, were sliced white-bread addicts. When they were told that the wholemeal bread was part of their treatment, they were prepared to grin and bear it. It wasn't very long before a majority of the patients began to prefer wholemeal to white bread, and new admissions to the ward were faced with propaganda from fellow-patients persuading them to start on the wholemeal bread on grounds of taste as well as health. There's no information about their ability to convert their families on their discharge from hospital – but if they succeeded as well with them as with their ward-mates there should have been a big reduction in digestive and other disorders in the locality.

As we've seen, the first step on the road to conversion to healthy eating can be to avoid convenience foods. That will cut consumption of fats, sugar and additives, and equally important, automatically increase consumption of fibre, vitamins and essential minerals. The next step is to begin to follow the suggestions in the lists on p. 265. Once that is achieved, you'll not only feel a lot better, but you will actually develop a distaste for most of the foods on the 'Avoid' list. (If you don't believe this, ask anyone who's given up taking sugar in tea. They'll tell you that even after a few weeks accidentally-sugared tea tastes positively disgusting and aversive.)

But the major reason for the changes suggested is that they will benefit your health in the long term. You will be less likely to develop heart disease, or, if you're already at risk, less likely to develop it sooner rather than later; less likely to develop some forms of cancer; less likely to suffer from digestive problems such as diverticulosis. And more likely to live to enjoy a healthy old age.

However, the picture of health we all want to present now and in the future involves more than eating a good diet. We'll go on to look at some other important factors.

# Exercise

### How much exercise?

The fitness boom in recent years is most obvious when we see every park or open space teeming with runners and joggers, and every high street with its exercise studio. Women who don't much feel like taking up some form of exercise or sport – and most of us are physically lazy or mentally over-stressed – comfort themselves with the stories of joggers dying of heart attacks and damage done to joints and muscles by over-enthusiastic aerobics. Who wants to court such trouble? Then there's the expense of special clothing and footwear, and the strong suspicion that some of the exercise studios are run by people out to make a fast buck, and untrained into the bargain.

No doubt about it: sudden and violent physical exercise can be harmful. Every responsible fitness expert suggests that if you're not used to exertion you should start very, very slowly, and that any programme of exercise should be geared not only to age but to general physical condition. It doesn't matter if it takes six months or a year to build up to a good exercise routine – the main thing is to make sure that you take *some* exercise on most, if not all, days of the week. You can do this in your own home and in your own neighbourhood, it needn't take up much valuable time, and you don't need to buy any special equipment or clothing or pay steep fees to some entrepreneur for training.

But what is it all about? What will you be aiming at? We'll be looking at the role of exercise in weight control later (see pp. 278–81) and it certainly should be part of any attempt at 'slimming'. But from the pure health point of view there are benefits to be gained whether or not you're overweight.

An exercise programme has three aims – to develop strength, mobility and stamina – and there are exercises which will achieve these aims. You can get some help from reading about the kinds of exercise you need in the Health

Education Council's booklet *Looking After Yourself* (see 'Directory'). Here we describe some 'warm-up' exercises for beginners – whether you go on to something more strenuous or simply stick with these is up to you. The bookshops are full of exercise books and programmes, women's magazines often have pages devoted to exercise routines, and there are audio and video tapes available in record shops. The merit of the latter is that they usually provide musical accompaniment, and that does make things go with a greater swing.

### Exercises for mobility

The aim here is to exercise the various joints in your body so that you remain supple or regain some of the mobility you may have lost through lack of full use of the joints over the years. In addition to the few minutes a day you'll need to run through the exercises shown on the following pages you can help yourself by keeping the joints mobile at odd times while you're sitting at a desk, travelling in a bus or standing at the kitchen sink. Working from the feet upwards you can clench and relax your toes, rotate the ankles, bend and stretch the knees and so on, right through the body, up to the neck and shoulders. Older women whose joints are quite stiff can feel an amazing improvement with just this kind of exercise alone. They do keep the worst effects of osteo-arthritis at bay. But for full effect, try to find time for the exercises we illustrate, at least three times a week.

### Exercises for stamina

Here's where caution is most important. If you're in any doubt about undertaking an exercise programme, check with your doctor. If you're over forty-five and inactive, check anyway.

But almost anyone can walk or swim, both forms of exercise can easily be graduated, and both are excellent for improving stamina. Get up 10 minutes earlier and walk part of the way to work or the shops, if you normally use public transport. If you have a good, safe open space nearby for walking make use of it, but some people find walking for walking's sake tedious, and if you walk to work or the shops at least you're going somewhere and possibly saving money into the bargain. Depending on your degree of fitness, start with, say, 10 minutes' fairly brisk walking, and gradually increase the time until you can walk for an hour without strain. You should try to do this at least three times a week, never allowing more than two days to pass without this walk. (For the effect on metabolism, see p. 280).

If you're well able to walk some distance or climb a flight of stairs without getting puffed you should be able to undertake some exercises for stamina. These could be slow jogging, very gradually increasing to a longer distance and increased speed; or running - again, be cautious. They *should* make you slightly breathless and raise your heart rate – the idea *is* to 'exercise' the heart, which is, in effect, a large muscle; you may be anxious about doing this. But there's a good way to make sure you're not overdoing it. Take your pulse – two fingers on the pulse point on the inside of the wrist – while resting. Use a watch or clock with a second hand, and count the beats over 30 seconds. Double the number to find your pulse rate per minute. It's probably about 74.

When you start to exercise, stop after a few minutes – when you begin to get slightly out of breath – and take your pulse. Do this at once. Assuming that you have no heart disease or other reason for not exercising – which you should have checked – the safe rate of heart-beat is calculated as follows: your age subtracted from 170 when you first start. When you've been exercising for longer, the maximum exercise heart rate should be your age subtracted from 200. So:

| | |
|---|---|
| If you're 40 your maximum heart rate when you start exercising will be: ....................170 − 40 = 130 | **Work up gradually!** |
| and when you're in better shape: ....................200 − 40 = 160 | |
| If you're 65 your maximum heart rate when you start exercising will be: ....................170 − 65 = 105 | **Work up gradually!** |
| and when you're in better shape: ....................200 − 65 = 135 | |

At first you should take your pulse at frequent intervals after this kind of exercise, and stop until the rate has returned to the 'resting' rate you've already discovered, before continuing. After you've been exercising regularly for a couple of weeks or so, it's enough to do this check once a week. This walking or stair-climbing suits most people. Although parks and open spaces teem with runners and joggers, you can reach a good degree of fitness without taking such vigorous excercise - and brisk walking for at least half an hour a day will make a tremendous difference. Wear suitable shoes, low-heeled and springy.

### An exercise programme

The suggestions here are intended to get you started on a three- (or more) times weekly routine of exercise. The first group of exercises (A to F) should be done before the running-on-the-spot, jogging, dancing, swimming or other

**A** Feet apart, arms at sides. Raise arms above head, breathing in. Lower arms, breathing out.

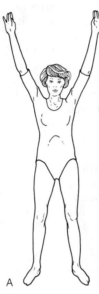

**B** Feet apart, bend sideways to left, keeping back straight, arm over head, left knee bent. Feel stretch. Repeat to right.

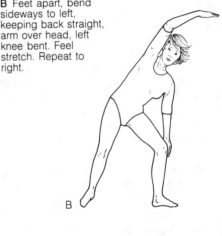

B

A

**C** Feet apart, arms at sides. Raise arms, palms together. Lower arms, turning wrists so that palms face outwards. Repeat at speed.

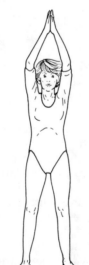

C

**D I** Feet apart, arms at sides, rotate shoulders. forwards and backwards.

**D II** Feet apart, arms at sides, raise and lower shoulders. Feel stretch.

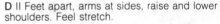
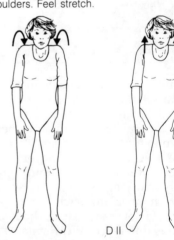

D I

D II

exercise you undertake to develop stamina. You should do them for about five minutes in all. They will warm you up and loosen you up for the running etc. part of your programme. You then wind down and cool down with the group of exercises (G to J).

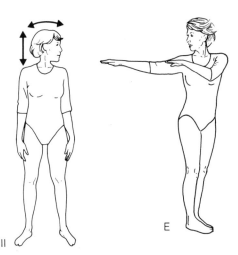

D III Feet apart, arms at sides, bend head slowly to left to look over shoulder, then right. Then bend head forward and gently back. Repeat.

D III

E Feet together, swing both arms left sideways, turning head. Repeat to right. Keep hips facing forwards and twist from waist.

E

F Sit on the floor, legs apart. Hands together, bend left to touch left leg as near to ankle as possible. Repeat to right.
Hands together, legs apart, bend to reach as far forward as possible.

F

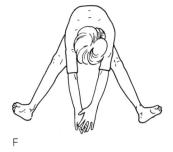

F

G Stand about 3 feet from wall, arms outstretched to touch wall. Bend arms until head touches wall.

H About 3 feet from chair-back, lean forward to hold chair, with bent back. Now lower back, stretching arms and straightening spine.

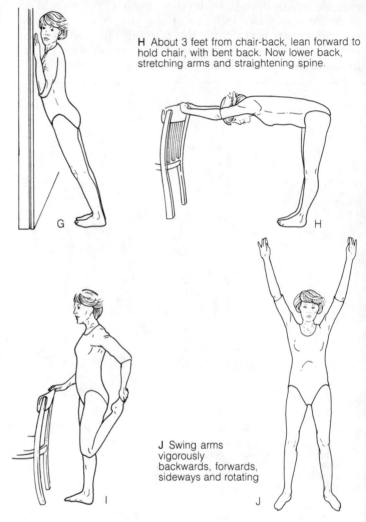

I Holding chair-back or table, raise leg backwards, bending knee and grasping ankle. Repeat on other side.

J Swing arms vigorously backwards, forwards, sideways and rotating

### 'It's such a bore'

There are all sorts of reasons for finding an exercise programme difficult to stick to, and lack of time and boredom must come top of the list. If there's an Adult Education Centre near you which offers keep-fit classes you should take advantage of it if you can; the company of others, the enthusiasm of a skilled teacher and the musical accompaniment which is normally provided will keep you going – though you should try to follow a modified version of the routines offered during the rest of the week on at least two other days. Exercising once a week is better than nothing, but won't have nearly such a beneficial effect as regular exercise. There are also commercially run exercise classes – check on the qualification of the teacher. Some are 'cowgirls'.

You can buy exercise tapes for an audio cassette recorder from record shops – these not only give instructions but provide a musical accompaniment. Or you can make use of radio or TV exercise programmes when they're available, or choose your own recording of suitable music to play while you're exercising.

The main incentive to continue, however, is the very great improvement in fitness and well-being that you will experience when you've exercised regularly for a while. Your breathing will be better – you can run for a bus without trouble, and climb several flights of stairs without strain. You'll feel physically stronger and more able to cope with sudden demands and stressful situations. And joint pains and vague niggles should be things of the past. Many women, too, report that they sleep better when they exercise regularly. Later in the chapter we'll look at ways of coping with the stress and anxiety that are behind most people's experiences of poor sleep.

## Can you say 'no'?

Eminent cardiologist Peter Nixon believes that important as diet, exercise and giving up smoking are in the prevention of heart disease, there's another even more potent factor. Stress in all its forms, emotional as well as physical, can push heart function to beyond its healthy limits. Anger, irritation, over-reaction to emotional problems, overwork, inability to say 'no' to the demands of others or oneself can lead to exhaustion of mind and body and consequent malfunction of the heart.

Nixon suggests that we shouldn't wait, as so many do, until our bodies tell us we've had enough. We should re-examine our lifestyles, learning to accept that we can be neither superpersons nor jills-of-all-trades who respond to every call made upon our time and energies. Unless we can learn to accept limitations, no amount of jogging and fat-reduced dieting will prevent heart disease in those at risk.

You may feel that as a woman on your own you can't easily shed any part of the load you're bearing. But it's worth evaluating just how important it is to work overtime, have your house in perfect order, take your children here, there and everywhere for out-of-school activities, attend meetings, rush, rush, rush. You're only human.

# A healthy weight

Since this is a chapter about health, any discussion about the 'ideal weight' or the 'attractive figure' is out of place. But isn't that sort of conception of 'beauty' something we can do without, anyway? Whose ideas of female attractiveness are we taking on board when we vainly try to emulate the model-girl image that bombards us from every hoarding, TV ad and magazine? Next to – but closely allied with – the putting-down of older women because they don't conform to some artificial idea of beauty, is this insistence that a woman is only attractive if her measurements are 'right'. But so powerful is this propaganda that very few women find themselves genuinely able to resist it. Even those who believe themselves to be unaffected by the male demand for the 'perfect figure' and who completely reject the sexism behind it, can actually dislike themselves as they are – too fat, too thin, bulges in the 'wrong' places, or whatever.

But, while trying to reject the stereotypical idea of a perfect shape, it's important not to reject also the well-established health hazards of being overweight, and the even more startling implications of disorders such as anorexia nervosa or bulimia. While there is a considerable degree of latitude in deciding what is a healthy weight for a certain individual, statistically someone whose weight deviates by more than about 10–14 lbs. above the average for her height is at greater risk of developing heart disease, diabetes, arthritis and other degenerative diseases. The grossly underweight woman – someone of child-bearing age whose periods have stopped, for instance – is also at risk. Her resistance to infections may be lowered, her capacity to recover from illness or accident impaired and, if she persists in losing weight, she can literally starve to death. If the choice were between some degree of overweight and some degree of below average weight – not that it usually is – the underweight woman is usually the healthier. But extremes are undesirable and possibly dangerous.

In recent years there's been a move away from calorie-controlled diets for the overweight. This has come from two sources – the feminist rejection of the stereotypical 'ideal' slimness which has so damaged the self-image of many women, and the school of thought that sees healthy exercise as a way of controlling not only weight but overeating. Contrary to popular belief, exercise does *not* increase appetite – rather the reverse.

## Your 'ideal weight'

In *Breaking the Diet Habit: The Natural Weight Alternative* Janet Polivy and C. Peter Herman (Basic Books, distributed by Harper & Row) the authors show that recent psychological, physiological and medical research raises doubts about the whole concept of chronic dieting. 'Natural weight', say the authors, is quite different from the 'ideal weight' shown on the usual weight tables. This is yet another apparently well-researched book that demonstrates not only that dramatic weight loss can be self-defeating, but suggests how the dieting habit can be broken and the right weight for the individual can be maintained.

### A feminist issue

A good deal of success has been claimed for weight control by means of a form of group therapy concerned with the whole question of over-eating, 'comfort eating', 'bingeing' and over-rigid dieting. Overweight women learn to eat only when they're actually hungry, and most are surprised to find that once they can accept this concept they just don't eat nearly as much as they have done in the past. The idea is that eventually they should cease to bother about calorie-counting, or entering into conflicts with themselves about whether or not to accept a cream cake – in fact, making eating the central point of their lives, as so many do. This is quite different from the old 'Weight Watchers' kind of group therapy. In its early days participants were weighed in public, praised or blamed for the amount of weight they'd lost or gained; this could increase the obsession with food that probably caused the problem in the first place. Weight Watchers now take a more sympathetic and individual approach, offering group support.

A full discussion of the implications of eating disorders and the role that therapy can play in normalising both food intake and weight is to be found in Susie Orbach's book *Fat is a Feminist Issue* and help is available through the Women's Therapy Centre.

### Weight and exercise

For many years the role of exercise in combating over-weight was played down. It would need a London-to-Brighton marathon, we were told, to provide the amount of exercise needed to take off 1 or 2 lbs. of extra weight. Small wonder that most overweight people accepted that taking exercise couldn't possibly affect the scales; and when, in addition, the weight they carried made exercise difficult and unattractive, they either resigned themselves to doing nothing about their fat or attempted – sometimes futilely – to control their weight by drastic dieting.

This simplistic theory about the uselessness of exercise as a way of losing weight has recently been very strongly challenged. It's pointed out that, though it's quite true that an impossibly huge amount of exercise would be needed to burn up enough fat in the body to make any appreciable difference to a person's weight on any given day, this is not the same as saying that exercise over a long term is ineffective. What matters is regular, much less drastic, exercise. This affects the body's metabolism – the rate at which it uses energy – and, as long as the regular exercise continues, there will be a gradual loss of weight, or maintenance of the person's normal, healthy weight, even though she is eating well.

Slimming diets, according to this school of thought – expressed most clearly in Geoffrey Cannon and Hetty Einzig's book *Dieting Makes You Fat* – are ineffective or counter-productive. In the first place, a drastic diet doesn't initially rid the body of fat, but of glycogen and water, essential to its vital functions. As soon as the diet stops, the first things to come back are the glycogen and water, so the weight is rapidly regained. Any 'slimming' diet will result in the loss of some fat, say Cannon and Einzig. But 'the metabolically active tissue lost on a diet has the effect of artificially depressing the body's energy needs'. Thus someone who over a dieting period has reduced her calorie intake from, say, 2,000 calories a day to 1,500, has to stick to that level of calorie intake, which her system has become used to, or she will put the weight back on again. Not for nothing is Cannon and Einzig's book called *Dieting Makes You Fat*. And the Royal College of Physicians' report on

---

## Exercise – eat more – lose fat?

A one-year study at Stanford University, comparing a group of previously inactive middle-aged men who were sedentary with a similar group who were encouraged to do regular jogging showed that those who had done most jogging lost the most body-fat. There was little or no change in the sedentary group. But more surprising – the jogging men who had lost the most fat increased their food intake most. None of the men had been asked specifically to try to lose weight, go on a diet or change dietary habits. As Professor Peter Wood of the Stanford University Heart Disease Programme says: more calories mean more food and hence more minerals, carbohydrates, vitamins and fibre, too.

---

obesity rubs home the message about slimming diets: 'Maintenance of weight loss beyond one year was less satisfactory and 11 longer-term studies have found that weight increases again in the majority of patients'; and it quotes a study that found that after one to five years 17 per cent of dieters were actually heavier than before. And the second important point about a slimming diet is that it is almost certainly deficient in necessary nutrients.

Cannon and Einzig's book suggests an exercise plan that involves regular running, which will cause steady, gradual weight loss but no loss of healthy, lean tissue. Another writer, 'Mary Ellen' (see 'Directory') suggests that an hour's brisk walk five days a week will achieve similar results. She has some dietary suggestions as well. If Cannon and Einzig are right, these needn't be followed too closely, because the good news is that, if you adopt the healthy diet outlined on pp. 265–9, you aren't consuming too many calories for health, anyway, and you're not depriving your body of the essential nutrients that almost any unbalanced, slimming diet is likely to lack.

**To sum up**
The truly balanced diet we've looked at earlier will achieve good results not only in terms of providing the right kinds of food and avoiding the ones likely to cause health problems now and in the future, but it will also cause weight loss in the over-fat, and weight gain in the unhealthily skinny. And exercise – again along the lines suggested – is essential for good health and the avoidance of some illness, with the added bonus of enabling the exerciser to eat well in every sense of the word without gaining weight. In other words, good food plus regular exercise equals optimum health; and that means a longer active life and the ability to survive successfully on your own.

# What about stress?

To keep us functioning at a level above the vegetable one, we need a certain amount of stress in our lives – in other words, some degree of challenge to keep us ticking over, cope with the environment, work, other people. But the majority of women face a good deal more than that – and none more so than the widowed, divorced or separated, who probably have to cope with lack of money, strained relations within their families, a work situation that may be far from ideal, and dealing single-handed with a huge number of domestic problems and chores. While it seems to be true that the least depressed sections of the population are single women, the group to which this book is addressed consists in the main of those who have been married (and married women tend to come high in the 'most depressed' groups in any study) and have gone through many traumas in the process of becoming 'unmarried'. Stress, and the feelings of lack of control of one's life that it so often involves, are very close to depression. We'll be looking more fully at depression in Chapter 17.

It hardly needs saying that a stressed woman is likely to be a woman with quite a few health problems. Tension and stress go together, and a tensed-up woman will suffer from neck, shoulder and back pain, which can be bad enough to cause severe and crippling disabilities. She can experience bouts of, or even chronic long-term, sleeplessness. Her resistance to infections can be lowered, and she may have digestive problems caused by unrelaxed meals. These are just some of the problems that are clearly related to stress. So intimately are 'mind' and 'body' related that a host of other disorders and malfunctions can be attributed, at least in part, to overstress.

### A change of lifestyle

Jessica's marriage broke up, leaving her with two teenage sons and an inadequate income. With some difficulty she managed to get a job as a secretary in a large construction company – bluffing her way through the first few weeks when she found that her old office skills had got a little rusty. Before long she found herself having to take on much of the work of an inadequate boss, and this often involved staying late, covering up for his deficiencies and holding the fort in his frequent absences. Her elder son was causing some worry – she found that he was 'bunking off' school and mixing with people she felt weren't good for him. The younger boy suffered from asthma. Her elderly mother needed help of a kind that only Jessica could give.

It wasn't surprising that Jessica, normally a competent, well organised person, became so tense and worked up, rushing from one job to another, one duty to the next, that she became totally exhausted. At first she would fall into bed and sleep until the alarm sounded, all too early, the following morning. But before long she began to sleep badly. She took an hour or two to get to sleep, slept fitfully for another two or three hours, then woke alert, anxious and unrefreshed, to face another day.

Seeing that this situation just couldn't go on, Jessica consulted her doctor. Luckily this woman doctor didn't – like so many GPs – dismiss her with a prescription for tranquillisers. She suggested that Jessica make an appointment to see her again out of normal surgery hours, and when she did, spent some time discussing ways in which the hectic lifestyle pattern she'd got into could be modified.

As a result, Jessica faced her boss and told him that if she were to continue in the job things would have to change. She couldn't work overtime – she had family responsibilities. She needed a proper lunch hour. If he expected her to continue to take so much responsibility she would need an assistant to do some of the more straightforward office jobs. All this was said with some trepidation – after all, jobs were difficult to find – but her boss was clearly so dependent on her and her organisational abilities that he accepted all her demands. With another person in the office, and a boss now anxious to please, Jessica for the first time could leave the office promptly at 5.30 p.m. and leave behind all the worries and anxieties, too.

This gave her more time to cope with her sons' problems. As her doctor had suggested, she had a useful talk with her elder boy's class teacher and head of his house, and between them they worked out strategies that provided him with more interest and incentive to stay at school. With his mother more available, the other boy's asthma attacks – which had so often happened when he was alone and frightened – became much less frequent. Then Jessica went to see her mother's GP, and arranged for her to be referred to a day-care centre, and allocated some home help.

All this took a great load off Jessica's shoulders – but the residue of sleeplessness and tension remained. A further suggestion from her doctor, though, began to make a great deal of difference. She advised Jessica to be 'kinder' to herself. The boys were old enough to be left alone one evening a week – so Jessica should visit friends, go to a cinema or concert, have fun. She could join a yoga or relaxation class, and learn to practise ways of relaxing tension at home. And the doctor advised her to put her organisational abilities to good use at home as well as in the office. 'Get things down to a routine,' she said, 'so that you don't have to think about every bit of shopping or domestic job. Get the boys to take on more responsibility – and make lists.' Although she felt a little doubtful, Jessica agreed to try out the doctor's suggestions.

There were a few problems in getting her sons to take on jobs they hadn't done before. But Jessica was tough. If they hadn't made their beds or tidied their rooms, she didn't do it for them. It was their job, not hers. If they failed to pick up some shopping on their way home from school, their evening meal was inadequate. In a few weeks they became more responsible and organised.

And Jessica took on board the idea of lists and found it very successful. She spent some time working out two weeks' menus, and the shopping lists that went with them, so that every week she simply took the relevant list to the supermarket with her and without thinking, worrying that she'd forget something vital or buy too little or too much, she was able to whisk through the shopping – and more important, relieve herself of the sort of trivial worry that had kept her awake – the 'I must remember . . .' syndrome that every insomniac experiences.

Finally, her doctor suggested to Jessica that a large part of her problem with sleeplessness was due to her worry about it. She asked Jessica to assess just how much sleep she actually needed to be able to function efficiently the following day, pointing out that many people manage very well on much less than the seven or eight hours generally believed to be necessary. Jessica realised that if she had five hours' sleep a night she could cope reasonably well with the demands in her life. She'd prefer to have more sleep, but would settle for five hours. The GP persuaded her to accept that this five hours' sleep was adequate, and normal *for her*, and suggested that she tell herself this over and over again until she felt that she had really absorbed the idea. To her surprise, she found that if she did wake, she no longer worried about the consequences of sleeplessness, and, having ceased to worry, she was very often able to go back to sleep again until she'd had her five hours – or more. If she did find that she was getting tensed up and anxious, she could put into practice the relaxation technique she'd learnt, and usually managed to drift off into sleep. The doctor's suggestions had paid off.

### Drugs are no answer

We've looked at Jessica's life in some detail because it not only illustrates the enormous burden that many women on their own find themselves carrying, but some of the ways in which such burdens can be lifted. Of course stress, tension and anxiety can be relieved by taking tranquillisers. Valium, Librium and others of their ilk have been and still are widely prescribed, and although there have been moves to reduce the number of 'repeat prescriptions' that some people get all too easily, there are thousands of women in Britain who have been on tranquillisers for many years.

It's generally recognised that tranquillisers are useful to enable someone to get over a really severe shock or crisis, but that they merely deaden emotional pain, without removing its cause, and should never be seen as a long-term solution to a problem in her life. And in recent years it's become fully accepted that, contrary to earlier opinion, they are physically as well as psychologically addictive. Moreover, addictive as they are, after a period of up to four months they don't, in fact, act effectively against the anxiety for which they were prescribed. The dose therefore has to be increased to obtain the desired effect – and the woman becomes even more dependent.

As with any addictive drug, withdrawal is a most painful experience, and it must be done very gradually. Sources of information and help in doing this are listed in the 'Directory'. If you are drug-dependent, though, it's important not to blame yourself for 'weakness' or to say that if only you could pull yourself together you could come off the drugs. They have been prescribed to you as a crutch – albeit a very inadequate one – to enable you to cope with difficulties in your life. And no one can suddenly throw away a crutch on which she has been depending.

You are right to want to discard the chemical crutch, which is doing you no good and which is leaving you with a muzzy head, deadened feelings and an inability to concentrate. Your aim, though, must be to reduce over a period of weeks or months, if necessary, the amount of the drug you are taking – and to be prepared for this process to cause you bouts of anxiety, sleeplessness and tension which may well make you tempted to reach for the bottle again. You *may* have bad experiences – but they will lessen in intensity and in frequency. And you *can* cope.

Further advice on stress and on coming off tranquilizers can be found in the 'Health' section of the Directory at the end of this book.

Since the problems that caused the symptoms may still be with you, your aim must be to replace the drug with positive action; this may be simple and relatively straightforward, as Jessica found. Or you may need help in reaching a solution or at least coming to terms with the difficulties in your life. In Chapter 17 we shall be considering where such help might be found.

# CHAPTER 16
# THE MENOPAUSE – AND AFTER

**Although for most modern women the menopause is less frightening than it was for their mothers, there's still an aura of anxiety about its effects. Here we look at the myths and the facts and see how a healthy life style can contribute to our well-being in mid-life.**

A birthday that marks the beginning of a new decade always seems specially significant. For a woman, reaching the half-century has a particular meaning, since it's around fifty that she can expect to reach the end of her reproductive life. By then, most women have been avoiding conception for at least ten years. Nevertheless, for those with a male partner, the possibility of conceiving has always been there. For a woman on her own, and especially one who has had no children, it may seem particularly poignant that all possibilities of having a child with a new partner are finally over. And women who believe – wrongly – that their sex lives are finished, and those who have always defined themselves primarily as mothers, can see the menopause as a cul-de-sac, rather than a crossroads that could lead to a stimulating and challenging future.

It may be difficult enough to cope with fears of the physical changes of the menopause, without having to cope with such false and hostile descriptions as those still occasionally appearing in the media too. It wasn't so many years ago that a male doctor – the author of popular works on sex – wrote that at this time 'a woman comes as close as she can to being a man. Increased facial hair, deepened voice, obesity, and the decline of the breasts and female genitalia all contribute to a masculine appearance. Not really a man, but no longer a functional woman, these individuals live in a world of intersex . . . sex no longer interests them.

'To many women the menopause marks the end of their useful life. They see it as the onset of old age, the beginning of the end. They may be right. Having outlived their ovaries, they may have outlived their usefulness as human beings. The remaining years may just be marking time until they follow their glands into oblivion.'

This woman-hating, fatuous nonsense was written by Dr David Reuben in a best-selling book of the 1970s. A long time ago? Perhaps, but a few 'experts' like him are still influential, and even more apparently open-minded and sympathetic writers like Dr Vernon Coleman can frighten women by references to 'an endless series of fractures' that could occur following the menopause when, he says, 'many women feel their femininity drifting away rather more speedily than they would have liked.' (*Women's Problems: An A-Z*, published in 1984 by Sheldon Press.)

But fortunately these stereotyped views are now being challenged and with them the negative attitudes towards ageing fostered by our society. We should be challenging, too, the assumption still held by many women that ill-health and emotional instability after fifty are somehow inevitable. Must women still be fobbed off by doctors who tell them that quite unrelated ills are 'just your age'? A woman without a man is even more likely to be offered some pseudo-explanation for the symptom that's brought her to the doctor: not only is she menopausal, but she's warped and embittered by her experience and thus there's a 'psychological' component, too, in her disorder.

## A gradual process

Accepting that there *are* a few menopausal problems, affecting 60 per cent of women to some degree, and around 20 per cent more severely – what can be done about them?

The menopause doesn't happen suddenly. Oestrogen and progesterone are hormones that trigger off the monthly shedding of the lining of the womb, and it's the ovaries that are the main source of these hormones. Over many years the ovaries gradually produce less oestrogen, and other glands partially take over their work. So it's quite wrong to assume that once the ovaries stop producing oestrogen the hormone is no longer present. The body can take about five years to adjust to the lower levels of oestrogen, but when it has adjusted, the menopause and its physical side effects are over.

In the early 1970s thousands of British women, and millions in America, became convinced that Hormone Replacement Therapy was the answer to all the physical and emotional problems they were facing at the time of the menopause. Doctors, influenced by the big drug companies and the researchers funded by them, rushed to prescribe

HRT not only as a remedy for clear problems but as some-thing to take 'just in case' a problem arose. They were ready to see lowered levels of oestrogen as producing a kind of 'deficiency disease' which could be 'cured', just as taking Vitamin C will cure the deficiency disease, scurvy.

But a reaction set in. There was a lot of bad publicity about the possibility that certain cancers could be the result of over-prescribing of oestrogen, and that stroke and heart conditions might be linked with oestrogen therapy. In America doctors became more cautious. In Britain, a more cautious approach had been evident all along, and a far smaller proportion of menopausal women were prescribed the hormone. Although many doctors believe that the dangers have been overstated, others think that HRT may have unacceptable consequences that may eventually appear.

The therapy offered today usually combines progesterone with oestrogen, and this, it is believed, will prevent the cancer of the endometrium (lining of the uterus) that was the main danger of oestrogen-only therapy. But some authorities are just as worried about the possible effects of progestogens, which have been linked with breast cancer in animals, though not, so far, in humans. The National Institute on Aging in the United States held a conference in 1979 at which a panel of experts felt that it was not safe to prescribe progesterone, and there has been a suggestion that there's an increased risk of heart attack in pre-menopausal women who have taken the oestrogen-progesterone combination.

Most British doctors who prescribe HRT believe that it should be started early in the menopause. Some think it should be continued for about five years, others that it should be given only when symptoms are severe and for the shortest possible period and in the lowest possible dose that's effective. Women on HRT must be regularly checked for undesirable effects.

# Three menopause symptoms

In its early days HRT was hailed as an elixir of youth, keeping women, as the phrase coined by one of its pioneers put it, 'feminine forever'. Wrinkles would disappear as if by magic, breasts regain their youthful shape, women would please their men by becoming even sexier. An article in the *Observer* as recently as March 1984, extolled the wonders of HRT, almost completely ignoring its possible drawbacks, and presenting it as a liberating panacea that had been unaccountably neglected by the women's movement.

Most responsible people, however, would not now claim that HRT turns back the clock or that it helps emotional ills. What is clear, though, is that hormone replacement is an effective treatment – in the short term – for the three recognised physical symptoms of the menopause: hot flushes, vaginal dryness and osteoporosis (fragile bones). And for women who want to avoid taking hormones, and for those with certain medical problems for whom they cannot be prescribed, there are various other ways of coping with these symptoms.

*Hot flushes* are probably the most troublesome, and it's been estimated that about 75 per cent of women in the menopause suffer from them at least occasionally. They range from a warm, glowing feeling to an intense burning sensation in the upper part of the body, with reddening of the face and neck, accompanied by profuse sweating, particularly at night. In the majority of cases HRT can be very effective in banishing the flushes – but of course only for so long as it's taken. Since they could trouble a woman for a few years, and many wonen wouldn't want to have HRT that long, the hormones may be seen as only a temporary alleviation of the problem, and alternatives could be tried. In a magazine survey in America, 2,000 women reported that they'd found Vitamin E supplements helpful in dealing with hot flushes and other symptoms of menopause, and it's also been suggested that Vitamin B-complex tablets might help.

But the flushes aren't dangerous, and are probably embarrassing only to the woman herself. It's a fact that other people seldom notice them, and some women don't dislike the feeling of 'glow'. Even so, hot flushes at night can be a nuisance because of the profuse sweating, sometimes followed by a feeling of chill. Menopausal women sometimes complain of insomnia – perhaps one reason for this is the necessity to get up and change sheets and nightwear which have become uncomfortably clammy. Having a change near the bed could make the interruption of sleep less prolonged. A cooling spray, used at night or during the day, is worth trying, too.

The second menopausal symptom, *vaginal dryness*, is also effectively treated by HRT. Some doctors prescribe oestrogen creams for local application to the vagina. However, if you are hesitant about taking a tablet, you may well prefer to avoid this treatment too. The oestrogen applied to the vagina does enter the blood stream; it isn't acting just as a lubricant but is actually affecting the tissues and making them produce the lubricating fluid that was produced naturally before the menopause. Once more, this effect lasts only so long as the cream is used. A solution that doesn't involve hormone therapy would be to provide a lubricant such as KY Jelly (obtainable from pharmacists) or a natural oil; saliva is also effective. But regular sexual activity is the best 'remedy' - and this includes masturbation, of course.

Through this lack of lubrication many women suffer pain or discomfort when having intercourse involving penetration. Furthermore, the fact that it's accompanied by thinning of the skin makes injury more likely, and menopausal women may find that they're more prone to vaginal and urinary infections. So it's more important than ever to wash the area frequently – plain warm water and no bath additives or soaps should be used – to wipe from front to back after defaecation, and to drink plenty of water, making it a rule to empty the bladder at two-hourly intervals.

*Osteoporosis* is the third condition that HRT can treat successfully. Women are more likely to suffer this at or after the time of the menopause than are men of the same age, and this does make it appear that hormone deficiency might be a factor. However, there may be more to it than that: as with so many ills, heredity and environment are implicated. Large-boned women are not so prone to brittle bones, black women suffer much less from osteoporosis than do white or Asian women, and well-nourished women who may even be slightly 'overweight' in terms of fashion are less at risk than skinny ones. Although HRT can undoubtedly stave off the development of the condition, once it's stopped, deterioration of the bones will continue. So it's unlikely to be a long-term solution.

Many doctors now believe that both diet and exercise have crucial functions in the prevention of osteoporosis. In pregnancy and when breast-feeding many women are poorly nourished, and begin to lose some of the calcium in their bones. They may continue right through youth and middle-age to eat insufficient, or the wrong foods, and gradually more calcium is lost.

Another cause of calcium loss may be too much phosphorus in the diet; this causes calcium to be drawn out of the bones. Bone strength depends on an equal balance between calcium and phosphorus, or slightly more calcium than phosphorus in the food we eat; dairy foods (especially skimmed milk and low-fat cheeses), spring greens, shellfish, canned fish with bones, and sesame seeds are high in calcium and relatively low in phosphorus.

Although bran is recommended as providing a good source of fibre in the diet, and is a suitable supplement for younger women, women who may be at risk of osteo-porosis should remember that wheat bran can impair the absorption of minerals, including calcium. It should there-fore be used in moderation, and substituting oat bran should be considered, while making sure that the natural sources of calcium are included. It has also been suggested that a diet high in animal protein draws calcium from the bones.

Calcium absorption is crucially affected by sunlight. This doesn't mean that you have to bake in the sun day after day. But you should take advantage of sunny days to be out of doors and with arms, legs and as much of the rest of the body as possible exposed to sunlight. The Vitamin D thus produced does build up in the body and a store of it will last through the winter until sunshine is available again.

A long-term study carried out in New York is designed to test the theory that supplementation of the diet with calcium and Vitamin D can prevent osteoporosis. The director of the project recommends that calcium tablets containing 1,500 mg a day should be taken by post-meno-pausal women, along with Vitamin D.

It seems to be likely that in addition to the hereditary and dietary factors, exercise is important in the prevention of osteoporosis. Although ideally a sensible exercise programme should be started no later than one's thirties, it's never too late for exercise to have *some* effect on bone strength. Physical exercise has been shown to slow down the rate of bone loss, and it may even build new bone tissue. Exercises that tone up the spinal and abdominal muscles – they don't have to be violent, but they should be done consistently – can help considerably. Walking briskly for at least half an hour a day, and swimming – which uses all the back muscles – is an excellent way of keeping fit as well as helping to keep the bones strong. Cycling, too, is good. The worst thing you can do is to lead a sedentary life. Women who are forced to do a lot of housework and gardening – as long as they avoid back strain by bending and lifting sensibly – get a reasonable amount of the right kind of exercise. If you're tied to a desk or a workbench all day you do need to compensate by deliberately seeking ways of getting exercise. So here's where the woman on her own may score – she may well have to do more physical work than someone who leaves the jobs that need effort to a man, and won't necessarily have to add a great deal of extra exercise to her daily timetable.

## Emotional problems

Older books when discussing the menopause usually offer a long list of troubles, far beyond the three physical symptoms we've been looking at, which are said to occur at the time of the menopause. And these 'menopausal troubles' are the subject of a great deal of anxiety. Even quite young women will attribute various ills they may suffer to the coming 'change' and it's often convenient for doctors to dismiss something they can't diagnose or treat as something to be borne because 'at your age it's only to be expected'. 'You're not as young as you were', they may add – not the most helpful of comments.

And so we get a catalogue of ills – insomnia, depression, anxiety, confusion, and inability to concentrate among them. There's no denying that these troubles do occur around the time of the menopause – though not only then, of course – and that they can be extremely distressing to the woman who suffers from them. They mustn't be discounted as unreal, hysterical, bids for attention and all the other labels that popular psychology may pin on them in the absence of overt physical symptoms. But there really is very little proof that they are actually directly attributable to the changes that occur at the menopause. The fact that they may *coincide* doesn't mean that they are *caused* by these changes. And lack of interest in sex, often seen as a 'menopausal problem' may have many other causes – and in any case isn't seen *as* a 'problem' by many.

The weary, uninterested doctor who believes that his patient's state is 'just her age' will be the first to hand out tranquillisers if she insists that something is wrong. If she doesn't he'll tell her to go away and pull herself together or count her blessings.

Six women who are going through the menopause or who had passed it are quoted on p. 293. It's interesting to note that of the women who suffered some form of emotional upheaval at the time of the menopause, every one had some other problem to cope with – a bereavement,

'I felt dreadful for two or three years. My marriage was breaking up and my mother died. I got very depressed. My doctor was no help at all. He told me it was just something I had to live with, that everybody went through things like this at some time in their lives and that I was taking it badly because women become unbalanced at the change of life. I think I only kept out of a mental hospital because my daughter needed me – she was going through a bad patch, too, and I couldn't desert her. Now whether it's because I finally decided on the divorce or whether it was because my hormones settled down, I'll never know; but suddenly the depression did lift, the headaches I'd been having stopped, and I began to sleep better. That was my menopause – I wouldn't want to repeat it.'

'I hope no one will think I'm smug, but actually I didn't have much trouble at all. It was inconvenient to have irregular periods for a year or two and once or twice I was quite scared that I'd got pregnant – I was living with a male friend at the time. However, apart from that I hardly knew anything was happening. Yes, there was some flooding – an awful nuisance, too – and I did have some hot flushes. But I carried on working and enjoying my independent life. Now that the menopause is over I feel more energetic than I've done for years.'

'My hot flushes are quite embarrassing – even on a cold day I get red and sweaty, and I don't like people guessing that I'm menopausal – my workmates and the boss all think I'm younger than I am. Also I have irregular bleeding and I don't know whether this is the menopause or something worse. My mother died of cancer just recently and I'm really frightened I might have it. I know it's silly but I daren't go to the doctor. If it is just the change he'll think I'm silly. If it's cancer I can't face it after the terrible time we had when my mother was dying. I suppose I'm still upset about that.'

'My only menopausal symptom was depression. I'm sure it was the menopause, because treatment with anti-depressants didn't help. They made me feel worse – muzzy-headed and peculiar. Then my doctor suggested HRT, and that did transform things for a few months. But she wasn't keen on my continuing with hormones indefinitely, so she wouldn't give me any more. I couldn't explain to her that I was having terrible problems with my son – I was afraid that if I told her the police would be involved. Perhaps it was because of him that I got so upset and depressed – but at the time it did seem a physical thing. I've got over it now, and he's settled down.'

**Six women speak about menopause**

293

*'I'm a lesbian. For years I've suffered from ill-health, and it all got much worse when I was going through the menopause. I got all sorts of aches and pains, attacks of anxiety so that I could hardly go out of the house, and a general feeling of 'lowness'. My lover was wonderfully supportive – she's younger and hasn't experienced the menopause herself yet, but I got so much help and understanding from her. She was so patient with me, so loving, and she helped me to come to terms with the changes in my body and the spell of unemployment I had just at that time. It's thanks to her that I feel now that I can cope.'*

*'At 49 I had one really bad period – I bled for three weeks, and began to feel quite weak. In fact because of this and because I never knew when the flood would come, I had to go sick from my teaching job. My doctor referred me for possible hysterectomy. The specialist agreed – he arranged a blood test and I was very anaemic. He thought I couldn't risk having many more periods like that. By this time it was the school summer holidays. I was put on a waiting list for the operation, and meanwhile went on the holiday I'd booked. I began to feel a lot better, and had a normal period, then, after term started, another. It seemed stupid to have a hysterectomy just because of one bad bout of bleeding, so when I got a notification that a hospital bed was available, I cancelled. After that I had two more normal periods, a few months apart – then nothing. I enjoyed my job, it would have been very inconvenient to have to be away for weeks over the operation, and it all seemed a fuss about nothing. I've had absolutely no physical or emotional upsets at all except for that one episode – and it's all behind me now.'*

---

marital breakdown or other difficulty. Although most of them believed that their main problem was menopausal, it would seem that anyone facing these difficulties at any time of her life would become depressed and anxious.

Middle age isn't easy for many people, and traumatic life-changes such as divorce or widowhood do frequently happen just at this time. Redundancy or difficulty in getting a suitable job after many years of child care can also coincide with the menopausal years. It's very difficult to disentangle all the various factors that can lead to emotional problems or breakdown. Menopausal problems are often by no means the only factors, though they may play a part.

One 'psychological' problem that's said to occur at this time is the 'empty nest syndrome'. Interestingly, not one of the six women quoted who were mothers had felt anything but relief when their daughters and sons left home, confirming the finding of American researcher Lillian Rubin that this 'syndrome' is largely a myth. Most women guiltily admit to feeling a sense of satisfaction when they're freed at last from the responsibilities of motherhood.

In this small sample, the two women who brushed aside their physical problems – which on the face of it seemed quite similar to the others' – were people who were fortunate enough not to experience major relationship problems at the time of the menopause, and were also occupied constructively outside the home.

# Hope for you

But there are women who aren't so lucky – and readers of this book may be among them. By circumstances – an unhappy marriage, for instance, or by social conditioning that has made them passive and inhibited – such women may not have been able to build satisfying, independent lives. Their health, by the time they reach their forties or fifties, may have been undermined by stress, unhappiness and illness.

If you're one of these people, there *is* hope. Every chapter in this book is for you. Even after years of neglect your physical condition can be improved: in Chapter 15 we've looked at the ways in which diet and exercise can help women of all ages to become healthier, and in this chapter we've concentrated particularly on healthy living for women of your age. With better physical health you'll be more able to cope with the psychological difficulties we've touched on here, but which we look at in greater detail in Chapter 17. Once you feel better, the ideas offered in Chapter 8 may help you to get back into education, a part-time job or voluntary work, even if full-time employment isn't a possibility.

The greatest support of all in these difficult years will come from other women. You may meet them at a yoga class, a further education group or a women's organisation. The Older Feminists' Network (see Chapter 12 pp. 232–3, and the 'Directory of useful organisations') has helped to stimulate the formation of local older women's groups which have proved extremely supportive to women in your age group. In a few areas women themselves, or concerned women health professionals, have started menopause groups, where women can discuss with each other any problems they may be facing, both physical and emotional. Some women attending such groups say that their lives – and this includes their personal relationships – have been transformed as a result. Sharing worries in a trusting environment often puts menopausal problems into perspective and enables a woman to tackle her difficulties – or, if her situation is intolerable, to gain courage to make a radical change in the way she is living.

This 'treatment' can be much more effective than tranquillisers or hormone therapy.

# Hysterectomy

It's around the time of the menopause that conditions may arise that make a doctor suggest that hysterectomy is necessary. Cancer may make radical surgery imperative; fibroids and consequent debilitating heavy bleeding when the woman is still menstruating can be another reason why the gynaecologist may suggest removal of the uterus. Disease or infection of the fallopian tubes may also cause problems that can be resolved only by hysterectomy.

In Britain very large numbers of hysterectomies are performed every year, but far fewer than in the United States, where it's been estimated that more than 800,000 women have a hysterectomy each year, and that if this continues, more than half of American women will have had the operation by the time they're sixty-five. Not surprisingly, a high proportion of these hysterectomies are unnecessary – as many as 40 per cent, it has been suggested, needn't have been done. In the United States women have been persuaded to have a hysterectomy 'in case of future trouble' and because their reproductive years are over and there's 'no point in keeping a useless organ'. Fortunately so far this epidemic is less likely in Britain, because surgeons working within the NHS don't stand to gain financially by performing a larger number of unnecessary operations.

This isn't the place to discuss in depth the medical reasons why removal of the womb may be advisable. But anyone to whom this is suggested ought to read up on the subject – we've suggested some books on p. 298 – and ask questions. Hysterectomy is not acceptable as a method of sterilisation – tubal ligation (a much simpler procedure) is greatly preferable. A prolapsed uterus – something that is more likely to occur a few years after the menopause – can be dealt with by a less radical repair operation. Small fibroids, which may cause increased bleeding before the menopause, are benign, and usually shrink after the menopause. The gynaecologist should also be asked whether it's really necessary to remove one or both ovaries at the same time as the womb is removed. If the ovaries are removed the woman may suffer a sudden menopause. In the natural menopause, as we've seen, ovarian production of hormones is taken over gradually by other glands. When the ovaries are taken away, the sudden withdrawal of hormones may result in exaggerated 'menopausal' symptoms – rapid bone loss or osteoporosis among the more obvious ones.

Many women fear the immediate and long-term results of a hysterectomy. Studies concerned with post-hysterectomy depression have come up with contradictory results, but there's little doubt that many women do believe that their hysterectomy is linked with quite severe depression in the year or two after the operation. It *is* major surgery, and like any such procedure, it's bound to need quite a long recovery period. It's not over-pampering yourself to behave as the semi-invalid you are for at least six weeks after you come out of hospital, and to go carefully for up to a year after that.

All-in-all a hysterectomy is a major event in a woman's life, and she needs all the support she can get. If you are faced with the operation, or you've just had it, there's a special group, the Hysterectomy Support Group, that can give you information and personal help, with telephone counselling and face-to-face contact if that's feasible. (For the address see the 'Directory')

When you've completed your recovery, (assuming that your hysterectomy was really necessary) you should feel very much better than before, able to resume your activities, take up new ones and enjoy sex. 'It's been a total success,' said one widow a year after her operation. 'I've taken on new responsibilities at work, despite my age. I've found the energy to go to pottery classes and keep-fit. I've even started an affair with a slightly younger man. I don't think we'll ever marry – but we're having fun and we like things as they are. Before the op I think I was a real drag. Looking back I can see I'm a different person now. Not bad at fifty-three'.

## Information and advice

The Hysterectomy Support Group, 11 Henryson Road, London SE4 1HL, may be able to put you in touch with a local member who can offer advice and support.

## MENOPAUSE: Further reading

*The Menopause – a Positive Approach* by Rosetta Reitz (Unwin Paperback). *Our Bodies Ourselves* edited by Angela Phillips and Jill Rakusen (Penguin) *A Women's Experience of Sex* by Sheila Kitzinger (Dorling Kindersley) *Prime Time* by Helen Franks (Pan).

## HYSTERECTOMY: Further reading

*Hysterectomy* by Professor Philips (Family doctor publications – from pharmacists or by post, 50p plus postage, from Family Doctor Publications, BMA House, Tavistock Square North, London WC1) *Hysterectomy and Vaginal Repair* by Sally Haslett and Molly Jennings (free from Johnson and Johnson, Slough, Berks. Send s.a.e., 8½ × 6 in).

# CHAPTER 17
# WHAT'S THE PROBLEM?

**Now we look at some of the worries and difficulties that individual women have met in adjusting to a new phase of life, and suggest ways of coping with them and of getting help.**

Surveys have shown that the 'best adjusted' people, those least likely to suffer from depression, are single women. But in your newly-acquired status of 'divorced' or 'widowed' perhaps you don't see yourself as coming into that category. To reach your present position you've probably had to go through many painful and upsetting experiences, making and breaking close relationships, and these will have left their mark. The very fact that you once weren't 'single' and had grown to depend on at least one other person has already changed you; now you have another adjustment to make and it may have been very difficult. The problems that almost everyone has to face at some time in her life may be magnified when you have no one with whom to share them; and there are others that seem to be closely related to your life as a woman on her own.

In earlier chapters we've discussed the adjustments you've had to make in the first days of separation or widowhood. The problems we discuss in this chapter are ones that have proved longer-lasting and perhaps more serious – the sort of difficulties that time and your growing sense of independence alone haven't been able to heal, or situations that have developed mainly as a result of your own reactions to the trauma of finding yourself suddenly alone. Some of these problems won't be ones you personally have met; others will seem only too real and pressing to you.

## Children and new relationships

In the months or years following your divorce or bereavement, you may have experienced what seemed like a total deadening of sexual feeling. Or, like other perfectly normal women, you may have been surprised and quite shocked to discover that your sexual needs have suddenly become very pressing in response to the emotional upheaval you've been through. Earlier in this book we saw how it's possible in this situation to rush into a new relationship, even if it's not a particularly promising one, and how this can sometimes – though not always – lead to a further complicating of your life.

But now that you hope the worst of the problems caused by your past experiences have been settled you are beginning to feel the need for a close relationship bound up with the need to satisfy the sexual feelings that, for most women of any age, are a very important part of their lives. In Chapter 13 we looked at the kind of relationships that can develop, both heterosexual and lesbian, and the ways in which a woman on her own can express her need for a satisfying sex life.

If you are really on your own, you have greater freedom to try out new relationships, reject those that prove to be wrong for you, without being responsible to anyone but yourself and your partner. It's rather different, you may think, if you have children still living with you. How can you best handle a situation in which, but for them, it would be perfectly reasonable to have your lover to stay overnight, go on holiday with you and generally take a share in your life? If he or she moves in, how will this affect your children? And if the relationship doesn't last, or was never intended to be a permanent one, how do you explain, how do you cope with yet another disruption in *their* relationships? Are you setting a 'bad example'? What will your, and their, friends say?

Moira split up with her husband while they were both in their early thirties. Their two children live with her. She's a lively, outgoing woman, who, though devoted to the children, didn't feel that she should distort her life to fit in with some possibly false image of childish 'innocence'. 'My marriage cured me of wanting a permanent relationship,' she says, 'though I suppose that if some amazingly wonderful man came along I'd have to think again. So far no one has. But I know and like a lot of men, I need sex, and as long as it's understood by both the man and me that there's nothing more to it than that, we go ahead and sleep together – it has to be at my house because I can't leave the children. So of course they've seen the man at breakfast and they know he's slept in my bed, and I think that, because I don't make a great thing of it, they've just accepted it as they would if *they* had a friend to stay.

They've always known the man in question before this happens – I make a point of inviting him to meet the kids several times before he stays the night. I give them a lot of independence, and I think that's why they appreciate that I must have mine, too. They've never asked whether so-and-so is going to be a new Dad, or anything like that. I'm sure because it's never entered my head, it's never entered theirs. I don't know what would happen if a man I liked didn't get on with the children – I suppose I would take that into account and not start anything with him. So to that extent I do care a lot about what they think!'

Not everyone would find it easy to adopt Moira's open, uncomplicated attitude. And of course with older children it may be necessary to explain more than she has found she needed to do, so that they understand what is involved and what their mother's sexual feelings are. If you find this difficult, because you believe that your behaviour is morally wrong and you're afraid that you will lose your children's respect and turn them into irresponsible, promiscuous teenagers or adults, perhaps you need to examine your attitudes towards 'sexual morality'. You may be a great deal happier to feel that you are right to be disturbed at the idea of not practising what you preach, and that to go against your firmly-held beliefs will ultimately be too destructive for you to cope with. The stress of concealing or denying something that you really believe is wrong and harmful to your children can be very great, and would probably poison any new sexual relationship in any case. But if, on the other hand, you believe that you, and your children, have the right to express your sexuality in any way that doesn't harm others, you can talk to them without guilt about your needs and theirs and expect the sort of respect for your independence that you in turn will give them.

# Re-marriage, step-parenting

In Chapter 13 we considered some of the reasons why many women hesitate to involve themselves again in a close relationship or a marriage. When there are children – yours or his – the situation may involve even more difficult adjustments on both sides than the 'simple' business of adapting to a new relationship between two adults.

It's estimated that each year in Britain 100,000 people become step-parents, and for most of them, and their children, this new situation is almost certain to cause some difficulties. This is especially so if the adults involved – the 'natural' father or mother – are still locked in a combative attitude over access, maintenance and past injustices. Most step-parents are only too anxious to settle down happily with their new family, but it's a mistake, say Emily and John Visher (counsellors working with step-families in the United States) to believe that once the initial ice is broken they can all get along together just like a 'normal' family. The relationship can be good, can be better than that of the original parents and children, but it's bound to be different. This is because everyone in the new family has experienced some kind of loss, whether it was divorce or bereavement that caused it. Step-parents, say the counsellors, tend to expect that with goodwill and good intentions everything will settle down quickly. They want to love their new family, but, to their surprise, they find that it takes time; and, when the love develops, it's not the same kind of love as they have for their own children. Expressing this love can become self-conscious and feel almost false. And the sort of quarrels, ups-and-downs every parent has with her own children, things that generally blow over quickly, can cause feelings of guilt and self-doubt, when a partner's children are involved. Women, in particular, are all-too-aware of the 'wicked step-mother' image, and may become too tolerant, too 'nice' in an effort to placate both children and partner.

To add to the complications, there's often the original father involved; as we've seen in earlier chapters, he may be associated in the children's minds with weekend treats and expensive presents. The step-parent – especially the stepmother – on the other hand, is easily seen as the 'baddie', the one who scolds and corrects, makes unwelcome demands and lacks the glamour of the less familiar parent. If the ex-husband has a new partner, she won't be seen as the conventional stepmother, but as part of this glamorous image, and it may be very difficult to tolerate the children's glowing descriptions of her kindness, competence and beauty when they are contrasting all this with the mundane behaviour and appearance of the mother they actually live with.

Every family has some problems along the way – and those of the step-family may be no different; though, because of the tensions brought about by the unfamiliar situation they may seem more serious. In some ways being a step-parent is like being an adoptive parent. You are inheriting someone else's child and possibly someone else's

'When I took on John I took on Gloria too. Of course I'd met her when we had taken Gloria out together some weekends, and she seemed a sweet kid, a bit quiet, perhaps, but I put this down to shyness. What I didn't understand was that the 'shyness' was really resentment and jealousy. John was anxious to break her in gently to the idea of our marriage – he felt he'd given her a raw deal by walking out on her and her mother, and that she needed careful handling. So I found myself in the ludicrous position of having to walk the streets every alternate Sunday while he had her to himself in our flat. If I arrived home before he'd taken her back to her mother I was treated to a display of rudeness and resentment on her part, and he did nothing to stop her. In the end I was driven to do something I hated myself for – telling him he'd have to choose between acting the doting father or having me go. It may seem trivial – after all, it was only those Sundays that were a problem – but it seemed to me that if he wasn't willing to make her treat me with reasonable respect he didn't actually respect me and my feelings.

'We went through some rough times after that, but he did make an effort to talk to Gloria and explain how I felt, and gradually she came round. I refused to go out every time she came – though I did occasionally – and after a while we had some good times together. She's still not altogether happy with me, I suppose, because she blames me for the break-up of her parents' marriage, but at least she's willing now to treat me as a human being. I don't think we'll ever be close – but perhaps that's too much to expect in the circumstances.'

'Lots of friends warned me about the difficulties I'd face in marrying a man with three children. I'd been married before, myself, but I had no children of my own, and I had absolutely no experience of handling them. Yet here I was, with a ready-made family who had been through a lot while their mother was ill and after her death. Perhaps because I expected trouble I got very little. The children had had to do a lot for themselves since their mother's death and were very competent and independent.Instead of seeing me as an interloper in the family set-up I think they were really relieved that now they were more able to relax and enjoy themselves while I took some of the stress out of their lives. I managed to cut down my hours of work to be with them more – I didn't mind, I rather enjoyed the whole business, it was so new to me. Anyway, it's all worked out very well; I've never felt I was compared with their mother or resented for my relationship with their father.'

mistaken handling, as well as the result of her genes. The difference is that enormous efforts are made on the part of social services and other agencies to match up adopters and adopted, and full back-up services continue right through the early days of adjustment. Step-parents, until recently, have been on their own. Recognising the problems, because she herself has suffered them, Elizabeth Hodder two years ago formed the National Stepfamily Association which held a conference of step-parents in London in 1983 and has gone on to form self-help groups and a telephone counselling service in some parts of the country. The very fact that this organisation exists has brought to the attention of other people the needs and difficulties of step-families – and doctors, social workers, teachers and counsellors are now much more aware of the problems. A potent cause of failure in second marriages may now receive the attention it deserves.

# Coping with depression and anxiety
## Depression
You're unusual if the upheaval and grief you have been through didn't cause you to become depressed for a while. How long that 'while' lasts varies, of course, with the circumstances of your loss. In the case of a bereavement, it is generally believed that the period of grief or mourning lasts for around two years, with upsurges of misery around the time of anniversaries and festive occasions perhaps, for the rest of the person's life. If the loss you suffered was less traumatic, or the sense of relief in getting out of a bad marriage is greater than the sense of loss caused by the failure of past hopes, you will have been able to recover within months or even weeks, and look forward to rebuilding your life in a positive way. Even if you were badly depressed in the aftermath of the loss, with time you should have recovered.

So here we're not considering your immediate reaction to a death, separation or divorce, but the sort of long-lasting, devastating feeling that's usually described as 'clinical depression'. Feeling low, hopeless, miserable, unable to concentrate, paralysed in mind, incapable of making any effort, trapped in a dark pit: these are descriptions, in their own words, of the condition of those suffering from what is generally believed to be one of the most widespread health problems, and one which is particularly prevalent, so it is said, among women.

A major problem when you are in this condition is precisely your inability to take the initiative in getting help. And this is where your family and friends can be most useful. However great the effort, you should try to talk to them about how you feel, and if they don't seem to understand just what you're going through, try to explain that exhortations to 'pull yourself together' or 'think of others worse off' are useless. There is nothing you'd like better than to be able to take yourself in hand and get out of the miserable state you're in – and nothing more difficult.

Once you and your friend or family member are convinced that help is needed, where do you turn? To most people, the GP is the person most readily available. You may be lucky and have a good relationship with a caring doctor, who will make time – perhaps by a specially arranged appointment – to talk to you, discuss possible treatment and generally provide the support you need. S/he may decide that rather than refer you on to a consultant psychiatrist it would be worthwhile trying out the effect of anti-depressant drugs, if these seem appropriate; and although you may quite naturally distrust drug treatment in general, it's worth knowing that in many cases a short course of anti-depressants is effective in taking the edge off your depression and enabling you to get into a better state to cope with any problems in your life, and make the changes that may be necessary to restore you to your normal equilibrium. These drugs don't act instantly – they can take three weeks to have full effect – but if they're going to help they will make you feel a lot better when you've been taking them for a while.

For some women anti-depressants plus the help of family, friends and a good GP can bring relief. It's when your GP is uncaring, too rushed or dismissive, or when what s/he has been able to offer has proved ineffective, that you and your friends have to decide the next step. At this point there may seem little alternative other than a referral to a psychiatric hospital or department. You may be advised that in-patient treatment is necessary, but in the majority of cases treatment is on an out-patient basis.

## Some interesting figures

More women than men suffer from depressive illness. But of 15,215 admissions to psychiatric hospitals in England and Wales, 68 per cent were men and 32 per cent women (1982 figures).

## Conventional psychiatry

Sadly, it's not possible to say that the treatment you get is necessarily going to 'cure' you. Psychiatrists, and the departments they run, vary tremendously both in the methods they use to treat their patients and in their attitudes and the atmosphere they provide. Some rely almost entirely on drug treatment with a small amount of psychotherapy ('talking treatment') on the side. Others will offer minimal drug therapy and much more individual or group psychotherapy. In some hospitals you'll see more of the psychologists. Unlike psychiatrists, psychologists are not medical doctors. They are more likely to use 'behaviour therapy' methods to help you overcome the problems of anxiety that are so often bound up with depression. Elsewhere the doctors are hostile to psychologists being involved in treatment and believe that the 'medical model' is the only appropriate one for treating 'mental illness'. So what it amounts to is that unless you know something about the methods and outlook of the particular consultant or department to which you are referred you will be unable to predict just what kind of treatment you're likely to get. All you can do, as one woman who has been through the process says, is to give it a go.

Your friends and relatives may be baffled by your state and the treatment or lack of treatment you seem to be getting. No one may bother to contact them or explain what's going on. Particularly if you're an in-patient, it's important that people should visit you regularly, and make their presence felt by doctors and nurses. They should know that even if you're not able to respond positively to their visit – and may even tell them not to bother – they should still come, making quite clear to everyone that there's at least one caring person outside who wants to know about your progress. If you seem to be getting worse rather than better, your visitor should be prepared to confront the staff in an unthreatening way, and ask why this seems to be happening.

You and your friends must always remember that as a voluntary patient in or out of hospital you don't *have* to put up with treatment that you find useless or upsetting. Despite the belief among some psychiatrists that you have to get worse before you can get better, if you find yourself leaving a consultation feeling more disturbed and upset than when you arrived, it's probable that something is wrong. From any form of treatment you should be able to walk away feeling that, even if part of the discussion you've

*'I discharged myself after a month. I was in a ward of zombies – everyone drugged to the eyeballs. People just sat apathetically all day, or slept on their beds. We were given no chance of exercise, not even any fresh air. The 'occupational therapy' was pathetic. I wanted to try some dressmaking but the OT couldn't get any materials for me and couldn't offer anything else. My consultant psychiatrist seemed kind at first, but he turned out to be an emotional bully, trying to make me accept his view of my problems, which didn't seem to fit. He reprimanded me for not standing up when he approached! Because I retained some vestige of independence I was regarded as an oddity. I could see that if I stayed any longer and took more of the drugs I'd land up as lost and hopeless as some of my fellow-patients – I wondered whether they'd come in in a relatively hopeful frame of mind, as I had, and had been beaten by the system. The staff told me they'd soon see me again as I said good-bye. They haven't.'*

**Psychiatry – two in-patient experiences**

*'The main benefit I got was from other patients. They had time to listen on an individual basis, and I found the group discussions, led by the psychiatrist, very supportive and revealing. There was something interesting going on all day and sometimes I found myself almost too busy, rushing from one activity to another. There wasn't any compulsion to join in, but I found after the first week I wanted to. I made some good friends and we keep in touch both through the group that still meets and through meeting each other socially. The staff made great efforts to contact my relatives and get their help, the social worker got me a part-time job even while I was still in hospital, and someone from the local group of MIND was put in touch with me, so that I had some ready-made back-up when I first came home. I'm still in the job, and one evening a week I do some secretarial work for MIND or chat with ex-patients who come along to the club that runs on the same evening. I won't say I never get depressed now – but I'm so much better and I don't think that would have happened if I hadn't been in hospital.'*

had was upsetting, there has been some positive result. You've reached some new insight or arrived at accepting a new, attainable goal. If this hasn't happened, and you're feeling more distressed, more depressed, should you consider at the very least explaining how you feel and be prepared, if you're met with platitudes or false reassurance, to end the treatment?

Although we've stressed the possibility that psychiatric treatment won't help you, it's just as necessary to say that many women do get real help from 'orthodox' medical sources and such possible help shouldn't be rejected without good reason. There are flexible-minded, genuinely caring doctors whose patients have every reason to be grateful for the help they've received. And where clinical psychologists or other non-medical staff have formed part of a team, or who have taken over the psychotherapeutic part of the treatment, they, too, can play a very positive role in a person's recovery from depression and anxiety.

### Feminist and self-help alternatives to conventional psychiatry

There are, of course, alternatives to 'orthodox' treatment for depression. A most useful section in the book *Dealing with Depression* discusses the options and explains the particular benefits that women fortunate enough to have experience with a feminist psychotherapist may derive. The book also examines the role and positive contribution that self-help groups – especially all-women groups – can make in enabling a woman to overcome her paralysing and threatening depression. The difficulty for most women, however, is the inaccessibility of such sources of help, though on p. 318 there's a short booklist and the address of a Women's Therapy Centre in London, which, even if you can't get to it, may be able to put you in touch with an individual therapist near your home.

But why have you got depressed in the first place? As we've seen, depression has been described as particularly affecting women. Since no one has been able to identify some peculiarly female physical reason for this, it seems probable that there is something in the way we live, or are expected to live, that causes much more depression among women than among men. And there's a fair amount of research to show that homebound isolation, the way in which women are expected to serve their men and their families and put their own needs aside, the expectation that we'll never show anger, the belief that so many women have that they're incompetent or worthless because they've been told it often enough – all these aspects of male-dominated society may cause all but the toughest or most fortunate to crack at some point of stress in their lives. Through the women's movement many have come to understand something of this and to find ways of overcoming the disadvantages of their upbringing and environment.

**Trapped at home?**

Depression and anxiety go together, and in fact some psychiatrists will see depression as the major problem in a given individual, while others will diagnose anxiety, with a depressive component. The sufferer herself is probably aware of both, and one of the most crippling ways in which extreme anxiety can show itself is a phobia – an 'unreasonable' fear of objects, places and people. The most common phobia is agoraphobia.

'Fear of open spaces' is how agoraphobia is usually defined, though it seems more commonly associated with fear of *crowded* places. Some experts say that around two-thirds, others as many as 90 per cent of agoraphobics are women. Various clinical researchers have described the typical agoraphobic as soft, passive, anxious, shy and dependent. But, as American psychologists Kathleen Brehony and Scott Geller point out, these are the sort of characteristics that are seen as 'typically feminine'. Women, they say, are generally viewed as 'relatively emotional, submissive, house-oriented, non-adventurous and desiring security'. Another researcher, I.G. Fodor, goes further. It's far more acceptable in our culture, he says, for a woman to be housebound than it would be for a man; and indeed 'homebound' women are actively rewarded by society, while those who choose careers outside the home may have suffered some 'social punishment' for not meeting traditional expectations. So, says Fodor, agoraphobia is just an 'extreme and exaggerated, yet logical extension of the stereotypical feminine role'.

Agoraphobia often first develops when a woman is suddenly plunged into domesticity for the first time of her life, with the birth of a baby. She gets into the habit of staying at home, and perhaps derives some sense of status and security from her new job, as a substitute for the sense of personal worth she had as a worker and wage earner outside the home. Through lack of contact with others in the same position, or friends and relatives who could take over the care of the baby sometimes, it may be that she literally can't get out.

If you've experienced this you'll know how devastating the feelings of panic can be when you *were* out and about – in a supermarket or a bus perhaps, surrounded by busy people. You may have felt you were going to have a heart attack – or at the very least, make a spectacle of yourself by fainting or being sick. You made your escape as best you could; you weren't actually ill, but the terror you experienced and the fear of that fear may have prevented you daring to repeat the experience. This was the beginning of your agoraphobia. You became dependent on others to do the shopping; you either couldn't go out at all, or only in the company of your husband or a friend; holidays were impossible. Your whole life, and possibly that of your family, too, was affected.

Perhaps with help or an increased understanding of what you might do to help yourself, you overcame this disability. But if you didn't, and you are now on your own, you'll be even more motivated to conquer your fear. Some women have even found that the very fact that they now have no one to protect them and *enable* them to stay at home has pushed them out to meet the situations they feared. But many more still feel trapped in their homes, paralysed at the thought of going shopping, to the cinema or to visit friends. And this group is joined by others who are experiencing anxiety of this kind for the first time in their lives, because they've found the world transformed from a place of security where joys and troubles could be shared, to somewhere alien and threatening. Loneliness and grief have encouraged a sense of isolation where the only sure thing in life seems to be the protection and comfort of home.

If this is how you feel, you do need help. As with the sort of depression we've looked at earlier, you may find it through medical channels. But since phobias are perhaps more limited and definable than depression, self-help groups using fairly well-tried methods have been formed. The group Action on Phobia (see p. 318) makes use of the 'behavioural' technique developed by some clinical psychologists, but the advantage is that the group leaders, trained in these methods, are themselves former agoraphobics. A number of local groups have been formed, and even if there isn't one near you, Action on Phobia can provide you with a rundown of self-help methods which are the next best thing.

Most psychologists agree that if agoraphobia is a 'learnt' response to a particular situation (in most cases, isolation at home, for whatever reason) then it follows that it should be 'unlearnt' – and this is the first line of treatment, whether from a psychologist or under the guidance of a lay group leader. First, you are taught a relaxation technique that you can summon up at need. This isn't just 'doing nothing', but a conscious programme of relaxing every part of your body – and your brain. The next step may involve just opening your front door and standing there for a moment or two while you relax in the way you've been taught. You have to learn to let the panic come, rather than fighting it, and concentrate on relaxing instead. Gradually your panic will fade and you'll be able to go to the door without fear. Then you're ready to take your first steps outside. Later you'll be able to go to the front gate, then out into the street, then to the end of the road, and so on. One day you'll manage to go greater distances unaccompanied. All this may take months, and you'll probably have to enlist the help of a friend or family member to work in partnership with the group leader. If you have absolutely no one to take on this role, Action on Phobia will help with a telephone 'link-line'.

The problem with some self-help groups is that members become too dependent on them for their social needs. A good group will measure its success by the number of people who are able to leave the group and join other organisations and activities. It's not a good idea, once you're better, to hang on to the regular meetings as your only outlet. That could be exchanging one kind of dependency for another.

### Anxiety and sleeplessness

In Chapter 13 we looked at the interaction of over-stress with tension and consequent sleeplessness. But some women are aware of constant feelings of anxiety apparently unrelated to actual events in their lives – what's known as 'free-floating' anxiety. They're not so anxious that, like those suffering from agoraphobia, they're actually prevented from going out, going to work, or leading a normal social life. But the feeling of apprehension, that some nameless frightening thing is going to happen, even, in some instances, that they're almost on the edge of a panic attack, can be very difficult to cope with.

These feelings are generally explained in terms of an 'unresolved conflict', and it may be that, if you suffer from this kind of anxiety, you can identify some problem – generally in your relationship with other people and your fear of handling a conflict with them – that can be resolved. Inability to face up to others isn't a sign of *general* cowardice – anxiety, like many other emotions, is very specific, as Gwen has found.

She's a divorced woman in her late thirties who has been very active in the peace movement. She's well-known in her group for her resourcefulness and her fearlessness, on occasion, in facing up to threats of violence on demonstrations and picket lines.

'I think my friends see me as almost reckless,' Gwen admits. 'I do get carried away, partly from what I believe to be the rightness of what I believe in, partly because I feel other people are depending on me. I'd never attack anyone or behave in a provocative way, but I will stand my ground and I won't let myself be pushed around. But at work it's quite different. I'm an abject coward – I let people walk right over me, even when I know I'm right. I lie awake at night thinking how I ought to handle some situation, or what I ought to have said to the manager. But when it comes to doing anything I just go under again. It's got to the point where every time I walk into the office I have this sickening feeling of fear – as if something frightful is going to happen.'

Gwen agrees that actually nothing terrible ever does. She's ready to defend others, take up issues for *them*; but when she herself is involved, her confidence evaporates. It was the same in her marriage; like the manager, her husband could say or do what he liked with never a comeback from her. Her anger and resentment were suppressed – either because she feared the consequences for herself and her children or because her upbringing encouraged the feeling that *she* didn't matter, that it was her place to accept and put up with the unacceptable, without complaint. Perhaps the 'unresolved conflict' she's now suffering is the conflict within herself between her need to assert herself and stand up fearlessly to injustice, and the pull of habit and conditioning.

## Tranquillisers

Publications for doctors frequently carry advertisements showing middle-aged or elderly women – never men – with expressions of misery, anxiety or downright terror on their faces. The advertisements, of course, are for drugs 'with minimal side effects' that will calm such a person down, make her less disturbed and anxious. And most women suffering from feelings of anxiety that apparently don't have a 'real' cause do consult their doctors and do find themselves with a prescription for tranquillisers to deal with the anxiety or make them sleep. As we saw in Chapter 15, and earlier in this book, tranquillisers can be useful, in the very short term, to enable a person to cope with a crisis. You may have reason to be grateful to your doctor for giving you something that helped you to sleep in the midst of some painful event. They didn't make the event go away, but they did take the edge off shock or grief.

The temptation, having had that experience, is to resort to tranquillisers again when you feel anxious, with or without obvious 'cause', or if a succession of bad nights has worn you down. Many doctors are beginning to resist patients' requests for repeat prescriptions, and are either prescribing a very short course of treatment or refusing to repeat a prescription unless the patient comes to the surgery for a consultation. But others will comply unhesitatingly with a request or themselves suggest that tranquillisers are the obvious remedy. Their patients may join the hundreds of thousands of people 'hooked' on tranquillisers.

In the back of this book there's a list of agencies that can help you if you're in this position. Information and support from others who really know the problem can be enormously helpful. But if you decide to try to help yourself, there are ways to overcome tranquilliser-dependence.

First of all, it's important to understand that the addiction in many people is a very powerful one – some experts say it's as bad as heroin addiction. So it's going to be very difficult to come off the drug, and it's not going to be an enjoyable process: see below.

## Come off gradually

If you have been taking tranquillisers or sleeping pills for more than 2–3 weeks, don't try to cut them out suddenly. If you do, you may have such a bad reaction that in desperation you'll start to take them again. So – take it gradually. You can:

Cut out one tablet a day (if you're on several doses per day). Try this for at least a week before cutting out one more tablet. Try this for a further week or several weeks; repeat this process until you are no longer taking any tablets.

Or divide one or more tablets into quarters (or ask for a lower-dose tablet) and start by taking ¾ tablet once or twice a day, with the full dose on other prescribed occasions. Try this for at least a week before dividing another tablet into quarters, and taking ¾ of that.

When all tablets are three-quarter strength, cut down equally gradually to halves and quarters and then to nothing.

Or if you are taking the tablets only at bedtime, cut out one tablet a week. Be prepared for a difficult night and day, but persist until the experience is less painful, and cut out another – and so on. You may decide to leave to the last the cutting out of a tablet on the night before a particularly difficult day: some people find Mondays stressful, so the last tablet to be missed is the one taken on Sunday nights.

*Remember that it doesn't matter how long you take to wean yourself from the drug: cutting down is still better than continuing the full dose indefinitely.*

## Alternatives to drugs

We've already looked at some of the practical steps you might take to cope with tension, anxiety and sleeplessness. Changing your way of life as Jessica was advised to do (see Chapter 15, p. 282) is one of them. Only you can judge how much this will help in your individual situation. Another is to try some self-exploration, with the help of an individual therapist or group – see p. 308. And many women have found yoga or learning a deep relaxation technique very useful in smoothing away 'free-floating' anxiety. You may find local classes, or you can buy useful books, records and cassettes that teach the technique. If you can't manage to get to a class, and you find it too difficult to follow the instructions on cassette or in a book, you could write to the organisation Relaxation for Living with a s.a.e. for information about their taped course – it's much more comprehensive than just one cassette can be, and if you meet any problems there are accompanying notes or someone to whom you could write about any difficulty.

Finally, if insomnia is your problem, have you considered improving your bedroom conditions? If you can't get to sleep or you wake early, it may be that there are some simple remedies, that will help even if your main problem is stress and anxiety.

*Is the room noisy?* Can you change rooms? Ask neighbours to make less noise after, say, 11 p.m? Have you tried thicker curtains? Can you afford double glazing? Have you tried wax earplugs? (Get BQ earplugs if you can, otherwise Boots own brand.)

*Is the room too light?* Have you tried thicker or heavily-lined curtains? Have you tried an eye-mask?

*Are you too hot or too cold?* Do you adjust bed-coverings according to temperature? Do you use a hot water-bottle or electric blanket?

*Is your bed comfortable?* Are you making do with an old mattress? (The one you've slept on for 20 years will be sagging and bad for your back. A new one should be priority – one of the first things you treat yourself to as a woman on your own, if you possibly can.)

*Are you getting enough air?* Can you control ventilation to prevent stuffiness or draughts?

*Have you tried reading/getting up/relaxation/listening to music?* (Each of these helps some people.)

If none of these ideas works for you, then try to take the worry out of insomnia by assessing just how much sleep you *really* need. Some people can forget about the so-called 'normal' seven or eight hours – these may not be normal for *them*. Especially if you're an older woman, your sleep pattern may be changing, and you actually do need less sleep than you did when you were younger. It could be futile, and just add to your anxiety, to 'try' to sleep as you used to.

# Looking back in anger

Jo is in her late fifties. She was married for thirty years and was devastated when she learnt that her husband had been having an affair with a younger woman over a long period, and that 'everyone' knew about it except herself. 'He would have been quite happy to leave things as they were,' she says. 'He was shocked when *I* wouldn't and started divorce proceedings. I was terribly angry to think that the shortage of money we'd been experiencing, despite his good job, was because he'd been keeping two homes going, and that I'd had to take a job I didn't enjoy, basically to pay for *her*. His 'business trips' turned out to have been jaunts with her. I felt I'd been made a complete fool of – his colleagues and our friends must have been laughing at me.' Now she suffers periods of self-hatred and depression.

Jo thought that once the divorce was through and she'd had time to get used to living alone again – only one of her children was still occasionally at home – she'd become reconciled to the situation, if not to her ex-husband. It hasn't happened. She feels as angry as ever. Three years later, she admits that anger and jealousy and hurt pride are still dominating her life. 'I live in the past,' she says 'and worry about the future. That means I can't enjoy the present, even though things have been going quite well for me since I changed my job and got involved in local politics.'

A feminist therapist is helping Jo to understand herself better, to admit to her overwhelming feelings of hatred and lost self-esteem, and to come to terms with what has happened, in a positive way. She's getting Jo to see that she's being unrealistic in believing that *everyone* knows about her 'humiliation' and despises her for it, pointing out that on Jo's own admission she has many good friends who have been most supportive to her. And Jo is beginning to realise that she didn't have any particular liking and respect for her husband's colleagues – she wouldn't have had anything to do with them, but for him – so that the fact that they've dropped out of her life doesn't matter to her. The therapist is enabling Jo herself to challenge the irrational beliefs that have been dominating her, and to accept that, yes, she had every reason to be angry when the break-up happened, but that in many ways her life is fuller and more satisfying now than it was when she was a (deceived) wife.

It isn't only in situations like Jo's that angry feelings can take over. If you've been badly treated, not, perhaps, by an individual, but by what 'society' has expected of you and your role as a 'good' wife and mother regardless of other aspirations, you've a right to be angry about it. But anger suppressed or unchannelled or directed against your family, rather than the concept of 'the family', is a negative and crippling emotion. It's never too late to protest, in actions as well as words. What's past is past. You can't change it – but you can change your future, and in understanding what has happened to you, and why, you can work with other women to ensure that your daughters and granddaughters have a real choice about the way they lead their lives. At the end of this book, and throughout its pages, we list organisations whose objectives, however diverse, are to do just that.

# Drinking too much?

When you're lonely, distressed and anxious it's very easy to slip into the habit of taking a drink to try to smooth away the trouble. And a glass or two does, undoubtedly, make your problems seem less pressing – for that moment. You feel more relaxed and at ease, sometimes more able to ride over a difficulty with increased confidence. If that's your experience, it's not surprising that you have recourse more and more often to alcohol, just as someone on tranquillisers may feel that they, too, help her through the day. The question is – are you becoming too dependent?

There may be cause for concern if:
• You automatically pour yourself a drink when you get home from work.
• You drink alone.
• Your only social life is centred round the pub.
• You find it difficult or impossible to stop drinking for a few days at a stretch.
• Despite good intentions, you can't refuse a drink.

If any of the above apply to you, you aren't necessarily on the way to becoming an alcoholic – but you are becoming alcohol-dependent, and if you're concerned about it (as you should be from the point of view of your general health and efficiency) your first step might be to try to resist drinking in whichever of these situations applies.

Ideally, whether or not to drink on any particular occasion ought to be a matter of choice. Some medical opinion suggests that one or two glasses of wine a day – or the equivalent – may actually be beneficial. If you can maintain that level of drinking, unless you're pregnant or a doctor has advised otherwise, you'll almost certainly come to no harm. Modern treatment for alcoholism or 'problem drinking' is tending away from a complete ban on alcohol towards 'controlled' drinking. In other words, the glass or two a day suggested above.

## Help with drinking problems

ACCEPT Services UK, Western Hospital, Seagrave Road, London SW6., Individual and group counselling, centres at Western Hospital and elsewhere in London and Home Counties.

Alcohol Counselling Service, 34 Electric Lane, London SW9. Counselling mainly in South London area.

Alcoholics Anonymous, 11 Redcliffe Gardens, London, SW10 9BG. Group addresses in London from 01–834 9779, in rest of the country from 01–352 9779. Best-known and largest organisation, many groups. Members encouraged to stop drinking altogether.

For local centres and groups contact your Social Services Department.

If you find this level of drinking impossible to maintain, you'd be wise either to see your doctor and come clean about what's happening, or to approach one of the groups suggested here. Another possibility is to consider some of the measures suggested earlier in this chapter, or group therapy of the kind offered by the Women's Therapy Centre (see p. 318) rather than a group specifically concerned with problem drinking.

There are some sources of useful information listed over-leaf, and remember to also look at the 'Directory' at the end of this book.

# Useful information

**Step-Parents: Useful information**
Contact the *National Stepfamily Association*. Mrs Elizabeth Hodder, Maris House, Trumpington, Cambridge, CB2 2LB.
**Books**
*Stepparenting* by Brenda Maddox (Unwin Paperback)
*How to Survive as a Second Wife* by Maggie Drummond (Robson Books)

**Agoraphobia**
Contact the following useful organisations:
Action on Phobia, 17 Burlington Place, Eastbourne, Sussex, BN21 4AR
(Send three second-class stamps for full information.)
The Phobics Society, 4 Cheltenham Road, Chorton-cum-Hardy, Manchester, M21 1QN
(Send large s.a.e. for helpful leaflets and contacts.)
The Open Door Association, 477 Pensby Road, Hewall, Wirral, Merseyside, L61 9PQ
Information service for agarophobics. Send large s.a.e.

**Books**
*Simple, Effective Treatment of Agorophobia* by Dr Claire Weekes (Bantam)

**General**
**Books to read**
*Dealing with Depression* by Kathy Nairne and Gerrilyn Smith (Women's Press)
*Outside In – Inside Out* by Leslie Eichenbaum and Susie Orbach (Penguin). A feminist psycho-analytic approach.
*A Complete Approach to Therapy* by Joel Kovel (Penguin)

**Useful Organisations**
Here is a list of useful organisations and women's therapy centres:
MIND (The National Association for Mental Health) 22 Harley Street, London W1 co-ordinates local mental health associations, and has a telephone informatoin (not counselling) service on 01–637–0741.
The Women's Therapy Centre, 6 Manor Gardens, London N7.
Pellin South London Feminist Therapy Centre, Pellin Centre, 43 Killyon Road, London SW8.
Oxford Women's Counselling Centre, Highcorft House, Tanners Lane, off Queen Street, Eynsham, Oxon.
Bradford Women's Therapy Service, tel 0274 400175
Samaritans – address and telephone number in local directory. In London ring 283 3400 for number of nearest service.

# CHAPTER 18
# HOLIDAYS

**Everyone needs a holiday – perhaps especially the woman on her own. We look at some of the problems and the possible solutions.**

Going on holiday alone can be terrific, if you are the kind of person who enjoys her own company and luxuriates in the freedom to go where she pleases and do as she likes. But you need plenty of self-confidence – and maybe even a stubborn, defiant streak – to start with. Some women have encountered difficulties:

'I quite like living by myself now that I've got used to it. But I work very hard and I would appreciate a good holiday once or twice a year. I've tried a conventional 'package' and although the place was lovely, I felt so conspicuous on my own in the hotel dining room, and it was even worse in cafés and restaurants in the town. I was actually actively discouraged by the man in charge of the sunbeds on the beach. He told me it was 'embarrassing' to accommodate a single person – all the sunbeds were set out in pairs. So I found myself sticking to the hotel pool and risking other people thinking I was trying to tag on to their parties. It really wasn't a very happy holiday.'

This woman's experience must be commonplace to many in her position. However much we may feel that single people ought to make a stand and insist on the same sort of welcome and service extended to couples and groups, it's not easy to brave offhand treatment, and stares from other holidaymakers. 'I felt that other people on the holiday were avoiding me, afraid that I'd tag on to them when they wanted to be alone with their partners or friends,' says another woman.

Unless you are starting out brimming with self esteem, it might be better to put off the truly independent holiday until you are feeling completely comfortable in your new identity. But what are the alternatives?

# Holidays with children

Women with children not yet old enough to go on holiday
without their mothers may not feel quite so conspicuous
in a world of 'happy families', and in some cases the children may get together with other children and thus bring
their mother and other parents into contact. Sheila,
however, found this a doubtful advantage when she took
her two children on holiday with her to a seaside hotel
that advertised special 'family holidays'. Her children got
friendly with another pair of similar age, and their parents
seemed pleasant people when they met up on the beach
or in the hotel. But before long Sheila found herself acting
as unpaid baby-sitter. The children were all so happy
together, suggested the parents, that it would be a shame
to take their two away when they went off for the day or
the evening. As Sheila wouldn't be going anywhere, would
she look after them all? Sheila had hoped for a quiet
holiday, but found herself tied to the children most days
and evenings – and, like so many women, managed to
feel 'mean' and 'guilty' when she suggested that the other
parents might take an occasional turn. After all, she *wasn't*
going anywhere by herself and she'd have to be with her
children anyway if the others hadn't been around. She felt
exploited and resentful.

Perhaps Sheila was unlucky. She stayed in a hotel where
there were very few guests, so she was confined to these
acquaintances. Many of the package holiday tour operators
offer special arrangements and price reductions for children, and a single parent booking one of these holidays in
a large hotel may have a better time – there are bound
to be large numbers of children when there are special
inducements, and therefore an increased likelihood of
meeting up with people with whom to share child care.
Any travel agent will help you select a suitable holiday for
yourself and your children.

Another idea is to join up with a friend to rent a cottage
for a self-catering holiday, either in this country or abroad.
You can get information about renting cottages (or flats)
from the National Tourist Board of whatever country you
are interested in. Avril hired a cottage in France
with another mother, who was not herself a single parent
but whose husband's job kept him at work in England:
'We had a wonderful time. We took one car between us,
with my two and Debbie's son in the back seat, and shared
the driving. The cottage was lovely and for some reason
my kids found it more acceptable to do their chores with

another child present – they all made a game out of it. And if Debbie or I wanted to go off on our own for an afternoon the other would happily babysit.'

There are also special organized holidays for single parents and their families which have proved very successful with some mothers. Started in connexion with Gingerbread, the organisation for single parents, these holidays are now operated by a separate company and organise holidays in Britain or abroad (see 'Directory'). There is a choice between self-catering and inclusive arrangements, and a Sharing Scheme which puts single parents in touch with each other to arrange to go away together.

Another possibility for those with children is a holiday at a centre that provides a variety of activities for children of all ages and their parents, ranging from 'hands on' computer courses for primary-age children to canoeing for adolescents and archaeology or keep fit for their parents. Different courses can be sampled each day at Millfield School Village of Education (see 'Directory') or you and the children can choose just one or two activities to carry you right through the week. At Loughborough University there's an emphasis on outdoor activities, and you can get information about other places in the 'Directory' at the end of this book.

# Unaccompanied holidays for children

Many mothers on their own feel particularly strongly that their children need to get away by themselves from time to time. Not only does their absence give the mother a much-needed break, but a holiday without a parent can encourage the independence that a single mother may think her children lack. But at what age is this reasonable?

It all depends on the child. For most, going away from home for the first time is a big adventure, and though they may look forward to it, it's probably with mixed feelings. Homesickness is always a possibility, less likely if your child has already stayed away from you with friends or relatives for a few days; but among strangers s/he can feel the absence from you and familiar surroundings more keenly. If your child is already showing signs of disturbance or insecurity as a result of a recent upheaval in your lives, it may be wiser to postpone a holiday on her own for another year or two. And most very young children find the experience a strain, to be avoided if possible.

## Children abroad

Secondary schools often organise school journeys to France, Germany and occasionally further afield. Unless your child's visit is intended primarily as a holiday experience, from the language-learning point of view an exchange arrangement on an individual basis is probably more satisfactory. The Central Bureau for Educational Visits and Exchanges publishes annually a list of organisations able to arrange exchange or paying guest visits abroad. This is the *Guide to Adventure and Discovery*, Central Bureau for Educational Visits and Exchanges, Seymour Mews House, Seymour Mews, London W1H 9PE, price £2.50 (1984).

Others, of course, revel in the freedom and companionship and the chance to learn new skills that the best of these holidays provide. Such children, who may have been quite apprehensive when setting off, come back quite in love with the life they've been leading, demanding to repeat the experience as soon as possible.

Only you can judge how your particular child will react or is likely to feel.

Some addresses of commercial and other holiday organisations are listed in the 'Directory', or write to the British Tourist Authority (address in 'Directory') for information about specialised holidays for unaccompanied children. In all cases, it's desirable to book early in the year: most of these holidays are in great demand.

## Special interest holidays for adults

If you have no children to worry about, what kind of holiday can you arrange for yourself? Most women would agree with the divorced woman quoted at the beginning of this chapter – conventional, hotel-type or package holidays can be frustrating and embarrassing to all but the most self-sufficient and confident. Teaming up with a friend may work well – for cheapness you're better off sharing a room, quite apart from the companionship you'll gain. But not everyone likes the degree of intimacy involved in room-sharing. You can still go away with a friend *and* have a room to yourself, however, if you can track down a holiday where at certain times of the year, or in certain resorts, there are 'single rooms for the price of doubles'. Your travel agent may suggest a particular tour operator who offers this arrangement – Sovereign Holidays is one such company.

But there is an increasing choice of holidays especially

uited to people on their own – 'activity holidays' as they're
enerally known. 'Activity' doesn't mean physical activity
though it can – but covers a huge variety of interests.
'he advantage of a holiday of this kind is that not only
vill you not find yourself isolated and conspicuous, but
rat you're likely to meet compatible people if you choose
omething that really interests you. In some of the centres
variety of courses go on at the same time, so that in your
eisure time you have a chance to meet an even wider
ross-section of people. And naturally you should come
way from such a holiday with increased knowledge or
kill of some kind.

Despite 'cuts', many Local Education Authorities still run
veekend or week-long courses, usually in rather splendid
ountry mansions they've taken over and adapted for the
urpose. In London the Inner London Education Authority
•ffers accommodation in student residences attached to
olytechnics, to enable people to stay cheaply in the capital
vhile they follow courses of study arranged by themselves.
)ther polytechnics – such as the Middlesex – arrange
ummer schools with a selection of education courses. And
ome higher education colleges offer residential courses
vith time to explore local towns and countryside. Finally,
here are a number of private commercial organisations
hat offer relatively luxurious accommodation and courses
n many subjects all the year round. These are particularly
.trong in arts and crafts, but music and drama also feature
n some programmes.

It's impossible to list here all the many educational,
ecreational and special interest holidays available, but
ources of information are listed in the 'Directory' at the
ack of this book.

## Getting a passport

f you haven't had a passport of your
wn, you will need one for any holiday
broad. The much more limited British
Jisitor's Passport may be adequate for
ne trip abroad – it's acceptable in
Western Europe and West Berlin, but
not for Yugoslavia or for overland travel
o West Berlin through the German
Jemocratic Republic (East Germany),
nd it's valid for only a year. You can
;et the Visitor's Passport from any main
post office (in Northern Ireland from
the Passport Agency, Belfast).

The full British Passport (soon to be
replaced by a European one) is applied
for on a form of application available
from main post offices. Send the
completed form, with the photographs
required, to the nearest address given
on the form. At busy times of the year
you should allow at least 28 days.

## Holiday insurance

Most tour operators offer holiday insurance as part of or in conjunction with their package arrangements. You don't have to insure with them or their insurance companies. Read the small print. You might get a better deal if you insured independently through your travel agent. Make sure you have adequate medical cover. Although there's an arrangement within the EEC and some other countries for reciprocal medical insurance cover, in some countries there's a large amount of red tape involved in getting repayments of expenses, and your holiday could be spoiled queuing up for the correct form, reimbursements, etc., quite apart from the illness or injury and the disruption it may have caused. You could need cover up to £50,000 for a serious illness or accident (1985). In the US the cost could be even more.

If you want to take a risk and cover yourself via the reciprocal Health Service arrangements, get leaflet SA 30 from the local office of the DHSS; this tells you how to apply for form E111, which tells you how to get treatment in EEC countries and gives advice on regulations outside the EEC. You must take E111 and the leaflet supplied with it (SA 36) with you when you go abroad, if you intend to claim free or reduced cost treatment should it be needed.

# Taking your car abroad

If you've been used to holidaying independently with a car and there's no package that appeals, you will probably want to continue to arrange your own holidays, with your family or friends or on your own. By far the simplest way to make all the arrangements is to book your ferry, arrange insurance, and get maps and route plans, if you want them, through one of the motoring organisations (see p. 325). They will also arrange to issue an International Driving Permit, if this is required in the country you'll be travelling to or passing through. British drivers holding full driving licence and over eighteen must have an IDP for Algeria, Bulgaria, Czechoslovakia, Hungary and Spain, and it is recommended for the German Democratic Republic, Morocco, Poland, Tunisia, Turkey and the USSR.

Motor vehicle insurance is compulsory throughout Europe – if you have insurance cover for the UK you're automatically covered in these EEC countries – Republic of Ireland, Belgium, Denmark, France, West Germany, Italy, Luxembourg and the Netherlands; and Austria, Czechoslovakia, German Democratic Republic, Finland, Hungary, Norway, Sweden and Switzerland although they aren't EEC countries, accept your British insurance cover. However, this only satisfies the minimum legal require-

# What to take

If you're taking your car abroad you'll need:
- First Aid Kit (compulsory in some countries)
- Warning triangle (compulsory in some countries, two in Cyprus and Turkey)
- Nationality plate
- Rear view mirror on the left, fixed externally
- Seat belts – note that in many countries it's illegal for children to travel in the front, even with seat belts.
- Spares (see below)

And remember to adjust your lighting:
Adjust headlights so that they don't dip to the left – you can buy beam deflectors from the AA or an accessory shop – remove them when you return to the UK. In France and Tunisia locally registered motorists must show a yellow beam from their headlights – if you don't want to be sworn at use amber lens converters or paint the glass with a yellow plastic paint (removable with solvent). In many countries it's compulsory to carry spare bulbs – and it's a wise precaution everywhere.
*The motoring organisations can offer full advice on regulations and what to take with you. The AA will hire you a spares kit for your make and model of car – in 1984 the charge was 55p per day plus VAT for members, with a returnable deposit of £25.00.*

ments in each country. Before going abroad you should ask your insurance company for advice, and make sure you are adequately covered. If in any doubt, you should ask for your UK cover to be extended to apply fully to the Continental countries you'll be visiting. They will issue a 'Green Card' which is accepted as evidence of insurance and is valid in most of Europe. You *must* have a Green Card for Bulgaria, Iceland, Morocco, Poland, Portugal, Romania, Spain, Tunisia, Turkey and Yugoslavia.

It's unwise not to book ferry space ahead at the height of the holiday season – either directly with the ferry company, through a travel agent or your motoring organisation – but you can take off on spec at less popular times of the year and you should find space. It's economical to fill your car with the maximum number of passengers allowed, even if you drop some of them off as soon as you land in Europe. Friends wanting to make their own arrangements abroad will be glad to share the costs of cross-Channel or North Sea ferries, making the whole trip much cheaper for all of you. You should just make sure that your arrangements for meeting up at the end of the holiday are cast-iron. Exchange holiday addresses and telephone numbers if possible, and check that the arrangements still stand, or arrange contact points or to leave messages with a reliable person or officer.

## Car insurance – and everything

If you've never taken a car abroad on your own, you might like to consider the all-in arrangements offered by the motoring organisations. Having the maximum possible cover for all possible emergencies could give you real peace of mind.

The AA '5-Star Service' for instance, is made up of three parts: vehicle security, travel security and personal security. Vehicle security gives access to the overseas emergency services for all kinds of difficulties, including vehicle recovery, legal assistance, spare parts delivery, and a free bail bond in Spain (where you can be held for an alleged motoring offence unless you pay a bail bond). Travel security offers you additional cover against unexpected accommodation expenses and unexpected travel expenses if you should break down and be delayed. Personal security gives the usual travel insurance cover for loss of luggage, medical expenses etc.. Additionally, the 5-Star Service now covers you against losses incurred through a tour operator, travel agent or ferry company going out of business, up to £1,000 per party.

Full information on this Service and other facilities offered by the AA for motorists holidaying abroad will be found in the free brochure *Motoring Abroad*, which you can get from any AA office.

# CHAPTER 19

# GETTING OLDER

**Retirement or qualifying for a pension may seem to mark the beginning of a new stage of life. But being 60-plus doesn't mean that active life is over: there may be problems but there are opportunities too.**

If you're over sixty you may have skipped some of the previous chapters. Perhaps when you've read this one you'll want to go back to them, because a great deal of what we've discussed and the suggestions that have been made apply to women of all ages. Whether you've been divorced for years or whether it's been a recent event some major adjustments were necessary – see Chapters 2, 4, 5, 6 and 11–13. If you're now alone because of a bereavement, read Chapter 3 instead of Chapter 2, but the rest will apply to you equally.

In the over-sixties group, bereavement is much more likely than separation or divorce to be the cause of finding oneself suddenly alone. This doesn't make it any easier to bear. But at least if the partnership was a good one it's possible to look back on many years of a happy relationship, at troubles faced and overcome with your partner's support, and to get some comfort from the knowledge that he or she had *your* love and support up to the end of life. As we get older most of us have probably considered the likelihood that we should have to face widowhood at some time – husbands tend to be older than their wives, and men still, on average, die earlier than women. We may have pushed these thoughts to the back of our minds, hoping that somehow death will come to both partners at the same time. But statistically this isn't likely, and a woman of 60-plus may have ten or twenty years alone before her still. Those years needn't be wasted.

'My biggest dread as I approached retirement age was unemployment,' says Grace. 'It may sound silly, but I do see retirement as being just like being out of a job – even worse in some ways, because an unemployed person is at least *eligible* for a job, even though the chances of getting one mayn't be good. My husband died more than ten years ago, and because I had very little money I was forced to go back to work. It was the best thing that could have happened. I got work I enjoyed and made a lot of friends I'd never have met otherwise. And I was *busy*. I did have some problems connected with the house which I had to tackle on my own – that was hard. But I couldn't let them get me down, and I had more than my own troubles to occupy me.

'So for a year or two before I retired I made what now look like rather frantic plans to involve myself in activities that I could carry over into retirement. I joined classes and societies and groups and I was out nearly every evening. I almost knocked myself out! Some of the groups I joined weren't really involved with things I was interested in, so the whole thing became a bit of a drag. Since I retired last year I've come to my senses and dropped some of this activity. I've concentrated on the one or two issues that really interest me, and they keep me busy enough, and allow me time to *enjoy* myself. You don't have to rush here there and everywhere and fill every moment of the day to feel both useful and relaxed in your old age.'

## Should you move?

In Chapter 7 we looked at some of the disadvantages of moving home, and many of these apply with particular force to someone on her own, and growing older. It's a well-known fact that many older people choose to move to an area they've visited on holiday. Dream cottages in the country or 'labour-saving' bungalows on the South Coast fortunately do tend to be beyond the means of most of those who fantasise about them. Fortunately, because they may come to trap rather than liberate. Unless the place you choose is accessible to family and friends, you know the area and its inhabitants well, and shops and medical and social services are easily available you could be in trouble. You may be perfectly strong and well at sixty or sixty-five: but will you be able to manage the garden, household repairs and daily chores in ten or fifteen years' time? Perhaps . . . but then perhaps not. What you gain financially by selling up and buying somewhere cheaper to live could be soon offset by higher prices and fares in a less-populated area. And what you may very well lose is the help from your adult children, friends and neighbours when you're in trouble. With the best will in the world if these people live many miles away they won't be able to pop in for a few minutes and make you a cup of tea if you're under the weather. And if you're really ill – could you be isolated, without help or anyone to contact the doctor or hospital on your behalf?

*At any point of transition in our lives, we have to stop and take stock. The sixties represent a crossroads, a time when we have choices.* It may not be easy when you're alone to make the right ones – but you do have options.

# What sort of a person are you?

Many people are just too busy while they're working or bringing up a family to stop and think what they really want out of life, what they really enjoy doing. If you've been having a hard struggle just to keep going, it would have seemed an impossible luxury to have time to consider more than the immediate present and the immediate task ahead of you. But now things have probably changed. You may have only yourself to think about; domestic responsibilities are reduced; your children can fend for themselves; meagre as it may be, you have a pension and, if you're not forced to leave work, at any rate you have a choice about it.

So take stock. What are your assets, not only in terms of housing or money but in terms of skills and abilities? Are you a very social person or can you tolerate or even enjoy being alone? Is there something – an interest, a political involvement, a hobby, a talent, you've never had time to cultivate, but would love to pursue now? In considering yourself and your needs you may feel you're being selfish. After all, most women spend a large part of their lives considering the well-being and needs of others, and it's difficult to break the habit! But just because you've always put yourself last, perhaps it's time for a change. And this isn't selfish. For one thing, in 'indulging' yourself by doing what *you* want to do you're likely to become involved with other people and you may have a crucial role to play in their lives, even though you're not consciously 'doing good'. For another, looking after yourself will keep you alert and healthy and thus no burden on others.

It's often helpful at a time of decision-making actually to sit down and draw up a balance sheet. You can do this when you're considering such relatively trivial things as the purchase of some object which you're not sure about,

## 60-plus checklist

• *How much money have I?* List income from all sources – pensions, interest on savings, part-time work, maintenance from ex-husband, building society account, etc.

• *Do I need more to maintain a decent standard of living?* List possible sources – social security, part-time work, housing benefit, sale of possessions, increased maintenance.

• *Should I move or stay put?* List advantages and disadvantages of a move. If plusses exceed minuses, consider where you could move to, and to what kind of flat/house. Be prepared to find on investigation that your assessment of the situation was incorrect (e.g. house prices or rents too high), then think again.

• *All the above satisfactorily settled, what would I really like to do?*

• *Is this realistic?* Take health and strength and energy into account.

• *If not, what compromises are possible?*

• *Are my plans realistic for now, but less so for the distant future?* If this is the case, perhaps you might err on the side of caution.

• *How far do I depend on family and friends for support, company?*

• *Can I tolerate a degree of loneliness?*

• *Do I prefer the company of younger or older people?*

• *If my wishes for the future aren't fulfilled, what would I do?*

• *Am I good or bad at taking social initiatives?*

• *Could I become interested in political action, adult education, old people's organisations etc.?*

• *Can I afford holidays, and if so, what kind?*

• *Who needs me, and what can I do about it?*

---

or the more important decisions about a house move; you can weigh up, for instance, the advantage of cheapness versus the possibility that the proposed purchase may result in increased costs of maintenance. In deciding about your future, it might be useful to make out a checklist; it will be an individual one, of course, but the questions listed above might help you make a start.

# Your money

Much of the information given in Chapter 6 applies to older women and it's worth checking with it again to see that you know what your rights and entitlements are, and that you're actually getting them. As far as Social Security benefits are concerned, the leaflets etc. most likely to apply to a widowed or divorced woman over sixty are:

NP 32 'Your Retirement Pension'

NP 32A 'Your Retirement Pension if you are Widowed or Divorced'

NI 184 'Non-contributory Retirement Pension for People over eighty'

NI 92 'Earning extra Pension by Cancelling your Retirement'

NI9 'Going into Hospital? What Happens to your Social Security Benefit or Pension?

P11 'Free Prescriptions'

(NP 35 and NP 36, concerned with widows' benefits, may not apply to women over sixty)

All these leaflets are available at your local DHSS office, and should be in your public library reference section and at the Citizens' Advice Bureau. If in doubt about entitlements, consult the CAB or the DHSS office.

See Chapter 6 for information about Housing Benefit.

# Work after sixty

### Can you go on working?

Many women, once they reach pension age, are only too glad to give up their jobs. Most are forced to do so, anyway, because a majority of employers fall in with the National Insurance retirement age for women – sixty. But what of the woman who has an interesting job which she feels quite capable of holding down? For her, retirement is likely to be a most unwelcome change.

'I find it difficult to accept that on a Friday I could do a demanding job which satisfied both me and my employers, but on the following Monday I'm out of work,' says Caroline. 'I've listened to all the "good reasons" why I have to go – make way for younger people, take a well-earned rest, etc. etc.. But don't those apply to men, too – and they can carry on for another five years? It's ludicrous, seeing that women live longer than men, and no one has ever proved to me that their brains deteriorate earlier!'

For a long time proposals have been in the air that a compromise should be reached on this point – general retirement at sixty-three is one suggestion, or the lowering of male· retirement age to sixty. But in the meantime, women like Caroline do find it harder than most to settle down to the life of a retired person. What are the chances of persuading employers to waive the official line on retirement at sixty, or of finding a new job?

If you're really indispensable – though we're always told that no one is – you may convince your employer that you should be kept on for a few more years. But it's very wise to try to come to terms with the inevitable: you will eventually have to go, and you should be preparing for this. In a time of high unemployment, unfortunately, the chances of getting another job at 60-plus aren't good – unless you have some particular skill or experience that's in short supply. An alternative would be to branch out as a freelance, doing something you're good at, but not necessarily your original job (see suggestions in Chapter 8), or to take on a consultancy. If this is a possibility, try to contact and keep in touch with people you've been associated with at work or in a professional capacity. If you're an obvious person to contact over some problem, work may come your way.

Someone with good secretarial skills, and living in a city, may get temporary work through an agency – not everyone's idea of a pleasant job, but it does bring in an income of sorts, and employers are often glad to have older women as a 'temp' as long as she's reliable and flexible. Shops often employ older women, part- or full-time.

Another possibility, especially if you're active and have experience with children, would be to take on the job of after-school care of the children of a working mother. You would be especially welcome if you were willing to come in full-time during school holidays or to help out with minor illnesses. This is the solution to the problems of two women, and it's been known to work very well indeed. An advertisement on a newsagent's board or in the local paper could bring results. You would have to be prepared to offer good references and to agree to fall in with the parent's wishes on discipline and diet. Going to the children's home, childminding regulations wouldn't apply.

**Voluntary work**
You may not want a paid job as a childminder, but if you have grandchildren nearby and their parents are both working they could be delighted to have you in daily on a similar basis. Much depends on the relationship you have with your daughter or son and your in-law, and whether you see eye-to-eye on the way you all think children should be brought up. If you don't – or you can't adapt to their ideas (s/he *is* their child) – then this situation could be fraught with conflict and everyone will suffer, not least the child. But if you're in broad agreement, you could really be tremendously welcome and valuable. You'll know yourself whether it's wiser to volunteer or wait to be asked. Even if you don't take on the job on a regular basis, you'll surely be much appreciated as a temporary back-up in emergency. Remember, though, that it's time that your own needs came first. It wouldn't be in your best interests to hold back from taking on a regular job or voluntary work just in case you might be needed to look after your grandchildren.

Many voluntary organisations are mentioned throughout this book and are also listed in the 'Directory' at the end, and most of them welcome helpers. (See pp. 341–3 of this chapter.) The important things to be sure about when taking on any voluntary job in retirement are, first, that you're really interested in the organisation and its aims, and second, that it's realistic to undertake the amount of help you're asked for or that you're tempted to offer. Better volunteer to do something limited to start with, and do it regularly and reliably, than promise many hours and find you can't cope. Voluntary bodies rely heavily on older women without too many home ties – and that's just the position you're in. Most will pay out-of-pocket expenses, and you shouldn't be shy about asking whether they'll pay fares or car running expenses before you commit yourself to something that involves travel.

## Women's organisations

For a list of those that cover all age-groups see 'Directory' But you may be particularly interested in one that is especially concerned with the lives of older women. This is the Older Feminists' Network. It meets in Central London about ten times a year, and some local groups have been formed. You can get information about the OFN from A Woman's Place (see 'Directory' for address).

# Further education

Elsewhere (see especially Chapter 8) we've looked at the Open University and other forms of adult education. 'It's never too late to learn' is a truism that applies particularly to you now that you're over sixty. Despite savage cut-backs in adult education budgets, local education authorities are still running popular courses in their centres, and in many areas these are available during daylight hours, suiting particularly those students who are retired or unemployed.

This is how one North London widow spends her week – she's lucky, of course, that so far the Inner London Education Authority has continued to provide these facilities and, for pensioners, extremely cheaply:

*Mondays* Mornings, Italian for beginners. Afternoons, Over-Sixties Keep-Fit.

*Tuesdays* Mornings, Art.

*Wednesdays* Mornings, Advanced cookery. Afternoons, Over-Sixties Keep-Fit.

*Thursdays* Morning, cooking for Lunch Club. Afternoons, Current Affairs.

On *Fridays* she does some shopping and housework.

Not every Adult Education Centre offers such a variety of classes, but just one or two a week could give some sort of structure to your life in retirement, keep your brain working, help you learn new skills or brush up old ones, and, above all, the chance to socialise with others who have the same interests. The camaraderie at the keep-fit classes is especially noticeable. Those attending often meet for a snack before going on to the class, and many have become firm friends.

The big objection advanced by many older people to attending evening classes or even some daytime ones is that they feel a bit out of place since so many of the other students are young enough to be their grandchildren. That's one of the reasons why Universities of the Third Age are beginning to take off in Britain.

That learning should be lifelong is the idea behind this development. It originated in France, where many thousands of older people are catching up with the education they missed in earlier years. If you're now sixty or more, it's probable that when you were young higher education wasn't for you – unless your parents could afford university fees, and to keep you for three or four years while you were studying. A few contemporaries got scholarships, but they had to be exceptionally clever, since these were so rare.

So you probably left school at fourteen or fifteen – and after that, unless you were willing to accept the grind of night-school after a day's work, your education was finished.

Of course in your age group there are others who were luckier, those who did have the chance of higher education. But they, too, may feel deprived. The educational path they followed may have been very narrow, and throughout their working lives they've been forced to stick rather closely to it. Now that they've retired, they form another group of people who would like to study something new.

Whichever group you belong to, it could be that the University of the Third Age (U3A) is for you. There are U3As in Cambridge (where the movement in Britain first started) London and a number of other cities, and others are planned. Each U3A runs itself, with no government finance, and the way they run is unique. It's called 'self-programming' or 'self-help'. Members form a sort of bank of skills, and it works like this:

# Further education

Information about local Adult Education classes should be available at your public library. Brochures normally are published in July or August, and enrolment takes place in September. It's best to start then, but if there's room for you, you can join at any time. See also Chapter 8. For information about the U3As send a 9 by 4in. self-addressed stamped envelope to Dianne Norton, 6 Parkside Gardens, London SW19 5EY.

A, a retired religious education teacher, offers to lead a course on comparative religion. But she's anxious to brush up the German she learnt years ago, so she chooses to go to a class led by B, a former refugee from Hitler's Germany. She, in turn, decides to follow a course in ancient Greek history, co-ordinated by C. C himself takes A's course, while D, who can't offer to lead any class, decides to go to a sketching group led by E, a successful artist who has no time to attend anything else but this class, but loves encouraging complete beginners. It sounds like a merry-go-round, but it works.

Although the emphasis is on learning, the atmosphere is informal, with lots of discussion rather than a rigid 'class' atmosphere. All the groups meet in the daytime, there are no entrance qualifications and students can attend any number of groups for the modest annual fee. This covers administrative costs only – the office, if there is one, is run by student volunteers. In some areas other educational bodies provide cheap or free accommodation for the classes.

## Learning in later life

In an Open University radio broadcast, psychologist Paula Allman was asked whether older people's belief that they learn more slowly than they did when they were young is because they were 'socialised' to believe this. She replied:

'I think there are structural implications within our society for why this is convenient for society. I think society needs to look at its practice . . . because we've got a change in age structure which is making the older-person group more visible.'

Ms Allman went on to express cautious optimism about the potential for development in older people: 'I wouldn't be half surprised if we do continue to develop at least in some way.'

Research in Australia in the learning potential of older people studying a foreign language, as compared with teenagers, showed that although they learnt a little more slowly, they retained what they learnt and examination results were comparable.

Don't be put off by the rather grand title. If 'university' sounds a bit daunting to you because you've scarcely had time to open a book in the last forty years, going along to one of the groups will soon reassure you. There are academic types, of course, and they're very useful. But there are other people who can offer rare skills, or none, who haven't had a formal education; and any group can include so-called 'ordinary' housewives, clerical workers, shop assistants, school teachers, manual workers.

The advantages of studying with a U3A are many – especially the social ones. Most have regular meetings of all members to hear lectures, play cards, or just socialise. Some arrange study visits to local museums and art galleries, concerts and theatres, and trips abroad for on-the-spot learning about the subjects they've been following.

## Fit over sixty

There's no reason why, just because you've reached pensionable age, you should assume that you can't follow the sort of programmes for diet and exercise we looked at in Chapter 15. If you are reasonably fit and active, good diet and plenty of exercise will keep you so. If you're not, unless there is some good medical reason why you can't follow a fitness programme, you can start gradually and build up energy, stamina, mobility just as younger people can. You may have to go at it a little more slowly, but the end result could be quite a considerable and enjoyable change for the better. And at the same time, if you are overweight you could slim down. There is absolutely no reason why someone in her sixties or seventies should weigh more than she did in her twenties. It isn't part of the ageing process to put on weight, though unfortunately many women do get stouter and heavier with the years, as a result of faulty diet and too little exercise.

Overweight is particularly hazardous for older women, not only because of the increased risk of heart disease and other ills that fat people are prone to. Osteoarthritis is a threat to older people, and carrying too much weight causes wear on the joints, especially of the hips and knees. So you'll be doing yourself a great favour, as well as looking better, if you can maintain a weight within 10 lbs. of the 'ideal' for your height and build. Weighing machines, magazine articles and fitness books will tell you what that is. Turn back to Chapter 15 for a fuller discussion of weight problems.

In the same chapter you'll find suggestions about healthy eating, and these are important to women of any age. If you're less active than you were – though you needn't be, except for medical reasons – you'll need to eat less than you did before. If you can take plenty of exercise, there's no reason why you shouldn't maintain health and a slim figure and still eat well.

*'If I'd known I was going to live this long, I'd have taken greater care of myself.'*
EUBIE BLAKE, American jazzman, on reaching 100.

## Eat well

Women with no income but a pension, and living alone, often complain that they can't afford to eat well. Certainly it's impossible to eat steaks, salmon and exotic fruit on a retirement pension, and restaurant meals are usually things of the past. But most women on their own have long learnt that such luxuries are not for them. What *is* wrong is that anyone should have to actually go short of essential food in order to pay her gas and electricity bills and the rent, and if you're in that position, turn back to our Money chapter (Chapter 6) for information about supplementary benefit. It's worth reminding you again that this is not a charity, that many people who are entitled to it are not drawing it, and that if you are finding difficulty in living on your basic pension – hardly surprising, if that is all you have – then you're entitled to the supplement.

However, the good news is that very often a healthy diet is in fact cheaper than an unhealthy one. Meat is one of the most expensive items in most people's food budget, and as we've already seen, most of us eat much more than we need. Even if you don't go vegetarian, you can cut down meat meals to about three a week and still be consuming quite enough protein. The substitutes for meat – peas, the huge variety of beans, and lentils – will provide you with enough protein if you make them the bases of your other main meals. The cheaper kinds of fish – herrings, mackerel, sardines – about three eggs a week, and low-fat cheese will nourish you very adequately, and are, in fact, healthier than fatty meat, sausages, bacon and other processed meat products. Soya beans – not the processed 'meat substitutes' which are quite expensive and which most people find unattractive – can be dressed up in all sorts of ways and are genuine replacements for meat in the diet.

Beans, peas and lentils do take longer to transform into appetising dishes than a chop or a piece of steak. You have to think ahead so that these dried foods are soaked overnight and cooked slowly. But they are far cheaper than meat or white fish, and have the great advantage that they're not fatty and they contain fibre. On p. 268 there's a list of recommended cookery books which would help you learn how to cook these foods to make appetising meals at low cost. If you have a fridge or freezer you can cook double the quantity you'll need for a meal for one, and keep half for a later meal.

### Keep exercising

The exercises described and illustrated in Chapter 15, (pp. 275–7) are quite suitable now you're over sixty – unless your doctor advises you against them. If you haven't done them before, build up slowly. It doesn't matter how long you take to reach a peak of fitness, as long as you're getting there.

Older women are particularly at risk of developing osteo-arthritis. A majority of older people do have some degree of arthritis, but this need not be crippling if you keep your joints mobile. (Rheumatoid arthritis is something different, and you'll have been told the correct treatment if this has been diagnosed.) To prevent osteoarthritis developing into something painful and disabling, you should pay particular attention to exercising all your joints, and on p. 272 we describe some of the ways you can do this.

The best way to start is with your feet and work upwards through the whole body. Sit on a chair or on the floor. Get your toes mobile by grasping each in turn, stretching it forward as far as you can. Then with your right hand, insert your forefinger between the big toe and its neighbour on the right foot, pushing the finger between the toes as far as you can, and continuing with the next finger between the next pair of toes, and so on, spread the fingers as far as you can, thus spreading the toes, then bend them so that you pull all the toes down towards the sole of your foot. Check this page to see that you've done all this correctly, then do the same with the other foot.

Then work up to the ankles, rotating them as far as you can in both directions, and, with legs apart (still sitting) move the feet outwards as far as you can, then inwards. Repeat several times.

You can exercise the knees by bending and stretching them and rotating them as far as you can, and you'll

'The highspot of my week is the Over-Sixties Keep-Fit class. We do about 1¾ hours of exercise and dance. It's really enjoyable. It's a very popular class – mostly women, but a few men. We're encouraged to do everything we can manage easily at first, working up to more and more difficult exercises as the weeks go on, but never straining. 'Never do anything that causes pain,' our teacher says. So if you can't lift your leg as far as someone else can, you don't worry – you just lift it as far as you can, and after a while you find you can take it further.

'I have a friend who goes to a different class and she tells me they do everything sitting on chairs! That's a joke when you see what we can do at our class – I think most of us move better than some people half our age. Of course if you're going to keep really fit you do have to do some of the exercises at home between classes. I do, but it isn't nearly such fun – you miss the company and the music. It's difficult to find a record that fits the exercises like our piano accompanist does.

'I'd advise every older person who can to find a class for pensioners – you can forget about embarrassment when you're with your own age group. You just need loose trousers, a track suit or a leotard, and gym shoes if you prefer, and the OAP fee is so little I think anyone could afford to go.'

strengthen the ligaments that surround the joint if you tighten and relax the thigh muscles a number of times. You can do this unobtrusively wherever you happen to be, not only when deliberately exercising.

Carry on up the body, consciously bending, rotating and flexing every joint, including the shoulders, and not forgetting the neck, which you should bend gently in every direction. You can exercise the fingers in many ways – typing, piano playing and so on, if appropriate, as well as performing similar movements without any 'apparatus', and clenching your fists. Shake your hands and wrists quite vigorously as well as rotating them.

### Take care
There are a few health-care points that need emphasising when you're in your sixties or seventies.

Question the need for drugs. It's your right to know what you are being given, why it's needed, and whether it has undesirable side-effects. It's unlikely that any drug is completely free of side-effects, and these may be more severe in older people. It's been estimated that a high proportion of elderly people in geriatric wards are there because of iatrogenic (doctor-induced) disorders. You should be particularly concerned if you're given prescriptions for several drugs to be taken daily – there may be a cumulative effect. Remember that tranquillisers and sleeping pills can affect concentration and judgment and if you're 'under the influence' of these you could either forget to take other medicines or forget that you'd taken them and thus take too many.

Many authorities believe that some supplementation of an older person's diet with vitamins and minerals is necessary, even if it shouldn't have been when they were younger. This applies especially to people living on their own on a low income. A multi-vitamin tablet with iron and other minerals taken once a day with a meal should ensure that you are getting at least the basics necessary for health.

Older women as we've seen (p. 290) are at risk of osteoporosis (brittle bones). There is strong evidence that extra calcium plus Vitamin D can help to keep bones stronger. Make sure you have plenty of calcium-rich foods in your diet, and that you get enough Vitamin D by exposure to sunlight or in your diet.

Continue to eat plenty of fibrous foods – fruit, vegetables, peas, beans, wholemeal bread etc.. But supplementation by wheat bran products may not be good: it interferes with the absorption of minerals, especially calcium. So make sure you get your fibre or 'roughage' from other sources or substitute oat bran.

## Take a holiday

You may feel that because you're not 'working' you don't need – or deserve – to take holidays. This isn't true. We all need variety of scene, different experiences, new people, in order to keep physically and mentally healthy right into old age.

If you have no friends or relatives to visit, you may think that holidays cost too much for you to consider. Don't give up before you've made enquiries, though. Your local Age Concern (see telephone directory) could tell you about any local schemes for pensioners' holidays, and some local authorities organise very cheap off-season seaside holidays for this age group. If you're interested in activity holidays – some not very costly – see Chapter 18, p. 322. And Saga Holidays have on offer a variety of good-value (though not necessarily cheap) holidays at home and abroad. Some of their winter holidays in popular resorts in Spain are particularly worth considering, because you can stay for 28 days or more at a cost little more than your outgoings at home would be. They're enjoyed by many pensioners anxious to get away from Britain in the worst months of the year. Don't expect summer sunshine, of course, but temperatures in these resorts in the winter are comparable to those in spring or autumn at home.

## Concessions to consider

Some local authorities offer special concessionary passes for recreational facilities to pensioners who apply. Ask about these at your public library, council offices or Age Concern. Cinemas and theatres may have special arrangements for pensioners on certain days, or for matinees. Many hairdressers give substantial reductions for middle-of-the-day services one day a week – usually Tuesday. A few shoe repairers also offer reductions, as do some dry-cleaners. And of course in many areas there are concessionary arrangements on public transport – sometimes free, sometimes at reduced prices. Travelling times are normally restricted, but this is seldom a real inconvenience to people who can be flexible when arranging journeys.

British Rail offer low-price travel to holders of their Senior Citizens' Railcards, available to everyone over sixty-five. The annual cost (£12 in 1984) can easily be saved on one long-distance journey, so if you are intending to travel any distance, even once a year, one of these cards is well worth having. A cheaper card for those only intending to go on day trips is also available. Get information from your local BR station, and when you apply for a pass take along a copy of your birth certificate, passport or other official document to confirm that you qualify for this age concession.

## Organising for action

We've already mentioned the Older Feminists' Network, but many pensioners feel they'd like to be involved more directly in political action for changes and improvements in conditions for older people. At a time when nearly one in four pensioners have incomes below the Supplementary Benefit level, when income tax regulations and the earnings rule discriminate against those who want to go on beyond

Getting older doesn't mean withdrawing from the issues of the day. Many political groupings would benefit from your skills and experience.

retirement age, there's certainly a lot of room for improvement. If you would like to contribute to this movement for change in the way society treats the increasing millions of older people, there are several organisations that would be glad of your active participation. They organise demonstrations, lobby MPs, get media coverage of issues affecting older people. Addresses to contact are given in the 'Directory' at the end of this book.

An alternative is to join a political party concerned with wider issues as well as matters directly affecting pensioners. Your public library will give you the name and address of the membership secretary of your chosen party.

You might also want to consider joining a pressure group which campaigns for an issue you feel concerned about.

For many older people becoming involved in political action is not only satisfying in itself, but provides the comradeship and companionship that may be missing in retirement, and a way of using skills and abilities developed during working years – the needs of any organisation are very wide. Organisers, clerical workers, canvassers, speakers – all of these and more would be very welcome.

# Where to live in old age

So far we've been looking at ways of making the most of life in the years following retirement. If you've managed to keep healthy and active, these years could be long and rewarding. But there must come a time when you're ready to ease off, when you may need help in running your life – and what to do about this is probably the biggest worry any ageing person has to face.

We've already suggested that if you planned to move house when you were in your sixties, it would be wise to consider just how you would be placed when you were less active in later years. Perhaps you weren't able to choose, or you made a choice that turned out to be less practical than you expected, given some infirmity that has developed since. If that has happened to you, or you think it may happen in the near future, you may now have to consider that different living conditions are needed. Or, like many other people living on their own, you may wish to remain where you are but call on the help that the local social services or health services can provide to enable you to carry on in reasonable safety and comfort at home.

Some form of 'sheltered housing' may be appropriate – a flat or bedsitting room with your own furniture and your own bathroom and cooking facilities, but with some communal services and a warden to keep an eye on you in case you need help. There are Housing Associations and other bodies able to provide sheltered housing of this kind. Waiting lists are long and so if possible you should apply well before you think you will actually need to move from your present home. Age Concern (local address in your telephone directory) or the Social Services department of your local council can give you advice, and see the 'Directory' at the end of this book for some specific schemes for elderly people.

If you need just a home help or some other social service, to enable you to manage in your present home, ask your GP to get in touch with the Social Services department's home helps service. Unfortunately you may not get as much help as you really need – cuts in the local budget have seen to that – but even a little help with shopping and housework will be worth having. Depending on your income, you will be asked to make a contribution towards the cost; but the service will be provided free if your income is very low. The doctor may also be able to arrange for a nurse or bathing assistant to visit regularly to help with baths, and s/he may also refer you to the appropriate Health Service centre or clinic for the supply of appropriate aids such as hearing aids, walking aids and wheelchairs.

Just as important, the local authority is empowered to make alterations and adaptations to your home. If you have been in hospital and the physiotherapist or occupational therapist advises the local authority that these are needed, you may get them fairly quickly. Unfortunately there is a longer waiting list for those who are referred by GPs.

If your disability is temporary, the British Red Cross Society (address in telephone book) can supply a variety of aids on loan, and it's worth contacting them if it appears that long delays are likely in the provision of aids by the Social Services department.

If you meet with any problems in the supply of needed aids and services, the Patients' Association (see 'Directory') would like to hear from you and may be able to offer help.

It may be that neither sheltered housing nor services to help you live at home will really meet your needs. At some point you may have to consider full residential care – a home for the elderly, whether run by the local authority or privately, or by some charity. This decision is often a very difficult one to take. How can you be sure that you will be treated with dignity, helped when help is needed but allowed as far as possible to run your life as you want?

If you feel that a 'home' is the only realistic option because you are no longer able to maintain yourself in your present conditions, you should start to make enquiries from your local Social Services department. They hold lists of registered homes. Choose several that appear to be in an area convenient to you and your family, and ask them to send you a copy of their brochure. This should provide more than just a catalogue of the facilities available. It ought to give you some idea of the aims of the people running the home.

The next step – and this is absolutely vital – is a visit to the home. If you can't get there by yourself, and there is no family member or friend to take you, ask the Social Services for help. And when you visit, the points to look for are listed below.

## Old-age homes: a checklist

● Life style – a good 'home' should offer residents the sort of way of life and general atmosphere that is congenial.
● Independence – it should recognise your need for privacy and autonomy.
● General standards of cleanliness with furniture and furnishings in good repair.
● Single rooms available; adequate bathroom and toilet facilities.
● Lack of unnecessary regulations and rules – e.g. about times of getting up and going to bed.

● Availability of medical care; arrangements in case of illness.
● Staff qualifications and attitudes; number of day and night staff.
● Fees and what they cover.
Fuller checklists, prepared by the Consumers' Association in conjunction with the Centre for Policy on Ageing, will help. You can get six copies for £3.00. Make your cheque payable to the Consumers' Association and send the order to *Which?*, Castlemead, Gascoyne Way, Hertford SG14 1LH.

It's a very good idea to arrange a trial stay. Even if you can't arrange this, *don't sell your house or give up rented accommodation* until you're absolutely sure you are going to want to stay in the home you've chosen. Some elderly people, especially those without close relatives, have found that the home they thought would provide them with the care and facilities they needed has proved disappointing, but, having given up their own home, feel trapped because there is nowhere else for them to go.

Your biggest worry may be that good residential care in a home or nursing home is going to be too costly for you. This need not be so. Although fees in private residential homes can amount to over £100 per week (1984), if your income and savings won't enable you to pay this, the DHSS arrangements with registered homes mean that your fees will be paid in part or in full, leaving you with 'pocket money' for day-to-day needs.

This arrangement is part of the Government's plan to privatise care, and it has led to the setting up of numerous commercially-run 'rest homes'. Some offer very poor standards of care – and that is why the checklist of points to look for is important. But there's another snag brought about by a recent Act of Parliament, and affecting especially those in homes run by local authorities. Under this legislation, expected to come into force some time in 1985, anyone provided with accommodation by the local authority has to pay for it, and the current arrangement is that if you are receiving the retirement pension and your capital is less than £3,000, the local authority takes the bulk of your pension, leaving you with £6.80 (1984 figure) for yourself.

Any capital above £1,200 is assessed as income, and if you own your own home this is taken into account as part of your income. If your house is worth £30,000 or £40,000 you could find yourself having to pay the full cost of council residential care, since it would be assumed that you were drawing income from the letting of the house, or the proceeds of its sale. Should you have passed on your house or money within six months of entering the residential home, either giving it away or selling the property, you or the people to whom you gave the house will be liable for the whole of the fees. Thus if your house is your major asset and you think that you may need residential accommodation in a local authority home later, and if you want your family to derive some benefit from your house and household goods and not have to contribute the proceeds to your support, you should consider transferring the property to them sooner rather than later, or make some arrangement for a trust fund, as some people do to avoid capital transfer tax. Consult your accountant or solicitor about this.

Information, advice and help with these problems is available from the local branch of Age Concern, or by writing to the Information Department at its headquarters. Counsel and Care for the Elderly is a fully comprehensive service of information about recommended residential nursing homes mainly in the South East, but they can put you in touch with other groups that can advise you if you live out of their area. They also offer help with fees if this is needed. The Centre for Policy on Ageing publishes information books and also runs a 'Homes Advice' unit which provides advice to 'non-statutory' residential homes with the aim of raising standards. Addresses of all these organisations are given below.

# Helpful Organisations

Age Concern, England, 60 Pitcairn Road, Mitcham,
Surrey CR4 3LL
Age Concern, Scotland, 33 Castle Street, Edinburgh.
Age Concern, Northern Ireland, 128 Great Victoria Street,
Belfast 2.
Age Concern, Wales, 1 Park Grove, Cardiff.
Counsel and Care for the Elderly, 131 Middlesex Street,
London E1 7JF.
Centre for Policy on Ageing, Nuffield Lodge, Regent's Park,
London NW1 4RS.

# DIRECTORY: useful organisations and addresses

## DIVORCE AND BEREAVEMENT – GENERAL

Divorce Conciliation and
Advisory Service
38 Ebury Street
London SW1
tel: 01 730 2422

National Council for the
Divorced and Separated
13 High Street
Little Shelford
Cambridge
Cambridgeshire CB2 5ES
tel: 92 22181

Coping with Separation
8 Sandon Avenue
Newcastle
Staffordshire
tel: 0782 611664

National Marriage Guidance
Council
Herbert Gray College
Little Church Street
Rugby
Warwickshire CV21 3AP
tel: 0788 73241

Widows Advisory Service
Chell Road
Stafford
Staffordshire ST16 2QA
tel: 0785 58946
(Offers support, help and
advice on all financial and
emotional matters faced by
widows. Can direct you to local
organisations.)

National Association of
Funeral Directors
57 Doughty Street
London WC1
tel: 01 242 9388

To check whether the
deceased held savings
certificates write to:
Savings Certificate and SAYE
Office
Durham DH99 1NS
and
Bond and Stock Office
Blackpool
Lancashire FY3 9YP

Cruse (National Organization
for the Widowed and their
Children)
Cruse House
126 Sheen Road
Richmond
Surrey TW9 1VR
tel: 01 940 4818

Gay Bereavement Project
Dudley Cave
46 Wentworth Road
Barnet
London W11 0RL
tel: 01 458 4212

National Association of
Widows
Chell Road
Stafford
Staffordshire ST16 2QA
tel: 0785 45465

## DIVORCE AND BEREAVEMENT – LEGAL

Law Society
113 Chancery Lane
London WC2
tel: 01 242 1222

National Association of
Citizens Advice Bureaux
115 Pentonville Road
London N1
tel: 01 833 2181
(Will tell you where your
nearest bureau is)

Oyez Publishing Ltd
237 Long Lane
London SE1
tel: 01 407 8055

Law Centres Federation
Duchess House
Warren Street
London W1
tel: 01 387 8570
(will give you the address of
your nearest Law Centre)

Rights of Women
52–56 Featherstone Street
London EC1
tel: 01 251 6577
(telephone Legal Advice
Services for women:
Tuesdays and Thursdays 7 pm
– 9 pm)

Women's Aid Federation
(England)
52–54 Featherstone Street
London EC1
tel: 251 6429
(federation of refuges and local
support groups for physically
and emotionally battered
women)

# FINANCIAL

**British Insurance Brokers Association**
Fountain House
Fenchurch Street
London EC3
tel: 01 623 9043

**British Insurance Association**
Aldermary House
Queen Street
London EC4
tel: 01 248 4477

**Consumers Association**
14 Buckingham Street
London WC2
tel: 01 839 1222

---

# MOTORING

**The Automobile Association (AA)**
Fanum House
Basingstoke
Hants RG21 2EA
tel: 0256 20123
(or see your local phone book for nearest office)

**The Royal Automobile Club (RAC)**
Head Office
P.O. Box 100
RAC House
Lansdowne Road
Croydon
tel: 01 686 2525

**Women's Motor Mechanics Project**
Bay 4R, 1–3 Brixton Road
London SW9 6DE
tel: 01 582 2574

---

# CHILDREN

**Child Poverty Action Group**
1 Macklin Street
London WC2B 5NH
tel: 01 242 3225
(offers free information, advisory and advocacy services and helps with money problems; publishes two invaluable guides – *The National Welfare Benefits Handbook* and *The Rights Guide to Non Means Tested Social Security Benefits*)

**Children's Legal Centre**
20 Compton Terrace
London N1 2UN
tel: 01 359 9392
(free information and advisory service on law and policy affecting children and young people)

**Family Rights Group**
6–7 Manor Gardens
Holloway Road
London N7 6LA
tel: 01 272 4231/2 or 272 7308

**Advisory Centre for Education**
18 Victoria Park Square
London E2 9PB
tel: 01 980 4596
(provides advice on education)

**Pre-School Playgroups Association (PPA)**
Alford House
Aveline Street
London SE11 5DH
tel: 01 582 8871

**Gingerbread**
33 Wellington Street
London WC2E 7BN
tel: 01 240 0953
(self-help association for lone parents and families)

**Institute of Family Therapy (London) Ltd**
43 New Cavendish Street
London W1M 7RG
tel: 01 935 1651
(offers clinical therapy: sliding scale of fees)

**London Youth Advisory Centre**
26 Prince of Wales Road
Kentish Town
London NW5 3LG
tel: 01 267 4792

**National Childminding Association**
13 London Road
Bromley
BR1 1DE
tel: 01 464 6164

**National Council for One Parent Families**
255 Kentish Town Road
London NW5 2LX
tel: 01 267 1361

**Organisations for Parents Under Stress (OPUS)**
29 Newmarket Way
Hornchurch
Essex
RM12 6DR
tel: 04024 51538
(can put you in touch with your local group)

**Parents Anonymous**
6–9 Manor Gardens
London N7 6LA
tel: 01 263 8918 (Hotline)
(a telephone service to help parents who feel they might abuse their children)

**Parents Enquiry**
16 Honley Road
Catford
London SE6 2HZ
tel: 01 689 1815
(counsels families of homosexual children)

**London FRIEND (Gay Counselling)**
274 Upper Street
London N1 2UA
(support and information for gay youngsters)

National Childbirth Trust
9 Queensborough Terrace
Bayswater
London W2 3TB
tel: 01 221 3833

Family Network
National Children's Home
85 Highbury Park
London N5 1UD
tel: 01 226 2033
(telephone advice for parents
with problems. Local
counsellors)

Family Service Units
207 Old Marylebone Road
London NW1 5QP
tel: 01 402 5175

Scottish Council for Single
Parents
44 Albany Street
Edinburgh EH1 3QR
tel: 031 556 3899

ALATEEN
c/o AL-ANON Family Groups
61 Great Dover Street
London SE1 4YF
(groups for teenagers with
drink problems or problems
with alcoholic family member)

National Campaign Against
Solvent Abuse
55 Wood Street
Mitcham Junction
Surrey (can put you in touch
with local groups)

National Youth Bureau
17–23 Albion Street
Leicester
LE1 6GD
tel:
(incorporates the National
Association of Young People's
Counselling and Advisory
Services which can direct you
to local counselling agencies)

## Books

*Children Under Stress* by Sula
Wolff (Pelican)

*Bringing Up Children in a
Difficult Time* by Dr Benjamin
Spock (Bodley Head)

*Surviving the Breakup* by
Judith S. Wallerstein and Joan
Berlin Kelly (Grant McIntyre)

*Divorce and Your Children* by
Anne Hooper (Allen and Unwin)

*Step-parenting* by Brenda
Maddox (Unwin Paperbacks)

*The Generation Gap: The View
from Both Sides* by Mary
McCormack (Constable)

*Your Body, Your Baby, Your
Life* by Angela Phillips
(Pandora)

---

# HEALTH AND WELLBEING

## Organise for Health

The College of Health, (see address below) is
concerned with prevention of ill health, self-
care, better use of the Health Service, and
helping to bridge the gap between orthodox
and alternative medicine. Its main aim is to help
ensure that we, the patients, are better
informed, and that doctors should learn how to
listen to us. The College of Health publishes a
journal, *Self Health*, produces educational
material, and runs meetings and conferences.
There is an annual membership fee.

The College of Health
18 Victoria Park Square
London E2 9PF

The Health Education Council
78 New Oxford Street
London WC1
tel: 01 637 1881
produces educational material on health
matters, distributed through local Health
Education Units. Highly recommended in their
booklet, *Looking After Yourself*

The Women's Health Information Centre (see
address below) produces information material
on a range of topics affecting women and their
health. Their main areas of interest are: the
menopause, contraception, cancer, tranquilliser
use, and pre-menstrual tension. They can also
put you in touch with local women's health
groups.

Women's Health Information
Centre
52 Featherstone Street
London EC1
tel: 01 251 6580 or 251 6589

The Women's Reproductive Rights Information
Centre is concerned with issues affecting
women's rights in pregnancy, childbirth, fertility,
abortion etc. and can provide information or
advise you about possible action.

Women's Reproductive Rights
Information Centre
52 Featherstone Street
London EC1
tel: 01 251 6332

Particularly concerned with black women's health are:

**Foundation for Women's Health, Research, Education and Development**
c/o The Africa Centre
38 King Street
London WC2

**Training in Health and Race**
18 Victoria Park Square
London E2 9PF

**Black Health Workers and Patients Group**
Annexe B
Tottenham Town Hall
Town Hall Approach
London N15

**Brixton Black Women's Health Group**
Black Women's Centre
41 Stockwell Green
London SW9

**Greenwich Black Women's Health Project**
St Mary's Hall
Green Law Street
London SE18
tel: 01 854 3766

**Sickle Cell Anaemia Society**
c/o Brent Community Health Council
16 High Street
Harlesden
London NW10 4LX
tel: 01 451 3293

---

## Health – general information

**The National Association of Community Health Councils**
362 Euston Road
London NW1
tel: 01 388 4943/4 or 388 4814

General information for London groups is available from:
London Community Health Resource
68 Chalton Street
London NW1 1JR
tel: 01 388 0241

### Books – recommended general health guides

*Our Bodies Ourselves*, ed. Angela Phillips and Jill Rakusen (Penguin)

*The Sunday Times Book of Body Maintenance* (Michael Joseph)

*The Sunday Times ABC Diet and Body Plan* by Oliver Gillie and Susanna Raby (Hutchinson)

*The New Women's Health Handbook* by Nancy McKeith (Virago)

You may also be interested in *The Patient Patients: Women and their Doctors* by Helen Roberts (Pandora)

---

## Healthline – a telephone information service run by the College of Health

Dial 01 980 4848 between 6pm and 10pm 7 days a week for recorded information lasting 2–6 minutes on a range of health topics and approved by a panel of medical experts. The service is free except for the cost of the telephone call. A Directory of the topics covered by the service costs £1.00 from the College of Health. Ask for the tape you want by number (if you have their Directory) or tell the Healthline operator the topic you want to know about. Have a pencil and paper ready to note down the information you require. In this book you will find some Healthline topic numbers listed under the appropriate heading, but there are many others, and if you have a health problem or you simply want more information about something not covered here, ring 01 980 4848 to find out whether there's a tape that could help you.

For general enquiries about NHS and other health services in your area, and for advice on complaints about hospital or GP services contact your local Community Health Council. Enquiries may be made to the office of the steering committee for the National Association of Community Health Councils (see above).

## Disability

**Aids (for Disabled) Advice Centre**
215 Grays Inn Road
London WC1
tel: 01 833 0084

**Disability Alliance**
1 Cambridge Terrace
London NW1
tel: 01 935 4992

**Disability Income Group**
28 Commercial Street
London E1

**Disabled Advice/RADAR**
Mortimer Street
London W1
tel: 01 637 5400

**GEMMA (Organization of disabled and ablebodied lesbians)**
PO Box 5700
London WC1N 3XX

**Royal National Institute for the Blind**
224 Great Portland Street
London W1N 6AA
tel: 01

## Books

*Better Lives for Disabled Women* by Jo Campling (Virago)

*Disabled Eve: Aids in Menstruation* by Brenda McCarthy (Disabled Living Foundation, 346 Kensington High Street, London W14)

*Images of Ourselves: Women with Disabilities Talking* by Jo Campling (Routledge & Kegan Paul)

---

## Drugs – alcohol

See also *children* for children's drug and alcohol problems

**Accept Clinic**
200 Seagrave Road
London SW6 1RQ
tel: 01 381 3155

**Alcohol Counselling Service**
34 Electric Lane
London SW9
tel: 01 737 3570 or 3579
(free counselling, women only)

**Alcoholics Anonymous**
11 Redcliffe Gardens
London SW10
tel: 01 352 9779

**Alcoholics Recovery Project**
68 Newington Causeway
London SE1 6DF
tel: 01 403 3369
and
6–8 Kings Cross Road
London WC1
tel: 01 837 2686
(womeon only Tues. 2–4 pm)

**Black Women and Alcohol Group**
c/o The Alcohol Counselling Service
tel: 01 737 3570 or 3579

**Consortium**
Cambridge House
Walworth Road
London SE1
tel: 01 701 2209

**Greater London Alcohol Advisory Service**
146 Queen Victoria Street
London EC4
tel: 01 248 8406

**Westminster Advisory Centre on Alcoholism**
38 Ebury Street
London SW1W 0LU
tel: 01 730 1574

**Women's Alcohol Centre**
254 St Paul's Road
London N1 2LJ
tel: 01 226 4581

Healthline 01–980 4848 tape nos. 1, 2, 3

## Books
*Women under the Influence* by Brigid McConville (Virago)

---

## Drugs – counselling

See also stress

**Blenheim Project**
7 Thorpe Close
London W10
tel: 01 960 5599
(includes women's support group)

**Release**
1 Elgin Avenue
London W9 3PR
tel: 01 289 1123

**Drugs, Alcohol, Women Nationally (DAWN)**
146 Queen Victoria Street
London EC4V 4BX
tel: 01 236 8125

**Lifeline Project**
Jodrell Street
Manchester M3 3HE
tel: 061 832 6353
(counselling service for long-term minor tranquilliser and other drug users)

**Tranx**
c/o Joan Jerome
2 St John's Road
Harrow
Middlesex
(for tranquilliser addiction)

**Open Door**
Drug Dependency Unit
University College Hospital
London WC1
tel: 01 348 5947

Healthline 01 980 4848 tape no. 7 (help agencies)

## Books

*Coming Off Tranquillisers* (free leaflet, send s.a.e.) Family Matters, Good Housekeeping, 72 Broadwick Street, London W1V 2BP

*Heroin* and *Women and Heroin* (free leaflets) from DAWN, 146 Queen Victoria Street, London EC4V 4BX.

*Trouble with Tranquillisers* (60p) available from Release Publications Ltd, 1 Elgin Avenue, London W9 3PR.

## nutrition and diet

### Whole Health Programme
40 Weymouth Street
London W1
(Telephone Nutrition Service
0844 52098 Tues. 4–9 pm)

Healthline 01 980 4848 tape
nos. 110 (diet and heart
disease), 119 (fibre), 120
(children)

### slimming

### Weight Watchers
635–637 Ajax Avenue
Slough
Berks
SL1 4DB
tel: Slough 70711
(commercial, local classes)

### Women's Therapy Centre
6 Manor Gardens
London N7
tel; 01 263 6200
(for group therapy)

### Overeaters Anonymous
PO Box 539
London W11 2EL
tel: 01 589 3157 Mon–Fri 9 am
– 6 pm, Sat 9 am – noon)

### Compulsive Eating Groups
organised by
Spare Tyre Theatre Company
86–88 Holmleigh Road
London N16

### Slimming Magazine Clubs
4 Clareville Gardens
London SW7
tel: 01 370 4411
(commercial, local classes)

### anorexia, bulimia

### Anorexia and Bulimia Nervosa Association
c/o Sue Chambers
12 Geneva Court
Manor Road
London N16

### Anorexia Anonymous
24 Westmorland Road
London SW13

### Anorexic & Bulimic Women's Groups
tel: 01 892 5945 (after 9 pm)

### London Anorexic Aid
c/o Sarah Vicary
Flat 3
Eve Court
127 Grosvenor Avenue
London N5 2NJ

### Books

*Fat is a Feminist Issue* by
Susie Orbach (Hamlyn)

*Breaking the Diet Habit* by
Janet Polivy and C. Peter
Herman (Basic Books)

*Mary Ellen's Help Yourself Diet
Plan* (Fontana Original)

*Dieting Makes You Fat* by
Geoffrey Cannon and Hetty
Einzig (Sphere)

*The Art of Starvation* by Sheila
MacLeod (Virago)

---

## MENTAL WELLBEING

### Black Mental Health Project
c/o Brent Volunteers Bureau
tel: 01 902 7204

### Bradford Women's Therapy Service
tel: 0274 401175

### COPE
Basement
11 Acklam Road
London W11
tel: 01 969 9790
(anti-psychiatry collective)

### Patients Association
Room 33
18 Charing Cross Road
London WC2H 0HR
tel: 01 240 0671

### Pellin South London Feminist Therapy Centre
43 Killyon Road
London SW8
tel: 01 622 0148

### Prompt (Radical Mental Health Pressure Group)
tel: 01 693 0011 (Mon, Wed,
Fri, 3–10 pm)

### Women and Mental Health
Box 21
Sisterwrite
190 Upper Street
London N1

### Women's Therapy Centre
6 Manor Gardens
London N7
tel: 01 263 6200

### Women's Alternative to Mental Hospitals
Box 33
Sisterwrite
190 Upper Street
London N1

### Mental Patient's Union
16 Clifton Gardens
St George's Road
Hull
N. Humberside

### MIND
22 Harley Street
London W1
tel: 01 637 0741
(has lists of local Mental Health

Associations, some of which
run clubs and groups for
former psychiatric patients)

Healthline 01 980 4848 tape
no. 91

Healthline 01 980 4848 tape
no. 90 (nervous breakdown)

### Books

*In Our Own Hands (A book of
self-help therapy)* by Sheila
Ernst and Lucy Goodison
(Women's Press)

*A Practical Guide to the Mental
Health Act* (MIND) from
address above.

*A Patient's Guide to the
National Health Service*
(Consumers' Association)
Chapters 8 and 9.

## assertion

Pellin South London Therapy Centre, see above.

Women's Therapy Centre, see above

For other assertiveness training (enclosing s.a.e.) to:
Anne Dickson
c/o Quartet Books
27/29 Goodge Street
London W1P 1FD

### Books

*The Cinderella Complex* by Colette Dowling (Fontana)

*A Woman in Your Own Right* by Anne Dickson (Quartet)

## agoraphobia

Action on Phobias
17 Burlington Place
Eastbourne
East Sussex
BN21 4AR
tel: 0323 54755
(local groups, telephone link-line)

The Open Door Association
447 Pensby Road
Heswall
Wirral
Merseyside
L61 9PQ
(information service)

The Phobics Society
4 Cheltenham Road
Chorlton-cum Hardy
Manchester
M21 1QN

### Book

*Simple Effective Treatment of Agoraphobics* by Dr Claire Weekes (Bantam).

## stress

See also *Drugs – counselling* for help with coming off tranquillisers.

Relaxation for Living
29 Burwood Park Road
Walton-on-Thames
Surrey
KT12 5LH
(local teachers, audio-cassette relaxation course)

Ursula Fleming
62 Godstow Road
Wolvercote
Oxford
(tape, Relax to Concentrate, available from above address)

Positive Health Centre
15 Fitzroy Square
London W1
tel: 01 388 1007
(teaches Autogenic Training and has list of therapists outside London)

For details of tapes for help on nervous suffering made by Dr Claire Weekes (author of *Self-Help for Your Nerves*, pub. Bantam), send s.a.e. to Mrs Keating, 16 Rivermead Court, Ranelagh Gardens, London SW6

Advice and exercises in relaxation and creative visualisation are given in the tape *Fighting Addictions* by healer Matthew Manning, available from Matthew Manning Cassettes Ltd, 34 Bisham Gardens, London N6 6DD.

### Books

*Anxiety and Depression* by Prof. Robert Priest (Martin Dunitz)

*Stress and Relaxation* by Jane Madders (Martin Dunitz)

*Ten and Tranquillisers* by Diane Harpwood (Virago)

*Trouble with Tranquillisers* a booklet available from Release Publications Ltd, 1 Elgin Avenue, London W9 3PR Claire Rayner's leaflet *Coping with Tranquillisers* is available from her, c/o Sunday Mirror Advisory Service, PO Box 125, Harrow, Middlesex, HA1 3XE. Send s.a.e., marking envelope "Tranquillisers'.

## depression

Depressives Anonymous
36 Chestnut Avenue
Beverley
N. Humberside
HU17 9QU
(national organization, local groups)

Depressives Associated
19 Merley Ways
Wimborne Minster
Dorset
BH21 1QN
(national organisation, local groups)

Healthline 01 980 4848 tape no. 124 (post-natal depression)

### Books

*Dealing With Depression* by Kathy Nairne and Gerrilyn Smith (Women's Press)

*Depression: the way out of your prison* by Dorothy Rowe (RKP)

*Outside In – Inside Out* by Luise Eichenbaum and Susie Orbach (Penguin)

## Loneliness

**National Federation of Solo Clubs**
Room 8
Ruskin Chambers
191 Corporation Street
Birmingham B4 6RY
tel: 021 236 2879

**Friendship (APS)**
7 Muirfield Close
Heywood
Greater Manchester OL10 2DS
tel: 0706 68503

**National Council for the Divorced and Separated**
13 High Street
Little Shelford
Cambridge
Cambridgeshire CB2 5ES
tel: 92 22181

## Lesbian line information

All kinds of information and help are provided by the various Lesbian Lines in different parts of the country. You can telephone the numbers given at the times indicated, or write to BM Box 1514, London WC1N 3XX. The London line is open on (01) 251 6911 on Mondays and Fridays from 2–10 pm and on Tuesdays, Wednesdays and Thursdays from 7–10 pm. All the following times are pm unless stated otherwise.

**Aberdeen Lesbian Line** (0224) 26869 – Wed 7–10
**Bradford Lesbian Line** (0274) 305525 – Thurs 7–9
**Brighton Lesbian Line** (0273) 603298 – Tue. 8–10, Fri. 2–5, 8–10
**Cambridge Lesbian Line** (0223) 256–3 – Fri. 6–10
**Cardiff** (0111) 374 051 – Thur. 8–10
**Colchester Lesbian Line** (0206) 870051 – Wed 8–10
**Coventry Friend Women's Line** (0203) 25991 – Tue. 7–10
**Coventry & Leamington Lesbian Line** (0203) 77105 – Wed. 7–10.
**Dundee Friend Women's Line** (0382) 21843 – Tue 7–0
**Edinburgh Friend Women's Line** (031) 556409–5. Thur. 7.30–10. Ask for a woman if a man answers – a woman is always available.

**Glasgow Lesbian Line** (041) 2484596 – Mon. 7–10
**Lancaster Women's Line** 63021 – Wed. 6–9
**Leeds** (0352) 453588 – Tue. 7.30–9.30
**Leicester Friend** (0533) 826299 – Tue. 7.30–10.30
**Liverpool Women's Line** (051) 7080234 – Tue & Thur. 7–10
**London Friend Women's Line** (01) 708 0234. Tue & Thur. 7.30–10.
**Manchester Lesbian Line** (061) 2366205 – Mon–Fri. 7–10.
**Merseyside Friend Lesbian Line** 7080234–Tue. & Thur. 7–10.
**Munster Cork** (021) 505394 Tue. 8–10
**Newcastle Lesbian Line** (0632) 612277 – 7–10
**North Staffordshire Lesbian Support Group** (0782) 266998 – Fri 8–10

**Nottingham Lesbian Line** (0602) 410652 – Mon & Wed 7–9.30
**Oxford Lesbian Line** (0865) 242333–Wed. 7–10
**Peterborough** (0733) 238005 or 265181 – evenings before 10 pm
**Plymouth Lesbian Line** (0752) 261251 – Tue. 7.30–9.30
**Preston Lesbian Line** (0772) 51122 – Mon & Wed. 7.30–9.30
**St Andrews Lesbian Line** (0334) 72604 – Mon 7–10
**Sheffield Lesbian Line** (0742) 581238 – Thu 7–10
**Swansea Lesbian Line** 467365 – Fri 7–9
**West Midlands (Birmingham) Lesbian Line** (021) 6226580 – Wed & Fri. 7–10
**Eire (Dublin)** 710608 – Thu 8–10

## Women's Organizations

**A Woman's Place**
Hungerford House
Victoria Embankment
London WC2
tel: 01 836 6081

**Older Feminists' Network**
c/o AWP
Hungerford House
Victoria Embankment
London WC2
tel: 01 836 6081

**Equal Opportunities Commission**
Overseas House, Quay Street
Manchester MC 3HN
tel: 061 833 9244

National Housewives Register
245 Warwick Road
Solihull
Birmingham B92 7AH
tel: 021 706 1101

National Association of
Housewives
30 Tollgate
Bretton
Peterborough
Cambs.
tel: 0733 262143

National Federation of
Women's Institutes
39 Eccleston Street
London SW1W 9NT
tel: 01 730 7212

Cooperative Women's Guild
342 Hoe Street
Walthamstow
London E17 9PX
tel: 01 250 4902

National Council for the Single
Woman and her Dependants
29 Chilworth Mews
London W2 3RG
tel: 01 262 1451

---

# EDUCATION AND RETRAINING

Educational Guidance Service for Adults. Enquire at your public library or education office – the service is available in different parts of the country.

TOPS. Ask at your local employment office or Job Shop.

Open University. Walton Hall, Milton Keynes, MK7 6AA. For non-degree courses ask for 'Guide to the Associate Student Programme'.

Open Colleges. Ask at the education office or a local college.

Universities. A new information leaflet for mature students is available from the Universities Central Council on Admissions (UCCA), P O Box 28, Cheltenham, Glos., GL50 1HY.

Polytechnics. 'Opportunities in Higher Education for Mature Students is available from CNAA, 344/354 Gray's Inn Road, London WC1X, 8EP.

Other organisations offering courses not mentioned in Chapter 8 are:

Sixth Form Colleges. Enquire locally.

Flexistudy courses. See National Extension College, below.

London University External Degrees. Details from The Secretary for External Studies, London University, Seante House, Malet Street, London WC1E 7HU.

Part-time university degree courses. A list from Margaret Korving, 270 London Road, St Albans, Herts, AL1 1HY – send £1.00 and state area of the country where study is required.

Business and Technician Council, Central House, Upper Woburn Place, London WC1H 0HH for Higher National Diploma courses in technical and business subjects.

Diploma in Management Studies. One especially for women at Polytechnic of Central London (1985), Marylebone Road, London NW1 5LS.

## Student grants

The Department of Education and Science issues an annual booklet, 'Grants for Students: A Brief Guide', which is available free from DES, Elizabeth House, York Road, London SE1

## Recommended Publications

Equal Opportunities – a careers guide for women and men, by Ruth Miller and Anna Alston (Penguin).

Simple Steps for Returners by Pamela Anderson (Poland Street Publications, 9 Poland Street, London W1V 3DG) is intended to help women explore all the paid or unpaid openings in employment available to them, and make decisions about returning – or not returning – to outside work. It is full of useful 'case histories' of women who returned to work, too further education or training courses or started their own businesses – and how they did it.

Second Chances available from:
The National Extension College
18 Brooklands Avenue
Cambridge
CB2 2HN
or from your public library.

# WORK

**Smaller Business Association**
108 Weston Street
London SE1
tel: 01 403 4066

**Small Firms Service**
telephone FREEFONE 2444

**Scottish Development Agency**
120 Bothwell Street
Glasgow 2
tel: 041 248 2700

**Welsh Development Agency**
Pearl Assurance Building
Greyfriars Road
Cardiff CF1
tel: 0222 32955

**Local Enterprise Development Unit, Belfast (LEDU)**
LEDU House
Upper Galwally
Belfast BT8 4TB
tel: 0232 691031

**Business in the Community**
227a City Road
London EC1
tel: 01 253 3716

**Council for Small Industries in Rural Areas (COSIRA)**
141 Castle Street
Salisbury
tel: Salisbury 336255

**Women in Manual Trades**
52–54 Featherstone St
London EC1
tle: 01 251 9192

# HOLIDAYS
## Holidays with Children

**One Parent Family Holidays** 25 Fore Street, Praze-an-Beeble, Camborne, Cornwall, TR14 0JX.

**Single Parent Holidays**, Edwin Doran Travel, Travel Headquarters House, 9 York Street, Twickenham, Middx TW1 3TZ.

**Millfield School Village of Education**, Millfield School, Street, Somerset, BA16 0YD.

**Holiday camps:** Not everyone's choice, but plenty of activity for children while parent relaxes. Travel agents and press advertisements are sources of information.

**Vacation Courses**, Loughborough University, Loughborough, Lincs.

**University accommodation:** Many universities now offer rooms with breakfast, or self-catering arrangements, in their vacations. Since some are situated in or near holiday spots, they could make excellent bases for family – or indeed single people's holidays. Cost from £7.50 a night (1984). Write to the British Universities Accommodation Consortium, Box No 214, University Park, Nottingham NG7 2RD.

## Holidays for children alone

**Colony Holidays, Linden Manor, Malvern WR13 6PP** Holidays for children 8–15, various centres, non-profit making. Transport to chosen centre included in cost. Free holidays for children from 'deprived' areas, sponsored by industry. Walking, swimming, games, cooking, crafts, music among many activities offered.

**Lakeland Training Group, The Promenade, Arnside, Cumbria LA5 0AD.** Children 9–15. Tougher, more outdoor activities. Sailing, windsurfing, canoeing, camping.

**PGL Young Adventure Ltd, Adventure House, Station Street, Ross-on-Wye.** Holidays in centres in UK and abroad, children all ages. Mainly outdoor activities.

**Barton Children's Holidays, West Woodyates Manor, Nr Salisbury, Wilts.** Holidays in a number of boarding school premises in different parts of the country. Outdoor and indoor activities. Somewhat more 'school-like' than some of the other holidays above, but plenty of organised fun.

**For more addresses** consult the current **Adventure Holidays** published by Vacation Work, 9 Park End St, Oxford – this should be available in the reference section of your public library. **The English Tourist Board Activity and Hobby Holidays** should also be in the library, or can be ordered from Admail 14. London SW1W 0YE, price £1.25 plus 25p postage (1984).

**British Tourist Authority**, 64 St James's Street, London SW1.

## Special Interest Holidays

The best source of general information on the wide variety of holidays available is the NIACE calendar. This is published twice a year and covers virtually all the Local Education Authority and commercial or non-profit making bodies offering week-end or week-long courses. Order from the National Institute of Adult and Continuing Education, 19B De Montfort Street, Leicester LE1 7GE – ask for **Residential Short Courses** – price 90p including postage.

**Activity Holidays in Britain**
(Farm Holiday Guides, 75p
from large newsagents or
booksellers)

**Leisure Interests Guide**
(Activity Holidays Associates
Ltd, £1.95 from large
newsagents or booksellers)

**Adventure Holidays** (Vacation
Work, £2.95)

**The Ramblers' Association**
1–5 Wandsworth Road,
London SW8 1LJ offers
walking holidays graded for
difficulty.

**The Information Section
(Courses)**, Crafts Council, 12
Waterloo Place, London SW1Y
4AU (tel (01) 930 4811) may
be able to help you find a
suitable crafts course at a
small centre.

For a full list of courses in
individual sports write with
s.a.e. to **The Sports Council
Information Service**, 16
Woburn Place, London WC1H
0QP.

Some hotel groups offer
special interest weekends –
not cheap but high standard
accommodation. Consult the

**Good Hotel Guide** (Consumers
Association/Hodder and
Stoughton) in your public
library.

The Consumers Association
magazine **Holiday Which**
tested **Health Farms** (May
1984) and found they
provided relaxation and
pampering with many
facilities and 'treatments' for
around £200 – £300 a week.
Obviously too costly for most
– but if you're interested, get
addresses from women's
magazines.

# GETTING OLDER

**Age Concern**
60 Pitcairn Road
Mitcham
Surrey
tel: 01 640 5431

**Help the Aged**
16–18 St James's Walk
London EC1R
tel: 01 253 0253
(provides a number of services
including grants for
pensioners' projects and help
with housing. Large range of
publications)

**Centre for Policy on Ageing**
Nuffield Lodge Studio
Regents Park
London NW1 4RS
tel: 01 586 9844

**Pensioners Link**
17 Balfe Street
London N1
tel: 01 278 5501
(social clubs, pensioners'
action groups, older women's
project, help for housebound
pensioners, health courses,
advice and advocacy work
and Reminiscence Projects)

**All Party Parliamentary Group
for Pensioners**
House of Commons
London SW1A 0AA
tel: 01 219 4082

**British Pensioners and Trade
Union Action Association**
97 Kings Drive
Gravesend
Kent
DA12 5BQ
tel: 0474 61802

**Pensioners for Peace**
7 Sandfield
Bromsberrow Heath
Ledbury
Hereford
HR8 1NX
tel: 053181 485

**The Standing Conference of
Ethnic Minority Senior
Citizens**
5–5a Westminster Bridge
Road
London SE1 7XW
tel: 01 928 0095
(day centres, clubs and
activities for members of
various ethnic groups)

**National Federation of Old Age
Pension Associations**
(Pensioners' Voice)
Melling House
91 Preston New Road
Blackburn
Lancs
BBN 6BD
tel: 0245 52606

**London Joint Council for
Senior Citizens**
c/o TGWU Retired Members'
Association
TGWU
Transport House
Smith Square
London SW1P 3JP
tel: 01 828 3806

**Forum on the Rights of Elderly
People to Education (FREE)**
Bernard Sunley House
60 Pitcairn Road
Mitcham
Surrey
CR4 3LL
tel: 01 640 5431
(co-ordinates local
organisations and produces
information bulletin)

**The University of the Third Age
(U3A)**
6 Parkside Gardens
London SW19 5EY
(see Chapter 19)

**Older Lesbian Network**
c/o London FRIEND
274 Upper Street
London N1 2UA

**Older Feminists Network**
c/o A Woman's Place
Hungerford House
Victoria Embankment
London WC2
el: 01 836 6081

# APPENDIX

On 10 June 1985, Norman Fowler, Secretary of State for Social Services, announced major proposals for changes to social security benefits. These proposals were published in a Green Paper entitled *Reform of Social Security*. The Green Paper is a consultation document on which the government are seeking views. They will publish their final plan for the social security system in the autumn of 1985, in a White Paper. The White Paper will be rapidly followed by a Social Security Bill which should become an Act of Parliament by July 1986.

None of the proposals in the Green Paper will come into effect before April 1987. We can also expect that many of them will be modified or dropped either during the consultation period or while the Bill is passing through parliament. There are many detailed changes which have not been included in the Green Paper which we can expect to be in the final legislation. It is therefore very difficult to predict exactly how the social security system will change in April 1987. The Green Paper does not contain any figures and it is therefore difficult to assess how the new benefits relate to existing benefits in their levels and scope. There has been much speculation in the press and elsewhere about winners and losers. Until there are figures and clear proposals, we can only speculate. But the government has made it clear that there will be no extra money for social security, and indeed, that it wants to cut housing benefit expenditure. We can therefore assume that few people will benefit from the changes, and that where the system is made more generous, such changes will have been paid for by reducing entitlement of some other group of claimants.

The government have promised that no one who is on a particular benefit in April 1987 will suffer adversely as a result of the changes. They will keep their existing level of benefit as long as they remain on that benefit. It will therefore be very important to ensure that you are getting all the benefits to which you are entitled *before* April 1987. The new rules will also mean, in some cases, that there will be benefits that you can claim in April 1987, that you couldn't get before that date. So make sure you don't miss out on them.

The main proposals set out in the Green Paper will, if they become law, affect entitlement to the following benefits:

**RETIREMENT PENSION AND WIDOW'S PENSION**. The basic pensions will not be affected, but it is proposed that entitlement to the additional pension – known as the state earnings related pension (SERPS) will be phased out for men aged less than 50 and women aged less than 45 in April 1987. The effect of this change wouldn't be felt for a long time and would primarily affect people who are under 35 at the moment. Women who are aged 35–46 in April 1987 would get some SERP when they retire but not as much as they could have had if the scheme had continued in its present form. The main effect from 1987 would be that everyone who is employed will have to have some form of occupational pension.

**SUPPLEMENTARY BENEFIT** It is proposed that the present supplementary benefit scheme be replaced by a new income support scheme. Weekly additions and lump sum payments – single payments – would be abolished. There would be no long-term rate of benefit under the new scheme. Instead there would be a basic personal allowance based on the age of the claimant, with a different rate for couples. Claimants would be able to claim certain 'premium' payments on top of their personal allowances if they have children, are elderly or disabled, or are a single parent. The Green Paper does not state the levels of weekly payments and it is therefore not possible to predict who would be better or worse off under the new scheme. However, there will be no extra money available and it seems clear that some claimants, particularly disabled people, would not get as much from the new premium as they currently get from their weekly additions.

Single payments and payments in emergencies, known as 'urgent needs' payments, would be abolished. Instead a new **SOCIAL FUND** would be set up to provide one-off payments in certain circumstances. Payments would be entirely at the discretion of the DHSS and there would be no right of appeal against decisions; many of the payments would be recoverable.

**MATERNITY GRANT AND DEATH GRANTS** would be abolished. Instead, people on low incomes would be able to apply to the social fund for help. A lump sum payment of around £75 would be available to meet maternity needs for families on the new income support scheme or the new family credit (see below). People on low incomes would be able to get a social fund payment towards a funeral, but may have to pay this back later.

**MATERNITY ALLOWANCE** would continue to be paid but the rules would change slightly. Women would have to meet a recent work test as well as a contribution test. They would have more flexibility to choose the period for which the benefit is paid.

**WIDOWS** Widow's allowance, now paid for the first twenty-six weeks of widowhood, would be abolished. Instead, widows would get either widow's pension or widowed mother's allowance from the first week of widowhood and a lump sum payment of £1,000. However, the age rules would change, so that widows aged 45–55 would only be able to get a reduced pension and widows aged 45 or less would get no widow's pension.

**FAMILY INCOME SUPPLEMENT** would be abolished and replaced by a new benefit called family credit. Unlike family income supplement (FIS) which is paid direct to the claimant by the DHSS, the new benefit would be paid by the employer through the claimant's PAYE code. We do not know how self-employed people would claim family credit. Claimants would have to be reassessed for family credit every six months, whereas FIS lasts for a year. The Green Paper does not give the rates for the new family credit so we cannot say whether it would be more or less generous than FIS. But families on FIS currently get free school meals. Families on family credit would not.

**HOUSING BENEFIT** The housing benefit scheme would continue to be paid by the local authority. But a number of changes to the method of financial assessment are proposed. The government has said that it wants to cut £500m from the housing benefit budget; so it is clear that the changes would reduce many people's entitlement to benefit. The main changes are as follows. The present financial assessment is different for housing benefit and supplementary benefit. The new assessment would be the same. This would mean that people with incomes below or at the new income support level (the new name for supplementary benefit) would get the same housing benefit whether or not they are on income support. But it would also mean that people at the higher income levels, for example, people with occupational pensions or average incomes from employment would get less housing benefit than under the old system. At the moment, people on supplementary benefit get 100 per cent of their housing costs met. This includes rent, rates, water rates and any obligatory services charges. Under the new scheme, they would get 100 per cent rent but only 8 per cent of their rates, no water rates and no service charges. These amounts would have to be met out of their weekly benefit.

**NEW CAPITAL RULES FOR HOUSING BENEFIT AND SUPPLEMENTARY BENEFIT** At the moment, anyone with capital over £3,000 cannot claim supplementary benefit; but capital is ignored when assessing for housing benefit. Under the new scheme capital below £3,000 would be ignored when assessing for income support and housing benefit. But capital between £3,000 and £6,000 would be taken into consideration. People with less than £6,000 would be able to claim, but they will be assumed to have an income of 40p per week for each £100 of capital between £3,000 and £6,000.

# INDEX